POLITICIANS AND THE WAR
1914–1916

The following books by Lord Beaverbrook
deal with the Lloyd George Ministry

Politicians and the War
Men and Power

LORD BEAVERBROOK

about to open the rebuilt Stornaway House, his old home which was
bombed during World War II.

LORD BEAVERBROOK

POLITICIANS
AND
THE WAR
1914-1916

ARCHON BOOKS
1968

First published by Butterworth in two volumes, 1928 and 1932
First published in one-volume edition by Oldbourne Book Co. in 1960
© Lord Beaverbrook 1960
Printed in Great Britain by
Cox & Wyman Ltd., London, Fakenham and Reading

CONTENTS

CONTENTS

CONTENTS

ILLUSTRATIONS

INTRODUCTION

This book is a reprint of two volumes published many years ago. The book is an account of politics and politicians in the First World War.

My work cannot be described as "a Political History". It is, however, an accurate record of the events attending the reorganisation of the Liberal Administration of 1915 and the formation of the First War Government drawn from all three political parties.

The fall of Prime Minister Asquith and his Coalition Government in 1916, and the rise of Lloyd George to power and fame, are all recorded in detail.

I have made no mention of my own activities during these political crises, except for the purpose of substantiating statements and accounts of events.

BEAVERBROOK

Fredericton, N.B.
September 1959

Book One

CHAPTER I

INTERVENTION

I HAVE had it in mind for some time to write a history of British politics during the Great War, and the period of reconstruction. With this object in view I have collected a large quantity of material bearing on home politics from 1914 to 1925, including notes I made at one period or another myself.

On reflection, I am of opinion that some part of this material may be utilised in the form of an outline sketch of the principal events and the outstanding characters of the period. Such a selection cannot, of course, pretend to be final in the view it takes either of events or individuals, but none the less its publication may be of value in fixing public attention while interest is still vivid.

Obviously, such a book is not history in the strict sense. It is merely a contribution to history. Neither is it a day-to-day record of politics. It deals in the high lights which shine on big events of the epoch and on the vital decisions of the personalities who took part in them.

These characters are in most cases interpreted

in the light of personal knowledge. I have
ventured to deduce some of their motives from
the views I have formed privately, and to indicate
the nature of my opinion by the anecdotes I relate
of them.

I publish this account in the hope that it will
interest, and in the certainty that it will do no
harm. In fact, in so far as it interests it may prove
of some public advantage. Democracy depends
to-day for its successful practice on the judgment
and knowledge of every citizen on the problems
of government. If that judgment is to be in any
way sound, it is of importance that people should
have accessible some guide to the conduct of the
war by their elected rulers, some picture of the
personalities which played a part in it, and still
play a part before us. Such an outline of history
must either be given promptly or not at all.
Nothing is so quick to fade as the immediate
memory of public events. Men know less of
what happened twenty years ago than of what
happened in 1880. A kind of twilight period
of boredom and forgetfulness soon supervenes,
and by the time the stage of authentic and final
history is reached only a few will read the page.
But to-day the events of the war are not so long
past, and most of us still have a lively memory of
those exciting days.

. . . . .

The week immediately preceding the outbreak
of war saw the two historic parties locked in a
fierce grapple over the Irish question. Attempt
after attempt at compromise had broken down

just as the protagonists seemed on the very edge of agreement. I mention this at the outset because the impression caused by the struggle over Home Rule was slow to fade from the minds of many of the politicians on both sides, and, during the early months of the war, exercised an important influence on the relations between the two parties from 1914 to 1916, which is the principal topic of this volume. This " Irish " atmosphere is therefore important, and I shall come back to the subject in the next chapter. But with the first vital threat of war with Germany it ceased to be the dominant factor in the complex of Liberal-Conservative relationship and faded into a side issue.

The problem which leapt into the forefront the moment that war was seen to be inevitable was that of Coalition. Was the War Government to be the Liberal Government then in Downing Street, or were the Conservatives and the Liberals to combine to form a National Coalition War Ministry ? Leading men on both sides gave opposing answers to this question, and indeed sometimes changed their minds as circumstances altered. But it is the dominating issue of the period with which I am dealing in this book. The reader who wants a sure guide through the labyrinth of the shifting policies and the conflicting personalities who figure in these pages will do well to take the idea of " Coalition " as a clue to much which would otherwise be mysterious or even incomprehensible.

There were three separate attempts to form such

a Coalition. The first was made by Mr. Churchill
in those days of July and August 1914, immediately preceding the ultimatum, when the unity
of the Liberal Cabinet seemed imperilled. The
attempt failed. The second attempt was made by
Mr. Churchill in March 1915, when he persuaded
Mr. Asquith to invite Mr. Bonar Law and Lord
Lansdowne to the meeting of the War Council
which offered to give Constantinople to Russia
in the event of victory. This failed too.

The third effort at Coalition was the result of
Lord Fisher's resignation from the Admiralty.
It was initiated by Bonar Law, welcomed by Lloyd
George and carried through successfully against
the wishes and interests of Mr. Churchill. I
trace the career of the Coalition so formed up to
the point when the outbreak of conflicting forces,
no longer based on party divisions within it,
prove its decay as a governing instrument and
point to its early dissolution.

The personalities engaged in these struggles
for or against Coalition assume sometimes
attitudes tinged with the drama of irony. Mr.
Churchill induced Lord Birkenhead to act as
mediator with the Tory leader in the first effort
to effect Coalition—and the plain proposition was
rejected. In the second attempt he induced Mr.
Asquith to approach Bonar Law with a concealed
offer, which was ignored. The third time he is
found fighting Coalition and trusting in Lord
Balfour to save him from the Tories. And when
Coalition comes, he goes.

Bonar Law, on the other hand, rejects Coalition

twice and on the third occasion he is the architect
of the First Coalition Government.

I am not suggesting, of course, that in either
case was there the slightest inconsistency. Mr.
Churchill was perfectly entitled to hold his view
that the introduction of a Tory element into the
Cabinet at the outset would strengthen the war
spirit in the Government. He was equally
justified later on in defending his own control
and administration of the Admiralty against Lord
Fisher—and this, as it turned out, involved, too,
fighting against the Tories and their inclusion in
the Ministry.

Bonar Law's position was completely self-
consistent in this matter. He had no abstract
objection to Coalition. On the contrary, he
thought it was the form of Government to which a
long and severe war must inevitably bring the
nation. But he considered this to be the last step
to take and not the first. So long as a Liberal
Government had credit for success and good
management, and a patriotic Opposition was
content not to oppose, all was well. While such
a national asset remained unexhausted why draw
on another ?

But if the Liberal Government failed, if the
party truce showed signs of being broken, why
then unity could be maintained and national
confidence restored by forming a mixed Ministry.
To make a Coalition at the start was like leading
the ace of trumps.

When one considers how in the course of the
four years of war the capacity and credit of

Ministry after Ministry was exhausted, it is clear that Bonar Law showed a penetration into the future which exceeded that of most of his contemporaries in the fateful summer of 1914, and a commanding wisdom beyond that of his age. So long as the Liberal Ministry could be defended he sustained it from the Opposition benches, but when its hour struck he made a Coalition in a day.

   .   .   .   .   .

The first crisis in party Government synchronises with the last night of July 1914, when the Conservative leaders were at Lord Wargrave's house, at Wargrave. There, by pre-engagement, I arrived very late to find Bonar Law, Carson and Birkenhead. The composition of the party suggested that it had been summoned to discuss Ulster and Home Rule. But the conference instantly found itself involved in a discussion of the attitude the Opposition should adopt towards the war and the Government. While this was proceeding news reached us of acute dissensions in the Cabinet on the subject of British intervention.

Churchill, in a word, was in communication with Birkenhead, and the first attempt to form a Coalition Government had begun. By this means the views of the Liberal interventionists in the Cabinet—for Churchill believed he had Grey's support in his action and the unspoken assent of the Prime Minister—were put before the leader of the Opposition. The information given Birkenhead was briefly this : Liberal Ministers,

THESE GLITTERING BIRDS OF PARADISE

Olive Edis, F.R.P.S.

THE CABINET ROOM, 10 DOWNING STREET

"In another week," Asquith said, "I shall have sat in this Chair for seven years."

like the Radical section of the country as a whole, were seething with doubt and agitation. While most of the leading Liberals were determined to stand by France, the majority of the Liberal newspapers were dead against war, and this view was finding such strong expression in the Cabinet itself that in the event of intervention some seven or eight resignations might be expected.*

In considering the list of the threatened seceders the formidable name of David Lloyd George immediately flashed through the minds of men. If these resignations took effect, would the Opposition be prepared to come to the rescue of the Government, not merely with parliamentary support, but by forming a Coalition to fill up the vacant offices ? Such was the message that Birkenhead conveyed to Bonar Law, and he added that he was informed that the knowledge of a favourable Tory decision in this matter " would affect the Prime Minister's mind." And indeed it is obvious that any Prime Minister faced with the prospect of a secession would be immensely strengthened in his own attitude by such a promise of Opposition support. He would be in a position if he chose to call in Tory support, and even Tory Ministers, to make good his own defections.

Bonar Law would give no encouragement to Birkenhead. He objected to Mr. Churchill as the medium, and commented on the fact that overtures were made through him. This method of indirect communication so common in political circles

*" The Cabinet was overwhelmingly pacific." " The World Crisis, 1911-1914," by Rt. Hon. Winston S. Churchill. Page 199.

never suited Bonar Law, and he would take no action.

The whole method of negotiation by Churchill through Birkenhead savoured too much of an intrigue to suit Bonar Law, who liked the plain, straightforward course. His view was that if any help or support was wanted from the Opposition it ought to be asked for openly and directly by Mr. Asquith himself, and in that case he would go to London. Matters, therefore, advanced no further than the acceptance of the general idea that the Tories should support the Government if it declared for war, and Churchill's effort, though well intentioned, failed.

The truth of the matter was that there were two schools of thought both in the Liberal and Conservative camp. The strong interventionists in the Government would undoubtedly have welcomed an accession of strength in the power of embarking on or waging war from the Conservatives in exchange for a number of Liberal Ministers who were in principle pacifist and not likely to shine in a metier they disliked.

On the other side, many of the Conservatives would have welcomed a direct inclusion of their party in the Ministry. Birkenhead, who was the only strong advocate of Coalition at Wargrave, could have obtained plenty of support for his opinion had he gone forward with it. There were many members of his party who were deeply disappointed at not being able to serve in a War Government. They had to content themselves as it was with very minor positions of service, while they considered that their talents gave them the right to higher places which they could fill to better advantage to the country than the Liberal occupant.

But the movement was checked at the very outset by the clear and unalterable view expressed by Bonar Law that he was opposed to Coalition. As long as the leader was of this opinion, colleagues or followers could really effect nothing in the contrary direction.

On the Saturday morning everybody wished to return to town at once. Bonar Law, however, suggested that it would be better to wait for further news, and that he should go to London later in the day, so that we could all go together. Eventually the whole party motored to town in the afternoon.

Churchill, on our arrival in London, was anxious that Bonar Law should dine with him and Grey that night, presumably with the intention of renewing his efforts to secure an offer of coalition. Bonar Law, however, was too prudent to accept, for the reasons already given. As a matter of fact, no question of a formal offer ever arose, because the situation in the Cabinet did not develop in the direction anticipated by Mr. Churchill, for reasons which will be understood if we consider the balance of forces and the trend of opinion within the Government circle.

The crisis in the Liberal Party was for several days acute. Three main groups of opinion immediately disclosed themselves. There were those who were against intervention at any price, those who were in favour of intervention, and those who were ready to engage in or abstain from war, according to conditions.   On the Friday, 31 July, the day that the Tories gathered at Lord Wargrave's house at Wargrave, the Liberals were still divided.   Lord Morley, Mr. John Burns, Sir John Simon, Lord Beauchamp, and Mr. Hobhouse were for an immediate declaration of neutrality without imposing any conditions on Germany.

Allied with this group were Lloyd George and the late Lord Harcourt, who were for peace, but were prepared to leave the door open behind us in case it became necessary to intervene. Beyond these, and shading off to the left of peace and the right of war, was a body of opinion represented by Lord Crewe, Mr. McKenna, and Sir Herbert Samuel, who were not definitely committed to either side. Viscount Grey was solid for intervention, and Churchill, going even beyond him, was pressing for instant mobilisation. The Prime Minister, while in his personal opinion leaning strongly towards Grey and Churchill, was chiefly anxious to maintain unity at all costs. In the ultimate resort he would have stood by Grey, but he hoped to avoid resignations and all ultimate expedients. So strong was the division of opinion in the Liberal Party that it seemed quite impossible to reconcile it on 31 July without resignations from the Government. But a rupture was avoided, and on Saturday it was decided to instruct Viscount Grey to inform M. Cambon, the French Ambassador, that our Navy would not allow the German Fleet to attack the French Channel ports. Mr. Burns would not even agree to this, and resigned as a protest against any course but unconditional non-intervention, but his resignation was by consent held back, and only announced after further sittings.

On Sunday morning, 2 August, the Cabinet met again to face letters of resignation from Lord Morley and Sir John Simon, but, none the less, the resigning Ministers attended the conclave. This Sunday morning meeting was in reality the decisive one. Lord Crewe, who throughout this crisis, and indeed in the war as a whole, showed remarkable moderation, judgment and patriotism, was at this period specially urgent with his colleagues that what was undoubtedly Liberal majority opinion should not separate itself from the policy of Grey and Churchill, behind which stood the threat not only of the resignation of these Ministers, but of the withdrawal of the Prime Minister, the disruption of the party, and the fall of the Government in the very moment of the most acute crisis which had threatened the British Empire for a hundred years ; events themselves would settle the issue.

He was successful. It was finally agreed to postpone the actual decision of peace and war, but to mobilise both the Army and the Fleet at once. This action undoubtedly decided the question, but when the final decision for war was taken only Lord Morley and Mr. Burns resigned,*

*Viscount Grey, writing in praise of Mr. Asquith's handling of the Cabinet at this juncture, says : " Had it not been for Asquith the outbreak of war might have found us with a Cabinet in disorder

Lord Beauchamp, Sir John Simon and Mr. Hob-house, no doubt for good reasons, preferring to continue their support of the Government. It will be observed at once from this narrative how small in numbers was the interventionist party in the Cabinet ; and it had, in addition, ranged against it several minor members of the Ministry who were in the Government but not in the Cabinet, and the great bulk of the Liberal Press.

Even inside the Cabinet itself a majority for non-intervention could certainly have been obtained if a strong man had stepped forward to lead the pacifists. It was a case of quality against quantity of opinion, and the Prime Minister himself, though temperament and judgment ranked him with Grey and Churchill, was handicapped by his position of chairman to the debates and weakened by a desire to maintain Liberal unity at all costs.

In these circumstances practically everything depended on the attitude of Mr. Lloyd George. The pacifists were strong in numbers, but without a leader they were helpless, as indeed the event proved. Would Mr. Lloyd George consent to fill the role of leader ?

Letters and diaries will be published in the future which will give a full account of Mr. Lloyd George's actions, of the various motives which swayed him, and of the conflicting emotions which surged in his mind. I will only say this much in anticipation of further evidence.

or dissolution, impotent to take any decision."—cf. " Twenty-Five Years," by Viscount Grey of Fallodon.   (Vol. II, page 242).

Those who insist on regarding Mr. Lloyd
George as the inveterate Jingo of the war from
start to finish are wrong in their facts and mistake
their man. The then Chancellor of the Exchequer
approached the prospect of intervention with the
greatest reluctance, and suffered far-reaching in-
certitudes of mind.

He consulted with those of his colleagues who
had pacifist leanings—or at least they consulted
with him. He brought forward a theory, held by
the existing French General Staff, that if the
Germans violated Belgian neutrality they would
pass only through the furthest southern corner,
leaving Brussels and the plains of Flanders north
of and untouched by their armies.

In the course of these conversations Mr. Lloyd
George demonstrated to his friends with a map
how small an infraction of neutrality such a
military move would imply. He marked on the
map with his finger the direction he thought the
German march through Belgium would take.
" You see," he would say, " it is only a little bit,
and the Germans will pay for any damage they do."

At the eleventh hour he came down on the
right side. When the Germans invaded Belgium
he was influenced in favour of the decision.
With this decision there vanished the last hopes
of the pacifists and any prospect of that kind of
anti-patriotic opposition which supported France
and Napoleon against the Ministries of Pitt and
his successors. Mr. Lloyd George alone had the
genius to play Charles James Fox, and he declined
the role.

It appears to me that both Mr. Lloyd George's hesitation and his final decision do him equal credit. He was reluctant to abandon the schemes of social amelioration he had devised and to plunge into war. He did not wish to put the future happiness and prosperity of all the people of the Empire on the hazard of a throw. But when he realised that his country was up against a Power which knew no moral scruples and was dangerous both to the Empire and humanity he took his decision firmly.

Once Mr. Lloyd George was in the war the very power of imagination which had given him pause gradually wrought him up to the fiercest activity in the struggle.

CHAPTER II

CHURCHILL

MR. Churchill was the leader of the War party in the Cabinet. His position at the Admiralty had long inured him to regard Germany much as a man in business regards a rival who is always cutting his prices. He would seem therefore to have been the natural ally of the Tories and their leader.

Yet how, as a matter of fact, was he regarded in the Opposition ranks?

It can only be answered, he was hated, he was mistrusted, and he was feared. Therefore, though he himself had decided to put all party considerations aside and play the great national role, should war break out, this decision was by no means tantamount to bringing such a truce in old quarrels into effect. It takes two sides to end a party feud.

It was also unfortunate for Churchill that there was not any real sympathy between him and Bonar Law. They were always in some ways at cross purposes with one another, both before and in and after the war. In fact, I shall show in these pages how often Bonar Law upset Churchill's calculations and destroyed his plans. There

seemed a kind of fate about these clashes, for if
Bonar Law had no friendship for Churchill he
had no enmity either. Churchill, however,
showed rancour in relation to Bonar Law. It
was the only instance in Churchill's career, as far
as I know, in which a complete reconciliation
could never be effected.

Bonar Law, on the other hand, never went out
of his way to fight Churchill, but he nearly always
took an opposite view of what the situation
demanded, so that this absence of understanding
between the two men had a vital influence on the
course of the war. And " misunderstanding " is,
I think, the right word. For Churchill never did
justice to Bonar Law's intellect and Bonar Law
always underrated Churchill's character—by which
I mean the power of holding resolutely to those
things in politics which one believes to be true.

Both had entered the House of Commons at the
same time, but they had never been intimate.

Bonar Law got office before Churchill, but the
latter would never regard him as an equal, and
always treated him in a patronising way up to
the outbreak of war.

For instance, on one occasion Churchill wrote
to him as follows :

" You dance like a will-o'-the-wisp so nimbly
from one unstable foothold to another that my
plodding paces can scarcely follow you."

In another letter Churchill says—

" The words which you now tell me you employed, and which purport to be a paraphrase,

if not an actual quotation, are separated by a small degree of inaccuracy and misrepresentation from the inaccuracy and misrepresentation of the condensed report,"

and in another communication he indulges in what might be termed a double positive. He wrote :

"I resist all temptation to say, 'I told you so ! ' "

The slightly acrimonious tone of these epistles does not mean that the two men met each other as enemies. I remember seeing a typical meeting between them in the hall of the Midland Hotel at Manchester. Churchill had stood at the famous bye-election at North-West Manchester as a Liberal and been defeated. Bonar Law became the prospective Conservative candidate for the same seat at the approaching General Election. Bonar Law was in Manchester prosecuting his campaign, and Churchill had been making a speech somewhere in the Manchester area. Returning from this meeting, he ran into Bonar Law, and went up to him with a great appearance of giving him warm welcome. I thought the geniality on both sides rather forced. Bonar Law said, "Well, Churchill, I suppose I had better speak to you to-night, because I imagine after I've read your speech to-morrow I shan't be on speaking terms." And the jest was not altogether spoken in earnest.

Had both lived and remained in opposite parties, their relations might have become comparable

to those of Gladstone and Disraeli. Had they both
been included in the same party all through their
careers, the relations between Lord Rosebery
and Sir William Harcourt would have afforded a
close parallel. In fact, had Bonar Law lived,
Churchill would have had no future at all in
Conservatism. I never heard the older man use
but one kind of language of the younger. " I
consider Churchill a most formidable antagonist.
None the less, I would rather have him in opposition to me than on my side."

Although this antagonism between the two
men necessarily influenced me, I had been dazzled
by the brilliant powers of the young Liberal leader.
I had dined at his house, had talked with him
unreservedly—of course with plenty of display
on his part of that kind of wit which contains the
promise of coming intimacy.

None the less, I was so far living in the Bonar
Law atmosphere of suspicion, that when Birkenhead offered to take me to Churchill's house at
the Admiralty on the Saturday night before the
war broke out, I went frankly as a critic.

We found Churchill there with a couple of
friends. While we were talking a message was
received announcing the postponement of the
German ultimatum to Russia.

I ignorantly regarded it as an omen of peace
and rejoiced in the prospect of escaping a European war. Churchill's opinion was to the effect
that this was only a postponement and that it was
bad news, not good news.

I argued that a postponement would be desirable

for it might result in composing national differences and avoiding the issue for ever.

" The German staff," Churchill said, " have absolutely promised their Government a swift military decision, first against France and then against Russia. They may be right, or they may be wrong, but if their Government believes them, it will declare war, whoever is against them."

He argued that the German menace had to be faced and fought out some time or another. It would be impossible for British statesmen ever to plan out a peaceful progress for the nation until it had been settled once and for all if Germany was going to control the German Ocean. You were not really avoiding a war—you were simply postponing it.

At this point, since some of us would have it that the crisis was ended, a rubber of bridge was demanded. Churchill took a hand in the game, but I was cut out and looked on.

Suddenly an immense despatch box was brought into the room. Churchill produced his skeleton key from his pocket, opened the box and took out of it a single sheet of paper, which seemed singularly disproportionate to the size of the box, just as the paper seemed too big for the brief message typed on it. On that sheet was written the words, " Germany has declared war against Russia."

He informed his guests. He asked me to take over his partly-played bridge hand, leaving me, I must add, in an extremely unfavourable tactical position. He rang for a servant and, asking for a lounge coat, stripped his dress coat from his back, saying no further word. We tried hard to concentrate on the bridge game, but it was impossible to make progress. Our thoughts were wandering. A cool observer would, I imagine, have formed a poor impression of our play.

Churchill makes a picture for me at this critical moment when he got the message which meant war.

He left the room quickly, as in duty bound, and forthwith the Navy was mobilised, in defiance of the decisions taken by the Cabinet early on that day. History has recorded the dramatic directions given by the First Lord that night.

For my own part, I simply saw a man who was receiving long-expected news. He was not depressed ; he was not elated ; he was not surprised. He did not put his head between his hands, as many another eminent man might well have done, and exclaim to high heaven that his world was coming to an end. Certainly he exhibited no fear or uneasiness. Neither did he show any signs of joy. He went straight out like a man going to a well-accustomed job.

In fact, he had foreseen everything that was going to happen so far that his temperament was in no way upset by the realisation of his forecast. We have suffered at times from Mr. Churchill's bellicosity. But what profit the nation derived at that crucial moment from the capacity of the First Lord of the Admiralty for grasping and dealing with the war situation .

We waited in Admiralty House long and

anxiously for Churchill to return with further news. But he did not come back, and it was nearly morning when we left for our homes.*

That Sunday morning, 2 August, was full of conferences. Lord Balfour, Lord Lansdowne and Lord Long, and probably one or two others, called at Pembroke Lodge to see Bonar Law, and the general attitude of the party, which was entirely for war, was finally defined in the sense I have already indicated. Bonar Law had drawn up the draft of a letter to the Prime Minister, and this was generally agreed and despatched to Downing Street.

The letter was couched in the following terms :

Dear Mr. Asquith,—Lord Lansdowne and I feel it our duty to inform you that in our opinion, as well as in that of all the colleagues whom we have been able to consult, it would be fatal to the honour and security of the United Kingdom to hesitate in supporting France and Russia at this present juncture ; and we offer our unhesitating support to the Government in any measures they may consider necessary for that object.

Yours very truly,
(Sgd.) A. Bonar Law.

This letter was in the first place intended as a record of the Conservative attitude. Further, it was meant to cover the point raised by Churchill that the Tories must strengthen Asquith's hand

*For Mr. Churchill's own description of that evening cf. " The World Crisis, 1911-1914." (Pages 216-217.)

against the pacifists in his own Cabinet. But it did not suggest giving any active assistance.

To this attitude of the official Opposition leaders towards the Government there was one exception. Lord Balfour was an ex-Prime Minister, an ex-leader of the Conservative party, the repository of the Salisbury tradition in foreign policy, and, above all, for many years the moving spirit in the Committee of Imperial Defence of which he was still a member.

These facts gave him both some freedom with his own party and closer touch with the Government. He was consulted by members of the Cabinet before the declaration of war, continued to sit regularly on the Committee of Imperial Defence, and subsequently on the Liberal War Council.

It was at this time necessary, in order to estimate Bonar Law's position in the party, to consider his relationship with Lord Balfour.

It would be hard to analyse Lord Balfour's attitude towards Bonar Law, his successor in the Tory leadership. It was not exactly friendly. Quite definitely it was not hostile. Never was there the slightest hint of an intrigue encouraged in that quarter against the new leader. And yet Lord Balfour was not helpful. The keynote seemed to be a slightly cold but absolute correctitude.

Bonar Law, as was natural to him, rated his predecessor's attainments very high in comparing them with his own. He could not see his own counterbalancing advantages. You could, he

used to say, put a case in which you believed to
Lord Balfour and convince him of its truth.
And yet he could make a better argument for the
side in which he disbelieved than you had made
for the cause in which you believed.

Although Lord Balfour was always perfectly
frank with Bonar Law, there seemed to be no real
point of contact between their temperaments.
All the formalities were observed, and yet the
relationship remained tepid. In this atmosphere
Lord Balfour's co-operation with the Government
filled Bonar Law with a certain amount of anxiety.
And he was right to be anxious. An ex-Premier
and ex-Leader of his own party closely linked
with the Liberals might, under certain circumstances, prove a real menace to Tory inde-
pendence.

Curiously enough, the event proved the fear
to be an unreal one. As I show in a later chapter,
when Lord Balfour did try to use his influence
with the Tories to save Mr. Churchill's place at
the Admiralty, he discovered himself quite impotent. With all his detachment Balfour had a
sincere affection for Churchill, but failed utterly
to save him from the wrath of the Tories.

Lord Balfour's is a curious mind. He does not
care for stories about politics or public men. He
likes to hear the episodes of the life of action—
and action to him seems to mean Finance. He
will be thrilled with the tale of a big coup in the
market place, and admires the successful promoter.
In this respect he rather reminds me of Kipling,
who adores the man of action too—only his hero

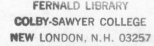

must be a soldier or a governor. The soldier, if he is a sensible man, is confused by this worship, seeing that he thinks Kipling, the man of letters, far greater than any of his contemporaries. I have seen the same sort of thing happen with Lord Balfour when he heard the tales of the leaders in finance about the time that New York began to dominate the money making markets of the world. The late E. H. Harriman was his hero. This makes it all the more curious that Lord Balfour should not appreciate Bonar Law more. For I have watched them together and realised that Bonar Law was politically the greater figure precisely because he possessed that capacity for action that Lord Balfour lacked.

I have always admitted to a difficulty in forming a proper estimate of Lord Balfour and of the late Joseph Chamberlain. I write them down below the level at which nearly all my contemporaries in politics value them. I cannot be convinced of error. For instance, Mr: Tim Healy, sometime Governor General of the Irish Free State, has always placed these two statesmen in a rank commensurate with any great leader he had known in the course of his long career. And Healy has always had a great influence on the political judgments I have formed. I began to listen to him quite early in my House of Commons career ; but it was just at the time of which I am now speaking that his influence was strengthened greatly by the following episode—

Healy and I left the House of Commons in the evening to walk along the Embankment to the

Savoy and to get a meal. It was at the most critical period of the Mons retreat. As we walked Healy was holding forth about the oppression of Ireland and the iniquities of British rule. I paid scant attention to what he was saying. I had heard it all before. My mind was oppressed by a foreboding of disaster—for I had seen a despatch which had just arrived from G.H.Q. in France.

At last we sat down at a tea-table in the Embankment Gardens, and I said, " I am tired of hearing about the grievances of the Irish—let me tell you something of the perils of the British army." From a somewhat retentive memory I was able to repeat to him that paraphrased despatch of the British Commander-in-Chief almost verbatim. " I mean to retreat to the sea. If the enemy remain in contact, this will be a very difficult operation. I advise you to look to the defences of Havre."

I looked at my companion, and suddenly I saw the tears streaming down Healy's cheeks. In a passionate and vehement flow of words he dedicated himself, before God, to the service of the Allied cause—as though I was not even there as a spectator of his outburst.

I have known Tim Healy—rebel, agitator, enemy of Great Britain—intimately since that hour, and he never violated the vow of service which he made that summer evening.

CHAPTER III

DISSENSIONS

NO sooner were the Liberal Government over their first difficulty in securing a large Government majority for intervention in the war when they were confronted with quite a new difficulty. Strong objections were raised to the despatch of the British Expeditionary Force to France, a proceeding which had for years been considered in British Military and Cabinet circles as represented by the Committee of Imperial Defence as the first step in the possible Continental War.

These objections came from unexpected quarters —both Tory and Liberal. Denial on the part of the authors of these protests would be useless. And after all, why should anyone now consider it an article of faith to deny what they thought or said at that moment ? The event proved that it was right to send the Expeditionary Force out. This does not prove that the counter arguments of fears were not honest.

None the less, the two main sources of these hesitations or objections were somewhat startling. Lord Northcliffe, on the Tory side, came to Mr. Churchill and protested strongly against this

movement of the troops. I would ascribe this
action in his case to a confusion of mind on military topics. Certainly his intervention did not
influence Churchill, who stood out strongly for
the despatch of the Expeditionary Force; all the
more strongly perhaps because of Northcliffe's
intervention.

Lord Haldane's attitude was far more complex
and peculiar. The whole foundation of the
modern British Army which he, as War Secretary,
and his military advisers on the war had created,
was precisely directed to the despatch of this
particular force to the North of France, should
the occasion arise. It had been asserted officially
over and over again, particularly as an argument
against conscription, that the Navy, the remaining
regular divisions, the Special Reserve and the
Territorials were a sufficient safeguard against
invasion. The Committee of Imperial Defence
had definitely declared in this sense. In all these
decisions Lord Haldane was a principal par-
ticipant. The creation of the Expeditionary Force
and its splendid training for foreign war is indeed
his greatest claim to be remembered gratefully
as a successful executive Minister.

It is clear, therefore, that in theory he was
absolutely bound to believe in the despatch of that
body. In practice he was found to be voicing all
the military doubts and arguments of those who
were in favour of retaining the entire British
Army at home.

Viscount Grey denies in his book, " Twenty-
five Years," that this charge against Lord Haldane,

frequently repeated, has any foundation. He asserts that Lord Haldane " was, from the first, for giving authority at once to send all six divisions to France in the shortest possible time."

It is true that Lord Grey was a colleague of Lord Haldane in the Government, and such evidence bears great weight. Yet I have before me a contemporary letter written by one Conservative leader to another, giving a detailed account of an interview with Lord Haldane at this time. Founding my view on this letter, I feel bound to say that Lord Haldane expressed different opinions from this Conservative writer. In substance he said :

(1) That if the Expeditionary Force were retained it might form the nucleus of a far more formidable force to be despatched at some future date ; (2) that its present accession to the French strength would be trifling ; (3) that its extinction would hamper us in the struggle later on. Such a stronger force might be used subsequently to cut across the German communications behind.

These arguments could hardly be taken seriously. The only formidable reason put forward was that this country would run the risk of invasion by the denudation of troops involved by the despatch of the Expeditionary Force. This last view had been definitely and formally dismissed, as I have said, by the Imperial Defence Committee, of which Lord Haldane was a prominent member.

At the actual crisis Lord Haldane appeared to be absolutely undecided. He used apparently

the arguments of others against despatching the
British Expeditionary Force—without definitely
pinning himself to them—and yet they were the
very arguments to which he himself was
apparently bound to make the most conclusive
of replies. The case against these arguments had
long ago been supplied by himself.

Other influences than Lord Northcliffe or Lord
Haldane were at work tending toward the same
end. The " Westminster Gazette " showed inside
knowledge of the struggle which was going on.
It denounced attempts " to drive us into the reckless project of embarking our Expeditionary
Force in continental warfare " quite regardless of
the fact that the military system organised by the
Liberal Government had for years designed it
specifically for this " reckless " role. None the
less, the " Westminster Gazette," as a Liberal
organ, had a perfect right to its own opinion.

The issue was further confused by a third school
who were anxious to change the military plans
in a different sense, and to land the British Expeditionary Force somewhere on the coast of
Belgium with a naval base behind it. From here
it would issue out against the right rear of the
German turning movement instead of placing
itself directly in the path. Mr. McKenna supported this idea, which contained within it the
germ of the Antwerp manœuvre.

The predominant view of our strategy in the
case of a war with Germany prevailed in the face
of these fears, doubts and remonstrances. But the
protests caused a considerable delay, and it was

not until some time elapsed that the final decision to despatch the Army was taken. Several days had been wasted.

It is not pleasant to reflect that the issue of the Mons retreat and the Marne, where a few divisions either way would have turned the scale, hung for some days on a hair, and that the timidity of journalistic, military and Ministerial minds nearly exercised a fatal influence on the whole future of their race and of the world. A detached and impartial friend who studied Lord Haldane's mind during these gyrations mournfully reported : " On the whole, I was rather depressed by a certain woolliness of thought and indecision of purpose which seemed to mark his conversation."

The declaration of war by no means put an end to the dissensions in the Liberal Party. In the third week of August the attitude of Turkey was a cause of profound uneasiness, and the question of active operations against her confronted the country. A keen observer has given a picture of how the various Liberal actors struck him at the time. Asquith appeared anxious, with the best of reasons, to avoid a split at any cost. Lloyd George now, for the first time, began to advocate that idea of a Confederation of Balkan States on the side of the Allies, to which, in spite of all his plunges from right to left into every controversy of the time, he remained faithful to the very end.

The rest my informant pictured to me only in a lightning sketch : Haldane, mystic and un-precise ; Simon, the last word in logic ;

Hobhouse, assertive and irrelevant; Runciman, precise in style and instructive in manner—the lesser luminaries of the party bewildered by the disagreement among its heads. As a matter of fact, war with Turkey was delayed for three months.

While these dissensions were rife within the Liberal ranks, an event occurred which destroyed all the good feeling between the leaders of the two parties and gave the Coalition conception a severe setback. This was the resurrection of the old pre-war Irish controversy due to the determination of the Government to complete the Parliamentary progress of the Home Rule Bill and to put it on the Statute Book.

Instantly the ghosts of ancient strifes and hatreds were resurrected in Westminster. Leaders flew to arms and the atmosphere of the House of Commons became charged with party suspicion. Equally in the constituencies the spirit of co-operation between Liberals and Conservatives which had arisen out of recruiting meetings and other common war activities was seriously impaired.

Looking backwards now after the lapse of years, such a violent gust of antagonism may seem hard to justify in the eyes of posterity. A generation which did not participate in the Home Rule struggle of the years 1910-1914 will be unable to understand the intense bitterness of the sentiment it evoked in Liberal and Conservative minds alike—so that even at the outset of the life and death struggle with Germany, any action of the

Government could arouse the old vendetta in full force.

I can perhaps explain the intensity of this feeling as well as any man because I acted as an intermediary in practically all the negotiations for a compromise settlement which took place between the two party leaders, during the months when the United Kingdom seemed to be drifting towards civil war. In all such transactions one felt the complete lack of understanding of, or sympathy for, the standpoint of the opposite side.

At one meeting which took place between Asquith and Bonar Law at my country house at Leatherhead both men had come to it desiring to avoid conflict. Both were men of a high degree of intelligence. Yet so constrained was the atmosphere—so full of irreconcilable antagonism—that no progress could be made at all. The whole negotiation looked like tumbling into ruins.

Bonar Law was harsh and Asquith subsided into silence. Asquith then tried to relieve the tension by walking to the window and expatiating on the beauty of the view as it extended across the valley to the opposite hill. There was nothing like it, he remarked, in the South of England except the view from Hindhead. Unfortunately, this kind of observation never had the slightest effect in rousing Bonar Law's interest. So this move failed.

It was at this moment that I had an inspiration. The " Daily Express " had just sent a special representative to Belfast to report on the threatened Ulster rising. I was even then on very intimate terms with the Editor, whom we all know affectionately as " Blum," and I had received a note from him describing the fate of this correspondent. He had been suddenly recalled, on account of a misunderstanding, from a land of Covenanters singing eternally "Oh, God, our help in ages past," and was kept waiting for an interview outside Blum's door for the whole afternoon while others passed in and out. At last he could stand the punishment no longer. He sent in a note by a messenger—

" Oh, God, our help in ages past,
   Our hope for years to come,
   Chuck out the dirty beasts within
   And let me see my Blum."

When I told the story to the Prime Minister and the Leader of the Opposition, humour came to the rescue and a contact of personality was instantly established.

I tell this trifling story because it illuminates the real basis of contact between public men. The leaders of parties live their lives among supporters, friends and subordinates who share their views and intensify their natural bias. When they meet their opponents it is as open foes in debate. In the course of time they lose their sense of perspective and become harsh and unbending in their attitude towards the viewpoint of the other side. This is especially the case with serious and honest men, and the only method of relieving the tension between them when they meet personally is to introduce some touch of humour or interest which makes them feel that the stage enemy may after all be human.

My own experience is that negotiations proceed better and national interests are more readily served when the negotiators on both sides are not too serious.

When, therefore, on 15 September, the Prime Minister announced his decision to carry the Home Rule Bill through its final stage, he was instantly accused by Bonar Law of an act of bad faith, and the accusation was couched in no measured terms. I will not try to estimate the rights and wrongs of the matter, or to repeat the arguments of the contestants. The issue is dead, and it does not possess a spark of life or interest to the reader of to-day.

My own opinion at the time was that it did not matter a rap whether Bills were put on the Statute-book or not. It was merely to fill in a post-dated cheque which had little prospect of being honoured. It was clear that much water had to flow under many bridges and rivers of blood over the fields of Europe before the question could be raised again, and by then who could tell what the situation would be ?

One thing alone was certain—it would be different. Bills on the Statute-book would be only sand castles against the sweeping tide of change. From this standpoint I thought Bonar Law had lost his sense of proportion in making so much of the incident in the middle of such military events as were occurring in France. He thought differently, and was quite angry with me for maintaining the opposite view.

The real explanation seems to have been that some men acquired the war mentality rather earlier than other members of the political fraternity, for Bonar Law's attitude was certainly not exceptional. It was shared, for instance, by Lord Carson, as the following story shows.

At this period there used to be regular meetings of the members of the Opposition Shadow Cabinet at Bonar Law's room in the House of Commons at which policy was discussed. But the chief attraction of these meetings was the reception and reading out of the secret cables from the front which the Government thus transmitted to the Opposition.

These telegrams were not sent in exactly in the same words in which they were received, but were first paraphrased in the War Office. I remember that this fact gave some Conservatives considerable offence—as suggesting either that they were not to be trusted, or that the Government were cooking the news. Of course, the real explanation was the danger of the cipher leaking out owing to one of these telegrams going astray.

It was at a period when Lord French was sending back a series of messages which were a source of alarm to the heads of the Government and of the Opposition. Whenever one of these documents, with Mr. Asquith's mark on it, reached Bonar Law, there was perturbation in the Shadow Cabinet. On one occasion Bonar Law's secretary brought in such a message marked in the well-known way to a meeting, and immediately left the room. His anxiety to hear its contents was, however, almost unbearable. He waited outside and waylaid the first person to leave the room, who happened to be Carson. He was struck at once by something ghastly in the Ulster leader's expression.

" For Heaven's sake," he exclaimed in alarm, " tell me what has happened ? What is the news ? " " The very worst possible, my dear fellow, the very worst." " But what has happened ? Is the news very bad ? " " Bad "— in a tone of tragic solemnity—" very bad. Asquith has decided to put the Bill on the Statute-book."

I do not tell this story imputing any blame to Carson. The Home Rule struggle had been his life issue, and if he took a little time to adjust his viewpoint to new conditions he was not the only public man by any manner of means who suffered from this defect. Soon he was to take the war very seriously indeed.

But at this time Carson might be regarded as a bulwark against Coalition. He fully shared Bonar Law's belief that Asquith had tricked them both by promising them that there would be no new domestic legislation during the War and then putting the Home Rule Bill through its last stages in direct defiance of his promise.

So it may be said with confidence that the attitude of hostility towards Coalition which had existed in the higher Conservative circles at the outbreak of war had been intensified by this quarrel over the Home Rule Bill.

CHAPTER IV

THE SECOND ATTEMPT AT COALITION

THIS chapter will be concerned with the internal difficulties of the Tory chiefs and with the second attempt made from the Liberal side to attract them into a Coalition Government. As in the previous instance, the protagonist in this Coalition effort was Mr. Churchill, who now occupied a position of very considerable influence in the counsels of the Government. In public prominence, at any rate, the First Lord of the Admiralty outstripped at this time any other Minister, except Lord Kitchener. His personality made a strong appeal to the imagination of the people. A striking speech of his at the Guildhall, consisting of only a few pointed sentences, had made a limited appeal to Conservative sentiment. And in October 1914 he had figured in the fiercely-discussed episode of the Expedition to Antwerp.

I propose to deal with this question only in so far as it had a political complexion. With its military aspect I am, of course, not concerned, though I believe that history will decide that the authors of the expedition had sound grounds for their action. In the world of politics the Antwerp affair nearly produced a striking change in the Cabinet, and one which might have profoundly modified subsequent developments in the Mediterranean. When Mr. Churchill hurried across the Channel to encourage the Belgian authorities to hold on to Antwerp until relief should arrive, he was so impressed with the urgency and importance of the situation that on 4 October he cabled to the Prime Minister from the beleaguered fortress in the following terms : '" If it is thought by H.M. Government that I can be of service here, I am willing to resign my office and undertake command of relieving and defensive forces assigned to Antwerp in conjunction with Belgian Army, provided that I am given necessary military rank and authority, and full powers of a commander of a detached force in the field. I feel it my duty to offer my services, because I am sure this arrangement will afford the best prospects of a victorious result to an enterprise in which I am deeply involved. I should require complete staff proportionate to the force employed, as I have had to use all the officers now here in positions of urgency. I wait your reply. Runciman would do Admiralty well."*

Lord Kitchener received this despatch from the Prime Minister. His comment was written in his own hand on the margin : " I will make him a Lieut.-General if you will give him the Command." But the Government did not accept the

*Mr. Churchill describes this offer of his to resign the Admiralty in " The World Crisis, 1911-14." (Page 351.)

challenge. Lovers of the curious in history may regret that the occasion was lost for producing the spectacle, unprecedented in modern times, of a Cabinet Minister stepping direct from the council chamber to high command in the field.

The autumn and winter of 1914 were, indeed, a stagnant period as far as politics were concerned. The new days had dawned of a " patriotic Opposition."

But though all was calm on the surface, the depths were frequently troubled. The Tory leaders in adopting the policy of silent support had undertaken more than the human nature of their supporters could always, one might almost say ever, bear.

Fresh from a fierce party conflict, these supporters distrusted Ministers profoundly. Several of the members of the Government they knew to be pacifists at heart. The Conservatives were no doubt burningly anxious to help to win the war, and they found their role reduced to one of negative endurance. There was only one thing which would really have satisfied them—the authority for their party to run the war—and since this could not be granted to a minority, many of them were none the less disturbed and discontented because what they demanded was plainly irrational.

Of all these thwarted desires the two Conservative party leaders—Bonar Law and Lord Lansdowne—had to bear the brunt. Some weeks it rained memoranda from members of the House, and the authors were firmly convinced that the

fate of the Empire depended on the acceptance
by the Government of their typewritten views.

The writers made the pills, and they expected
their leaders to administer them to a harassed and
recalcitrant Ministry. The national service members wanted at least a compulsory cadet system.
G.H.Q. in France found a kind of spawning pond
for its grievances in the Opposition ranks at
Westminster.

Every month a suggestion for a debate which
must either have been futile or revealed valuable
military facts to the world had to be crushed
without giving offence.

In these circumstances Bonar Law was for-
tunate in the temperament of the man on whom
he most depended. The great need was to keep
one's judgment calm and one's temper in check,
and yet not to achieve a sort of cold superiority
on some height inaccessible to the rank and file.

In calmness Lord Lansdowne shone. In 1914
he was wise and unruffled, bringing the serenity
of a high, unchallenged position, a long experience
of government in all parts of the world, to match
Bonar Law's sober-minded and middle-class
placidity.

Lord Lansdowne was cautious, too cautious,
if you like, but he displayed a consistent and
absolute refusal to " get the wind up." I like to
think of him in this light. The two men set their
faces like flint against the fussiness of colleagues
and the indignant surgings of the rank and file.

Under these circumstances the discontented
Tories—who were really the political ancestors

of the present Die-hards—turned for countenance
and leading to the late Lord Long. This was
natural enough. He had been their candidate for
the leadership as opposed to both Sir Austen
Chamberlain and Bonar Law. He was understood
to stand for a Toryism more agricultural and
crusted than was usually found in the industrial
constituency of Conservatism. It was just as well,
perhaps, that he was selected as the chief of revolt
—for he was conspicuously loyal by nature, and
capable of forgiving the triumph of a younger
rival.

Long was *par excellence* the country gentleman
in politics. He aspired to be no more. In fact,
he was a kind of second Lord St. Aldwyn, but
without the ability or acidity of that statesman.
His strength lay in character, and yet he had no
firmness of purpose. This may seem a hard saying,
for character in politics is generally regarded as
constancy in clinging to a fixed opinion against
all odds. Long, on the contrary, often changed
his views, and would express two different sets of
opinions at the same time because he had not yet
fully realised the fact that he had changed. For
his mental process was not sufficiently rapid or
clear to let him see at every moment exactly where
he stood, or allow him to grasp a contradiction.
Yet none the less I maintain that the essence and
value of the man lay in his character—in the good
humour which covered the occasional roughness,
in his sincerity of purpose, in the absolute quality
of his personal honesty.

As a matter of fact, he tired in the course of time

of the men who stood behind him—those whom nothing could satisfy but a purely Tory Cabinet, for which there was no popular support.

As his knowledge of the real problems of the war increased and the environment of office gripped him, he tended to march from right to left across the field of ideas, leaving his tail to Lord Carson and becoming more and more the protagonist of the doctrine that his Majesty's Government must be carried on. But this is to anticipate.

As Lord Balfour pointed out very wisely and temperately at the outset of 1915, the dilemma of the Opposition was not to be eluded. You must either have silent, even uncritical. support, or you must have Coalition. You could not have loud discussions of military plans, nor give private advices to Ministers when the facts were not before the advisers.

Under these circumstances the second attempt to originate a Coalition Government was made. This movement, like its predecessor of August 1914, was started by Mr. Churchill, who had a curious passion for bringing the Tories, who were fundamentally hostile to him, into the Ministry. How was he to recapture the spirit of co-operation between parties which he believed to have existed at the outbreak of war ? His friend Birkenhead was in France and not available any longer as a means of communication.

But the naval bombardment of the outer forts at the Dardanelles had proved a striking success. Constantinople seemed to be almost within our grasp, and the future of Constantinople had become a topic of serious consideration between the British and the Russian Governments. It was suggested that as a means of strengthening the War Alliance, the British Government should promise that coveted prize to Russia in the event of a successful issue.

Immediately another question arose. Could a single British party which might be out of office when Peace was declared pledge Britain to this course ? Must not the Opposition be consulted in order to assure the continuity of British policy over Constantinople ?

Mr. Churchill grasped eagerly at this opportunity. He counted Constantinople as being already in his gift. It might be used as a lure to catch Russia first and the Opposition leaders afterwards. He urged the Prime Minister to invite Bonar Law and Lord Lansdowne to a Conference. He imagined that the Tories would say, not without reason, that they could not take responsibility for such a plunge into European commitments unless they had at their disposal, as the Government had, full knowledge of the reasons which dictated the policy. From that attitude it would appear easy to draw them on one step further—namely, to a decision that they should share power if they were to be asked to share responsibility.

The Tory leaders were accordingly summoned to the War Council to discuss the cession of Constantinople to Russia, should it be in the gift of the Allies at the making of peace.

The event turned out very different from the anticipation. Bonar Law had no knowledge at all that he was being invited tacitly to step into a Coalition Government. None the less, with his customary acuteness, he suspected that something lay behind the invitation, and he behaved at the meeting with even more than his habitual caution.

The Prime Minister, on his side, was not in the least forthcoming. He found it in those days almost impossible to treat Tories as equals. The Tory leaders appeared to him to sit silent and hungry at the board. Inwardly they were registering a decision never to accept such an invitation again. For it was absurd to suppose that they would take responsibility for Ministerial policy when only the conclusion, and not the facts on which it was based, were put before them.

On leaving the War Council, Bonar Law and Lord Lansdowne determined that while they would meet the Prime Minister in private and listen to anything he had to tell them, they would never again fall into such a trap as the Conference on Constantinople had seemed to open before them.

Mr. Churchill's efforts, therefore, so far from promoting a working agreement between parties, leading towards a Coalition which would, as he firmly believed, strengthen the instrument for waging war, had in reality a precisely opposite effect.

CHAPTER V

A KITCHENER CRISIS

THE Government no less had its troubles and dissensions, as I have pointed out. There was far more harmony below than at the top. The brotherhood of man and of arms might embrace the rank and file, but not the Cabinet. In the country Liberals and Tory members of Parliament were speaking once more from the same platform at recruiting meetings. They even met socially in a way they had not done in all the years I sat in Parliament before the war. Especially after the Irish troubles had been forgotten Ministerialists and Opposition began to consort with each other again. There had always been, of course, a group which ignored public animosities for the sake of the pleasures of private intercourse, but it had never been a large one.

Now all this was changed. I remember distinctly my surprise in finding myself dining in the House of Commons with a set of Liberal politicians. This dinner was only the beginning of a general breaking-down of barriers to which I owe many of my present-day Liberal friends. But this atmosphere of brotherly love did not extend to Downing Street and Whitehall.

The early months of the year 1915 were marked by serious disturbances inside the Cabinet over the question of the supply of guns and ammunition to the Army in the field.*

The outside view that this question never became vital or prominent until the time of the fall of the purely Liberal Government in the Spring of 1915 and the Press campaign of that period is entirely contrary to fact. In the course of this narrative I shall have to describe three phases of what is known as the Shell controversy.

The first phase, which we have now reached, embraces the controversy beginning in October 1914, and ending with the appointment of the Shell Committee in April 1915.

The second phase is the quarrel between G.H.Q. in France and the War Office at home on this same issue, which began after Neuve Chapelle, in March 1915, and lasted till the fall of the Government on 19 May of that year.

*For the position inside the Government on this question and particularly in its effect on the relations between Mr. Lloyd George and Lord Kitchener, cf. "Twenty-Five Years," by Viscount Grey of Fallodon. (Vol. II., pages 242-243.) "When munitions ran short and he had realised what the needs were and how they would grow, he made the question his own, though it then belonged entirely to the War Office. Kitchener's principle and practice was to leave the work of other people alone, and to tolerate no interference from others with what he regarded as his job. When he found the activity of Lloyd George entering his department he barred the way. The torrent of Lloyd George's activity foamed against the obstruction, and for a time was delayed ; but it ended by sweeping before it that part of the War Office that dealt with munitions and depositing it elsewhere. In short, a separate Department of Munitions was formed, and Lloyd George's method was to get things done by searching out the ablest men for his purpose, wherever they could be found, and throwing them into the work."

The third phase may be described as the influence, such as it was, that this source of trouble had on the crisis which produced the first Coalition. For the moment I am only concerned with the first phase.

As early as October 1914 Mr. Asquith was seriously concerned with the ammunition problem. He had not reached the point of realising that in the teeth of all military advice it would be necessary to call in civilians and new firms to make good the supply, but he did consider putting the armament firms under Government control, and he appointed a special committee of the Cabinet, consisting of McKenna, Runciman, Lloyd George, with Lord Kitchener as chairman, to deal with the problem. The results attained proved, however, disappointing, because Lord Kitchener and the War Office were firmly resolved that a civilian body should not interfere in the ammunition question.

On the last day of the year Lloyd George wrote to the Prime Minister complaining about the Shell situation and criticising Kitchener on account of his neglect of the Russian position. The letter appeared to take the form of general complaints and indicates dissatisfaction and irritation with the War Office. It is as follows:

December 31, 1914.

My dear Prime Minister,

I am uneasy about the prospects of the war unless the Government take some decisive measures to grip the situation. I can see no

signs anywhere that our military leaders and
guides are considering any plans for extricating
us from our present unsatisfactory position.
Had I not been a witness of their deplorable
lack of prevision I should not have thought it
possible that men so responsibly placed could
have displayed so little forethought. You remember the guns and ammunition incident.
When I raised the question in the Cabinet the
War Office had only ordered 600 guns in all.
Those were to be delivered before next
September. The immense manufacturing resources of the country had not been organised
for cannon, rifles, or ammunition, and America
was not even explored. As a result of the
activities and suggestions of the Cabinet Committee, 4,000 guns are now promised before
that date. Ammunition has also been provided
for these guns.

     .   .   .   .   .

No real effort has been made until this week to
ascertain the Russian position. Now K. has
invited a Russian officer to come over to confer
with a view to helping Russia with ammunition.
Two months ago I pressed it on the War
Office. Had it been done then, we could have
helped Russia while Archangel was still open,
and saved her from the perils of exhausted
caissons.

Sincerely yours,
(Signed) D. Lloyd George.

By the beginning of March 1915 Lloyd George

was continuing his agitation and his campaign had taken on a controversial form. His dissatisfaction with the Shell position had increased.

On 6 March he told his friends that he intended to resign unless a Shell Committee with adequate powers was appointed. Most of March was spent in an attempt to deal with the situation created by this threat. On 18 March Asquith considered appointing Lloyd George Director of War Contracts, or something of that kind, and relieving him of his duties at the Exchequer. This was the first suggestion of a Ministry of Munitions. But nothing was done and the controversy was allowed to drift on.

Towards the end of March Mr. Asquith had summoned Lloyd George, Lord Balfour, Churchill and Montagu to a meeting which he declared would consider the whole question of putting munitions on a proper footing and of creating a committee which should have real powers to deal with the matter. It was significant that Lord Kitchener was not invited to this conclave.

On 28 March matters came to a direct issue in the Government, Kitchener indicating resignation if the committee contemplated were appointed, and Lloyd George adhering to his own threat of retirement if it were not. The end of the month found the Prime Minister still struggling to arrive at a settlement between the civilians, who felt that the military had not grasped the full import of the situation, and the soldiers at home, who regarded the intervention of the civilians with contempt.

One potent voice was, however, raised in favour of the appointment of the Shell Committee. Lord Balfour expressed grave discontent with the failure of the Government to carry into effect the opinion of the meeting which he had attended in the third week of March, and on 8 April the Shell Committee was finally constituted, and announced in the House of Commons on 15 April. It consisted of Lloyd George (as chairman), Lord Balfour, Harold Baker, George Booth, Sir Stanley von Donop and Edwin Montagu.

The last named supplied much of the hard executive work which this committee contributed to the problem set it. Montagu's abilities were extraordinary. He became the rising hope of Liberalism, the visible successor of Lord Rosebery, at almost too early an age for the hope of the morning to last into the afternoon. At twenty he had almost ceased to be young ; at thirty he was middle-aged ; at forty he already represented a maturity of judgment which accompanies real age. Unrivalled in his mental equipment, he seemed to lack the courage to take the responsibility for his own projects, sound as they invariably were, and as a consequence tougher but less able men reaped where he had sown. His early death was an irreparable loss to the State in this dreadful age of mediocrities.

The Committee was appointed, but none the less matters can hardly be said to have proceeded smoothly. Colonel Repington, speaking of the dissensions over the supply of guns at this period, writes : " Lord Kitchener did not comprehend the importance of artillery in the war, took no effective measures to increase our supplies of it, and concealed the truth of the situation from his colleagues in the Cabinet." I have never seen any refutation of this charge—though it is really quite unsubstantiated. It is founded on an incident which took place when a number of the authorities on the Shell question were together in a room, and one of the clashes Lord Grey has recorded between Lord Kitchener and Mr. Lloyd George took place.

Just before the Shell Committee was appointed Lord Kitchener had been asked by Mr. Churchill for some relative figures between men and gun material.

Kitchener turned to Asquith and said, " Must I answer ? "

Asquith said, " Yes."

Kitchener said, " I will give you the figures next week."

He did so.

In the meantime a practically identical question had been put to Sir Stanley von Donop, who also put in a return. Lloyd George, with von Donop's return before him, immediately challenged Kitchener with the bold accusation that he was being treated to cooked figures. The whole thing was probably due to a misunderstanding which could have been explained quite easily. But on the occasion of Lloyd George's attack feeling between the various supporters of the protagonists to the dispute began to run high.

Then ensued a scene truly remarkable in itself and more remarkable still in the dramatic consequences which might have flowed from it. Kitchener behaved with great dignity. He rose from the table and declared that as he appeared to have lost the confidence of some of his colleagues, who were supposed to be working with him in the supply of ammunition, he would retire. Such an action could, of course, mean nothing less than resignation from the Government. Had he succeeded in carrying out his intention, the whole history of the political direction of the war would have been altered. For so great was his external prestige at that time that his resignation must have brought about the immediate fall of the Government. Under such circumstances all the Liberals must have resigned together, and a Conservative Ministry, though in a minority in the House of Commons, must have taken office.

That this did not happen was due to two facts—that the door of the room opens *inwards*, not *outwards*, and that Mr. Pease happened to be present. He was the Postmaster-General and an ex-party Whip, and therefore a man of prompt decision in a political crisis. Pease got up and practically raced Lord Kitchener for the door. So near a thing was it that had the door opened outwards, Lord Kitchener would have passed through before Pease could have stopped him. The Postmaster-General acted swiftly, and placing his back against the door, and spreading his arms right across it, he made it impossible for Kitchener to get out—except by resorting to physical violence. During the interim some realisation of the devastating consequences of what was, after all, largely an outbreak of temper on all sides, came home to everybody. Apologies were made, and the crisis was averted.

The Prime Minister displayed some humour in pouring oil on the troubled waters. The War Office, he explained, kept three sets of figures, one to mislead the public, another to mislead the Cabinet, and the third to mislead itself. But though concord was restored to all outward appearance, Lloyd George for some time declared that it was useless for him to argue with Lord Kitchener again.

The War Secretary undoubtedly had a motive for the extraordinary secrecy he so often displayed. He used to declare facetiously that politicians talked State secrets to their families, and that on the rare occasions when he moved in society he found the women far more conversant with military facts and movements than was pleasing or expedient. It is not necessary to identify further the political and social group to which this jest applies. " My colleagues," said Kitchener, " tell military secrets to their wives, all except ——, who tells them to other people's wives."

The Shell Committee was therefore brought to birth with great pangs and labour in the Government. Yet, on 15 April, Lloyd George was chairman of the new body—and this he mainly owed to the support of Mr. Asquith, with whom he was for the moment in close accord. Indeed, when, at this period, the " Times," the " Morning

Post," and the " Observer " indulged in some severe criticism of the Prime Minister, Lloyd George assured him with tears in his eyes, and no doubt with complete sincerity, that sooner than join any cabal against him, he would prefer (1) to break stones on the road, (2) to dig potatoes in an allotment, (3) to be hanged, drawn and quartered.

And the new Shell Committee was undoubtedly believed by all who took part in it at this time to possess real powers. It has, indeed, since been claimed for it that the adequate supply of shells which appeared in France in the late summer and the autumn of 1915 was the product of its labours, rather than of the Ministry of Munitions, which five weeks later took its place. On the other hand, the chairman complained that the War Office refused it information as to the real needs and demands of the generals in the field.

Mr. Lloyd George was chairman of the committee ; it was his threat of resignation which had been chiefly instrumental in forcing the creation of the body on an unwilling War Office. There is little doubt but that if he had pressed for the necessary information with the same pertinacity he would have succeeded in obtaining it.

Finally, it should be said in fairness both to the Ordnance and to the original Shell Committee that they stated a case to prove that no orders and no exertions on their part could have produced a more adequate delivery of munitions until machinery for making shells had itself been created. They contended that this machinery was not ready until the " Shell Crisis " was over.

CHAPTER VI

"DRINK AND THE DEVIL"

IT would have seemed at this period that the Shell controversy in the Cabinet, described at the end of the last chapter, was bound to come at once to a decided issue. But events took a quite unexpected turn owing to a strange vagary on the part of the Chancellor of the Exchequer.

After the battle royal of March 1915, and a week before the final ratification of the committee's powers, Mr. Lloyd George had become obsessed with a totally different aspect of the same problem —the slow rate in the production of munitions, which he ascribed to drink. His agile mind flew off at a tangent, and all through April he was more concerned with his scheme of State purchase of the liquor trade than with compelling Whitehall to give the Shell Committee full information on the needs of the Army.

His energies became directed rather to seeing that the working man got less beer than to making certain that the soldier got more shells. The abolition of vodka in Russia went to the Chancellor's head, and he determined to carry State purchase and control in England in order to promote war efficiency.

Having not only conceived this startling ambition, but actually fired the cautious moderation of Bonar Law into agreement, it must be said that he went about the business with commendable worldly prudence. He summoned Lord Birkenhead to advise him how the country, or at least the Tory part of it, would regard such a plan.

By the beginning of April 1915 Mr. Lloyd George had divulged his idea to Radical temperance reformers and Tory front-benchers alike, and obtained for it rather a mixed reception. Bonar Law, as has been said, was favourably disposed, but he would not commit either himself or his friends in advance. This was as well, for a rising note of opposition and criticism soon began to make itself heard.

Lord Lansdowne, though using the terms of great moderation, still rather resented action which was in effect a plea of guilty to a charge of national insobriety.

Lord Long also shared the resentment of working men at this wholesale charge. He was sceptical of the practicability of the whole plan, because of its effects on Radical unity. The Radical temperance extremists, such as Whittaker and Leif Jones, would never, in his opinion, agree to a reasonable scheme of compensation. Nor would the brewers of any class support the proposals.

This review of the situation turned out to be correct. Sir Thomas Whittaker gave the plan his blessing, but Mr. Leif Jones was apparently regarded by Mr. Lloyd George as too righteous for redemption, and was not made the Chancellor's confidant.

The whole essence of any such scheme was, of course, its finance. Was the country justified in embarking, at the height of a great war, on a colossal outlay, and could the detailed application of the purchase system be made with any fairness to the various interests concerned and to the reasonable satisfaction of the trade ?

Sir Austen Chamberlain was by no means prepared to object to the plan *in toto*. He was, in fact, more sympathetic to it than the majority of his colleagues. Without prejudicing the practical issues, he was not willing to oppose the scheme if the Government declared that it was necessary for the successful prosecution of the war. At the same time, he regarded with anxiety the financial liability involved, and doubted the efficiency of State control and management.

Finally, he distrusted the Chancellor of the Exchequer's tendency to dash at big decisions without sufficient thought and preparation. This, indeed, was the crux of the whole difficulty. Mr. Lloyd George was more replete with enthusiasm than detail, and, in fact, about this period Sir Herbert Samuel was discovered proceeding to a meeting with Mr. Lloyd George charged with the somewhat belated task of producing a practical scheme.

Lord Younger and the brewing interest remained, after an interview with the Chancellor, hostile to the general conception, and their influence was probably decisive in a scale already sufficiently weighted against a somewhat rash and quixotic undertaking.

What is really interesting about this abortive proposal to nationalise the drink trade is the ameliorating effect produced on the relations between the two parties. Much of the bad effect produced by the Home Rule Act controversy was undone when the Liberal Chancellor of the Exchequer entered into consultation with all the important Opposition chiefs. It is true that Lord Birkenhead and Bonar Law were favourable to the plan, and Sir Austen Chamberlain, Lord Long and Lord Younger were not, but this division of opinion really anticipated the conditions which were certain to arise under a Coalition. The great point was that there had been free and intimate consultation between the second man in the Government and the Opposition chiefs on an important national issue. A feeling of friendliness was restored—and though the issue passed, the impression it had left behind did not. The " Drink " problem smoothed the way towards Coalition.

The next step towards nationalizing the Drink traffic was to appoint a committee, which included Lord Balfour, Bonar Law, Mr. Henderson and Sir Austen Chamberlain, to consider the proposal further. This had already begun to sit when, on 12 April 1915, the " Daily Express " burst the outlines of the scheme on the public, and asked an astonished world whether " England

was to be drowned in beer or methylated spirits."
The publication of this news led to a crisis.
Lord Birkenhead sent me an urgent message,
asking me to meet him at the Marlborough Club.
He told me there that Lloyd George held me
responsible for the publication of the news in the
" Daily Express," since he considered that
newspaper to be my organ. I was thus
" dishing " Lloyd George's plan by publishing it
in advance.

I was able to repel the accusation. I had no
substantial connection with the " Daily Express "
in those days except a small block of shares and
my personal friendship with R. D. Blumenfeld,
the Editor. It was not until two years later that
in order to protect my existing interests I took
over financial responsibility. I took no part in
policy until 1 January 1919.

But the blight of publicity proved the final
ruin of the proposal, and when Mr. Redmond also
entered a strong objection, all was over, though
Bonar Law was left mourning to Mr. Asquith
over its loss as late as the month of June 1915.

Faced with this situation, Mr. Lloyd George,
speaking in the House of Commons on 30 April
1915, abandoned his scheme with the same daring
rapidity with which he had adopted it. One
moment State purchase filled the whole bill—
the next it had vanished as though it had never
been. One may marvel at, if one can hardly
admire, the light-hearted way in which Mr.
Lloyd George picked up this vast new plan as
one might pick up a sovereign from the pavement,

and then dropped it again as quickly as if the sovereign had turned out to be a hot potato.

There was no State purchase, and the morals of England, in the long run, were left to the tender mercies of Lord D'Abernon and the Liquor Control Board, whose measures met with a considerable degree of success, even if his successors occasionally fall into the error of confusing Carlisle with Paradise.

Of all the wild and visionary schemes which flitted across men's minds during the great disturbance of the war, this, I should imagine, was the most impracticable. Its author buried it with almost indecent promptitude, and the funeral party hastily dispersed to deal with more pressing problems. This was the last big question which arose in home politics before the crisis which led to the formation of the first Coalition. It was not until 19 May, after the Liberal Government had fallen, that Lloyd George turned back again to the Shell problem from which he had allowed his attention to be diverted, and indited a vigorous attack on our past deficiencies in the supply of ammunition. But it will be convenient to postpone the discussion of this memorandum of 19 May until the actual crisis of mid-May has been dealt with.

While all appeared to be quiet on the surface, something was moving in the depths of the waters more potent to affect the ultimate result of the war than German submarines. Lloyd George was undergoing a subtle change of view and character. He had been seen in the past as a pacifist—the opponent of " swollen naval estimates," the protagonist of social reform, who went into the war reluctantly, almost as though impelled by some force outside himself. The man of peace was now at war. The new environment began to act on that responsive temperament, and nerves hitherto quiescent in that complex nature began to tingle into life. His moves from the Exchequer to Munitions in 1915, and from Munitions to the War Office in 1916, simply mark his march through the years from the pacifist doubter of 1914 to the greatest War Minister England had seen for over a hundred years.

The Queen's Hall speech in September 1915 was the first outward sign that Mr. George the semi-pacifist had ceased to exist. In that splendid oration he, too, like the generation of which he spoke, had to renounce and recant much, and to make a new dedication of spirit " to the great everlasting things that matter for a nation—the great peaks of honour we had forgotten—duty, patriotism, and, clad in glittering white, the great pinnacle of sacrifice pointing like a ragged finger to heaven." Terrible as it would have been to the Prime Minister to have found in Mr. Lloyd George the leader of a peace-at-any-price party in August 1914, his new development was hardly less disquieting.

Hitherto, if Asquith had been the directing brains of Liberalism, Lloyd George had been the strong heart sending the fresh blood of new policies coursing through the party veins. But how if head and heart ceased to work in unison ?

Throughout the year Lloyd George studied the development of events and listened to the rambling and cryptic discourses of Lord Kitchener. The experience left him profoundly disquieted. By the opening of 1915 he was a discontented colleague within the Cabinet, pointing to weaknesses and demanding remedies. He was no longer the animating soul of the Government as in the good old days of peace— but its terror—the spirit which denied all the facile promptings of optimism. Worse than his discontent was the fact that he let it be known outside. Wise Liberal heads were shaken over this vagary of a second-in-command, sure, if he would only keep quiet, to succeed to the Premiership somewhere about 1930.

Already, as early as January 1915, the idea of mobilising peace industries for the production of munitions of war was beginning to stir in his brain, and in opposition to Kitchener he had little belief in the Russian Army if it was not stiffened and supported by a constant flow of shells, guns, rifles and cartridges. While Lord Fisher was urging his Baltic adventure and Churchill was preaching the Dardanelles crusade, Lloyd George was for Salonika, the Balkans, and an attack on Austria—a scheme from which he never swerved from start to finish.

He was earnestly advocating aggressive action on behalf of Serbia, and a letter was written at the end of January, as follows :

January 29, 1915.

Dear Lord Kitchener,

You will, I am sure, have seen telegram No. 14 in last night's sections from Sofia. It is so obviously the German interest to crush Serbia in order to detach Bulgaria from the Triple Entente and to free a way to Constantinople, that it is risky to doubt the accuracy of the telegram. The French delayed assistance to Antwerp until it was too late. This time the responsibility is ours, and we shall not be held blameless if a catastrophe occurs.

Ever sincerely,
(Signed) D. Lloyd George.

It was natural, therefore, that our handling of King Tino of Greece, the great stumbling block to British Balkan policy, should incur his special wrath : " Tino," he said, " is the Kaiser's chief spy in Europe, and we write him lawyers' letters ! " But he secured more unpopularity by the trenchant expression he gave his views than support for the views themselves, and in February was observing gloomily that " while the whole Press is describing the war as an unbroken success, the facts are precisely the contrary." The early spring, then, was marked by this rising note of warning, menace, and appeal from the new strategist.

Yes, singular as the fact is, Lloyd George had a genius for strategy. Whence comes the instinct for war ? While Churchill in his young days was slaking his thirst for military glory on the fields of India, Egypt, and Africa, Lloyd George was defending Nonconformist trespassers on Church property and slowly rising to fame as the hope of the stern, unbending pro-Boers.

Yet both men possess the same aptitude for war. And there was a further resemblance—a defect—in their military mentality. Once they made up their minds they were immovable—no argument, no contention that the facts had changed since the original opinion was formed could move them in the slightest degree. Thus, neither of them was at any time a Westerner, and while Churchill always believed that the War could be won through Gallipoli, Lloyd George was equally constant in his conviction that it could be won in the Balkans.

He wrote on 7 February 1915 to Sir Edward Grey summarising his whole attitude on this issue. A copy of the letter will be found in Volume I of " War Memoirs of Lloyd George " and should be read by those interested in the Eastern or Western schools.

This fixity of idea was all the more curious in Lloyd George's case—because in many respects his mind was so fluid and impressionable.

Somewhere in the recesses of Lloyd George's mind there moved a strange instinct, not always given to field-marshals, but to middle-aged civilians, like Cromwell, for knowing what was happening on the other side of the hill, or, in this case, across the sea and on the other side of Europe. As the compass turns to the north, so Lloyd George's instinct always turned in the direction of the menace. Conversation after conversation attested this uncanny prescience. But in the opening stages of the war his was the fate of Cassandra—to foresee and to be disbelieved on the word of the nearest major-general.

But the man who simply sits down and prophesies correctly—and Lloyd George, too, like everybody else, made plenty of mistakes, notably on Russia and over man-power—is not destined to be the national standard bearer in a supreme crisis. Lloyd George had not only the energy of words, but the energy of action. He was full of offensive and defensive plans to meet the emergencies he foresaw.

Once he had taken up war as his metier he seemed .to breathe its true spirit; all other thoughts and schemes were abandoned, and he lived for, thought of, and talked of nothing but the war. Ruthless to inefficiency and muddle-headedness in his conduct, sometimes devious, if you like, in the means employed when indirect methods would serve him in his aim, he yet exhibited in his country's death-grapple a kind of splendid sincerity. And he was thrifty of human life. He would not press failures at the cost of huge butcher's bills. He was against prolonging the agony of the Dardanelles; he protested against the final and futile horrors of Paschendaele in 1917.

When confronted with the statement that German companies were by that date reduced to the strength of 70 men instead of 200, and that G.H.Q. therefore thought success certain, he brushed it aside as a truth-loving judge might a lawyer's formal plea. Of course, it may be said that in both these decisions he was influenced by his dominant idea of a campaign in the Balkans, but that does not alter the facts.

But what must be our main judgment on the personality itself, which more and more as this story proceeds casts the shadow of its influence over the troubled waters ? A combination of enormous physical ability joined to a mentality so voracious of experience and so sensitive to atmosphere as to attain to greatness by the very variety and immensity of its attributes ; a physique so constituted that sleep comes at will at any hour of the day, and that illness is only a high temperature—such are the capacites which make Mr. Lloyd George.

His is, no doubt, the practical mind lacking the broad philosophic view which makes Lord Balfour tower above his contemporaries, or the power of lucid and ordered argument in which Churchill shines, and yet, taking it all in all, in the sum of its qualities, its passions, its knowledge, its expression, its understanding of a whole nation, greater than Balfour's or than that of Churchill either.

Perhaps his most valuable asset is the amazing charm of his personality. Men will go in to him in a frame of mind charged with suspicion, believing him capable of any villainy. They will come out saying, " We have been misinformed ; whatever that man is, he is no scoundrel or impostor."

In a word, he understands how to deal with the personal factor. He resembled Mr. Asquith in that he was always intensely interested in the personalities of his colleagues in office—but the interest of the two successive Liberal Premiers differed in its quality. Mr. Asquith was interested in the mental attainments of his friends and subordinates, and his appraisement was often touched with a certain intellectual contempt, as of a superior mind detecting weaknesses. On such topics he would be ready to talk freely. Lloyd George, on the other hand, looks at his colleagues on the human and social sides. He would ask not what a man's brains were, but what his habits, his preferences, his private virtues or vices. As a consequence, his distribution of offices sometimes seemed almost haphazard.

Finally, he is a good friend while it lasts, but there are no lasting friendships at the very summit of politics. Once he is estranged, there is none of that lingering afterglow which makes us still cherish memory and hesitate to strike the sometime companion.

Lloyd George goes right-about-face like a flash, and by this means re-establishes his position even more firmly over the fallen body of his quondam ally. On the other hand, reconciliations with him are equally facile ; but death alone can secure his lasting praise. This is well seen in the case of Lord Rhondda, who was his opponent and then his friend, and has been since so canonised by Lloyd George that no praise of him can be too high. It is his military aptitude shown in personal politics ; no hesitation, no tenderness ; make up your mind swiftly, and hit hard. It would be interesting to inquire how much of the mentality which makes him great in war springs directly from his long training and pre-eminence as a political tactician. Much there is in common between the two arts. Both require prescience and insight into the mind of the enemy ; both a careful calculation of existing resources, adaptability to meet new conditions pushed to a supreme degree, dazzling rapidity of movement, cold caution at one moment and stark courage at the next. Not that Lloyd George is one who makes up his mind over-quickly and then repents.

Until the actual moment of decision he sways visibly between various alternatives and is plainly influenced by the advice given him. Once his decision is taken, all is over, and further talk is so much waste of breath.

Yet when Lloyd George boasts himself as the last word in " political strategy," he does himself at once something more and something less than justice. He has made plenty of mistakes which would have ruined another man. When he has escaped the penalty he has done so by his genius for theatrical management, which always makes him withdraw a piece which has failed before it is actually hissed off the stage.

He knows that the people see high politics much like a film picture ; they will forget that you have fallen down the stairs in the last reel if you are doing something brilliant in the present one. But though he may be a master of this game, the massive weight of his personality raises him far above the level of the mere political strategist.

He lives for fame ; vices he has none, simple tastes many, unless ambition be a vice—in which case "he is the most offending soul alive." For fame is the passion of his soul and the light of his life ; it has supported him in his terrible labours, and nerved him against cruel attacks. To be popular in both senses of the term, to be one with and adored by the people, to be at once a patriot, a hero, and a democrat, so that all three attributes mingle in the atmosphere of a single blaze of glory, such has been the desire of a lifetime achieved.

Nor has this career necessarily reached its zenith ; there lie beyond it other heights which he has set himself to scale, and the record of his past and the still unabated fires of his late middle-age promise him the fulfilment of his further desires. And, indeed, as long as he is alive he will never cease struggling upwards. Mr. Asquith once described Bonar Law as "mildly ambitious." Strike out the epithet "mildly," and you have Lloyd George. And if he can be contrasted with Bonar Law on the score of ambition, he differed from Asquith no less in the character of his personality. Asquith's intelligence and mentality were sufficiently simple for him to be able to describe himself and his own process of thought with complete accuracy. Lloyd George's are so complex that he never can. No description, therefore, of his mind whether given by himself or by another, can hope to satisfy him ; for what is true of him in one of his Protean shapes must of necessity be false of him in another. Such was the character who, loaded with a legacy of Tory hate, and rapidly adding to the burden of growing unpopularity among his more passive Liberal colleagues, set out to save his country.

How far he succeeded in realising his ideals this narrative will show.

But before I break off from the subject of Mr. Lloyd George and his activities in the Spring of 1915 I will quote at length from a letter written to the Prime Minister, from which I have eliminated nothing except a personal reference to Major-Gen. Sir John Hanbury Williams and General Sir Arthur Paget.

Treasury Chambers,
Whitehall, S. W.
Feb. 18, 1915.

My dear Prime Minister,

The situation revealed by Lord Kitchener's statement at this morning's Cabinet meeting is a grave one, and I strongly urge that the War Council should take it into consideration at once. After seven months' war we do not even now know approximately the position of the Russians. Sir John French told me that he had been assured by the Russian officers who visited him that Russia would have 3,000,000 of men fully equipped in the field next month, and that they could then sweep back the German and Austrian armies opposed to them. The War Office compute the Russian forces now at

1,200,000. If Sir John French's information be correct the Russian reinforcements available in March would come to 1,800,000. Now we learn that the Russians have no rifles to equip their new men with, and that they can only turn out rifles at the rate of 40,000 per month. At that rate they can only bring 500,000 more men into the field by this time next year. The Germans are capturing more than 40,000 Russians with their rifles each month. What is the truth about their equipment ? We surely ought to know. Our fate depends upon it.

I ventured in October last to express my doubts as to the Russian equipment, and I suggested then that we should take definite steps to ascertain how they were situated. I thought then it might be possible to arrange a meeting between the three War Ministers—or responsible representatives.

. . . . .

We ought to have a searching and candid survey of the whole military situation, with a view to devising the best means for meeting it—otherwise we shall drift into irretrievable disaster.

There has been a deplorable lack of coordination between East and West, and as long as it lasts the Germans will continue winning. Mere optimistic bluff is not going to float us through this hurricane.

Ever sincerely,
(Sd.) D. Lloyd George.

. . . . .

An attack of pneumonia brought me home from France in the early spring, and on my way out again at the end of April I met Churchill. He told me with great indignation that Bonar Law had thought fit to give him a lecture on his conduct of the Admiralty, " rating me like an angry Prime Minister rebuking an unruly subordinate." Churchill seemed utterly unaware that Bonar Law had very good reasons in what was going on inside the Tory party for giving the First Lord a caution. But he took the hint in bad part, oblivious of the shadows of doom now creeping upon the Government and his own administration, and sublimely ignorant that he was the principal object which was casting that shadow.

In May I received a warning that trouble was ahead from a telegraphic message, which reached me at St. Omei, telling me that a crisis in the Admiralty was approaching.

Events were fast moving towards some momentous development.

CHAPTER VII

SHELLS

IT was common knowledge that an acute difference of opinion had arisen between the Higher Command in France and the military authorities at home as to responsibility for recent failures to advance, and that this dispute centred round the supply of ammunition.

The Shell controversy was occupying the minds of Ministers. I have described in a previous chapter the attempt at increasing supplies by means of a Committee presided over by Mr. Lloyd George and appointed in opposition to the views of Lord Kitchener.

Bonar Law's attitude towards the agitation over Shells was this. He thought that the whole method of supplying munitions should be rectified. But this should be done, first of all, by a private inquiry on the part of the Opposition leaders into the Ministerial plans, and not by a vote of censure in the House of Commons, which would cause national scandal and danger. Should private representation fail, then, and only then, ought the Conservative party to resort to public attack. Such representations he pressed on the Government with vigour. He was strengthened in this view by the fact that negotiations were on foot which ended in Italy joining the Allies within the month. He firmly believed that a Shell debate might damage or imperil the relations with Italy. He intended to impose this view on the free-lances of his party, and was quite sure that he could do so.

I will now relate in greater detail the story of the " Shell Scandal " in the Spring of 1915.

The " Shell Scandal " really began at the battle of Neuve Chapelle, 10 March 1915. No doubt, deceiving himself, and certainly misleading others, Lord French represented that action to the public as a triumphant victory. I was in the battle area at the time, attached to the Canadians, and the plain truth is that it was a horribly costly failure.

This truth began to percolate to England by way of soldiers' letters and officers on leave, and in a few weeks was the common talk of the mess and the canteen at home, whence it began to reach the public as a whole. In the meantime, the second battle of Ypres, lasting from 22 April well into May, and succeeded by the great attack on the Aubers Ridge (variously known as the action of Festubert, Givenchy and Fromelles) which began on 9 May, had clearly revealed the deficiencies in our ammunition supply and the power of the German defensive.

Lord French was, in fact, faced by failure, and by failure which at the beginning he had represented as success. He stood to his defence, and that defence was that he had to break off the action of Neuve Chapelle just as it was going to succeed, because his gun ammunition had run out.

The answer to any such excuse from a general is that you ought not to enter into an offensive battle unless you have enough ammunition. The commander who miscalculates is seriously to blame.

I well remember a soldier and member of Parliament at General Headquarters—Captain Stanley Wilson, M.P.—describing to me in those critical weeks, with great prescience, exactly what form this policy of the offensive-defensive against the home authorities would assume. " We have failed, we have lost many lives." This was the gist of the G.H.Q. case. " There may be a popular outcry—very well, then, let us concentrate it quickly on the home authorities."

It is quite true that the Army had not enough ammunition, certainly not enough high explosive ; it is by no means clear that the military authorities at the front were not as much responsible for this state of affairs as the War Office or the Government. On this point I shall have more to say in discussing Lord Kitchener's whole career during the war.

It was while affairs were shaping in this way that Colonel Repington came to stay with Lord French, not as a correspondent, for no war correspondents were permitted, but as a personal friend. Colonel Repington was a very clever man, and his advice and assistance would be of great value to the Commander-in-Chief in finding the way out of the difficulties in which the latter's description of Neuve Chapelle as a victory had involved him. The attack on the Aubers Ridge began on 9 May, and it was of the fighting at Richebourg and Fromelles that the " Times " published the statement on Friday, 14 May: " The shortage of high explosive was a fatal bar to our military success."

I have already described in a previous chapter how much anxiety the Shell question was causing in the mind of the Government, even as far back as 1914, and how Lloyd George had threatened to resign over it in March. The weakness in our munition supplies was therefore perfectly well known, both in France and Westminster, for a very considerable period before the crisis of May arose. We have been told by Lord French how Colonel Brinsley-Fitzgerald and Captain Guest came home on a mission from the Commander-in-Chief and interviewed prominent politicians on this very question. But it was not merely that Guest saw Lloyd George and Fitzgerald interviewed Bonar Law. They and other officers and members of Parliament attached to G.H.Q. talked to every member of the Commons who could be got to listen to them—and this kind of conversation had been going on for weeks before anything serious was published in the Press about a lack of high explosive. A few guarded comments had appeared in the newspapers, but that was all.

The first result of this agitation was a somewhat mild and inconclusive debate in the House of Commons on 21 April on the subject of the organisation of the munition supply. Professor

Hewins, Bonar Law and Lloyd George all took part. It centred, however, chiefly round the questions of " Drink " and " Trade Union Rules " —although Bonar Law said one or two sharp things about Ministerial secrecy, and remarked that he was continually being told by supporters that he did not criticise the Government enough. Anyone, however, who tries to treat this debate as any real form of censure connected with a Shell shortage scandal is reading history backwards. All the suggestions put forward by the Opposition were tentative in character and expressed in mild tones.

Another result of this secret agitation from G.H.Q. in France was to stir into activity the Unionist Business Committee, of which Sir Ernest Pollock, now the Master of the Rolls, was chairman, and Sir William Bull secretary. Professor Hewins drew up a form of motion, to be put down in the name of Mr. Sanderson, now Chief Justice of Bengal, calling the attention of the House of Commons to the shortage of ammunition in France.

Bonar Law, maintaining his attitude of " patriotic opposition," objected to the motion. Sir Ernest Pollock saw him, and he then went and talked to the Business Committee. As a consequence, all action in the matter was postponed. Bonar Law, in fact, quelled the movement and would have kept it in subjection easily enough until he had satisfied himself that Ministers were not ready and able to abolish the Shell scandal themselves, and in any case until the

Italian question was settled. This interview took place before 13 May, on which date the House rose.

When, therefore, Colonel Repington published his despatch on Friday, 14 May, his statements were old news to the Opposition members and contained no information for Whitehall or Westminster.

There would not have been any rumpus at all over what was a defence of Lord French rather than an attack on the Government had not one astute mind at least seen in a single phrase in the " Times " despatch potential political dynamite. Mr. Lloyd George grasped at once that if the general public were told with sufficient vehemence that we were failing in France for lack of gun ammunition he would be powerfully aided in enforcing his own munitions policy on the reluctant soldiers. He therefore inspired Lord Northcliffe to take up the question.

That agitation itself began in the mildest manner by his newspapers calling attention to Colonel Repington's statement in the " Times " of Friday 14 May. These articles were published during the few days, almost hours, which marked the fall of the Liberal Government and the formation and announcement of the new Coalition Ministry. They were not very deadly, and at any rate, they were directed against a corpse. It was not until after the formation of the first Coalition Ministry had been formally announced in the House of Commons that the real Northcliffe Shell agitation began.

The Liberal Government fell from a set of causes totally unconnected with Shells. What these causes were will be set forth in the following chapter.

Lord Northcliffe did not bring that Government down—what he did was to make certain of the creation of a Ministry of Munitions with powers adequate to the conceptions of its first head— Mr. Lloyd George.

This was not the first time that Northcliffe had contemplated a drastic intervention in the conduct of the war. We have seen that he had threatened the strongest opposition if the Expeditionary Force left the country, but in practice did nothing when his opinion was disregarded. The Shell Shortage agitation was conducted with great vigour, and undoubtedly had a good deal to do with the improvement in the position in this respect. This campaign was merged into that directed against Lord Kitchener.

Northcliffe undoubtedly believed sincerely that Lord Kitchener's removal from the War Office was a matter of the most pressing national importance. He knew also at the time of launching it that Kitchener was getting unpopular in the Cabinet—but he failed to realise the extent to which the War Secretary had retained his prestige with the man in the street. For this latter reason Northcliffe never carried out his full original intention with regard to the campaign. This, he told me one afternoon at the Ritz Hotel, was to go on attacking Lord Kitchener day in, day out, until he had driven him from office. But he was,

like all public men, too sensitive to an unfavourable atmosphere to push the matter through.
After a time he drew back, and the attacks
ceased.

Thus, in the period under review in this book,
Northcliffe had three disagreements with the
Ministry on grave issues of policy, namely—
Expeditionary Force, Shells and Kitchener.

On the first one he was silent—the second one he
pushed home successfully with the assistance of
certain members of the Cabinet. In the third
instance he began an assault, but did not charge
home.

Northcliffe was a man of great ability and
attractive character. He was very agreeable to
talk to, though he could not place his arguments
in a sequence which led to an inevitable conclusion, but on the contrary, jumped at the
conclusion at once and then simply reiterated it.
He was hampered during the war by the fact that
while he had profound knowledge of newspapers
and publicity, he had no realisation whatever of
the political temperament. Thus, he had no first-
hand experience of the medium through which he
was trying to work.

In his early life the politicians would not accept
him. To them he was simply a man newly risen
from the ranks, who owned newspapers, many of
which possessed no political influence. They
refused to recognise either his great gifts or his
coming power. They tried to treat him as the
Minister dealt with the old-time journalist—some-
body to be given little tit-bits of news as a present

in return for flattery and Press support. These methods naturally led to an estrangement.

When it was too late for the politicians to alter their attitude the tables had been turned. When they were willing and anxious to consort with Northcliffe he would have none of them. He often told me that he was better off as a journalist because he did not consort with Ministers or ex-Ministers, and that for his own part he never wanted, as a private individual, to have anything to do with them.

This deliberate abstention from one source of knowledge was a great weakness to him when he had perforce to deal with politicians and politics during the war. He did not know political dynamite when he saw it. At least, he did not know where to place it, or where to explode it. It was this fact which led to his failure to bring down Ministries of which he sincerely disapproved. If he had known what dynamite in politics was, he could have overturned the Liberal Ministry of 1914-1915 easily enough. But because he had not this knowledge he had nothing to do with its overthrow. When in turn he became keenly anxious to upset the First Coalition Ministry which followed, he had no idea how to set about it—although the task was not very difficult. So that his contribution to the change of Government in 1916 was an indirect one. He desired it greatly, and he prepared public opinion for the change.

Again in 1918 he could have destroyed the Lloyd George—Conservative combination at the very outset if he had taken the right course. He disliked the Coalition sincerely enough, but he did not grasp the particular appeal to the constituencies which would have ruined it. His idea was to be a kind of Clemenceau—the wrecker of incompetent Ministries. But he never could achieve this ideal, because he could not lay his mind side by side with the political mind and so pierce through to the human side of the problem. Even when a Minister or leader was quite ready to come to an accommodation with him, he could not grasp the moment for a deal. He would lecture eminent public men as if they were somewhat refractory schoolboys—and this attitude broke the touch between him and them.

On the other hand, he was successful enough in his assaults on the reputations of particular Ministers in the war, and by sheer pertinacity dragged more than one to the ground.

To all broad principles Northcliffe adhered unflinchingly, once he had fully grasped them. He was absolutely dauntless in his belief in victory, and it was really inspiring to talk to him in bad hours. Nor was this a pose as it was in the case of some of the statesmen.

But he was capable of amazing confusion of mind, as in the case of the despatch of the British Expeditionary Force. I can give another instance. At the end of the war he put out an immense manifesto to be published in his own newspapers, and as an advertisement in others—laying down what the conditions of Peace ought to be. I am told that this was prepared for him in the Enemy Propaganda Department which he controlled.

His staff brought it to him and said that it ought to be published under his name. Northcliffe replied : " Well, let's hear it." As the reading of this vital document continued, it became increasingly clear that Northcliffe was not listening with attention. In reply to an enquiry as to whether he approved of the substance, he gave his staff to understand that his mind was fully occupied with distribution and means of attaining publicity. Thus a document of great importance to his reputation was given to the world with the utmost carelessness as to its meaning, but with vast ingenuity in securing that it should be read.

Northcliffe was, as I have said, a potent force, and proved again and again a powerful factor, compelling the Government to recognise public opinion on war issues. But that was not his ideal. He desired to hold high office, and his associates told him they believed he would attain to a War Premiership.

Whatever the political world may think of Northcliffe, one fact can never be disputed. He was the greatest figure who ever strode down Fleet Street. He had created the character, type and temper of every newspaper which he owned— and there have been few changes of importance in Fleet Street since he left. He established his conceptions of journalism, not only by the direct influence which he brought to bear on that part of the Press he controlled, but indirectly by the example which he set to his competitors.

CHAPTER VIII

THE FALL OF THE GOVERNMENT

WHAT was the real cause of the fall of the Liberal Government in the Spring of 1915 ?

To put the truth boldly and bluntly, it had nothing whatever to do with the Shell scandal and was produced solely and entirely by the dissensions at the Admiralty between Mr. Churchill and Lord Fisher, which culminated in Fisher's resignation.

The idea that the shortage of shells was the cause of the Ministerial collapse has become so ingrained in our mentality that men who knew better have thought this was so themselves.

There are several natural reasons for the existence of this delusion.

By a pure coincidence the " Times," owned by Lord Northcliffe, published a dispatch from the Front exposing our weakness in gun ammunition, on Friday, 15 May. That was the actual day of Lord Fisher's resignation. A few mild articles on the lines of the Repington protest appeared over the week-end in the " Daily Mail." But during this week-end, as I shall prove in this chapter, the Liberal Government had fallen dead by agree-

ment between Asquith, Lloyd George and Bonar
Law. On the Monday, 17 May, Bonar Law wrote
a formal letter announcing the decision of his
colleagues to take a part in the Government
precisely because of what had happened at the
Admiralty. On Wednesday, the 19th, the new
Government was announced. None the less the
old Government, to the popular mind—which
knew nothing of internal causes—appeared to
fall to the accompaniment of a series of cautiously-
worded statements in the popular Press which
merged (*after the Ministry had fallen*) into a real
shriek about a Shell scandal.

This thoroughly confused the outside judgment,
which soon began to believe that the Government
had fallen *because* of these attacks.

But, apart from the public, not even some of the
men most intimately concerned with these events
knew the truth. I refer especially to the late Lord
Northcliffe and Mr. Churchill, who in one degree
or another countenanced the delusion that the
Shell scandal was either a factor or the deciding
factor in the fall of the Government. Northcliffe's
reiterated assertion, of course, spread the legend
to millions of people until it absolutely swallowed
the truth.

I do not question the honesty of the convictions
Northcliffe and Churchill respectively entertained
on the subject. Neither of them was aware of
what was happening in the inner political ring.
Lord Northcliffe knew nothing of any change of
Government until the night of Tuesday, 18 May—
four days after Fisher had resigned, and after

a Coalition had been definitely arranged. Next day, however, Lord Northcliffe's organ did summarise the causes of the collapse, in this order : (1) Resignation of Lord Fisher, (2) Trouble over Shells. But the first cause—in reality the only one—was soon forgotten by Lord Northcliffe.

Churchill was ignorant, too, as to what was going on. He had been kept in the dark by his own colleagues. He was not told of the negotiations with the Conservatives. In fact, he was treated shabbily. So he might be forgiven for misunderstanding the course events actually took, seeing that he knew nothing about the crisis at all until he came down to the House of Commons on the Monday afternoon.

However, writing years after the event, he ascribes the causes of the collapse to (1) Shells, (2) Fisher's resignation—and he reinforces this statement by saying that the leaders of the Opposition had given notice that they intended to demand a debate on Shells. The official Conservatives, as we have seen in the preceding chapter, never at any time contemplated such a course. Therefore Mr. Churchill is quite mistaken, not only in enumerating Shells as the primary cause of his disaster, but in mentioning them as a cause at all. Possibly both Northcliffe and Churchill were subconsciously swayed in the direction of thinking that Shells brought down the Government because both would have liked it to be true.

Northcliffe would naturally believe that he had destroyed a Ministry through his newspapers. It would be as naturally unpleasing for Churchill to feel that his conduct of the Admiralty had brought down the administration of which he was a leading member—however sure he was that his policy was right.

To anyone who examines impartially the evidence contained in the following narrative it will be abundantly clear that Shells did not produce the fall of the Liberal Ministry, but that the quarrel at the Admiralty did.

I will now resume the sequence in point of time of my narrative of events. I left it at Friday, 14 May—the day on which Colonel Repington's article on the shortage of munition supply at the front had been published. On that day something had occurred at the Admiralty which led directly and instantly to the downfall of the Liberal Government. On that Friday, Admiral Lord Fisher resigned in protest against the action of Mr. Winston Churchill, First Lord of the Admiralty, and within five days of his resignation the First Coalition Government was formed.

It was the clash between these two powerful intellects which overthrew the first British War Ministry—and therefore the story of their friendship and disagreement is worth recording.

Lord Fisher's appointment was originally due to a weakness in Mr. Churchill's position at the Admiralty, which came to a head in the October of 1914, when Prince Louis of Battenberg was retired. Mr. Churchill would far rather have kept Prince Louis as First Sea Lord—and, in fact, did keep him, in face of racial popular clamour, long enough to damage himself.

In addition, Mr. Churchill was blamed, largely unjustly, for the loss of the three torpedoed cruisers, for Antwerp, and for the despatch of the untrained Naval Brigade, and the internment of so many of them in Holland.

Finally, he made an ill-advised speech at Liverpool about digging the Germans out of their holes like rats, which had been seized on by his political enemies.

This last episode points, indeed, to the root cause of Churchill's subsequent troubles at the Admiralty—a failure to keep himself in touch with existing political opinion, owing to the immense energy he devoted to his immediate official duties. But of this I shall have more to say later. Anyhow, a cold wind was blowing on him in October 1914, and he has since recognised the fact. He therefore pressed hard for Fisher's appointment as a support to his own position—which was really another mistake.

Churchill co-opted Fisher to relieve the pressure against himself, but he had no intention of letting anyone else rule the roost. Here, then, were two strong men of incompatible tempers both bent on an autocracy. It only required a difference of opinion on policy to produce a clash, and this cause of dissension was not long wanting.

Fisher's master notion in the war was a landing in the Baltic behind the German lines ; the Russians were to supply the troops and the British Navy to land them, perhaps within a hundred miles of Berlin. This idea of a blow at the heart of Germany seems to have originated with the successful invasion by sea carried out by the Russians against Frederick the Great in the course of the Seven Years War. It was impossible to say that the plan was impracticable, but it required a violent act of faith to believe in it and its consequences, involving immense preparations of quite new types of vessels. These Fisher set about preparing with his customary energy, and Churchill raised no effective objection at the outset. Then came the Dardanelles expedition, and the whole situation changed. There was only a certain amount of men and material to go round, so that the Baltic scheme was always pulling against the Dardanelles adventure, and vice versa.

Here, then, were two men in a single department, each with a rival project—Fisher bent on the Baltic plan, and Churchill firmly believing that the Dardanelles was the better way.

This divergence was in itself quite sufficient to produce a rupture. There was another cause for the Admiral's discontent, not specially directed against Churchill, though touching his interests. The special and privileged position held by Lord Kitchener—a soldier sitting in the Cabinet—was a source of irritation to the distinguished sailor. Why should the Army have a member in the inner ring of the Government while the expert head of the Navy was only an adviser ? And was not Fisher as good a man as Kitchener ?

Fisher could not realise the unique position which Kitchener held in the British Empire, so that in his own lifetime he had become more of a mythical demigod than a mere man. Lord Fisher was, of course, a great man, but he was nothing more, and therefore constitutional rules were not broken in his favour. None the less, the grievance rankled, and in conversation with his friends he frequently declared that Churchill should go and that he ought to succeed him as First Lord.

Fisher's resignation was therefore not only a trial of strength on definite naval issues with Churchill, it was directed against the Government as a whole and the subordinate position he occupied under it. A new Government was to make him First Lord and right the Navy's wrongs. And this fact perhaps explains the violence of his method of resigning. He did not merely wish to defeat Churchill over the Dardanelles and Baltic issue. He was waving a flag and courting a wholesale crash.

Thus, after a time Fisher became a voluminous correspondent, and his letters of complaint were expelled with the rapidity and force of machine gun bullets and found targets in the breasts of Opposition members of the House of Commons. Indeed, he had written long letters over his signature denouncing the Dardanelles operations root and branch—and this was well before his resignation.

The wounds festered in the breast of a party which, in any case, viewed Churchill by this time with distrust. Fisher was the apostle of Toryism, the Dardanelles expedition was unpopular, and Fisher was known first to be lukewarm, and later actually opposed. Furthermore, the Tory opposition said that while a strong and famous man was First Sea Lord some check was imposed on Churchill, while an ordinary sailor would be helpless.

But what if Fisher were to go ? The Conservative party would not tolerate a tame Board nominated by Churchill and subservient to his policies. Churchill did not know it, but he was like a man chained to an enemy—so that both must live or die together. If you throw your chained enemy into the sea he pulls you after him.

As has already been mentioned, enough ferment had been worked up on the Opposition side by the end of April 1915 to induce Bonar Law to give Churchill a warning, which was disregarded. In May the long-delayed explosion took place. Lord Fisher privately tendered his resignation to the Prime Minister. There were several conjoint causes for his action, and he received encouragement from devoted and influential persons. On 12 May the " Goliath " had been sunk in the Aegean—another sacrifice to the Dardanelles—while the fate of the " Lusitania " indicated to the First Sea Lord's mind that we were not putting a sufficient proportion of our efforts into the mastery of the northern seas and into suppressing the submarine menace. The actual point of conflict was the diversion of men and material by Churchill to the Dardanelles against the wish of Lord Fisher.

If Lord Fisher had contented himself with a simple resignation in the ordinary form, it is quite certain that he would have succeeded in ousting Mr. Churchill and would have remained at the

Admiralty in his old position. Indeed, he might have become First Lord. Instead of this, on the Saturday he pulled down his blinds with a dramatic gesture and, walking over to the Treasury, caught the Chancellor of the Exchequer just as he was starting for the country. To him he simply announced that he had resigned and that, further, he was not going back to the Admiralty at all. Lloyd George was thunderstruck. The news came to him as an absolute bombshell, for he was utterly unaware that Lord Fisher had the slightest intention of resigning.

The Sea Lord said to Lloyd George that the long-delayed crash had come over the diversion of certain units and material to the Mediterranean, which had taken place, in Lord Fisher's opinion, without due notice having been given him.

Mr. Lloyd George drew Lord Fisher into his room and sent for Mr. Asquith, who came. But in spite of the remonstrances and entreaties of the two men that Fisher should at least remain at his post for the time being, they utterly failed to shake him in his decision not to remain.

Another intermediary was then sent for. Mr. McKenna had been First Lord of the Admiralty when Lord Fisher was a First Sea Lord, locked in a technical strategic and political battle to the death with Lord Charles Beresford. It was the cordial support of McKenna which had then saved Fisher from destruction at the hands of his enemies, and consequently he had considerable influence with the distinguished sailor. All other means failing, and Fisher remaining locked in his room at the Admiralty and refusing to see anyone from the Government, McKenna was despatched as a private friend to try and get him to see reason. The blinds were indeed down in the First Sea Lord's room, but McKenna caught Fisher's eye peering out at him from behind the cover. After that he would take no denial and was finally let in.

In a long argument that followed McKenna completely failed to convince Fisher that he was pursuing a mistaken course. The First Sea Lord handed his keys over, so to speak, but resolutely declined to sit down again at his desk.

Lord Fisher departed for Scotland and left the Admiralty without a First Sea Lord at the very height of a great war. This action made it absolutely impossible for any Ministry to recall him to office, and thus, though Churchill went and the Government fell, no profit accrued to Lord Fisher.

Mr. Asquith at first decided to support his First Lord, Mr. Churchill, and gave permission for a new Board to be appointed, with Sir Arthur Wilson at the head of it, and this would have to be announced when the House met in the following week. But the Prime Minister had forgotten the Opposition.

It is now necessary, therefore, to examine Lord Fisher's action from the standpoint of the Tory camp.

Just as the Opposition members were aware of the Shell trouble between Lord French and Lord Kitchener, so many of them were intimately informed of the progress of the conflict between

Lord Fisher and Mr. Churchill at the Admiralty.
Lord Fisher had seen to that. Lord Wargrave
led the Tories who supported the First Sea Lord,
and Bonar Law knew quite well how extended
and formidable his activities were, and that the
resignation of Lord Fisher would be the signal
for an outbreak of hostility to the Government
which he would be quite unable to control.

On the Shell scandal Bonar Law had his followers well in hand, as has been proved in the
last chapter. On the Admiralty crisis he had not.
And here in the main he sympathised with his
own followers. He believed that a Shell scandal
might keep Italy from coming into the war on
our side. He thought the news of the dismissal
of Churchill from the Admiralty might actually
encourage Italy—for he had no belief in Churchill
as a responsible administrator.

One thing he knew for certain. If Churchill
came down to the Commons on Monday, 17
May, with a new and tame Board of Admiralty
in his pocket, the Tory party would revolt instantly. The Truce of God between the Liberal
and Conservative parties would come to an abrupt
end.

This was precisely the contingency that Bonar
Law was most anxious to avoid. He had endured
much since August 1914 in order to keep his
promise of a silent and patriotic Opposition, but
the limit of his resources had now been reached.
An acrimonious debate on high questions of
naval policy would be an indecent picture in the
middle of a great war. And the debate would be

followed by a division, with the Opposition voting against the new Admiralty Board. But the leader of the Opposition decided to face the facts.

Supposing the Government fell, could the Conservative party alone support an Administration ? It was improbable. But to coalesce after defeating the Government would immensely increase all the difficulties in the way of a Coalition. Bonar Law had never been greatly enamoured of the Coalition idea for its own sake, but it seemed to him that matters had come to a point which he had foreseen some months before, when a partially discredited Government could only be rescued by a new infusion of blood. He did not like Coalition, but it seemed the least of possible evils.

Bonar Law would not see Fisher, who sought out a personal interview through an intermediary. He was determined that he would not be drawn into the consideration of the personal quarrel between Fisher and Churchill. He would only deal with public issues. Further, he was annoyed with Fisher for the method chosen for imparting the news of the resignation to various members of the Opposition. The plan selected for informing Bonar Law himself was indeed original.

The leader of the Opposition lived at Pembroke Lodge, in Edwardes Square. There he received by post a singular missive.

It was simply a marked cutting from the " Pall Mall Gazette " in an envelope addressed in Lord Fisher's hand, stating that " Lord Fisher was received in audience of the King and remained there about half an hour." The form of the letter convinced him that the sender was Lord Fisher himself, and that Fisher wished him to know this fact. Bonar Law came to the conclusion that Lord Fisher had resigned. Other Tory friends of Fisher were also informed of the resignation, and it was clear that soon after the House met on Monday the storm would break.

Bonar Law immediately saw Lord Lansdowne, wrote to Mr. Asquith, and made an appointment to see Lloyd George. The object of the interview was this, and this alone : Bonar Law was going to tell Lloyd George that if Fisher had really resigned, the Tory party would not permit Churchill to turn Fisher out and to remain himself. His first question to Lloyd George was, therefore, whether the resignation was an accomplished fact. Lloyd George said it was.

Bonar Law replied : " Then the situation is impossible." He pointed out to Lloyd George that Fisher was the darling of the Tory party, Churchill had become its bugbear. Was the first to go and the second to stay ? The rank and file of the Opposition. would not tolerate it. When the House met again on Monday the new list of the Admiralty Board would have to be read out. Then the tempest would break with uncontrollable violence, and the Opposition would once again begin to oppose. Bonar Law finally told Lloyd George plainly that of his own personal knowledge he was convinced that he could not hold his followers back, even if he wished to.

Lloyd George saw the position in a moment

when faced with the alternative between Coalition and open rupture.

" Of course," he said, " we must have a Coalition, for the alternative is impossible," and, taking Bonar Law by the arm, he led him through the private passage which runs from the back of the Treasury to Nos. 10 and 11 Downing Street, and brought him to Mr. Asquith.

From the moment that the two men exchanged these sentences the Government was dead and the leading articles on Shell shortage in the newspapers of the next few days were only bullets fired into a corpse from which life had already departed.

This is the exact way in which the Liberal Government of 1915 fell.

Bonar Law, after rejecting Coalition twice— once consciously and once unconsciously—had seized on it the third time. A critic might say that he had been driven into this step by the feelings of his own supporters. This is not the case. To begin with, he sympathised on the whole with the views of the Tory back-benchers on the issue at the Admiralty. But in any case, the conditions he had laid down in his own mind and expressed in private in August 1914 had now fulfilled themselves. The Government was falling and discredited. The party truce could no longer be kept. The time for a Coalition, the possibility and necessity of which he had long foreseen, had now arrived, and as his decision had been formed for months, he was able to act on it with his usual sureness and promptitude.

Never, perhaps, has so important a political

decision been carried out so quickly. Mr. Asquith supported the plan for a Coalition at once. Immediately after the conversation with Asquith a meeting of as many of the Tory leaders as could be collected at short notice was held at Lansdowne House. Bonar Law informed his colleagues of Fisher's resignation and of conversations with Lloyd George and Asquith.

The following letter was sent to the Prime Minister :

Lansdowne House,
17 May, 1915.

Dear Mr. Asquith,

Lord Lansdowne and I have learnt with dismay that Lord Fisher has resigned, and we have come to the conclusion that we cannot allow the House to adjourn until this fact has been made known and discussed.

We think the time has come when we ought to have a clear statement from you as to the policy which the Government intends to pursue. In our opinion things cannot go on as they are, and some change in the Constitution of the Government seems to us inevitable if it is to retain a sufficient measure of public confidence to conduct the war to a successful conclusion.

The situation in Italy makes it particularly undesirable to have anything in the nature of a controversial discussion in the House of Commons at present, and if you are prepared to take the necessary steps to secure the object which I have indicated, and if Lord Fisher's resignation is in the meantime postponed, we shall be ready to keep silence now. Otherwise, I must to-day ask you whether Lord Fisher has resigned, and press for a day to discuss the situation arising out of his resignation.

Yours, etc.,

(Sgd.) A. Bonar Law.

This letter shows with finality that it was the Churchill-Fisher quarrel and not the question of Shells which brought the Liberal War Government to the ground.

When the real Shell agitation began, several days after the fall of the Government, it took a dual form.

As I have stated, Lord Northcliffe launched hs campaign in order to arouse the public. Mr. Lloyd George, too, was busy in Cabinet circles. Behind both manifestations lay a common purpose—to take the supply of munitions right away from Lord Kitchener and the War Office.

On 19 May 1915, the day that the formation of a new Ministry was announced in the House of Commons, Mr. Lloyd George wrote to the Prime Minister to this effect—He must reconsider his position as Chairman of the Shells Committee. Such a Committee functioning through a Department of the War Office had no real executive authority and he would not go on with what had proved an unsatisfactory arrangement. In other words, the Shells Committee must be a department in itself.

This letter is as follows :

May 19, 1915.

My dear Prime Minister,

Certain facts have been brought to my notice on the question of munitions which I have felt bound to call your attention to. I write to you, inasmuch as my appointment as chairman of the Munitions Committee came direct from you.

In order properly to discharge our functions as a committee it was essential that all information as to the character of the explosive most urgently needed and the present supply available should be afforded to us. I am now informed, on what appears to be reliable information :

(1) That in order to attack highly developed trenches, protected by barbed wire entanglements, shrapnel is useless, and high explosive shells indispensable.

(2) That those who are responsible for conducting operations at the front have for months impressed this fact upon the War Office, and asked in the first instance that 25 per cent. of the shells sent to France should be high explosive, and that afterwards this percentage was increased to 50 per cent.

(3) That, notwithstanding these urgent representations, the percentage of high-explosive shell provided for the 18-pounders has never exceeded 8 per cent. ; that when the great combined attack to break through the German lines was made by the French and British armies last Sunday week, the French prepared the attack with an overwhelming bombardment of high explosive, which utterly demolished the German

trenches and barbed-wire entanglements, thus enabling the French to penetrate the German lines for four miles without any excessive loss of life. In spite of the fact that the French spent their high explosive munitions lavishly, they have still in reserve hundreds of thousands of shells of the same kind for the purpose of continuing their operations. On the other hand, our armies had less than 45,000 high explosive shells in all; of these about 18,000 were 18-pounders. They therefore had to rely on shrapnel, so that when our troops advanced to the attack the German fortifications were barely pock-marked. The Germans rose in their trenches and mocked at our advancing troops, and then calmly mowed them down in thousands. The Germans themselves have barely lost 200 men.

I am also told that the attack on Saturday last had to be made by night—a risky operation—because of the deficiencies in high-explosive shell, and that after the battle there were not more than 2,000 high-explosive shells left for all our guns.

(4) That a full report on ammunition was sent to the War Office weeks ago from Headquarters in France, and that then later on another report on guns was sent. Neither of these reports on guns has ever been shown to the Munitions Committee, and I gather they have not been seen by you.

If these facts are approximately correct, I hesitate to think what action the public would insist on if they were known. But it is quite clear that the proceedings of a Munitions Committee from which vital information of this character is withheld must be a farce. I cannot, therefore, continue to preside over them under such conditions. It is now eight months since I ventured to call attention of the Cabinet to the importance of mobilising all our engineering resources for the production of munitions and equipments of war. In October of last year I brought a full report from France showing how the French Ministry for War had coped with the difficulty. The Cabinet at that date decided that the same course should be pursued here, and a Cabinet Committee was set up for that purpose. We met at the War Office, and it was there agreed, with the Secretary of State in the chair, that steps of that kind should be taken in this country. I regret to say, after some inquiry, that action on those lines has not been taken even to this hour except at Leeds.

A Cabinet Committee cannot have executive power ; it can only advise and recommend. It is for the Department to act. They have not done so, and all the horrible loss of life which has occurred in consequence of the lack of high-explosive shell is the result.

Private firms cannot turn out shrapnel because of the complicated character of the shell, but the testimony is unanimous that the high explosive is a simple shell, and that any engineering concern could easily produce it. That has been the experience of France.

(Sd.) D. Lloyd George.

On Friday, 21 May, when the new Government was being formed, the " Daily Mail " began its real " Shell Campaign," making use of the word " scandal " for the first time in flaring headlines. A violent attack on Lord Kitchener and the War Office management of munitions was also launched. The Kitchener attack was instantly abandoned, but the Shell agitation was carried on with immense vigour for ten days and then dropped. The object, which was to force the creation of a Ministry of Munitions and to make an atmosphere which would afford an excellent opportunity to the new Minister, was achieved by that time.

CHAPTER IX

" OFFICES "

THE distribution of offices was the next, and not very agreeable, task of the new Government. It was settled at once in principle that the Conservatives and Liberals should divide the posts equally between them. Churchill was, of course, the principal sufferer in a *debacle* of which he had been the primary occasion. He was very loath to leave his great work and office.

I think I am right in saying that it was on the night of Tuesday 18 May that I dined with Birkenhead, who took me to see Churchill at the Admiralty. Churchill had only been told when he actually came down to the House in the afternoon of the day before to read out his new Board that the Coalition would be formed, that the Ministry would be reconstructed, and that no new Board could be appointed for the present.

It was certainly rather terrible to have this news of defeat in the hour of apparent victory broken to one suddenly behind the Speaker's Chair !

What days that Monday and Tuesday must have been for Churchill ! Has any man ever gone through such a hail of incidents, such rapid alternations of hope and despair, such a succession of good news and bad news, in the course of two days ? Consider the direction that events took. The First Lord came down to the Commons on that Monday full of confidence. Lord Fisher had been removed from his path—to all appearance without any evil consequence. Henceforward, he would be sole master at the Admiralty. The list of his new Board was in his pocket, and had been approved by the Prime Minister. None of the senior naval officers showed any disposition to refuse promotions and appointments on account of Fisher's mutiny. Assured of Mr. Asquith's support, he did not believe that the Opposition could do anything effective against him, nor did he anticipate any great storm in the Commons— whose members were now waiting for him as an audience attend the rising of the curtain and the entrance of the principal actor.

Suddenly he is told that his new list must not be announced. Mr. Asquith and Mr. Lloyd George together inform him of one crushing piece of news after another. A Coalition is about to be formed : the inevitable implication is that one of the conditions of the compact is his de- parture from the Admiralty. Thus all the bright hopes of his morning are rudely dissipated.

Later, his two principal colleagues come forward with a new proposal. The suggestion of the Colonial Office was put forward by the Prime Minister in the presence of the Chancellor of the Exchequer. Mr. Lloyd George brought his imagination into play. What had been lost on the sea might be regained on the land. A Colonial

Secretary with Mr. Churchill's military talents might marshal the hosts of the races of Africa and the Dependencies, and rush them to the assistance of the Empire.

While this offer was being made—in fact, it was accepted—the conclave was suddenly interrupted by an urgent message from Mr. Churchill's own office. The gist of it was, " Please come to the Admiralty at once—important news." Mr. Churchill left immediately, and received the startling information that the German High Sea Fleet was coming out, apparently intending battle. Instantly, all thoughts of other matters such as Ministerial employments must have vanished from Mr. Churchill's vision. Here in the great battle in the North Sea would be the vindication of his naval policy—a triumph such as few lifetimes afford any man. Instead of the bald announcement that Mr. Churchill was no longer First Lord of the Admiralty and that his successor had been chosen, there would be a tense scene in the House of Commons, in which white-faced members listened in strained attention while Mr. Churchill announced the greatest victory which the British Navy had ever attained before or since Trafalgar. Would a First Lord who had played Barham to the new Nelson be allowed to go into retirement ? And if he did go, he would leave the Admiralty in a manner which would make his exit an imperishable event in British history.

Such, at least, would have been the reflections of any ordinary man in Mr. Churchill's position.

But as confidence, on that eventful Monday, had been replaced by despair—so depression was now succeeded by the growing light of an immense hope. All that afternoon and evening he was rushing towards the probable scene of action every battleship, battle cruiser or torpedo boat that he could lay hands upon. He had no First Sea Lord at the time, and was acting as head of the Admiralty. He sent messages to the Harwich force and to the flotillas and to the submarine and destroyer flotillas at Dover and Yarmouth. He ordered them to proceed to the probable scene of action. He threw his whole naval hand in at once. He held back nothing. If only the Germans would come on ! So Monday evening lengthened with hope. Mr. Churchill slept a little, and rose at 7.0 a.m. on Tuesday to learn that the Germans seemed to be receding towards their base. By 9.0 a.m. it was clear that all was over— and the German High Sea Fleet beyond our reach.

There was an end of the matter. The offer to Churchill of the Colonial Office was afterwards withdrawn owing to strong Tory protests and weak Liberal support, and the failure of the new Trafalgar to eventuate relegated him to the Duchy of Lancaster.* I conclude as I began this story— " What days ! "

*There was an interlude of six months, only to be mentioned because it shows Churchill's boundless fertility of invention and his determination to be in the line of action somewhere. He suggested that he might be made Governor-General and Commander-in-Chief in East Africa, so as to unify all the operations against the Germans in that area. This proposal, too, though somewhat favoured by Bonar Law, Colonial Secretary, finally met with strong opposition and failed to eventuate.

Churchill was thus, on the Tuesday night I saw
him at the Admiralty, a man suddenly thrown from
power into impotence, and one felt rather as if
one had been invited to " come and look on fallen
Antony."

What a creature of strange moods he is—always
at the top of the wheel of confidence or at the
bottom of an intense depression.

Looking back on that long night that we spent
in the big silent Admiralty room till day broke, I
cannot help reflecting on that extreme duality
of mind which marks Churchill above all other
men—the charm, the imaginative sympathy of
his hours of defeat, the self-confidence, the arro-
gance of his hours of power and prosperity. That
night he was a lost soul, yet full of flashes of wit
and humour.

But all those days of our acquaintance were his
bad times, and then one could not resist the charm
of his companionship or withhold from him the
tribute of sympathy.

That Tuesday night he was clinging to the desire
of retaining the Admiralty as though the salvation
of England depended on it. I believe he would
even have made it up with Lord Fisher if that had
been the price of remaining there. None the less,
so little did he realise the inwardness of the whole
situation that he still hoped.

He was anxious that the Tories should support
him in this, although it was obvious that it was
precisely the Tory backing of Lord Fisher that
had thrown him down. He negotiated with Lord
Balfour to act as intermediary and as his interpreter

to the Tory leaders. Balfour in his new role was
unfavourably received and in fact severely criticised by his colleagues.

My sympathies were entirely with Churchill, for
I had heard his speeches and read some of Lord
Fisher's letters, and I was more impressed by the
lucidity of the speeches than by the volubility of
the letters.

None the less, I had to tell him plainly that in
my opinion there was no hope.

Churchill refers to this conversation in his own
book, when he says that he received a message
to this effect from a sure source of information.
He was right in his valuation. For Bonar Law
had informed me earlier in the day that he and
his colleagues would not and could not countenance the re-appointment of Churchill to the
Admiralty. I pressed Bonar Law very strongly
to retain Churchill at the Admiralty on account
of the immense abilities he had already displayed
there.

Bonar Law replied that it was useless to argue ;
that the Tory party had definitely made up its
mind not to have him there—and that, in fact,
any attempt to retain Churchill at the Admiralty
would result in the complete and sudden collapse
of the substructure of the new Coalition Government. He added that Churchill had also lost the
confidence of his own Liberal associates. Finally,
he authorised me to tell Churchill the substance ot
his observations.

Yet Churchill still made an appeal on Thursday
night to some of the Tory leaders, asking to be

allowed to retain his office, and explaining that his conduct and motives had been greatly traduced, and that there was no real reason for Conservative hostility.

One of the arguments he used in conversation with me was ill calculated to serve his ends with the Tory chiefs. He said that Sir Arthur Wilson had agreed to serve under him and would not serve under anyone else, and he indicated his intention to create exactly that kind of Board to which his opponents most strenuously objected. But as a matter of fact, it made no difference, for the issue was really settled from the start, and in a day or two he realised that the worst had definitely happened.

But as late as Friday, 21 May, he wrote to Bonar Law, setting out in such a vigorous, coherent and concise manner his whole case for desiring to remain at the Admiralty, that I now print it in full :—

Admiralty,
Whitehall.
21.5.15.

My dear Bonar Law,

The rule to follow is what is best calculated to beat the enemy and not what is most likely to please the newspapers. The question of the Dardanelles operations and my differences with Fisher ought to be settled by people who know the facts and not by those who cannot know them. Now you and your friends except Mr. Balfour do not know the facts. On our side *only* the Prime

Minister knows them. The policy and conduct of
the Dardanelles operations should be reviewed
by the new Cabinet. Every fact shd. be laid
before them. They shd. decide and on their
decision the composition of the Board of Admiralty shd. depend.

It is not in justice to myself that I am asking for
this ; but primarily because of the great operation
wh. is in progress, and for wh. I bear a tremendous
responsibility. With Sir Arthur Wilson's professional aid I am sure I can discharge that responsibility fully. In view of his statement to the Prime
Minister and to the naval Lords that he will serve
as First Sea Lord under me, and under no one
else, I feel entitled to say that no other personal
combination will give so good a chance.

If this view of mine shd. prove to be true it
affects the safety of an Army now battling its way
forward under many difficulties, and the success
of an operation of the utmost consequence for
wh. more than 30,000 men have already shed their
blood : and I suggest to you that it is your duty
to refuse to judge so grave an issue until you
know the facts.

My lips are sealed in public, but in a few days
all the facts can be placed before you and your
friends under official secrecy. I am sure those
with whom I hope to work as colleagues and
comrades in this great struggle will not allow a
newspaper campaign—necessarily conducted in
ignorance and not untinged with prejudice—to
be the deciding factor in matters of such terrible
import.

Personal interests and sympathies ought to be strictly subordinated. It does not matter whether a Minister receives exact and meticulous justice. But what is vital is that from the outset of this new effort we are to make together we shd. be fearless of outside influences and straight with each other. We are coming together not to work on public opinion but to wage war : and by waging successful war we shall dominate public opinion.

I wd. like you to bring this letter to the notice of those with whom I expect soon to act : and I wish to add the following :—

I was sent to the Admiralty 4 years ago. I have always been supported by high professional advice ; but partly through circumstances and partly no doubt through my own methods and inclinations, an exceptional burden has been borne by me. I had to procure the money, the men, the ships and ammunition ; to recast with expert advice the war plans ; to complete in every detail that cd. be foreseen the organisation of the Navy.

Supported by the Prime Minister, I had last year for 4 continuous months of Cabinet meetings to beat down the formidable attack of the Chancellor of the Exchequer backed by 3/4ths of the Cabinet upon the necessary naval estimates. On the approach of war I had to act far in excess of my authority to make the vital arrangements for the safety of the country. I had to mobilise the Fleet without legal sanction and contrary to a Cabinet decision. I have had to face 9 months of war under conditions no man has known, and wh.

were in the early months infinitely more anxious than those wh. confront us now.

Many Sea Lords have come and gone, but during all these 4 years (nearly) I have been according to my patent " solely responsible to Crown and Parliament " and have borne the blame for every failure : and now I present to you an absolutely secure naval position ; a Fleet constantly and rapidly growing in strength, and abundantly supplied with munitions of every kind, an organisation working with perfect smoothness and efficiency, and the seas upon wh. no enemy's flag is flown.

Therefore I ask to be judged justly, deliberately and with knowledge. I do not ask for anything else.

Yours very sincerely,
Winston S. Churchill.

Bonar Law replied on the same day :—

21st May, 1915.
My dear Churchill,
I thank you for your letter, which I shall show to my friends, beginning with Austen Chamberlain ; but, believe me, what I said to you last night is inevitable.

Yours sincerely,
A. Bonar Law.

Churchill, failing his own retention, was keenly anxious about his successor. He preferred Lord Balfour because that statesman had, on the whole, agreed with his Dardanelles policy, and was conversant with all the facts in connection with it.

Here, at any rate, he had his desire, and the virgin soil of the Admiralty was immediately fertilised by Lord Balfour's subtle intelligence. I often wonder what the sailors thought of him, though no one could doubt that he would be immensely popular with his subordinates. Sir Henry Jackson became First Sea Lord in Lord Fisher's place.

Such was the amazing story of the struggle at the Admiralty—one which in peace time would have been high comedy of the most exquisite character ; but which, occurring in the middle of a great European conflict, is nothing short of tragedy. I can think of no parallel in history. The First Sea Lord himself vanished, and for some days the British Navy was without an official expert head, and it is surely the last tribute to Lord Fisher's hold on the public imagination that he should still have retained so large a position in the public eye after his proceedings of Saturday, 15 May. But if there was one thing more astounding than his action when he pulled down his blinds at the Admiralty it is this—that he still confidently expected to be recalled to office after it !

It therefore remains for us to add to the Fisher maxims yet another motto, " Don't draw down the blinds."

And here I must break off my narrative to give an analysis of Churchill's conduct and character as it was displayed in the war up till May 1915.

His attitude from August 1914 onwards was a noble one, too noble to be wise. He cared for the success of the British arms, especially in so far as they could be achieved by the Admiralty, and for nothing else. His passion for this aim was pure, self-devoted, and all-devouring. He failed to remember that he was a politician and as such treading a slippery path ; he forgot his political tactics. He thought of himself not as holding a certain position in relation to Liberal colleagues and a Tory Opposition, but as a National Minister secure of support from all men of good-will. Or if he knew that there were pitfalls lying before the man who thought in this way, he walked on careless of them because of his belief in his own objective. If it was a mistake it was the error of a big-minded, though self-willed, man. Actually the rocks were under his keel the whole time, and finally he struck one in the course of his daring pilotage.

To begin with, all his Liberal colleagues did not like his view that the war was the only issue. There was Home Rule, for instance. I can imagine him expressing the opinion that to discuss Home Rule now was " tosh "—because it would settle itself in some quite different way when the war was over. This would give offence to serious-minded Liberals who were still as deeply interested in the Home Rule Bill as were some of the Conservative Shadow Cabinet from the opposite standpoint. At any rate, he never made any

concession to Liberal party feeling, but stuck
grimly to the Admiralty.

At the same time, he failed to realise that the Tory
opposition did not regard him as a National
Minister at all, but still cherished against him a
resentment born of pre-war political differences,
that they did not trust his conduct of naval affairs,
and were quite determined to support in the most
violent fashion any sailor who differed with him
on an expert question. It would be too long a task
to enter into all the ideas which animated the
minds of the Conservative rank and file at this
moment, but it is true that belief in the naval
and military experts and intense opposition to
Churchill were dominant articles in their creed.

Churchill did not understand all this, largely
because he shut himself up in the Admiralty and
hardly ever went to the House of Commons except
as a form. As he worked devotedly at his own job,
the currents of political opinion slipped by him
unnoticed. If he went out to speak at all, it was at
meetings in the country. This was patriotic of
him—but, as we have seen in the case of the
Liverpool meeting, he laid himself open to attack
by his enemies even in this endeavour. If he failed
in 1915 it was because he showed himself too
confident to be prudent. He neither tied the
Liberals to him nor conciliated the Tories.

If Churchill was avid of power and office
during the war, and intensely depressed whenever he was excluded from active official
participation in its conduct, the blame can only
be attached to his assurance and self-confidence.

He cared for the Empire profoundly, and he was honestly convinced that only by his advice and methods it could be saved. His ambition was in essence disinterested. He suffered tortures when he thought that lesser men were mismanaging the business.

I do not say that he was always wise—but his patriotism burnt with a pure flame throughout. Hard fighter as he is in debate, he is a man almost devoid of rancour. A defeat does not sour him, even though it depresses him, nor does it turn him into a hater of the successful half of political mankind. And he possesses another virtue—exceptionally rare in politics—or, for that matter, almost anywhere. He is strictly honest and truthful to other people, down to the smallest details of his life. He will not even tell what is usually known as a " dinner lie " to get out of a distasteful engagement. Yet he frequently deceives himself.

The announcement of the formation of the Coalition Government was made by Asquith and Bonar Law in the House of Commons on Wednesday, 19 May 1915. The whole crisis had taken well under a week.

The Coalition had a very tepid reception from the Press. The Liberal rank and file were annoyed by what seemed a kind of inexplicable overthrow. Old friends had to be excluded from office to make room for the newcomers—a painful business. The stalwart Tories thought the Government should not have been saved, even in part, and

that their own side would then have had a mono-
poly of office. The leaders on both sides also had
to adjust themselves to the new situation.

The principal Unionist leaders gave a shining
example at once of patriotism and disinterestedness. They were burningly eager to take office,
not for its own sake, but because they honestly
thought that their inclusion in the Ministry would
infuse a new vigour and efficiency into the conduct
of the war. They had chafed at the impotence
to serve their country which Opposition imposed.
They believed that they had talents which could
be put to great national use and that a combination
of the best men on both sides in office must be
stronger than a one-party rule. If some of these
ideas turned out to be fallacious, this does not
reflect on the zeal and integrity of the men who
entertained them.

That such professions were not merely the
cloak of concealed ambition is proved by the
readiness each individual showed to stand down
for any other colleague whose abilities might be
adjudged greater than his. Lord Lansdowne was
ready to stand out altogether if his inclusion would
prejudice the chances of Lord Curzon or Lord
Selborne. Sir Austen Chamberlain was most
anxious that no question of his claim should stand
in the way of the party leader becoming Chancellor of the Exchequer in the event of his not
preferring or securing the new Ministry of Munitions. I shall come in a moment to Bonar Law's
own act of self-abnegation. Lord Long also
indicated his complete willingness either to serve

or stand aside, as circumstances might dictate. He added that he was inclined to take exception to two important Liberal personalities as members of the joint Ministry, namely, Lloyd George and McKenna. And in this he showed a curious prescience—for they were the two Ministers whose internecine feuds caused the head of the new Ministry some of his most severe trials. Long finished by assuring Bonar Law that, office or no office, he should have his unswerving support as a private member of Parliament.

I will finish the list with the striking example of Lord Finlay, who had by prescription the highest claim to any law office which was within the power of the Conservative party to offer him.

Lord Finlay placed his claim for office at the absolute disposal of his leader, and paid the price for his renunciation without a murmur. On the Liberal side there were some similar acts of self-sacrifice. Sir John Simon refused the great prize of his profession, the Lord Chancellorship, in order to stay at the Home Office, and other Ministers announced their willingness to fall into any arrangement which would make the formation of the Coalition Ministry easier.

CHAPTER X

THE FIRST INTRIGUE

IT is regrettable to have to relate that this general attitude of sacrifice was not shared either by the Prime Minister or one or two of his principal colleagues. These approached the formation of the new Ministry, not in a spirit of frank union with their late opponents, but with the intention of doing the best they could, if not for themselves, at any rate for their party. Briefly the object of this intrigue of May 1915 was to keep the Conservatives, and especially their leader, out of their fair share of the great offices in the Cabinet. It was this original move which made the whole edifice of the first Coalition shaky from the very beginning and ultimately prepared the way for the ruin of Mr. Asquith as Prime Minister.

Let us consider the situation. The Premiership was not vacant, nor was the Foreign Office, nor the War Office. But there were besides two positions of great importance—the Chancellorship of the Exchequer and the Ministry of Munitions. It was obvious that Bonar Law, as leader of an equal force in the Cabinet, had a prescriptive right to one or other of these offices. Mr. Lloyd George, as Chancellor, had no doubt an equal

right to remain where he was if he wished. That
was all. The Liberal Leadership, on the contrary,
decided that by one method or another Bonar
Law was to be kept out of both these offices—
so that the Liberals would hold the Premiership,
the Foreign Office, the Exchequer, and the Ministry of Munitions—obviously a monstrous in-
equality in the distribution of power.

Mr. Asquith's first proposal to keep Bonar Law
out was to take the Exchequer himself in addition
to the Premiership, and send Lloyd George to
Munitions. The duplication of the Premiership
and the Treasury in the middle of a great war was
so obviously inadmissible that it was at once
objected to and abandoned.

The Prime Minister then summoned several of
those of his Liberal colleagues who were to have
Cabinet places in the new Administration to a
meeting and explained the position to them. He
had, he said, the names of the Conservative
members of the Administration to be. The Opposition claimed and would have half the seats in
the Cabinet—that was settled. There remained the
question of the distribution of offices. There was
a general concurrence that none of the Tories
were to have any of the big places—or to put it
more particularly—the problem was to prevent
Bonar Law from being made either Chancellor
of the Exchequer or Minister of Munitions.
Those who were present and had a personal
acquaintance with Bonar Law knew that in his
simple patriotism they had the surest instrument
to effect their purpose.

When the conference was over, several of the Liberal leaders adjourned to Mr. Lloyd George's room to discuss details. It was there that one of them proposed a definite plan. Lloyd George should go to Munitions, and some Liberal should take the Exchequer on condition that he was ready to vacate if Lloyd George wished to take it back in the future. This was agreed to. Mr. McKenna was selected to be the warming pan. The Prime Minister sent for him and offered him the Treasury on these precise terms—explaining that it was necessary, since the Liberals representing the majority in the House of Commons ought to hold the great offices. Mr. McKenna replied in effect that he felt himself bound to acquiesce in any request the Prime Minister made to him, and to accept any conditions imposed on him in a grave national emergency. In taking this attitude he was undoubtedly perfectly sincere. He never thought, however, that the condition under which he was bound to resign the Treasury was ever likely to be fulfilled. He felt sure that Mr. Lloyd George would not in any case return to the Exchequer—and so it proved.

I cannot but reflect with some little amusement on the irony which crowned this event. McKenna never vacated the Exchequer, but, on the contrary, was within a little over a year fighting Lloyd George implacably and successfully in the War Cabinet. Lloyd George was appealing to Bonar Law to come to his help, and the latter was for some weeks restrained from doing so because of the deep impression this episode of the offices had left on his mind. Lastly, when Mr. McKenna was at the Treasury he passed a Tariff which gave all the orthodox Free Traders the shock of their lives—though it had been especially asserted that a Tariff Reformer like Bonar Law should not be Chancellor.

The proposal of the Liberal chiefs now agreed to was sufficiently amazing. The Conservatives, the greatest individual party in the Commons, had with great reluctance come to the rescue of a falling Government ; its members came in not as subordinates, but as allies ; not because their presence was desired, but because it could not be spared.

The head of that party in the House, therefore, entered the Ministry not as an ordinary subordinate, but as an independent potentate, capable of dealing on almost equal terms with the Prime Minister. One breath of his could destroy the Government in a night.

Even if he held his hand for ever there might come a day when he would need every ounce of status and authority which the highest office could give him to keep his own followers in line.

Later on Mr. Asquith and his friends had to pay a bitter price for joining in a game which tended to depreciate Bonar Law's status in his own party, to weaken his authority over it, and so to render the first Coalition more susceptible to attack from the Die-hards of the Tory Right. From the very moment that the scheme for this transaction over offices was set on foot in Downing Street the first Coalition was doomed.

If Mr. Asquith had possessed the ears to hear with he would have recognised that the death-knell of his Administration was set ringing by this intrigue.

It remained to carry the plan into effect. First of all, a story was put about that Mr. Scott, the well-known and highly-respected Editor of the " Manchester Guardian," had declared, as an uncompromising Free Trader, that nobody of Bonar Law's fiscal opinions could be made Chancellor of the Exchequer by a Liberal Prime Minister. That difficulty, of course—if it ever existed—could have been surmounted by sending Bonar Law to Munitions. In fact, both Lord Balfour and Lord Kitchener indicated a preference for the appointment of Bonar Law to Munitions—since it never occurred to them to imagine that the Leader of the Opposition had no choice open.

Finally, it dawned on Bonar Law that he was to be jockeyed out of both the big vacant posts. The Prime Minister was in a difficulty, for he could not form a Ministry at all without Bonar Law's concurrence. He suggested an interview between Bonar Law and Lloyd George. Here Lloyd George made to his competitor that kind of appeal to his shining qualities of disinterestedness and patriotism which Bonar Law could never resist even though he ought to have done so.

He yielded to the appeal, but on returning to Mr. Asquith to announce the sacrifice, he remarked truly enough : " You mustn't think I am doing this because I am compelled to. I know very well I can have what I want simply by lifting

my little finger. But I won't fight. I am here to
show you how to run a Coalition Government
by forbearance and concession." With this
renunciation the Tory leader departed to the
dignified obscurity (in war time) of the Colonial
Office.

When Bonar Law went out that morning to the
meetings with Mr. Asquith and Mr. Lloyd George
which I have just described he promised his
friends that, whatever happened, he would not
give way; he returned to inform them that he
had done so! The truth of the matter is that
over and over again in his career Bonar Law
would have given rein to this passion for self-
abnegation if others had not held up his hands.

If Bonar Law would not contend for his proper
position himself it was at least the duty of his
Conservative colleagues to make a stand on his
behalf in the interests of their own position in and
influence on the new Government.

As it was, the Conservative meeting at Lansdowne House ratified the appointments and concurred with hardly a murmur in a decision which
put a slight on the party chief and damaged both
his authority and the prestige of the party. When
I asked one colleague to make an effort to have
things put right, he said: " It's all settled now,
and it's too late to do anything."

Neither the Liberal nor the Conservative leaders
saw that Conservative prestige and authority
might be wanted badly some day, for already
there were anxious mutterings among the Tory
rank and file.

The number of claimants for the smaller posts were innumerable, and there was a great scarcity of offices in the second grade.

The Tories had imagined that the fall of the Government was certain to take place if their own leaders did not hold out a helping hand. They believed that a dissolution would have followed and returned them to office independent of all other sections whatever, and that in any case such a course would have given them a larger share of the spoils of office even in a Coalition Government. Long and loud were the complaints of those who were marked out for office in the old days but were now excluded through lack of room.

Some amusing discussions took place while the Lloyd-George-Bonar-Law controversy was still unsettled, and it was thought that one would go to the Exchequer and one to Munitions.

In this the Press, or rather, some editors, took a lively but secret part. The Press is divided into two schools, those of open and secret diplomacy. The open diplomats, of whom Lord Northcliffe was then the chief, enforce their demands by a public agitation. The secret diplomats are the editors who try to get their way by influence, cajolery and argument ; and these, at moments of political disturbance, carry far more weight than the most eminent private Member of Parliament.

The battle for the smaller positions on the Conservative side was, as I have indicated, far more fierce than anything which took place at the top, where self-abnegation ruled.

I may say this without offence because personally
I did not take advantage of such opportunity of
minor office as was open to me.

One ought not to be too ready to blame the
contestants. The Conservatives had been out of
office for eight or nine years. In that period
men who had worked assiduously at politics all
their lives saw themselves passing out on the
wrong side of middle-age without any official
recognition of their hard work and real abilities.
They were mostly too old for active soldiering,
they were desperately anxious to serve their
country in some tangible and obvious form, and
they were knocking in crowds at a narrow gate.

One noble gesture, however, was made by all
the Conservative aspirants for power from the
highest to the lowest. It was called the self-
denying ordinance—because it laid down that no
Conservative member of Parliament serving at
the front should be eligible for office. This had
the double advantage of maintaining the strength
of the firing line, and diminishing the queue
waiting outside the portals of Whitehall.

The Law offices, of course, are things standing
apart. For some reason or another the distribution
of these offices always seems to evoke the most
terrible contentions. No one disputed the claim of
Lord Carson to a big position. On the contrary,
Liberals and Conservatives were united in the
belief that he was certain to prove a most effective
Minister in war time. And in any case he had
already held Law office in a Conservative Administration. He was clearly indicated for the

Attorney-Generalship. But if Carson was Attorney-General, only one other legal post was open to a Conservative. A Coalition could not appoint a Tory Lord Chancellor, a Tory Attorney-General, and a Tory Solicitor-General. The inclusion of Lord Birkenhead as Solicitor General deprived an old-time Conservative peer of office, for the Liberals flatly declined to take in a single other Tory.

Birkenhead owed his promotion to Bonar Law, who was determined to provide for him, even in the face of great difficulties. But after all, Birkenhead was a bigger figure in politics than most of his competitors. His appointment meant that the Lord Chancellorship must go to a Liberal. Mr. Asquith made the first offer of the position of Lord Chancellor to Sir John Simon, who by his record at the Bar and in the House of Commons was fully entitled to the post. Simon declined the proposal, thus showing that he was determined to remain in active politics and wanted to be Prime Minister before his career was ended. In default of Simon, Mr. Asquith turned to Buckmaster, the Solicitor-General in the late Government, as the next available Liberal. It is no exaggeration to say that this appointment was a great surprise. Lord Buckmaster was a very young man for the post. He had made no special position for himself in the House of Commons. He had succeeded Lord Birkenhead at the Press Bureau—an awkward but not important office.

But there it was ; political exigencies had to be

satisfied. Carson must, of course, as the senior, have the Attorney-Generalship, and if, as Bonar Law insisted, room had to be found for Birkenhead as Solicitor-General, then Buckmaster must go upstairs. In this indirect way Bonar Law really made Buckmaster Lord Chancellor.

This almost accidental appointment turned out an excellent one. Buckmaster proved a splendid Lord Chancellor—and not only as a lawyer. He became the principal Liberal speaker in the House of Lords—one of the greatest orators I have heard there in my time. Listening to him there, it was impossible to understand why I had failed to appreciate his speeches in the House of Commons —yet such was undoubtedly the case.

The Ministry was by now pretty well complete, but, strange to relate, one quite unimportant incident almost wrecked it when all was settled. I have told of the keen desire for office which animated some of the older Tories, and the case of the Irish Chancellorship was a queer outcrop of this frame of mind. This had been promised to Campbell (now Lord Glenavy), whose position at the Irish Bar gave him a right to expect the post. But, Mr. Asquith going on forming his Ministry without filling the appointment, and Mr. Redmond objecting, he was finally told that he could not have it.

At this there was an uproar as if the heavens or the Empire were about to fall, and several prominent Ministers, including in particular Bonar Law, actually threatened to resign and break up the new Administration. The best comment on the whole matter was made by Mr. Birrell. " It is admittedly a comparatively very small matter for either side to hold out about, and were a rupture to follow upon it I do not think that outsiders could be got to believe that it really occurred on so contemptible an issue."

By the middle of June the agonies of Cabinet-making were over, and on the 14th of that month I returned to France, pondering on the stability of the new Government and wondering what its fate would be.

So was formed with little enthusiasm on the part of its creators and in an atmosphere of doubt and hesitation, the first Coalition Government. With its Liberal predecessor discredited, it seemed that if this Ministry failed too the resources of Parliamentary government would be exhausted, and that nothing, therefore, except this frail bark stood between the nation and the Atlantic Ocean of chaos. How little can any man foresee, and who could have believed in May 1915 that it would not be till this Government had fallen into decrepitude and finally into ruin that the hope of England would rise, and that a far stronger, more active, and more efficient successor would carry the Empire through the conclusion of a triumphant war to the celebration of a victorious peace ?

CHAPTER XI

FRICTION

THE summer of 1915 was marked by one episode of special political significance. With the frequent and inevitable absences of the Prime Minister from the House of Commons it became necessary to make a formal appointment to the Deputy Leadership of the House. Considering the sacrifices that Bonar Law had made in May and the obvious justice of the view that the Tory leader in the Coalition should act as second in command, there is no doubt but that Bonar Law had a reasonable claim to the appointment. He certainly, however, set about obtaining it in rather an unfortunate manner, which gave Mr. Lloyd George the legitimate cause of complaint that Bonar Law and the Prime Minister were settling the whole affair over his head and without his knowledge. Lloyd George pleaded that as Chancellor of the Exchequer he had in fact been for years Deputy Leader, and should not be deprived of his post. Finally, Lloyd George made the old appeal to Bonar Law's besetting virtue, and once again Bonar Law retired in Lloyd George's favour. The effect of the episode was a separation between Lloyd George and Bonar Law, both of whom were showing a tendency to combine in complaining of the mismanagement of affairs, especially at the War Office.

As the summer drew on and the Liberal and Conservative Ministers began to become acquainted with one another as working colleagues, certain re-alignments took place. Nor were the various frictions which were set up those of party against party. Rather they cut clean across old party distinctions. As the very composition of the Government had originally been due to an intrigue, so its life was being continually weakened by the growing dissensions of little groups within it—Liberal often allying with Tory against Tory, or Liberal fighting Liberal.

Of the first type of mischief, a salient instance was the Prime Minister's continual exaltation of Lord Curzon at the expense of Bonar Law, with which I shall deal more fully in a sketch of Lord Curzon's character. Why, if Mr. Asquith wanted some kind of Conservative counterpoise to the official Tory Chief, he did not select Lord Lansdowne, the Leader in the Lords, it is impossible to say. The fact remains that he preferred Lord Curzon.

The Prime Minister proposed about this time to appoint a Cabinet Committee to deal with the issue of Compulsion. At first he submitted a list which included the name of Bonar Law. Then he designated a Committee composed of Curzon, Chamberlain, Selborne, Crewe and Churchill. Bonar Law was angry, particularly when he was informed that the Prime Minister had actually consulted Curzon as to the composition of the Committee. Any other Minister would have resigned. Bonar Law always effaced himself.

The battle of Liberal against Liberal was a far more serious matter. We have seen that Lloyd George and McKenna had agreed amicably enough to part Bonar Law's Ministerial heritage among them. Here their agreement ended—and a conflict arose which lasted as long as the Ministry and was one of the principal factors which accounted for its fall. This tension between the new Minister of Munitions and his successor at the Treasury continually increased.

On one occasion Asquith invited Lloyd George and McKenna to meet him in the Cabinet Room for the express purpose of effecting a reconciliation. The attempt failed. It appeared the meeting would end in disaster. Asquith was sitting in the chair which he always occupied at the Cabinet.

" In another week," he said, " I shall have sat in this chair for seven years. If I have the slightest reason to think there is anyone among you who has the faintest suspicion about me I will glady abandon it."

Asquith has written an account of this interview. He says the natural anger of the irreconcilables dissolved like frost in a sudden thaw when he uttered these sentences. They both exclaimed :
" The day you leave that chair the rest of us disappear, never to return."

The only other person who seems to have made

any real attempt to keep the peace between the protagonists was Lord Reading.

Had Lord Reading cared to resign the Chief Justiceship, he might have held almost any Ministerial post. He seemed, however, content with the influence he could exert on others, and with the exercise of his judicial functions, which he continued to perform. He had been a non-official adviser of Lloyd George at the Treasury, but on the change of Chancellor he still continued this task and used to help McKenna. He was, therefore, well placed to act as mediator between old Chancellor and new, and never ceased to preach peace and pursue it.

The Financial Secretary to the Treasury was Mr. E. S. Montagu (later Secretary of State for India), and had he joined his potent voice to Lord Reading's in advocating compromise and agreement, the fatal dissension between Lloyd George and McKenna might have been healed. Montagu unfortunately did not look on the matter in this light. He belonged to the central Asquithian group in the Cabinet, to which McKenna too was allied, and as an Asquithian he preferred to support McKenna rather than Lloyd George. So another chance of avoiding disruption was missed.

Finally, both the contending Ministers were surrounded by a group of henchmen consisting of voluntary political assistants. These sometimes had differences of their own which helped to exasperate each potentate against the other. For instance, a bitter quarrel which was carried on between Lord Riddell, who was the friend of Lloyd George, and the late Sir Hedley Le Bas, who was giving McKenna valuable assistance at the Treasury, was not helpful in promoting cordial relations between their respective chiefs.

Of all the actors concerned in this struggle the role assumed by the Prime Minister was the most amazing. He watched the feud develop and intensify with the kind of mild interest with which a hardened first-nighter may witness the development of a problem play. He showed no sign of realising that his own fortunes and those of his Ministry were at stake.

In those summer months Mr. Asquith still possessed prestige and power sufficient to quell disputants. His inclination was to McKenna. He was then strong enough to face even Lloyd George's resignation.

Obviously it was a matter of vital concern to him that he should either bring about a reconciliation between the opponents, or that he should utterly crush one or the other. Instead of this, he did nothing for peace, favoured McKenna just enough to irritate the Minister of Munitions, and took no steps whatever to ensure that the irritated Minister should be rendered harmless.

We all know that in the ultimate struggle which took place at the end of this year Lloyd George proved victorious. But I cannot withhold a tribute of sympathy with McKenna in his difficult succession to the Treasury.

Life at the Treasury was not made easy by the attitude of the Governor of the Bank of England.

The late Lord Cunliffe, who presided over the Bank, had found its importance, and consequently his own, swollen out of all proportion by the advent of war conditions. He became practically a dictatorial authority. In Lloyd George's time at the Treasury, the Chancellor and the Governor had worked amicably enough together. This was rather surprising, because Lord Cunliffe was a shrewd, hard-headed man, gruff and unpopular with his own directors, and with no temperament. One would not, therefore, expect him to find much in common with Mr. Lloyd George. Yet the fact remains that they got on well together, probably in virtue of the Governor having his own way entirely.

On the other hand, Cunliffe soon became a thorn in McKenna's side. The new Chancellor, who possessed a natural aptitude for finance, did not pursue Lloyd George's methods with Cunliffe. The latter, satiated with complete power, did not welcome a different type of Chancellor, who had his own views in many matters previously left entirely to Lord Cunliffe. And whenever the two men had a disagreement McKenna was reminded of the good old days when Lloyd George was Chancellor. Thus Lord Cunliffe unwittingly and accidentally intensified the feeling between the two statesmen.

Eventually McKenna asserted the claims of the Treasury, though it was not until Bonar Law's Chancellorship that a final pitched battle took place, which resulted in Lord Cunliffe's ultimate retirement.

McKenna's first victory is enshrined in a
dramatic story. The Chancellor was oppressed
by the immense obligations in expenditure which
we were incurring in the United States for the
purchase of war stores of all kinds, and felt the
urgent need to acquire dollars. In fact, towards
the end of his time at the Treasury he was spending
60,000,000 dollars a week in America. He would
frequently urge on Lord Cunliffe the necessity
of providing more bank balances for the Government in the United States, or, in other words,
cash in hand for immediate payments. Lord
Cunliffe would reply invariably, " Mr. Chancellor,
this is a matter of exchange, and the responsibility
here lies with me "—a strong hint not to meddle.

So matters went on until one hot summer
afternoon, when Lord Cunliffe sought out the
Chancellor of the Exchequer in the House of
Commons. There was perturbation and a sense
of crisis in the air—and, indeed, he had to disclose
a most serious situation. He produced two
telegrams from Morgans in New York, the
financial agents of the Government in America,
to Morgans in London. The gist of them was that
orders for £52,000,000 worth of war material
had been given by the British Fighting Services
in the United States ; that the contracts waited
to be signed ; that before signature £13,000,000
or 65,000,000 dollars, must be paid down. The
telegrams added that any delay in payment would
affect British credit adversely.

The message was alarming, because there were
no Government balances in the United States to

meet this demand for 65,000,000 dollars. Unless
prompt payment—the essence of sustaining credit
—was made, a dangerous and damaging blow
would be dealt to the financial prestige of the
British nation in New York. What had weakened
would slip towards the abyss.

Such was the tale of Lord Cunliffe. McKenna
replied : " But, Mr. Governor, this is what you
call a matter of exchange. Is it not for you ? "
It was a natural, if too severe, retort. " Oh,
don't talk like that," replied Lord Cunliffe—an
answer which would avert the wrath of the most
hard-hearted of Chancellors. " What is to be
done ? "

Finally McKenna said, " Leave it to me."
And in that sentence was contained the nullifica-
tion of the late Lord Cunliffe's claim to supreme
control over the national finance.

McKenna certainly acted with extraordinary
courage and energy on that stifling summer
evening. He sent instantly for the heads of the
Prudential Assurance Company—Sir Thomas
Dewey, Mr. Thompson, Sir Joseph Burn, and
Sir George May—and asked them how much the
Prudential had got in American securities. The
answer was 40,000,000 dollars. " Will you give
them to me and let me settle later ? " said the
Chancellor. The directors instantly replied that
they would. " Then let the Bank of England have
them by ten o'clock to-morrow morning." The
Bank of England supplied another £5,000,000
in gold. The whole 65,000,000 dollars was
promptly paid into the Morgan House in London

—the contracts were signed, and the situation, as grave as any which occurred on the Home Front, was saved.

The Prudential had deserved well of England that day. So had the Chancellor of the Exchequer.

What is Mr. McKenna's character and nature ? His abilities are brilliant and his logic remorseless. He is angular, emphatic, and positive. He likes to assert his view, and if you run against some projecting bump in his opinions you must merely nurse a bruise. McKenna has the satisfaction of believing that among politicians whose judgment on politics is almost invariably bad his opinion is always the best. Yet this self-assertiveness and strength of opinion and conviction go hand in hand with a most lovable disposition. One might almost say that the more McKenna infuriates you by his intellectual decision, the more you feel drawn towards him personally. He evokes affection naturally. That is the reason why he received daily doses of warm approval from Reading and Montagu at the Exchequer. And because of this same disposition he can also give flattery with devastating effect. The best judge of a man is his own family. McKenna need not fear this last judgment in a circle in which he is regarded with devotion.

Yet he has been as unlucky a politician as Lloyd George has been lucky. On every crucial occasion the gods have loaded the dice against him—and through no perceptible fault of his own judgment. In the Dreadnought campaign of 1908 he was unmercifully and quite wrongly abused by the pacifists and the Big Navyites alike—and finally superseded. In 1915 and 1916 he found himself in rivalry with the most powerful political force which England had seen since the days of Gladstone. He might have been Prime Minister after Bonar Law's death, but for a trifling electioneering difficulty—or, at least, a little deflection of the helm of judgment at a critical moment. That he would have made a most efficient Prime Minister of modern times no one can doubt.

Lastly, of all the political colleagues of the Liberal group that Bonar Law had to deal with in 1915 and afterwards, McKenna became his closest and most intimate friend.

CHAPTER XII

GALLIPOLI

THE responsibility of various soldiers, sailors, and Ministers for the inception of the Dardanelles adventure has been definitely and publicly fixed by the Report of the Dardanelles Commission. And even to give a summary of the military operations would be tedious. The narrative in this chapter will therefore be confined to the struggle in the Government to secure evacuation after the failure of the Suvla Bay operations in August 1915.

On this subject the Cabinet was divided into two opposing groups with here and there a Minister shifting backwards and forwards between them. This issue absolutely obsessed the minds of Ministers all through the late summer and early autumn of 1915. Important as it was, it yet relegated to the background matters even more important.

This obsession was perhaps due to the fact that the fight inside the Government took on all the zest of a pre-war combat between parties. Anti-Evacuationist fought Evacuationist with a sort of partisan will and was repaid in kind.

Bonar Law was the leader of the group which favoured retirement, and Churchill, who was consistent in his advocacy of the Dardanelles adventure throughout, led the section which was for going on to the bitter end.

Here Churchill found a powerful reinforcement for his "forward policy" among the Tories who had been admitted to the Government in May 1915. The Tory dwells greatly on "prestige," particularly in the East; the national honour is dear to his heart, and the idea of British soldiers retiring before Turks was odious to all.* This group still thought that another push might do the trick, and favoured a dogged persistence in the Peninsula. Its adherents were Curzon,† Balfour,‡ Birkenhead, and, curiously enough in the light of after events, Lansdowne. Carson occupied a position all of his own in relation to the question of the hour ; his view was that you must either collect large reinforcements and make a great effort or you must evacuate. This policy of " get on or get out " made him susceptible to

*Lord Kitchener had said as long back as Feb. 24 : " The effect of a defeat in the Orient would be very serious. There could be no going back." cf. First Report Dardanelles Commission, p. 32.

†As the result of a conversation with General Robertson, Colonel Repington writes on Oct. 21, 1915, as follows : " Curzon and one or two others oppose the withdrawal from the Dardanelles on account of the loss of prestige and the resulting danger in Egypt and India." cf. " The First World War, 1914-1918," by Colonel Repington, Vol. I., p. 51.

‡Mr. Churchill had been especially anxious that Lord Balfour should succeed him at the Admiralty, since they saw eye to eye on naval questions. cf. " The World Crisis, 1915," by the Right Hon. Winston S. Churchill, p. 366.

appeals from Churchill and the Die-hards; on the other hand, it was in practice an advocacy of retirement because there were no great reinforcements available. Bonar Law was the pioneer of evacuation; Chamberlain followed him in the end, and so did Long, with some searchings of heart.

The Tory party was therefore split almost exactly down the middle.

Signs of dissension among the authorities directing the war began to appear above the horizon in September 1915. This cause is not far to seek. In the Balkans a series of events were maturing which promised succour to the Turks, danger to our men in Gallipoli, and threatened us with the need of a new Mediterranean Army. On 17 September Belgrade was evacuated before an overwhelming Austrian force. On the 25th Bulgaria declared war against the Allies, and it was obvious that unless something drastic could be done a few weeks would see the linking-up of Berlin with Constantinople. Already in the first week of September Lord Carson, as he indicated subsequently in his resignation speech, was brooding uncomfortably over the situation in the Balkans. He had begun to enter protests against further sacrifices in Gallipoli, and had denounced our lack of knowledge and method in the Eastern campaign. At that time he made no mention of Serbia at all; but he did indicate that resignation might soon prove for him the better part. But by the end of September Serbia had become a kind of pendant to the dispute in the Government over the evacuation of the Dardanelles, if only because a relief force for Serbia must in the main come from Gallipoli.

The first real crisis occurred in October. Already, on 5 October, two divisions had been diverted from Gallipoli to Salonika as a kind of belated effort to help the Serbians, who were now in headlong retreat before the Austrians on the north and the Bulgarians on the south-west. But our experts could hold out no hope of a sufficiently strong army being brought in time from the West, either to save the Serbian Army or to block the Germans on the Constantinople railway.

The advocates of evacuation in Gallipoli now came out in full force. Bonar Law took the view that a very short time would see German munitions and officers pouring into Constantinople, and that our men on the shell-swept sea-coast would be in the gravest danger if they were not removed promptly, and a term put to an enterprise which had obviously failed. Furthermore, the Salonika expedition was likely to draw heavily on what limited resources we could spare for the Mediterranean. He made no condemnation of the expedition to the Dardanelles as such; he simply said it had failed, and that to avoid disaster we must cut our losses.

Lloyd George was with him, though his point of view was different. He was not a Dardanelles man, neither was he a Westerner; he was a Balkanite. During this critical time he was fulminating in private with a kind of terrible eloquence against those

who would spare forces for the Dardanelles or
forces for the West, but would not spare a soldier
to hold Greece and Rumania to our side and save
Serbia and the Constantinople railway.

Therefore, though he was for evacuation, and
though he denounced those who, instead of
coming to a clear-cut decision, sent out a general
" trawling round the Mediterranean for a policy,"
he had not Bonar Law's singleness of purpose ; he
would come to the fence, but wouldn't jump it.
He appeared half-hearted over the business, and so
we have the curious picture of Lloyd George,
the fighting man, sound enough in view, but
refusing to fight, and Bonar Law, the man of
peace and good-will, fighting to the death !
It is fair to say Lloyd George's friends declare in
defence that he was so busily engaged in producing
munitions that he had no time at all to spare for
anything else.

I always understood that Lord Long's private
views coincided with those of Mr. Lloyd George.
Sir Austen Chamberlain was, in principle, inclined
to support Bonar Law. The main opposition was
led by Churchill and Kitchener, with their Tory
Die-hards. The Prime Minister sat on the fence,
anxiously struggling to avert the disruption of the
Government. It was finally decided to recall
General Sir Ian Hamilton (14 October 1915) and to
send out General Monro to report on whether we
should evacuate or not. Bonar Law protested
vigorously against the waste of time involved in
this proceeding, but such devices were dear to the
heart of Mr. Asquith when facing a storm.

On the 15th October 1915, Lord Carson tendered his resignation, thus adding to the prevailing stress, but his explanation was not presented to the House of Commons until 2 November. He gave a variety of reasons, such as the failure to evacuate, the failure to help Serbia, our lack of general grip in the war, and the monstrous debates of a swollen Cabinet. The general impression that he gave one at the time was that he was suffering from a vague discontent with the whole administration of the war, a kind of foreboding of disaster, and was anxious to produce a crisis from which a better state of affairs might emerge.

As it turned out, his resignation was unfortunately timed. The only means of helping Serbia was to clear the Army out of Gallipoli and land it in Salonika. His single-handed resignation was not sufficient to effect this, whereas if he had stayed on he would have been of the greatest assistance to Bonar Law in fighting the decisive battle for evacuation. By putting his resignation alongside his leader's he would have immensely strengthened his hands and possibly helped to expedite the whole proceedings. Resignations in echelon, like attacks, are always a mistake.

On 31st October General Monro telegraphed home a report strongly favouring prompt evacuation.

In the first week of November everything rushed to an acute crisis. On 5 November the remains of the Serbian Army were making their last stand in the region of the Babluna Pass, and the Allied Expeditionary Force, though it got to within ten miles of them, was too weak to effect anything. After that the Serbians retired westward and our men back to Salonika.

November 3 and 4 were stormy times for the Government, and for four days a grave state of crisis existed. General Monro's report had to be considered. It was out-and-out for evacuation on purely military grounds. Asked by telegraph for the opinion of the corps commanders, he reported Byng and Davies for evacuation and Birdwood against. General Birdwood, however, based his opinion on political grounds. The Evacuationists pressed strongly for immediate action upon this report, as will be seen from the subjoined letter of Bonar Law.

None the less, so formidable was the opposition, that the Prime Minister made another attempt to secure a postponement of the decision. This took the form of a proposal to send out Lord Kitchener on a mission to do over again what General Monro had just done. The supporters of retirement made this concession with great reluctance. Consent was wrung by the force of surprise, even from Bonar Law. After the meeting I had a conversation with him and Carson at the Hyde Park Hotel. Bonar Law's situation was difficult; his state of mind peculiar; and his final action the most interesting thing that I have ever seen in politics.

He believed that he had been rushed at the Cabinet into consenting to postpone evacuation until Lord Kitchener had reported. He was quite certain that the decision was a wrong one.

He felt that in the discharge of his public duty he was responsible for thousands of lives, which might be lost by his original error and by his present inaction. Yet he had undoubtedly consented to the view of the Cabinet. If he went back on that consent, he would lay himself open to all kinds of damaging, because in part well-founded, charges. Colleagues would say that such changes of mind were intolerable, and that it was impossible to do Government business on such a basis at all.

And, indeed, all this and more was said by opponents. He had placed himself, in fact, in the weakest possible position from which to launch an ultimatum. If he did so, he must either be inexpressibly damaged or incredibly strengthened. People might either say " Here is a man who will not abide by his agreements and he is worthless " ; or they might say, " Here is a man with so strong a conception of his moral duty that he dares to sacrifice even his reputation for an honourable consistency in the cause that he thinks right."

Once Bonar Law was convinced that to wait for Lord Kitchener's report was to gamble for no real object with life on a vast scale, he took his decision and never flinched again from it. He drew up and despatched the following letter to the Prime Minister.

My dear Prime Minister,
    When you read to us yesterday General Monro's report, I expected it would be followed

ɔy the decision to make preparations for the evacuation of the Dardanelles with the utmost possible rapidity. You proposed instead that Lord Kitchener should do once again the work which had already been done by General Monro, which involves a further delay, and this proposal was agreed to by the Cabinet.

I felt that we were taking this very course, but there was so little time for consideration I acquiesced in the decision. I have now had time to give further thought to the subject, and am convinced that the decision at which we arrived is not only wrong, but indefensible, and this view is confirmed by the report which was given me last night by Mr. Lloyd George that our Ambassador at Rome has informed us that the Germans have already established communication with Constantino- 'e.

As soon as it became evident that we could not prevent this communication I was convinced that our position at Gallipoli was untenable, and that we ought to abandon it. I circulated a memorandum to the Cabinet putting this view as strongly as I could, and you will perhaps remember that when it was proposed that General Monro should be sent out I stated to the Cabinet that in my opinion we ought to decide at once to evacuate the Peninsula, that I only refrained from pressing this proposal because I knew that I could not obtain the support of a majority of the Cabinet, and because, from the nature of the case, it was impossible to discuss the subject in Parliament and obtain a decision of the House of Commons.

I therefore consented to the delay necessitated by General Monro's visit, and now it is proposed to have a further delay, for which there is, I think, no justification, and which is only explained by the desire to postpone a disagreeable but an inevitable decision. Nothing seems to me more certain than that the Germans will regard the destruction of our forces in Gallipoli as the main object of their operations in the Balkans. They will not delay, and if, as I believe is the case, the whole Cabinet realises now that we must withdraw from the Dardanelles, then every moment is precious, and the delay of ten days at least involved in Lord Kitchener's visit is, in my opinion, a fatal error.

If, as is at least possible, this delay may result in the destruction of our force, a weight of responsibility will rest upon the Cabinet which I am not prepared to share. I therefore earnestly request you to call at once a meeting of the Cabinet so that a definite decision may be taken on the subject.

Yours, ——

This letter was the announcement that Bonar Law would resign unless the Cabinet rescinded its decision of the 4th November 1915. The great difficulty about this was that Lord Kitchener had already started, and at the meeting of 6th November the strongest advocates of evacuation blenched from the idea of reversing his mission

behind his back. Some public men had also other
reasons for wishing him well away in the East,
to which I shall refer when I come to deal with
Lord Kitchener's relations with his colleagues.
Bonar Law, therefore, utterly failed to find a
single supporter for his plan for reversing the
previous decision.

Nevertheless, he decided to persevere and to
resign alone. The consequences of his resignation must have been the disruption of the
Ministry, for Bonar Law was not simply an
individual, but the leader of the strongest party
in the House of Commons. Appeals and remonstrances couched in the friendliest terms
were showered on him, especially by his Unionist
friends and colleagues, but they did not shake
his determination.

The opponents of evacuation certainly made a
most strenuous fight. On the very night of his
departure as an impartial commissioner to report
to the Cabinet, Lord Kitchener put up a new
scheme with the Admiralty for a purely naval
attempt to seize the isthmus behind the Turkish
armies at the neck of Bulair, and declared that he
absolutely refused to sign orders for evacuation
on the ground that it would lead to a terrible
disaster. But the Navy fought shy of the scheme
and Kitchener was obliged to modify his first
declaration and to state that he did not see his
way through the problem, and that it would be
better to work out a scheme for getting the troops
away, should this prove necessary.

Lord Kitchener then left for the East, where

he did not find the position in the least satisfactory. On visiting Egypt he discovered members of the Headquarters Staff comfortably installed in Cairo and the vicinity, and with no personal contact with the Palestine front against Turkey. He remarked to these officers in Egypt : " I thought you were here to protect the Canal. It seems to me that the Canal is protecting you."

After the Cabinet meeting of 6 November Bonar Law stood absolutely alone. Chamberlain, who agreed with him and who behaved with a most punctilious sense of honour, felt bound to take the ground that, having agreed to the departure of Lord Kitchener to report, he could not resign until that report had arrived. He did not think himself in the least likely to be convinced by any arguments which Lord Kitchener might advance against evacuation, but he would not pledge himself to resignation in advance of these arguments. November 7th therefore passed in interviews and perturbation. The disruption of the Government appeared imminent, for Bonar Law was oppressed with a sense of his public duty and could not be deflected an inch.

On that day Bonar Law had a meeting with Asquith—at the Prime Minister's request. Bonar Law made it clear that this conversation was a final one—and that either evacuation or his own resignation must follow at once. He amply atoned for any irresolution he had shown in his original attitude towards Lord Kitchener's mission. In the face of every persuasion employed by a veteran in the art he remained firm. At the conclusion, the Prime Minister promised to support Bonar Law in his demand that the troops should be withdrawn forthwith. The crisis passed. Bonar Law did not resign ; the troops were withdrawn from Gallipoli.

Probably no other man then in British politics could, after his original error in council in agreeing to the Kitchener mission, have pulled off such a stroke. It required a man not only of commanding titular position, but of unimpeachable moral character, combined with a reputation for meaning what he said. If any other Minister had threatened to resign under such circumstances the challenge would have resulted in the destruction of the Minister and not of the Ministry.

Even after 7 November the Die-hards continued to give trouble. But their cause was lost. Lord Kitchener's mission was now nothing but a journey to the spot for the purpose of arranging the method of evacuation.

On 15 November Lord Kitchener reported from the East. He was full of praise for what had been accomplished in the Dardanelles—there were many dangers in retirement—but the reason for retaining our forces there was no longer so strong as it had been—Egypt could be covered from another base—and careful and secret preparations for evacuation were being made, and this operation might be carried out with less loss than had been anticipated by himself. On 22 November he sent a message to say that German assistance to the Turks now made our position untenable. On 23 November the War Committee, which was the old War Council and the old Dardanelles Committee, counselled retirement on the strength of Lord Kitchener's views.

Their decision was reported to the Cabinet. It was obvious that all was over, and that nothing now remained save to ratify evacuation. But Lord Curzon, with his well-known partiality for Die-hard causes, still struggled to delay the inevitable. He asked for time to draw up a document depicting the terrible consequences of retirement. And, indeed, he did succeed in producing a kind of film picture of the massacre of the rearguard boatloads retiring from the Dardanelles. Bonar Law replied to the film. He pointed out that the War Committee had reported for evacuation. If the advice of this Committee and Lord Kitchener and General Monro was to be disregarded under the circumstances, our method of carrying on the war was a farce. There were still other gyrations of the Die-hards, but they are not worth recording. Evacuation was inevitable, and took place with great success, and with none of the horrible consequences anticipated.

No estimate of the moral firmness displayed by Bonar Law throughout the Dardanelles crisis would be complete which did not picture the kind of arguments with which he had to contend. He was reminded that he knew nothing of war that expert after expert predicted a loss of thirty or forty per cent. of the troops as the price of evacuation ; that he was setting his uninformed opinion against the best military minds, and that the stake at issue was the lives of thousands of men. Horrible scenes of slaughter by the seashore were conjured up for his edification. Bonar Law was asked whether he would like to have this terrible burden on his conscience ; and, so to speak, if he would be able to sleep at night with the curses of the dying in his ears.

Fortunately, or unfortunately, for him, he was not the sort of person to attract any theatrical expression of gratitude. He never turned from his course, and the consistent strength of his attitude saved many thousands of lives. He fought the Prime Minister, he fought the erratic genius of Churchill, he fought the immense prestige of Lord Kitchener, and he won. One Liberal colleague once let fall a remark which better than any other explains that victory. " Ah," he said, " Lloyd George is always threatening to resign, and we don't believe him. Bonar Law said he would resign, and we knew he would."

The prominent part played by Lord Curzon in the Dardanelles controversy on the opposite side was due entirely to his qualities in Council and not to his strength of character.

Lord Curzon occupied no very important position in the public eye at the outbreak of hostilities. The Tories regarded him as the man who had sold the pass over the Parliament Act. His day was generally regarded as over. But that was not his own view. From the very outset of the first Coalition Government he began to try to displace Bonar Law from the leadership of the Conservative party. He used perpetually a subtle argument that the leadership of the Opposition had lapsed *de facto* with the accession of Conservative Ministers to the Government. Mr. Asquith, as Prime Minister, was their head—everybody else in the Government was on an equality. As Lord Lansdowne's influence began to wane that of Lord Curzon grew, and though Bonar Law's position was never in danger these covert attacks were none the less persisted in.

Lord Curzon held at one time in political circles a general brief to watch over the interests of the Air Force, for fear this Cinderella of the Services might be ground to pieces between the contending demands of the Army and Navy, to which its several sections were subordinate. So when the War Secretary or C.I.G.S. had told his colleagues the news from the Western Front, and the First Sea Lord had responded for the Navy, Lord Curzon would take up the tale for the Air Force. This gave him an opportunity for the exhibition of that pomposity which was his outstanding, but by no means his only, characteristic.

His rhetoric in making his statements was so lavish that sometimes it almost approached the ludicrous. "And now," he would say, "I must tell you about the bombing operations of the Air Force. There are two kinds of bombing operation. One is made by day, and one by night. The advantage of day bombing is that the object of attack is visible. The unfortunate disadvantage is that the assailant is also visible to the enemy. Now, on the other hand, in night bombing the precise reverse is the case. The object of attack is not visible to the assailant, but, on the other hand, he cannot be seen by his opponents," etc., etc.

It is rather marvellous that his colleagues stood this kind of thing at all. Certainly he exercised over Mr. Asquith's mind an influence quite disproportionate to his real abilities, whereas the Prime Minister hopelessly underrated Bonar Law's talents and character from the start to finish of the first Coalition.

But apart from push and pomposity, Curzon had some other qualities which made it impossible to treat him simply as a political mediocrity and bore. He was a first-class dinner companion, and possessed of a shining wit. How the same man could be both a wit and a bore is hard to understand. In Curzon's case it simply was so—and this fact had a restraining effect on the adverse judgment of colleagues who were not inclined to like him.

On one occasion he gave a wonderful exhibition of his duality at a gathering in Paris under the third Coalition, and after the signing of the peace.

He had long been dinning into the ears of Ministers the necessity of keeping troops in Georgia and Azerbijan, and protecting the liberties of these infant republics. Some of his colleagues laughingly suggested that his interest was based on the fact that he knew where they were, and could pronounce the names correctly, whereas they could not—and that he was showing off his book knowledge and travel experience of the Middle East at their expense.

On this occasion he was particularly eloquent

in calling on his audience to save a people rightly struggling to be free, sacrificing their blood for their national ideals of centuries—small nations, indeed, but, above all, brave men.

Lord Birkenhead made a pointed attempt to check the flow and prick the bubble of rhetoric. He interjected : " Lord Curzon has laid great stress on the bravery of these peoples. Can he tell me the names of any battles the Georgians and Azerbijanians have ever won in history ? "

There was a shout of laughter from the whole table. The barque of Curzon's eloquence seemed to have foundered. Curzon recovered instantly with a sharp rejoinder : " And can the Lord Chancellor tell us the names of any battles they have lost ? "

It was Curzon's wit that won in the encounter. Of such a strange mixture was Curzon's character compounded.

So closed the Gallipoli episode—a strange picture of blood and mismanagement, glory and failure. There was one man who did not wait for the public news of the evacuation. Churchill had, on 15 November, anticipated the announcement, and on 18 November made his resignation speech to the House of Commons, left the Duchy of Lancaster, and retired to the command of a battalion in the trenches of France.

CHAPTER XIII

FIRST AND SECOND KITCHENER

AS the echoes of the conflict over the evacuation of the Dardanelles died away and the Government, by the mere process of time, began to find its legs, Ministers came to take first-hand stock of each other. Some strange developments then became apparent. There was a re-grouping of personalities largely independent of original party distinctions. Some of the Tories rallied round Mr. Asquith. The Prime Minister, indeed, seemed to make a particular appeal to the older and more feudal elements in Toryism as exemplified in Lord Lansdowne, Lord Curzon and Lord Long. Apart from this, many Liberal and Conservative Ministers found themselves quite adrift from old associations and entering into new friendships and alliances with men they had previously distrusted or detested.

Lord Kitchener was unquestionably the second figure in the Cabinet—so that the attitude of individuals towards him assumed immense importance. When the Conservatives first entered the Government they were willing to give him unquestioning support against any of his Liberal critics. They regarded him as an appointment largely forced on the Premier by the Tory agitation of 1914. Not being as yet broken to the realities of war as seen from the inside, they imagined, no doubt, that their task would be to line up behind " a great soldier " against Liberal civilian criticism. This romantic view of the situation did not last long, chiefly because Lord Kitchener himself never encouraged it. On the contrary, his attitude and method was highly discouraging to any such conception. The Tories began to understand why some of the Liberals had failed to appreciate Lord Kitchener.

It must be remembered in fairness to all the people concerned that Lord Kitchener's presence in the Cabinet was in itself an amazing anomaly.

No soldier, as a soldier, had ever sat in a Ministry since Monk and the Restoration, for Marlborough had been on the Council before he took a prominent part in a great war, and Wellington only after his soldiering days were finished. The source of such an anomaly in our political life requires explanation—just as do the somewhat unhappy consequences which flowed from it.

When Lord Kitchener was snatched off the Dover boat at the outbreak of hostilities and made Secretary of State for War, the appointment was made in deference both to the overwhelming pressure of public opinion and of the Press, and to the views of the Opposition. Mr. Asquith at that moment had just taken the seals of that office from the hands of General Seely, and Lord

Haldane was deputising there for the Prime Minister. It was clearly absurd and impossible that the Premier should be War Secretary in the face of a European war. On the other hand, neither the nation nor the Tories would have Lord Haldane there at any price. His reputation for a tenderness towards Germany was a fatal bar to his prospects.

What were the reasons for the appointment of the first great general since the Duke of Wellington to hold high civil office, and what was the nature of the man in whose favour this breach with ordinary tradition was made ? The two questions are really indisseverable, for it was the personality of Lord Kitchener which gave him the immense prestige which compelled the Government to employ him at any cost. All this immense reputation was partly substance and partly that longer shadow which concrete objects cast in the rays of a setting sun. Lord Kitchener was a great and obscure figure. He had always been successful in everything which he had undertaken in distant lands.

The overthrow of the Khalifa, the final pacification of South Africa, the re-organisation of the Indian Army, the kindly and successful despotism he practised in Egypt, stood as bright and solid milestones marking the progress of his career. Other men have perhaps achieved as much without achieving adoration. But Lord Kitchener was the best advertised man in the Empire, because he refused to advertise ; he had found a royal road by which the Press was compelled to talk about him, if only in sheer annoyance at his silence. And something of the mystery and fatalism of the East was added to the hard practicality of his mind.

He was a stranger in England, and had the power and attraction of strangeness. On the Christmas Day of 1914 a visitor found him as usual during the war in his own large room at the War Office. Two huge fires blazed at either end, and the room was hot and sluggish. The newcomer commented on the appalling state of the atmosphere. " Very likely," said Kitchener, with a shiver. " I have not spent a Christmas in England for forty years." This touch of loneliness always struck the mind of the people, and also explains much in his Whitehall career. The low haze of the desert mist concealed his feet, and threw the rest of the figure up in huge proportions till it loomed gigantic above the mirage like a fabled and superhuman being in some Arabian tale.

The people did not reason about Kitchener, they just trusted, and that mere trust was a priceless asset in days when life was being torn up by the roots and the firmest mind might well fall into doubt or fear. Men simply said : " Kitchener is there ; it is all right." The final proof of this contention is to be found in the myths which surrounded his death. In all the black ages of time men have looked for a deliverer, and when the deliverer has died with his work only half accomplished, his real death has always been denied, and his return confidently predicted.

The belief comes to us from behind the earliest dawn of history, and education has fortunately tried to kill these credulous hopes in vain. It is the last crown of popular worship, and when people said that Lord Kitchener was really a prisoner in Germany they ranked him with King Arthur and all the other heroes who come no more.

All this was the source of his strength, and of his appointment to office. He added to his prestige immensely by his prophecy of the scope and duration of the war. No other Secretary of State would have imagined it, and so no other would have prepared for it ; certainly no other man could have induced his colleagues to act on his conclusions or the public to accept them. A short war was in every one's mouth. But as events worked out at the outset along the lines he predicted—as the Germans failed to reach Paris, while the Russian steam-roller, instead of rushing upon Berlin at the speed of a motor-car, reeled back in confusion from Tannenberg, and the lines settled down in the west from the Alps to the sea, his outside reputation for prophecy rose to a towering height.

A subtle touch of the dramatic in the way in which he did business added to this impression, even in the inner circle of Government. In the first days of August the Government proposed to ask the House of Commons for power to increase the Army by 50,000 men. When the requisition came to the War Office Kitchener simply struck out the figure 50,000 and wrote in 300,000 ! And if his prestige in England was great, so was his position in Europe. The French and Russian Ambassadors, M. Cambon and Count Benckendorf, gave him their complete confidence and received his in return.

But when one has said this one has drawn the picture at its brightest ; henceforward the lights begin to fade, and the rest is a melancholy story of the gradual whittling away of an immense reputation. From the very start the presence of Lord Kitchener produced a curious atmosphere in the Government. The wit who invented the tale that after a long exposition of the military position Kitchener leant back, lit a cigar, and remarked to the assembled Cabinet : " And now let's talk about the Welsh Church," did not get altogether away from the truth. Kitchener was frightened of the politicians, and ill at ease with nearly all of them. He had the soldier's professional and professed distrust of the class— and only Grey and Asquith surmounted the prejudice. Consider his career, his military upbringing, his prolonged absences from English life, the Oriental reticence in which he had dipped his mind. To him the men of law, of persuasion, of the energy of speech, were like some strange animals out of another world. Mr. Asquith seemed to understand him.*

Kitchener was a shy man, and though on some

*" Asquith had the confidence, even the attachment, of Kitchener in a way that no one else in the Cabinet had then." cf. " Twenty-five Years," by Viscount Grey of Fallodon," Vol. II., p. 241.

unbidden occasion sentences of great power and simplicity would rise suddenly to his lips in the intimacy of a private conversation, he added to the soldier's inability to explain that curse of nervousness which prevents a man speaking at the very moment when he should and must speak if he is to prevail in council. This failing produced by degrees a dismal impression. Lloyd George once said to me that Kitchener talked twaddle, and then, as though striving to be just, added : " No ! He was like a great revolving lighthouse. Sometimes the beam of his mind used to shoot out, showing one Europe and the assembled armies in a vast and illimitable perspective, till one felt that one was looking along it into the heart of reality—and then the shutter would turn and for weeks there would be nothing but a blank darkness."

Shyness led to reticence, and the appearance of reserve injected a natural but unjustifiable irritation into the minds of colleagues. He was accused of secretiveness, sometimes with justice, sometimes only because he was suffering from a lack of the power of expression. When pressed for further explanations he would circulate extracts from telegrams—a proceeding which only increased mistrust. In a word, Ministers wanted to know what was going on in Lord Kitchener's mind—a thing he was unable or unwilling to explain to a crowded circle. By slow degrees their impression even of a lack of straightforwardness grew in strength, and one by one they began to drop away from his support.

All this might have mattered little if there had been no real ground for criticism. But, as the Dardanelles Commission reported : " Lord Kitchener did not sufficiently avail himself of the services of his general staff, with the result that more work was undertaken by him than was possible for one man to do, and confusion and want of efficiency resulted."

Consider the work of the War Office. First of all there was all the ordinary routine of that office in peace-time immensely augmented by the mere fact of war. Then there was the raising of the New Armies and the supply of vast additional quantities of military material. Finally, there was the supervision of the actual operations in the field. All these branches Kitchener attempted to take into his own hands, and he frequently issued personal instructions which were not known to the departmental chiefs.

His attitude towards the Imperial General Staff was particularly unfortunate, because that body had been robbed of nearly all its prominent members by the original Expeditionary Force and badly wanted nursing and encouragement. As it was, the late General Wolfe Murray simply became the War Secretary's technical adviser, with no independent power of initiative and judgment. Wolfe Murray failed because he was old, timid and ignorant of the changing conditions of warfare. Kitchener was always looking out for a successor to him and never making a selection. Nor was Wolfe Murray ever appointed permanently to the post of C.I.G.S.

This autocratic centralisation was not due to the

vanity of power.   Kitchener was too sure of himself to be vain, and when subsequently he was convinced by argument that he was undertaking too much he submitted to the subdivision of his authority, first with Lloyd George on munitions and then with Robertson on strategy, with a good grace.   It was simply that he had always done things in this single-handed way, and it did not occur to him to alter his habits.   In Egypt it had been practicable ;   in India his special capacity for work made him seize for himself as Commander-in-Chief powers under the burden of which his successors broke down.

At the time of the change of Government in 1915 a proposal was made to transfer Lord Kitchener from the War Office and make him Commander-in-Chief—an office which has always possessed very vague powers.   Some of the Tories were attracted by the idea, which they confused absurdly enough with a military dictatorship.   On the other hand, Sir Austen Chamberlain raised a cry of alarm.   Kitchener himself had often toyed with the idea, and used to discuss it with his friends up till the early months of 1915. But after the attacks of those months in the Press, which hurt his feelings bitterly, he never mentioned the subject again.

The Conservative members of the new Cabinet started, as I have mentioned, with a strong prejudice in Lord Kitchener's favour.   But by the autumn of the year 1915 the confidence of many of them was heavily overclouded, if not absolutely destroyed.

The Dardanelles controversy explains a part of this feeling. There were other reasons. It is a hard saying, but it is one which must be accepted, that the only test of military advice in war is success or failure. The blood-stained failures of spring and summer began to soak into men's minds ; summer and early autumn brought only nibbling advances. And even when the New Army and adequate munitions were ready in the autumn, the first wild and brilliant rush at Loos was marred by faulty staff work, and the final failure to hold the objectives paid for with a fearful death-roll. In fact, the war was not going well, and Lord Kitchener and Lord French both suffered a diminution of authority in consequence.

At the War Office, however, Kitchener's power from start to finish never suffered any variation or shadow of turning. Nor was this due to fear of an unpopular chief. Lord Kitchener there was not the sort of bogey, now brooding in some inner apartment, now sallying out to harass the staff, which has sometimes been depicted. There punctually every morning at nine o'clock, and seldom even going out for lunch, he was assiduous, but also accessible—to the kind of people he wanted. Civilians he would not see, nor fussy old generals, but the active and rising young officers of any rank could always gain admittance. Sometimes he spent, or possibly wasted, whole days in these kinds of talks, for he was, beyond anything else, the champion of the rank and file and of the young officers—of the men who do the rough work.

Of course, he had his favourites, chiefly those who had served under him with success in his early wars.   After all, it was equally said of Napoleon, " No one had a chance of his baton who had not been with him in Egypt." The soldier who had the greatest influence with him in England was undoubtedly the late General Sir John Cowans, the Quarter-master-general, whose advice he almost invariably took.

And if he had his favourites, he also had his bugbears—one of them the unfortunate official who had to sign all War Office letters for which he was not really responsible. " That man ——," Kitchener used to say, " will sign anything." But he was by no means the " terror " portrayed in the popular Press. In great things he cultivated patience almost as a fetish ; in small things not infrequently he betrayed a sudden irritation. Once it was pointed out to him that he had rebuked a junior officer unjustly.   " No matter," said Kitchener, after reflection, " that fellow has an obstinate face."

On one occasion at least he found himself passionately engaged in a controversy which one would have imagined was foreign to his interest.   The High Church party discovered that the Principal Chaplain at the front was a Presbyterian, and that Anglican priests were in military subordination to a Nonconformist.

Lord Kitchener took up with zeal this injustice to the orthodox Church.   He called Bishop Gwynne, of Khartoum, to the rescue, cut the

Episcopalians out from under the guns of the Presbyterian, put them under the bishop, and made him a major-general. The Presbyterian minister was only a colonel, and Kitchener was forcibly appealed to to redress the balance and make him a general too. " I will make him a general," replied Kitchener with real anger, " when you make him a bishop." But this, surely, was an eccentricity of genius.* He stood the greatest test of character in that he was worshipped by his entourage, and repaid their devotion in kind. Colonel Fitzgerald, who died with him, knew him better than any man, and was that kind of invaluable aide who will on occasion stand up to his chief in argument, adored him. When the news of Hubert Hamilton's death was burst on him by surprise Kitchener broke down and wept.

What Lord Kitchener had needed all along was someone in the Cabinet who could gain his confidence and put his ideas in a coherent and argumentative form. At one time he seemed to lean on Mr. Asquith, but the Prime Minister somehow did not fill this role.

Lord Birkenhead formed a friendship with Lord Kitchener, and undoubtedly aspired to be his interpreter to the Cabinet. He would have been ready to supply the fluent words for the War Minister's somewhat obscure cogitations and incoherent utterance. To a trifling extent he did this—but the main plan failed of accom-

*When Mr. Lloyd George became War Secretary the Presbyterian Chief Chaplain became a major-general. Mr. Lloyd George never was open to the influence of the Episcopalians.

plishment.   Why it was never carried through would be hard to say.   Perhaps Lord Kitchener looked on Lord Birkenhead as a politician pure and simple.   The more probable explanation is that the soldier had given his whole confidence to Mr. Asquith, and did not desire any other mediator in the Cabinet.*

Considering the great position Birkenhead has occupied in the public estimation, it is necessary to try and explain the way in which the light of his genius was obscured during the war period. This was certainly not due to any lack of judgment on his part on military matters.   On the contrary, he was generally clear and wise in counsel.

In the first place, his immediate power was occluded.   He had been the democratic orator-in-chief of the Tory party.   Whenever he came to speak vast crowds assembled to listen to him. But democratic oratory came to an end with the outbreak of hostilities.   It could only be employed for the purpose of recruiting, and here Bottomley could beat Birkenhead every time.

With this reputation behind him Lord Birkenhead's opinions were not always listened to with the attention which the soundness of his views ought to have commanded.   It was not until the time of Lloyd George's later Premiership that his essential wisdom in counsel was recognised.

As it was, in 1914 and 1915 the war atmosphere was unsuited to him.   He had no place anywhere.

*None the less Kitchener had a great personal regard for Lord Birkenhead. Sir George Arthur in his life of Kitchener relates that more than once Kitchener said " F. E. has been a comfort in Cabinet to-day."

The Press Bureau was a dangerous and thankless job. When Birkenhead went out to G.H.Q. in France he appeared as a major without any knowledge of a major's work.

In technical experience of war he was a lieutenant in the Oxfordshire Yeomanry. None the less, he was a Privy Councillor and a national personality. He could not be given the command of a regiment and he could hardly revert to his original rank. Birkenhead never understood the military view of his position. The result was a series of misunderstandings for which I blame the generals concerned far more than I blame him. There was a complete confusion of values. On one occasion General Seely, then in command of a brigade, went to the late Lord French, as Commander-in-Chief, and asked for permission to visit the King of the Belgians with Birkenhead as his companion.

The Commander-in-Chief asked for an explanation for the request. General Seely said that they had a private message for the King of the Belgians from Lord Kitchener. This infuriated Lord French, who declared that all representations from the Government at home to the officers commanding the Allied armies in the field must be made through him. The backwash of his annoyance was vented on Lord Birkenhead, who had in reality very little to do with the matter.

Lord Birkenhead's views on the war were, in the main, extraordinarily sound. He was neither enthusiastic about new ideas, nor unduly suspicious of them—but he could not understand generals.

His valuation of his own services and prospects always varied greatly. When I first knew him before the war, his desire was to be the equivalent of Lord Randolph Churchill—the Tory Democrat, who would yet beat the Old Gang. After that his aspirations soared higher—and he would talk about Lord Palmerston as an enviable personality.

But in the interval of the war there was a distinct slump in the height of Birkenhead's ambitions. Afterwards, when post-war events gave a favourable chance for his vast abilities, he began to talk of Disraeli—long before Mr. Baldwin had made a habit of mentioning the late Earl of Beaconsfield with respect.

Lord Birkenhead's chief enemy has always been his own biting and witty tongue, which spares no man. He often gives offence in this respect to people whom he really loves and admires. G.H.Q. in France was about the worst place in the world in which to employ this particular instrument.

I remember myself making what I considered a few harmless jests there—and being astonished at their reception. A major-general became as violent in his fury as though I had been laughing at a funeral. But as a rule I avoided the military hierarchy.

Birkenhead did not—and was inclined to talk at St. Omer as if he were at the Carlton Club.

There still lingers in Pall Mall the story of Birkenhead's dealing with the well-known shipping magnate of Liverpool, the late Mr.

Welsford, who rather astonished everybody by leaving a million pounds behind him. Welsford was a good-hearted individual, but rather fond of talking and boasting. He became, in fact, the club bore.

Birkenhead came to loggerheads with him as a partner over the bridge table. " Do you know who is the most unpopular member of this club ? " " I suppose," replied Welsford, " that you mean me." " No, I don't," said Birkenhead. A silence followed. " Do you know who is the most unpopular member of this club ? " repeated Birkenhead. There was no answer. " Well, I am, because I proposed you for membership."

Such methods of conversation did not endear Lord Birkenhead to the military. When Birkenhead came home he met some lady who professed to have an intimate acquaintance with General Tom Bridges,* then attached as liaison officer to the staff of the King of the Belgians. " Tom Bridges," said the lady, " can make the Belgians do anything he likes." " Really, can he ? " replied Birkenhead. " Of course he can," said the lady. " Could he make them fight ? " " Of course he could." " Then," said Lord Birkenhead, " why doesn't he ? " From a mere major this was blasphemy. This style of wit did Birkenhead an incalculable amount of damage before he had reached an assured position in the political world. Afterwards it mattered far less to his prospects,

---

*Lieut.-Gen. Sir George Bridges, K.C.M.G., K.C.B., made Governor of South Australia in 1922.

for he had acquired a prescriptive right to a certain amount of latitude.

But the soldiers treated Birkenhead very foolishly in not making any adequate use of his talents. He has got the best brains of any man among my contemporaries. If all his other qualities matched his intellect he would be the biggest world figure of our time.

CHAPTER XIV

FIRST AND SECOND KITCHENER
(*continued*)

THE last chapter has been a melancholy story of the decay of the great military reputation of Lord Kitchener in the eyes of an inner ring of colleagues while its lustre still remained undimmed in the eyes of the nation. Conservatives had followed Liberals into the camp of doubt.

But all this time the decay of real power and influence went on. By the early autumn of 1915 Lloyd George and Bonar Law, the two most powerful men in the Ministry, had both, working from different ends, arrived at a state of profound dissatisfaction with the military administration at the War Office, and were considering together the advisability of informing the Prime Minister that unless an improvement took place a change would have to be made. Action was not long delayed.

Already by September Lloyd George was beginning to manifest signs of impatience with the general conduct of the new Government and a distrust of the personnel, methods, and machinery by which it was being carried on. With that kind of uncanny insight into the heart of the future which marks his daring, erratic, and yet practical mind, he had seized on three main improvements which must be carried into effect—conscription, a small War Cabinet, and the removal of Lord Kitchener from the War Office.

Of these three things, one came by agreement, one by a death, and the third by the fall of a Government. Bonar Law marked his uneasiness, and told Lloyd George that he was on the verge of falling out with Mr. Asquith—a *denouement* which would be disastrous to both men and a calamity to the country. He offered to go to Mr. Asquith and persuade him to do something to meet Lloyd George's views, adding with considerable humour, " I only want to see you two on the same good terms you were when you combined to do me out of the Chancellorship of the Exchequer in May." But we are only concerned with these matters here in so far as they affected Lord Kitchener.

Mr. Asquith was in a position of great difficulty. He did not really need pressing by his two principal lieutenants at all. He himself was firmly of opinion that there ought to be a change at the War Office, and agreed with them that Lord Kitchener's habit of acquiring all the military information and keeping it to himself often made it quite impossible for the Government to come to any decision at all—except one gained by leaping blindly in the dark. But the Prime Minister could not, and did not, disguise from himself the fact that Lord Kitchener's immense prestige made it impossible for the Government to dismiss him without a popular upheaval he was not yet prepared to face.

In addition, he was not greatly impressed with the idea, then put forward, of Lloyd George as the new War Secretary, on the ground that his administrative record was a poor one. So his attempt to remove Kitchener came to nothing.

However, a strange missive remains as a memento of the movement—so vigorously initiated and executed with such a lack of determination and energy.

It is a copy of a letter written by Bonar Law to Lloyd George. It is undated, and is in Bonar Law's own handwriting. The copy is transcribed on Colonial Office note paper, and bears the following endorsement :

"Written from recollection after letter was sent."

My dear L.G.,

Have you any objection to my telling the P. M. that you had said to me that in your opinion as long as Lord K. was at the W. O. nothing but disaster was in front of us, that you had told me that you had written to the P. M. that you could not continue to share responsibility if conditions at the W. O. were unchanged and that I had replied that if this question were raised as a clear issue I should be compelled to take the same course.

Yours, ——

But nothing could keep Lloyd George and Bonar Law long apart on the question of War Office administration, because it was always a question on which from start to finish they were in essence absolutely agreed. And then there was the Dardanelles controversy, ever growing fiercer and fiercer as the weeks of October 1915 slipped by, to keep the differences between Kitchener on one side and Bonar Law and Lloyd George on the other alight and glowing. The opposition to Kitchener said that he went to the War Office so early and worked so hard there that by the time the evening came he was quite unfit to discuss anything, while the " Evacuationists " resented a statement of the War Secretary, probably made in the heat of the moment, that it would be better for our prestige to lose the Gallipoli army than to withdraw it.

In the first week of November, as we have seen, the crisis over the Dardanelles became acute, and Lord Kitchener's whole position, bound up as it was with the refusal to evacuate, tottered. A day or two before General Monro's report was considered by the Government Lloyd George and Bonar Law renewed their demands for Kitchener's resignation, but in far more stringent terms. By this time Mr. Asquith, who cordially agreed with them that Kitchener must go, had so far nerved himself against popular opinion as to be ready to act.

But the method by which he sought to effect the common purpose was indirect. He did not dismiss the War Secretary ; he sent him to the East and became Acting Secretary in White-hall.*

In describing Lord Kitchener's part in the Dardanelles adventure I have pointed out the curious circumstances which surrounded his departure for the Mediterranean. Why was he sent to the East, an advocate of keeping the troops in Gallipoli, to report on the question of retirement, and the policy of evacuation decided on in Bonar Law's favour almost as soon as his back was turned and before he had time to report ? The answer is that Mr. Asquith was trying to kill two birds with one stone. By sending out Lord Kitchener to report he postponed the disruption of the Government and he also got away from England a War Secretary whom he was determined to dismiss without scandal if he possibly could.

*Lord Kitchener's biographer tells us that the War Secretary was under no illusion as to the underlying motive of the mission assigned him. " Candid friends had hinted to him that some of his Ministerial colleagues would be content to see his chair empty or otherwise filled, and would rejoice in any incident—or accident—which might prolong or perpetuate his absence. " Perhaps if I have to lose a lot of men over there, I shall not want to come back," was his remark, when the Cabinet approved a mission fraught with grave responsibility and capable of indefinite extension. On the morrow of Kitchener's departure the air was thick with rumours of his supersession."—cf. " Life of Lord Kitchener," by Sir George Arthur, Vol. III., p. 185.

†" At this meeting the desire of certain Ministers to effect Lord Kitchener's removal from the War Office was very prominent. When he left for the Dardanelles they had hoped that some pretext could afterwards be found for keeping him away from London permanently, and when his mission was terminated by the decision to evacuate, the question of delaying his return to England was raised at once. The first proposal made was that he should be asked to remain in the East so as to exercise a general supervision

Mr. Asquith never intended that Lord Kitchener should return to Whitehall ; on the contrary, he proposed to make him Viceroy of the East, with full command of all our Expeditionary Forces in the Mediterranean and in Asia. " Malbrouk has gone to the war," said a witty Liberal member of the Ministry. " Who knows when he will return ? " Kitchener himself had some suspicion of the plan, but he believed quite erroneously that the seals of office could not be transferred in his absence. But, in fact, by this time he was altogether out of favour. He passed through Paris on his way out, and had an interview with Joffre at Chantilly.

Field-Marshal Sir Henry Wilson—that shrewd over the evacuation, and my opinion was taken as to the desirability of that step. There was only one answer. The operation—an extremely difficult one—must be under the direction of one authority only, otherwise nobody would know who was responsible for anything. If Lord Kitchener was to remain, then he must be appointed Commander-in-Chief in place of General Monro. If not so appointed, then the farther he was away from the Dardanelles the better, so that there might be no misunderstanding as to who was in charge. But the Government could not well order him, a Field-Marshal, to take the place of Monro, a Lieutenant-General, and therefore another expedient had to be found. After several unsuccessful attempts to evolve one, it was suggested that he should be asked to go as a temporary measure to Egypt, where his presence would be valuable when the moral effect of the evacuation was being felt. This suggestion, put forward by a Minister who shall be nameless, was warmly welcomed, and was conveyed to Lord Kitchener at the same time as he was informed that evacuation had been provisionally approved, and that (following the advice I had given) the method of carrying it out " must be left, of course, to the judgment of the commander on the spot." Lord Kitchener replied that he ought to be " back in England, as time is passing, and I can do no good here. I have arranged with McMahon (the High Commissioner) to quiet the effect in Egypt as far as possible."
—cf. " Soldiers and Statesmen, 1914-1918," by Field-Marshal Sir William Robertson, Bart., Vol. I., pp. 140, 141.

hand in all such matters, a schemer and intriguer both, who possessed throughout the war
an importance quite disproportionate to his military status because he was endued with the
political mind, and could and did talk the language
of the politicians—was quick to note the altered
values. He indicated both Joffre and Kitchener
as still the strong men of each nation to the popular
gaze, but both in reality under the shadow of
displacement. The Field-Marshal must have had
a special interest in Lord Kitchener because both
dealt in military prophecy.

But while Kitchener was at least right in
1914, Sir Henry Wilson's abundant and por-
tentous prophecies were mostly disproved as
soon as uttered.

At the very moment when he was writing these
reflections on Joffre and Kitchener he declared :
" We have no longer anything to fear either
in the West or in the East from the enemies'
armies. On the contrary, it is they who have
cause for anxiety in the future."

In fact, the frequency with which the predictions
of the military failed in any way to correspond with
the event was as much a source of embarrassment
to the Government as the dogmatic tone in which
they were uttered was a cause of irritation to its
members. To-day in the ranks of the Higher
Command there is only one kind of prophet left—
the man who puts nothing in writing. But this is
by the way.

Mr. Asquith then was Acting War Secretary
while Lord Kitchener was in the Mediterranean

THE RT. HON. REGINALD MCKENNA

"Leave it to me."

EARL OF BIRKENHEAD AND THE RT. HON. WINSTON
CHURCHILL

Churchill "retired to the command of a Battalion in the trenches
of France."

but it had been clear even before Lord Kitchener's departure that some permanent new appointment had to be made. Lloyd George was not anxious to succeed to the War Office, though he was ready in the ultimate resort to assume a responsibility which he felt to be mainly his. He must have perceived, however, that any politician succeeding Lord Kitchener must be suspect in the popular judgment, and that this kind of suspicion would greatly limit his usefulness as War Minister. Suddenly Mr. Asquith announced that he was ready to assume the post in permanency himself, and at first he persuaded Bonar Law to his view. Lloyd George would not agree.

On reflection, however, Bonar Law decided that it was impossible for one man to be at once Premier and War Secretary, and he wrote Mr. Asquith a formal protest. Immediately after this Lloyd George in his turn changed his mind and agreed to Asquith facing as War Secretary the first blast of the storm which was certain to follow the eminent soldier's resignation. Bonar Law thought this change of front an instance of Lloyd George's instability, but the historian might say that no one concerned showed any marked consistency of opinion. What the upshot would have been it is impossible to say, for no new appointment was made.

The whole scheme for removing Lord Kitchener came to nothing. It was apparently upset by one of those lesser accidents which rule the destinies of nations. The story came to the late Charles Palmer, afterwards a member of the House of

Commons, then editor of the " Globe " newspaper, in that somewhat perverted form which
news passed through several intermediaries often
assumes.   The " Globe " promptly announced
on 6 November—that is, after Lord Kitchener
had started for the East—that there was serious
trouble between Lord Kitchener and the Cabinet,
and that the former had tendered his resignation.
Instantly Lord Birkenhead, as Attorney-General,
and Sir John Simon, as Home Secretary, brought
the heavy artillery of Dora into action, and the
" Globe " was suppressed.   But when the errant
newspaper was closed down the plan to change
War Secretaries was closed down with it.   The
Government did not lose the services of Lord
Kitchener, though it wanted to ;   but the
" Globe " did lose the services of Mr. Palmer,
though it did not want to.

It is amusing to reflect that the action taken was
tantamount to an admission by the Government
that the statement that there was a disagreement
between the Cabinet and Lord Kitchener, cul-
minating in the latter's resignation, was likely to
cause " disaffection."   The newspaper was permitted to publish again in a fortnight's time on
confessing that it accepted the Government's
assurance that Lord Kitchener had not tendered
his resignation—which was the truth—and also
" that there were no grounds of dissension between Lord Kitchener and his colleagues such as
to affect their future Ministerial co-operation,"
which was truth of a highly technical variety.

Lord Kitchener therefore returned to Whitehall.

But he himself was aware that his real reign was
over, and he pointed to Lloyd George as the
prime mover in producing this new situation.
Two aspects of his decline became apparent in
two simultaneous series of developments.   In
the first place there was Lord Kitchener's inclination to retire of his own volition, and in
the second place there came the proposal to divide
the functions of the War Office, and to set up the
old division which subsisted (until Lord Palmerston abolished it during the Crimean war) of a
Secretary at War and a Secretary of War.   If it
will be remembered that these two moves were
really going on together, it will be possible to
describe them one by one.

In the second week of December Lord Kitchener
intimated to the Prime Minister that he was
aware that he had lost the confidence of the
Cabinet, and that he wished to retire and take over
the command in Egypt.   The Premier was, of
course, agreeable to this course, but—who was
to succeed ?   His own succession had been ruled
out ; we have seen that Lloyd George was unwilling to be the new Secretary of State, and time
and reflection seemed to have stiffened him to a
definite refusal.   Bonar Law, for one reason or
another, was not offered the post, and when the
Prime Minister wished to appoint Austen Chamberlain this course, too, was objected to.   The
truth of the matter appears to be that the shadow
of the forthcoming Kitchener-Robertson agreement, which would devitalise the powers of the
new civilian Secretary, hung heavily over the

whole transaction, and robbed the office of its attractions.

Finally, as no successor could be found, Lord Kitchener consented to remain ; but he did so at the price of submitting to a further truncation of his powers.

Up till 1855 the Secretary at War discharged what might roughly be described as the administration of the War Office in times of peace. On the outbreak of hostilities, however, the Colonial Secretary suddenly became the Minister of War, and took over the responsibility for active operations. It was now proposed to revert to something analogous to this system by making the Chief of the Imperial Staff a kind of Minister of War responsible for strategy and the conduct of the armies in the field. The C.I.G.S. would thus cease to be the mere echo of the Secretary of War, and would become a real power and personage. Field-Marshal Robertson was the man indicated for the new appointment.

Something had happened in France which made Field-Marshal Robertson available for this post. Lord French had been recalled. Lord Kitchener had very little to do with this action. The question was on what terms would Field-Marshal Robertson come. Kitchener saw him in Paris after he came back from the East, and, indeed, they travelled together. In the course of the journey the two men got to understand one another, and cordial personal relations, never broken, were established between them.

The powers it was now proposed to give the

C.I.G.S. were in all conscience sufficiently extended. As has been suggested, the duties of the War Office were to be cut in half, and in reality two Secretaries of State appointed. One, Lord Kitchener, with the nominal leadership, was to discharge all those duties which would appertain to the Secretary of State in time of peace, the other, Field-Marshal Robertson, was to conduct the war. So long as these two co-equal monarchs agreed together in general policy and in respecting each other's boundaries, such a system might possibly work for a time, as, indeed, it did with Robertson and Kitchener. Robertson, indeed, absolutely played the game by his official superior but real colleague ; he behaved to him as if he acknowledged his subordination, and all friction was avoided. None the less, before he accepted the post of C.I.G.S. he had demanded and obtained direct access to the Cabinet. This privilege made his position practically co-equal with his colleague and far superior to the position of the First Sea Lord towards the First Lord of the Admiralty.

But the system of the Kitchener-Robertson agreement was a fundamentally wrong one, as Lloyd George discovered to his cost when he succeeded Kitchener a few months afterwards ; and it required a convulsion which destroyed a Government to rectify the blunder. Lloyd George, indeed, threw down the Government to do this— became Prime Minister—and promptly appointed Lord Derby Secretary of State under precisely the same vicious conditions.

Lord Kitchener, therefore, returned from Paris to find himself only in control of one of three branches of work with which he had started. Munitions and strategy had gone ; there only remained recruiting and the administration of the War Office.   Here he continued all-powerful until the end.

These last days were not without one touch of glory. At the invitation of the late Neil Primrose and Sir Henry Dalziel, he agreed to meet the members of the House of Commons face to face and brave the politicians in their very lair. The dissatisfaction of the inner ring had spread outwards, and he was doubted at Westminster. The meeting was a triumphant success, and Kitchener basked in a kind of Indian summer of a spontaneous popularity in the House.   But what the outer ring thought about the soldier could not affect the opinions of the Cabinet.

I have said that this is a story of diminishing lights, and now nearly all the candles but one—that of life itself—are out.   Even Kitchener's great popularity had not survived altogether intact the hard and disastrous year of 1915. Neuve Chapelle, Loos, the Dardanelles were not names of good omen ; and the strain of war was beginning to tell. In the early days the crowds had come down in the morning to see him enter the War Office ; they came no longer. Partly, no doubt, his manner discouraged these demonstrations ; he did not seem to care whether people gazed at him or not—hardly indeed to be aware of their presence ; unlike Lloyd George, who bor-

rowed an open car to drive from Downing-
street to the Mansion House because he could
not be seen in a closed one ! So the crowds, too,
fell away as the Cabinet Ministers had done.

To him the Russian Mission was a disguised
banishment—for he knew that from it he would
never return to Whitehall. He did not conceal
from himself that the sun of his military activities
was setting, although he could not foresee with
what suddenness it would be plunged into darkness.

So on a day in June, unnoticed, uncheered,
almost unattended, the greatest living soldier of
the Empire, a man who had become even in his
lifetime a legend both to East and West, drove
down to King's Cross. He arrived a minute and
a half before the train was due to depart, and on
the platform Kitchener had one of his curious
and sudden gusts of impatient irritation over the
delay. Then the engine pulled out, and the train,
with its load of human greatness, vanished into
the night.

CHAPTER XV

THE LAST PHASE

IT will be observed that nothing has been said
on the question of compulsory military service,
which, with the advent of 1916, became at last a
living issue. I do not propose to discuss the
history of the question in detail. The advocates
of compulsion have been shown definitely by the
logic of fact to be right and its opponents wrong.
No one believes to-day that we could have won
the war on a voluntary basis. But nearly all the
politicians held such transient views on the advisability of applying compulsion at any given
moment that they could adduce evidence to show
that they were in favour of it at one time or
another. To trace all the ramifications of their
beliefs would be tedious in the last degree.

Three outstanding facts may be noted :

.(1) The Tories declared themselves theoretically
for compulsion before they joined the first Coalition Ministry in May 1915, but did little to effect
it in office.

(2) Mr. Lloyd George, a Radical, was from start
to finish the leader of the compulsionist movement.

(3) Everybody up to the summer of 1915
tended to rely on Lord Kitchener to give a sign

—and Lord Kitchener seemed to be waiting on the Prime Minister to tell him whether to give a sign or not. So nothing happened.

Further, there were always three divisions in current opinion—though men passed backwards and forwards between them with bewildering rapidity. There were the people who were for conscription, whether the country wanted it or not ; there were the people who were for it if the country would agree ; and there were the people who were against it anyhow.

The middle section really had the most wisdom. They wanted to prove to the people that compulsory military service was the only possible course, and they had to show voluntaryism was breaking down before they could do so. The Die-hard compulsionists replied that this was a dangerous and wasteful process because the voluntary system put men into wrong places and killed off the best ones first. This, they contended, was a waste of national energy. The answer was that a great reaction against the war, due to a premature application of conscription, would waste more energy still.

The Derby scheme was the test. As soon as its failure was manifest to the country the Military Service Act was passed and accepted by public opinion. The proof that it was not a burning political issue is contained in the fact that only one Under-Secretary resigned because compulsion was not carried, and only one Minister resigned because it was.

Otherwise the internal politics of the greater

part of the year 1916 were, from the public point of view, singularly devoid of interest.

In France there was the lull which marked the preparation for the Somme offensive. The first great event was the tragic death of Lord Kitchener in June 1916. The War Office thus became vacant without any of the disabilities which had so far clung to the succession. The struggle over the vacancy is of great importance because it led directly to events of a far more serious character. The question at issue was simply this : Was the new War Secretary to be one of the strongest men in the Government or was he to be a Minister of the second magnitude in the political constellation ?

There were several people who for varying reasons held very much the same view on this matter—the soldiers holding higher commands at the War Office and the Prime Minister ; both were against Lloyd George.

Field-Marshal Robertson's position as the *de facto* leader of the soldiers' party was perfectly intelligible. It has been pointed out how strange a division of power had been created at the War Office under the Kitchener-Robertson agreement. It was clear that if the Chief of the Imperial Staff secured an agreeable civilian head as colleague he would be Secretary of War in all but name. If, on the other hand, Lloyd George was appointed, everyone might look out for squalls. Several soldiers were at that time taking a considerable part in what may be roughly described as war politics, and believed themselves to be,

or were at least told by others that they were,
the new strong silent men, the latest heaven-sent
saviours of their country in the long succession
of those soldier-statesmen.

The soldiers, therefore, put in a nomination
which they thought would meet their require-
ments. But the whole idea on which they acted
was absurd, and they vastly overrated their
influence as political strategists in these, to them,
new-trodden realms, unless—and it is a very
big " unless "—they knew that they had the
Prime Minister behind them. It must be clear
that in the normal course of events the great
position of War Secretary, which still retained
its prestige in name, if not in fact, would not be
allowed to fall to any but one of the most powerful members of the Cabinet. The war was going
badly, and the public would be likely to be dissatisfied with the nomination of a mere figure-
head to Whitehall.

Yet when it was suggested to the soldiers that
either Bonar Law or Lloyd George was certain to
go to the War Office, and that as they would probably find the former easier to get on with, they
had better make a virtue of necessity and ask for
him, they would not take the advice, but clung to
the idea of a smaller man, and so rushed finally
on their fate.

Now, the Prime Minister did not want Lloyd
George there either, and it seems probable therefore that the soldier-statesmen were at least
strengthened in their attitude by the knowledge of
this fact. They were, they said, keenly anxious to

avoid uninstructed or over-zealous civilian interference, particularly in the direction of the Quartermaster's and Adjutant's departments. What was the inner motive for the Premier's attitude ? In the course of this book it will be necessary to consider Mr. Asquith's character and record as a Minister in time of war, for, with the struggle over this appointment, another shadow of impending doom began to fall across his path. For the moment all that need be said is this : he never trusted Lloyd George, and therefore didn't like him. Mr. Asquith's distrust may have been due to political events of the past, or it may have been due to some accident of temperament. We do not, after all, trust or distrust men by logic.

But in describing the continual contests with his colleagues in which Lloyd George was involved, and the distrust and even animosity which he succeeded in arousing, first in the breast of many of his old Liberal colleagues, and then of his new Tory ones, we cannot help feeling that there is an aspect of his character which has not been squarely faced. Why did these perpetual stirrings of combat and distrust charge the whole atmosphere in which he moved ?

The answer might partly be found in his own rapid march from the pacifist wing of Liberalism to the left of extreme militancy. And in the original Asquith Government this explanation might account for the facts. Thus he began in 1914 at cross-purposes with Churchill because the latter was the head of the fighting school, and he finished the year by alienating the more

old-fashioned Liberals as a result of the vigorous
war measures he proposed.

But if this is the true and sole explanation of
the troubles which beset him, why was it that he
started with the confidence of his Tory colleagues in the May of 1915 and had largely lost
it by the end of the year ? Why did Bonar Law
say, " When we joined the Cabinet there was no
man we disliked more than McKenna and no man
we trusted more than Lloyd George. Now the
case is precisely reversed " ? Surely Lloyd George
did not alienate Tory sentiment because he was
in favour of a vigorous prosecution of the war.
The explanation will not hold water, and we must
probe still deeper into the events and discover
what common view united so many diverse
political elements in opposition to Lloyd George
within the Cabinet.

If you could cross-examine all those who were
at one time or another hostile witnesses, their
complaints would probably resolve themselves
into one single set of ideas—that Lloyd George
always had too ready and too complete answers
to every possible objection which might be
brought against his conduct, as though he had
considered in advance that his actions might lay
him open to charges of selfishness or insincerity ;
that he was, in fact, always thinking far too much
of himself and far too little of the team ; that a
brilliant stroke for himself outweighed in his
eyes lack of smooth running in the Government
machine ; that he was, in a word, always " on the
make."

There is no question but that this view was held by a large number of independent colleagues who had little in common among themselves. This mere fact does not, of course, prove that this interpretation of Lloyd George is the correct one. But the observer must note one tremendous piece of corroborative evidence. What caste Lloyd George had lost with many Ministers while he was only one among equals he regained almost at a stroke the instant he became Prime Minister. In a word, his team play became perfect the moment he was made captain, and the original source of every disturbance, the target of every mistrust, became a unifying influence in the Cabinet and an object of unbounded confidence. From this fact history must draw its own conclusion.

In any case, Mr. Asquith was firmly determined not to exalt Lloyd George's fortune further by granting him his ambition to go to Whitehall, and his mind turned in the alternative direction either of a weak man or a satellite. It is fair to say, however, that Mr. Asquith fully realised the strained feelings existing between Lloyd George and the Generals, and honestly feared that serious friction would follow on Lloyd George's appointment.

It has been pointed out already that Lloyd George and Bonar Law had in the past acted in concert on War Office questions. They were of the same mind now ; they did not think that the War Office should fall to one of the lesser lights, and so the position practically lay between the

two of them. Lloyd George was anxious, Bonar
Law was willing, to take it. If the latter had been
strongly pressed by the Prime Minister at that
time to take the vacant post things might have
turned out very differently, but he was not so
pressed.

There can, however, be no suspicion of an
intrigue against the Prime Minister, for at this
time Bonar Law and Asquith were working
in the closest harmony, while Bonar Law's attitude to Lloyd George was distinctly cold. It
cannot be stated too plainly or emphatically that
here, and in practically every matter in the period
under review, if Bonar Law's judgment was with
Lloyd George, his general sympathy was with
Asquith, and that it was always with the greatest
reluctance that he opposed the Prime Minister's
views. Lloyd George and Bonar Law simply
happened to agree on the facts of the War Office
situation. The truth of the matter is that to any
rational judgment Lloyd George was the obvious
man to succeed Lord Kitchener.

When matters stood in this posture a meeting
took place between the Minister of Munitions
and the Colonial Secretary at my house at Leatherhead to discuss what action should be taken. The
day was Sunday, and Bonar Law was to go to
France next morning.

The two Ministers arrived quite early. The
conversation between them began extraordinarily
badly, as is often the case between two public
men who are not on close terms of friendship
with one another. Bonar Law stated his com-

plaints against Lloyd George as a colleague quite
frankly. In effect he recapitulated the Asquith
case against the Minister of Munitions.

Lloyd George met, or rather avoided, these
accusations, with great tact. He did not attempt
a rebuttal of the charges. He treated the past as
something not worth discussing. There was
only one question that mattered, he said, and
that was how to deal with the vacancy at the
War Office. Either a satellite of Asquith or a
weak man agreeable to the soldiers would be
appointed, or the War Office must fall to one of
the strong men of the Government. This, he
thought, limited the choice to Bonar Law and
himself. Since a weak appointment would be
fatal to the conduct of the war, he offered to
give Bonar Law his unqualified support for the
post.

Yet even to this gesture Bonar Law did not
respond very readily. It was only in the afternoon
that the two men seemed to get into real touch
with one another. Then, after a prolonged discussion, Bonar Law promised to back Lloyd
George's claim to the War Office.

I had arranged to travel to France with Bonar
Law next morning, but all plans had to be changed
in order to carry out the new decision. Otherwise
the War Office appointment might be made
before Bonar Law and Lloyd George could
bring their joint influence to bear. Bonar Law
therefore determined to motor straight down to
Sutton Courtney, the Premier's Berkshire residence, and bring him to book on the War Office

KITCHENER LEAVING THE WAR OFFICE

"And now nearly all the candles but one—that of life itself—are out."

THE RT. HON. H. H. ASQUITH AND THE RT. HON. SIR
EDWARD GREY

"His relations with Grey were of that distant but friendly kind
which an ocean might have with a contiguous mountain peak."

issue. He was very humanly annoyed by the fact
that he had previously tried to arrange a meeting
with Asquith in London and had been told that
if he wished to see the Premier he must follow
him into the country.

I went with him, and sat in the car outside
while he went into the house. No sooner had
Bonar Law informed Asquith of the War Office
discussion with Lloyd George than the Prime
Minister said, " I offer it to you." Bonar Law
replied that it was too late. Last week, he said, if
he had been pressed he would have taken it.
Now he was pledged to support Lloyd George.
Furthermore, he had come to the conclusion on
reflection that Lloyd George was the best appointment and must have the post. Asquith then
agreed to make Lloyd George War Secretary.

Bonar Law and I crossed to France that Monday
evening. He stayed with me for the night at the
Canadian Headquarters at Hesden. He told me
to let Lloyd George know the upshot of the
Sutton Courtney interview. I sent Lloyd George
a telegram, vague in form but clear enough in
meaning. It was intercepted for a time by the
military censorship. This used to happen quite
frequently, although I was at that time the representative of the Canadian Government.
Messages to my own Canadian Prime Minister
were sometimes intercepted. The desire was, I
fear, only to show a little brief authority, for the
telegrams were always despatched in the end.

It was clear that the decision to appoint Lloyd
George to the War Office had been forced on

an unwilling Prime Minister by the joint action of the two strong men of the Government. This fact alone was sufficient to give cause for reflection ; but there was another curious and ominous feature about the actual terms of the appointment. Lloyd George was, of course, fully conversant with the nature of the Kitchener-Robertson agreement, and he had very rightly and naturally declared to all his friends over and over again that he would not take office so long as that agreement subsisted unaltered. In fact, to do so was simply to court trouble. None the less, in the following week he *did* accept the seals on exactly the same terms as his predecessor, and so became ruler of only half the War Secretary's field. Apparently, an interview with Field-Marshal Robertson gave him a fallacious assurance that no friction was to be anticipated.

Two aspects of a single fact stood out in glaring light from this transaction : the Prime Minister had made a forced appointment, and he had done it in such a way that it was almost certain to bring the new Secretary of State into conflict with the soldiers, who wanted him there no more than did the Prime Minister. Here we have the situation which contained within it one of the potent causes of the downfall of the second Asquith Administration, of the disruption of the Liberal party, and, gathering a momentum of results in its course as a falling boulder sweeps down an avalanche, finally produced the second Coalition Ministry.

But if the Kitchener-Robertson agreement was one of the proximate causes of the final explosion,

far more significant to the seeing eye was Asquith's
retreat from the position he had taken up.
Previous distribution of offices had been to
him either matters of his own choice or else
more or less matters of indifference and of
accommodating the desires of others. Now a
possible rival had been imposed on him against
his will.

Here was the situation. In the formation of
the Coalition Ministry Asquith had deliberately
depressed Bonar Law's position by giving all
the important offices to Liberals. It was this act
which set the warning death-knell of his administration ringing. I mean by this that if from the
very start he had treated Bonar Law not as simply
one of a group of Ministers, but as a partner and
a co-equal, he could have prolonged the life of
his Ministry almost indefinitely.

He had only to make Bonar Law Deputy
Leader and the real manager of the affairs of the
Government to secure a smooth passage for his
administration and his own titular supremacy.
For Bonar Law had no objection to working
with Asquith. Bonar Law liked him and admired
him ; it was the incompetency of his war administration to which the Conservative leader was
opposed. And this defect could have been rectified
by an administrator of the Bonar Law type in a
position of authority.

Even after the original error made by Asquith
in " the First Intrigue," there was still plenty of
time for him to repair his mistake, because Bonar
Law, though damaged, felt no resentment against

the Prime Minister. Asquith failed to take this chance. He dealt with Bonar Law as an ordinary subordinate colleague. Consequently, the original and essential instability of Asquith's administration remained.

In addition, the Ministry developed a secondary but very serious weakness in the growing intensity of the quarrel between Lloyd George and McKenna, which Asquith did nothing either to conciliate or to quell.

Lastly, and on this point I would lay the greatest emphasis, he was utterly defeated over the choice of a new War Secretary—and that by a combination of the powerful Tory chief, whom he would not take into partnership, and of the second greatest figure in his Ministry, whom he would neither conciliate nor dismiss. Such a formidable alliance showed that the end was in sight.

CHAPTER XVI

MR. ASQUITH

A PRIME Minister who has been beaten once may be beaten again, and more than one personality sat down to reflect on the possibilities opened up by the exhibition of weakness over the choice of a new Secretary of State for War.

And yet it may be said that in many ways Asquith's work had been well done and that the charm of his character did not court enmity. It is quite certain that mere jealousy had no part in his attempt to restrict the powers and activities of Lloyd George. His sense of his own superiority protected him from such a small yet poignant emotion. He was the greatest member of the House of Commons of our time, and Lord Balfour, despite Asquith's own generous compliment, must rely for his natural pre-eminence on other titles to fame than this. The reasons for his attitude of repression towards Lloyd George were almost certainly based on a quite different view. Since war broke out he had seen his second-in-command fight his way ruthlessly from office to office, and he had come to the conclusion that any favour conferred on him was merely a prelude to a further demand ; he was not alone in accepting the " selfish hypothesis " of Lloyd George's career.

Mr. Asquith is hard to describe, because within his own limited sphere, the management of Parliament in quiet times, he was perfection, and he was a failure because outside those limitations, and yet within his own range of time, lay a world of battle, murder, and sudden death—and that time called for men of a different range of genius. And more than most politicians of our period Asquith looked often to the past, always to the present, and seldom to the future. He was the last of the school of Gladstone, and with all their fundamental differences of temperament he possessed much in common with his old leader— so much that possibly only an old-time Liberal can really understand him.

Mr. Gladstone had so great a veneration for the Crown, while he constantly appealed to the people, that his attitude often gave offence to his more radical supporters. So Asquith, while he cared nothing for that society which is supposed, somewhat erroneously, to centre itself round the old landed aristocracy, considered himself the Prime Minister of the people, but the servant of the King, regarded the office of the Sovereign with veneration and received his personal attention with pleasure. Mr. Gladstone used to address crowds standing on the platform of a railway carriage. Mr. Asquith, though quite devoid of the ordinary intense desire of the politician for the limelight, had a similar pleasure in these station demonstrations—these spontaneous by-products of party or national enthusiasm.

And yet he had in him an element of shyness which made him push through such a crowd with an almost glum appearance of displeasure. In the House of Commons he was much the same, though his apparent roughness was not misunderstood and never diminished his popularity with his own supporters. It is perhaps permissible to dwell on some of the idiosyncrasies of so well-known a figure instead of leaving them to be disinterred by the biographers of 1970.

From the public point of view Asquith's mentality was a curious one. He used his immense capacities for tearing the heart out of a mass of material in a few minutes to bolster up his intense intellectual laziness. Reading and assimilating with great rapidity, and gifted with the capacity for re-expressing the result in a lucid and ordered way, he gave to his speeches the very minimum of preparation. The danger of this method in war time was that the conclusion reached might be purely superficial. And there is no doubt that he was remiss in dictating or dealing with long official memoranda and documents. Yet, like the late Lord Salisbury, but in a busier age, he would write an infinite number of short letters in his own hand—so painstaking was he in one thing, so careless in the other. It is not suggested that Asquith did not know his war facts and did not form reasoned judgments upon them. He did so in the same way in which a lawyer reads and judges the facts of a brief.

It was indeed marvellous how he attained to the knowledge he displayed. He devoted so much of his time to conversation, companionship, and even to social pursuits that it would have appeared impossible that the remaining hours of the day could have been sufficient for him to get through the immense amount of work which fell to his share. Even allowing for his splendid memory, one can only suppose that the hours given to trivialities were not really wasted, but that his subconscious mind was all the time working and pondering over grave issues and presenting him at the end with a completed process of thought.

In private, he possessed the quite well recognised habit of repeating at intervals certain cycles of stories or remarks if a certain cue were given him. Thus, if a guest called attention to the portrait of Charles James Fox on the wall at Downing Street, it was quite well known that he would on every occasion make precisely the same remarks—and the test was frequently applied. So if he saw a familiar face, even after a lapse of four or five years, it would at once recall to his mind some old joke or episode connected with the man, and he would tell him this again at intervals whenever he met him. That this was no vagary of age is proved by the fact that he always possessed this trait—a pretty useful one for a politician. Making, as he did, almost a fetish of loyalty and friendship, he was much beloved in his own intimate circle and among a wide and varied entourage of friends.

Such was the dominant figure of the old school

—of whom, probably, no two men will ever agree as to how far his subtlety was a weakness or his strength a mere refusal to face facts.

The political developments of the war from the very outset presented him with two sets of difficulties he peculiarly disliked—disunion in the Cabinet and the necessity for parting with old friends. As an individual and a patriot, it was easy enough for him to stand up for the honour of England in August 1914; as the promoter of Liberal unity he was agonised to see the split in the Cabinet, and hated to receive the resignations of the pacifists. For he was loyal in supporting a colleague in trouble even beyond the limits of prudence—and this in spite of his habit of discussing the shortcomings of Ministers in a rather detached and superior way.

Again, the first Coalition Ministry was from the start a tangled mass of dissensions always liable at any minute to break into a flame. Its very birth necessitated the violent expulsion of several tried and trusted colleagues, always a painful business to Asquith. It must be said, however, that once he had made up his mind that a Minister must go he acted firmly and promptly. "Well," he would say, " the axe must fall." And when his Coalition Ministry was formed it was a case of guillotining Liberals in a batch. And as the severed heads rolled in the sawdust he had to embrace a new committee of alien Tory colleagues.

From the personal and social point of view Mr. Asquith knew nothing of the Tory party.

For Lord Balfour, indeed, as one of the last monoliths of his own epoch, he had the greatest veneration, and, as we have seen, called him early in the war into close consultation. But Tories as a class he regarded from the orthodox standpoint as either fools or knaves. Of Bonar Law he had at the outset a very poor opinion as an uncultured person who had reached prominence by an accident, and the Opposition Leader's display from 1911 onwards of an unexpected strength of wrist in Parliamentary dialectic was simply an annoying surprise.

In the Coalition Ministry of 1915-1916 he underestimated Bonar Law utterly, and indeed never appreciated him until he had lost him. Yet there was no temperamental reason why the two men should not have come together. They had in common a certain cautious way of looking at life. Bonar Law recognised this appeal in Asquith and was always ready to work with him. But his offers of loyalty met with no real kindred response from the Prime Minister, who, in spite of demonstration after demonstration of Bonar Law's commanding moral and political strength, could not realise either his wisdom or his power. It was only after Bonar Law's departure that Asquith applied to him the honourable and touching epithet " shrewd and gentle."

Unquestionably, this underestimate of Bonar Law's capacities at the beginning of their relations led Asquith to acquiesce far too readily in his exclusion from the Chancellorship of the Exchequer or the Ministry of Munitions on the

formation of the Coalition Government in May
1915, and if the main initiative in this act of
exclusion came from Lloyd George, Asquith
undoubtedly played second murderer. His mistake, handsomely repented afterwards, was that
he thought Bonar Law's capacity and intellect
had never soared above the Glasgow iron market.
But the whole incident brought out a certain
tendency to amiable and indecisive language
which gave rise to misunderstanding. The Prime
Minister succeeded in giving some of the Tories
the idea that he favoured Bonar Law for the
Ministry of Munitions and the Liberals the impression that he was supporting Lloyd George.
There is not the slightest doubt that in reality
he lent his weight to Lloyd George throughout,
gave him Munitions, and promised to keep the
Exchequer ready for him when he cared to return.
In high politics misunderstandings about appointments are far more common than accusations of
bad faith in matters of policy, and Asquith was
not exempt from the common lot and subject to
the trials which await Prime Ministers in such
matters.

His own personal friends in the new Ministry
were naturally of the Liberal persuasion : Crewe
—whose judgment he with many wise men greatly
esteemed in opposition to the popular verdict—
Haldane, and Montagu, his one familiar of the
younger generation. His relations with Grey
were of that distant but friendly kind which an
ocean might have with a contiguous mountain
peak. Lord Reading, another friend, was apt only

to appear as a storm petrel, to prove that there was
a divergence between Asquith and Lloyd George,
and, changing rapidly into a dove, to bring the
peace of healing.

In the course of Cabinet intercourse with Tories
many of the old party prejudices melted away, and
Asquith's conduct of affairs was undoubtedly
regarded with approval by some of the stoutest
upholders of the Tory tradition. But neither his
ability nor their adherence could deflect the current
of events. He supplied his own epitaph when he
said, an hour before his defeat in East Fife was
declared, " It is hard to win the confidence of
the people—but, once won, you must be very
unwise to lose it."

A new and harsher world produced situations
which could not be met by mere evasion or delay,
and which would not wait on the necessities of
compromise. The master of the old school of
fencing met the difficulties with all the accustomed
weapons. But as the world surged more and more
fiercely about him his strokes began to go wide.
Parties and precedents vanished, and the Cabinet
and the nation became divided between those who
were anxious to win the war slowly and by rule
and those who were determined to win it at any
cost and to win it quickly, because delay spelt
ruin. The new school of reality therefore gathered
not out of political principles, but out of sheer
preservative instinct, round the new man who
strode on to a battlefield which suited his adaptive
genius. Asquith fell because he was by nature a
Conservative. But the beginning of his fall dates

from the struggle over the War Office, and when
Lloyd George went to Whitehall as War Secretary
the crisis of 1916 had in fact begun.

Book Two

Book Two

CHAPTER XVII

THE DUNKIRK CIRCUS

IN the summer of 1916 Asquith's position as
Prime Minister, supported by a Coalition
Government of all parties in the House of Commons, was being steadily undermined. He himself
must have been unconscious of the fact, because
the principal causes of his growing weakness must
be sought in his own method of conducting affairs.

People have sometimes talked and written as
though his downfall in December 1916 was a
sudden inexplicable catastrophe—or only to be
explained as the result of a secret intrigue hastily
engineered by unscrupulous rivals. Nothing could
be further from the truth. Ever since the spring
of 1915 the Premier had been engaged in knocking
the props from under him or in watching them
fall without replacing them. He had neglected
Bonar Law and exalted Curzon. He had alienated
Lloyd George without disarming him. He had
driven into an unwilling alliance of discontent
the man with the most glittering gifts and the man
with the most formidable moral power within his
Government. Worse than that, he had let this
combination beat him over the appointment to
the War Secretaryship.

Such errors were, however, retrievable. What could not be retrieved was Asquith's own way of looking at a world at war. This proved fatal. His complete detachment from the spirit of the struggle; his instability of purpose; his refusal to make up his mind on grave and urgent issues of policy; his balancing of one adviser against another till the net result was nil; his fundamental desire to have a peaceful tenure of office in the midst of war, could in the long run have only one result. The men who were in tune with the atmosphere of war—the bold, the eager, the decisive spirits—first fell away from him and then combined against him. And while all this was going on, he was immersed in his own social circle and engaged in responding to the devotion of his friends.

His colleagues would observe him in the midst of the transaction of affairs laboriously writing, in his own hand, long letters to private correspondents. He was violating one of the first canons of politics—that no man can afford to neglect business.

Outwardly, his position still seemed to be free from any serious menace. He had a group of supporters of his own in the Cabinet, such as McKenna, Runciman and Crewe, on the Liberal, and Curzon, Cecil, Lansdowne and Austen Chamberlain on the Conservative side. He was still held in general respect by the public at large—who were then only just beginning to grasp the fact that there was something essentially wrong with the central direction of the war. But this outside support is failing throughout the time covered by this narrative.

He was especially trusted by a very strong element in the community, consisting of the highly placed socially, the eminent intellectually and the respectable morally. These included, no doubt, the accomplished hypocrites, but the group was none the less important for that. To any criticism on the conduct of affairs these replied that Asquith was indispensable.

The other argument—and one naturally congenial to Asquith himself—was the necessity for national unity. As a matter of fact, there was unity in the nation at large. But there was disunity in the Cabinet—and Asquith's main task was to try to conceal the fact both from his colleagues themselves and the country. The blessed word " unity " was invoked on all occasions.

Asquith thus sits dreaming of his Peace in War. Of the more fiery or earnest spirits, Carson has resigned, Churchill has been extruded from the centre of power, Bonar Law is achieving within himself quite a new orientation of thought towards the war, while Lloyd George chafes more and more visibly day by day. And Lloyd George is getting dangerous. Yet the more he chafes, the less the Prime Minister likes him.

Why did not Asquith simply take up Lloyd George and make him his executive arm, while retaining the titular authority ?

In this summer the answer to the question is a simple one. Asquith would not promote Lloyd George, for the same reason that he had come to distrust Churchill, even to the point of permitting his dismissal the year before. Asquith was the man of peace in the war—these Ministers of nervous action fretted his very soul. He did not want them about him—always hustling and hurrying and driving. This tendency of his seems to have increased as the war went on.

To understand his attitude towards Lloyd George, it is necessary to compare it with his previous behaviour towards Churchill.

At the beginning of the war, Asquith admired Churchill immensely. He placed more reliance on him than on any Minister except Kitchener. He supported him heartily over Antwerp, both in the inception of the affair and after the effort had failed. It is true that here he showed a sign of his customary instability of purpose. For, having praised Churchill up to the skies for his well-intentioned efforts to save the doomed city, he hears later his own son's version of the affair. He then thinks the whole business was dreadfully mismanaged. None the less, Antwerp did Churchill no serious damage, either with Asquith or with anyone else—even if his colleagues did greet his request to be given the command in the field with a great shout of laughter.

What began the process of destroying Churchill's credit with the Prime Minister? The primary cause in my opinion was what Asquith christened the " Dunkirk Circus." And for this reason that hitherto practically unknown episode will be given a certain amount of prominence. It was not in itself a vital affair regarded from any military standpoint. It was encouraged by Joffre and supported originally by Kitchener so that the whole responsibility for the proceedings involved must be shared by other people with Churchill.

Churchill's own account of its inception is as follows :

" On September 16, Marshall Joffre telegraphed to Lord Kitchener asking whether a Brigade of Marines could not be sent to Dunkirk to reinforce the garrison and to confuse the enemy with the idea of British as well as French forces being in this area. Lord Kitchener asked me whether the Admiralty would help in this matter. I agreed to send the brigade if he would also send some Yeomanry Cavalry for its local protection. He sent a regiment. I was thus led, though by no means unwillingly, into accepting a series of minor responsibilities of a very direct and personal kind, which made inroads both upon my time and thought and might well—though I claim they did not—have obscured my general view."

But this narrative is not concerned with its military but with its political importance. This was great because it first shook Asquith's faith in Churchill's judgment. Asquith's opinion in the matter may have been absolutely erroneous. But that he ended by getting a complete scare over Churchill and the Dunkirk Circus is proved by document after document—and his conversation was full of the same topic.

If ships were lost like the three cruisers, or a battle lost like the Coronel, or an enemy raid successful like the Dogger Bank, Asquith would simply say " Bad luck for Winston " or " This will be a blow to Winston ; I am sorry for him." He did not in the spoken or written word show any irritation with the First Lord over purely official naval misfortunes. Nor again did he do so over the inception of the Dardanelles adventure, though he must have been sorely tried at times.

It was something peculiar in the Dunkirk Circus which attracted Asquith's attention and made him doubt in the long run whether Churchill was a wise counsellor in war. If it be answered that this was an irrational view for the Premier to take I cannot help this. It is a fact and no one can tell how deeply it affected Churchill's fortunes.

What was the Dunkirk Circus ?

Very few people would be able to answer that question to-day—and its existence was, indeed, hardly known to the war public of the time.

The Dunkirk Circus was begun with a landing and re-embarkation of marines at Ostend as a demonstration to make the Germans fear for their lines of communication in Belgium. The idea underlying it was really the historic policy of British armed intervention in Europe—most strikingly practised during the Napoleonic Wars. This was not to place a huge army in line with our continental allies, but to land smaller forces by means of sea power wherever they could upset the military plans of the enemy, and to withdraw them again by sea if their situation became dangerous. Churchill, however, could not claim to be an out-and-out supporter of this historic school of thought, for he was in favour of sending out the Expeditionary Force and placing it in line with the French army—instead of using it for the purposes of amphibious warfare.

The marine force disappeared from Ostend only to reappear in stranger guise at Dunkirk.

It was a portent, because it was a land army controlled not by the British military authorities at all, but by the Admiralty. It was thus a considerable source of irritation to the military. Its composition was extraordinary. It consisted of marines as infantry, of a regiment of yeomanry as cavalry, of a set of private motor cars Churchill had acquired and armed with maxims, and of a fleet of motor buses.

The object of this strange army was to encourage the Belgians and alarm the Germans by making a great parade of force without fighting any general action. The cars, the buses with infantry on board, and the cavalry, therefore, dashed in and out of such Belgian towns and villages as were not in possession of the enemy and played a kind of game of military hide-and-seek. They were here one moment and gone the next—ubiquitous, like their creator—a witness to the fertile and romantic imagination which had called them into being.

Had the matter stopped there, the trouble might have been confined to a growing irritation in the War Office and at G.H.Q. in France. But presently peculiar stories began to percolate to Ministers, who seem to have been at the outset very little informed as to what Churchill was doing on the Belgian coast. The Prime Minister told a story that Churchill had met General Seely (a former War Minister) in Dunkirk and had offered to run him back in a destroyer for a day's visit to his old colleagues. To this offer—so ran the tale—Seely had replied that he had sworn never to leave the soil of France so long as it was profaned by the foot of the invader.

Asquith's attitude towards the Dunkirk enterprise at this period may be gauged by the fact that he was so pleased with this story that he repeated it continually.

Then there were, on more than one occasion, unexplained absences on the part of the First Lord from the Admiralty, which were often inconvenient and caused a growing sense of annoyance among other members of the Government.

The Prime Minister, who, at the outset, had approved of the creation of the " circus," found himself tolerating these absences and trying to conceal the whereabouts of his colleague from other Ministers. Subsequently he discovered that he must take charge at the Admiralty during an absence of Churchill. On a later occasion still he could not find the First Lord when the date of the sailing of the New Zealand contingent was at stake so that, Asquith complained, a very serious delay in despatching this force occurred.

This at any rate was Asquith's opinion. It is easy to reply that the Premier could have operated through the First Sea Lord (Admiral Sir H. Jackson) in this matter during the absence of the First

Lord of the Admiralty. Again it is the subjective impression produced on Asquith's mind with which this narrative is concerned. The Premier was obviously irritated by the incident and it weakened Churchill against the crisis of the following year when everything depended on Asquith supporting him against the Tories. In fact Asquith's views about the Dunkirk " circus " began to alter. It did not seem quite so amusing.

At last the Prime Minister expressed the pious hope to a third party that Churchill would have learnt by past experience, and that he would wind up the " circus " and transfer it to the proper military authorities. It never seemed to have occurred to him that he might long before have spoken in this sense to Churchill himself and with authority. In fact, he never did so, but went by a roundabout way to Lord French and induced the somewhat unwilling Commander-in-Chief to lay his hands upon the concern.

Lord French could find no other use for the fleet of derelict motor cars than to take the quick firers out of them and give them to his infantry. So unlucky was Churchill in the whole affair, that he was embroiled with Lord Kitchener over this transaction. The War Secretary complained to the Prime Minister that Churchill had offered the " circus " to Lord French behind his back.

We have seen the development of Asquith's view towards the " circus." It goes through three phases—that of hearty support—that of amused tolerance—and finally, that of growing irritation.

To put it in a different way, the Premier had begun by encouraging the First Lord in his policy of independent activity. Then, though he had ceased to believe in the policy, its executor's tirelessness intrigues him. Finally, this very activity becomes a source of annoyance to his own peace. He wishes the man of action out of his life. When strong pressure from outside is exerted to put Churchill out, the First Lord is flung away easily because the citadel of trust and confidence which might have supported him has already really been betrayed from within. Asquith himself had passed over to the ranks of Churchill's critics by the time the Tories demanded his resignation.

All this was really not quite fair to Churchill. At least, it seems a pity that the Prime Minister could not have handled him differently.

Churchill's pugnacity, his exuberance of imagination, his mental and physical restlessness and keenness, were great national assets. What they needed, were pruning and directing. Was not this the natural task for the calmer mentality of an older man ? Churchill, checked here and guided there by a man who was his official superior, could have been kept in office and his invaluable qualities turned to the most useful national purposes.

These qualities became uncontrolled. Churchill tried to work everything single-handed. This in a way was his fault. It was also the misfortune of the nation. What he needed was careful coaching—a steady supporting hand in return for the right of control.

What he got from the Premier was a free hand altogether—leave, so to speak, to make or damn himself. As this freedom develops into licence, the man who might have been his mentor is simply amused. Then the whole business begins to bore him. Other colleagues make trouble about it. Here is another of these men of action, always trying something new, always creating situations which demand impossible decisions. If Churchill must fall, then his fall will be a positive release.

So Churchill went, and in his place, to be the main new source of irritation, came Lloyd George.

That statesman had indeed, in 1915, come perilously nigh landing on his Gallipoli when he wanted to buy up the Drink Trade in England. Fortunately for him, all sections of opinion and all interests had rushed down to the beach in a mass and driven him back to the safety of the open sea. Since then, his two ventures—to obtain munitions and to attain the War Office—had been successful. He had committed no further imprudences.

CHAPTER XVIII

MEN LIKE GODS

THE second weakness which Asquith developed was not his fault. It might be described as the loss of the support of the Generals and the Generals' party. Asquith had been from the outset identified with what might be described as the " men like gods " theory of the higher command. The Generals regarded it as the chief duty of a civilian Minister to listen respectfully to the oracles which proceeded from the mouths of the men of war. They wished to reduce the idea of civilian control and authority to the very minimum. Had the Generals justified this theory by success in the field; had they refrained from quarrelling among themselves; had they even given united loyalty to Asquith, his position would have proved unshakeable.

Unfortunately for him, they did none of these things. The first General to turn against him was Lord French, who set the Shell agitation going against the Government in order to cover his own failure to advance at Neuve Chapelle.

Sir Henry Wilson was all along conducting independently a virulent campaign against the Prime Minister. Wilson wrote and spoke continually to the Conservative leaders, urging them

236

to turn Asquith out. In fact, he devoted much of his energy to fighting the Prime Minister.

It is a matter for reflection that although Asquith was well informed of what Wilson was doing, he never came down on him. While outwardly to the world he kept the pose of Olympian indifference, he showed himself inwardly a good deal hurt and disturbed by these military intrigues and yet unwilling to take steps to end them.

He describes Wilson as " the serpent." He relates that he believes him to have set afloat a particularly malicious story that Kitchener had asked the French Generals whether they would not like Lord French to be superseded by Sir Ian Hamilton—and that this had destroyed good feeling between the British Field Marshals.

Finally, he ascribes various attacks on the position of Sir A. Murray, French's Chief of the Staff, to Wilson, and to his desire to succeed to the post. This Asquith vows Wilson shall never do, come what may. Sir A. Murray comes home, but Field Marshal Sir William Robertson takes his place. The next retirement is that of Lord French himself, which is brought about chiefly on the representation given by Lord Haig of what occurred at Loos.

Thus, by the summer of 1916 the war is not going well—the Generals are quarrelling among themselves quite as violently as the politicians— and Asquith has lost the unanimous support of the Generals' party.

People may wonder now at the absolute lack

of self-assertiveness, amounting almost to a com‾ plete abdication of authority, which marked Asquith's attitude towards the Higher Command. It is only fair to recognise how widespread was this feeling of the inferiority of the highly-placed civilian to the highly-placed soldier, both at the outbreak of war and for many months or years afterwards. In fact, in many cases it may be said to have lasted for the whole duration of hostilities.

The fact of the matter is that the Generals at once damaged and intimidated the politicians from the outset by the attitude they assumed towards them. This attitude was no doubt honest and natural enough in Army men; the Generals are not to be blamed. But no one could have a true picture of the war in his mind who did not realise the action and re-action upon the politics of the period produced by this "superiority" complex of G.H.Q. and by the acquiescences of revolts it produced in Downing Street or Whitehall.

The picture of Ministers which the Generals drew to themselves and which was reflected to some extent to the public, was something like this.

The Minister sat in a leather-bound armchair in a room where even the faintest hum of outside traffic was hushed, and pulled at a long cigar while he languidly superintended the activities of the secretaries. From this repose he would cheerfully give an order speeding " glum heroes up the line to death " by thousands—although he knew nothing of war. He then rose to go out to dinner, with others of his colleagues who had been similarly employed. If the Minister ever did show any activity, it was of that inconvenient kind by which an ignorant civilian interfered with the superb expert efficiency exhibited by the General. And in the meantime, too, the General, instead of smoking a cigar, was daily qualifying for a V.C. by the hardships he endured and the dangers he ran.

Anyone who will take the trouble to read those London newspapers of the period which reflected the Generals' standpoint, will recognise the picture.

Now, the majority of the politicians were absolutely cowed by this presentation of the relative merits of St. Omer (Headquarters of The British Army in France) and Downing Street. The soldiers remained to the politicians as " men like gods," while the politicians were mere men—and one does not argue with the gods, even if one thinks them wrong.

After a bit, however, some of the more independent and realistic minds among the Ministers of various administrations who had been to France fairly frequently began to have doubts about the validity of the Generals' argument.

They found these officers just as snug and safe at St. Omer and other places behind the line as anyone in Downing Street or Whitehall. Like Ministers, the Generals took decisions which resulted in other people running the risks.

In fact, the Generals in their attitude towards the politicians were confusing themselves quite honestly with the men in the trenches, who, as a matter of fact, disliked them just as much as they did any civilian Minister. G.H.Q. was in essence no more or no less personally heroic than the Cabinet. The only question was whether it could claim to be wiser in other ways.

The Generals' Press, however, insisted that the politicians were a nasty back-biting lot, thinking of nothing but personal advancement, whereas the Generals considered only the honour and glory of the country.

The more realistic Ministers, after a prolonged experience of Army generals, did not reach this conclusion.

But even the coolest of these observers were very slow to shake off the glamour which the Generals enjoyed in August, 1914. The Higher Command were particularly foolish in turning on Asquith, because he, more than any other possible successor, clung to this romantic view of civilian subordination to the last.

Two of the most important members of the Ministry who were shortly to take complete control of affairs were conscious of military disputes at home and in the Higher Command at G.H.Q. They had already revised their views on the godlike capacities of Generals when an event occurred which, though trivial in itself, had far-reaching consequences.

This episode, which brought the extraordinary mentality of the Generals home to the politicians, was the arrest* of Lord Birkenhead in France.

* General Sir Nevil Macready declares that the order issued by him was not to arrest the late Lord Birkenhead but to bring him back.

Many amazing versions of this affair were circulated at the time and possibly still linger in the memory.

The main fact was a simple one. Owing to a disregard of a formality on the part of a high Law officer (Lord Birkenhead), or in the alternative, owing to a piece of impudence or carelessness on the part of someone on the staff at G.H.Q., a Minister of the Crown was arrested, ignominiously treated, and brought back as though he was a common prisoner or deserter, and confined by the Military authorities.

One might have judged the story incredible if one had not had previous experience of G.H.Q. in France.

I was at G.H.Q. as the Military Representative of the Canadian Government. I was, of course, really a civilian travelling in military uniform because it was impossible to get about in the war zone at all in other guise.

To understand the Birkenhead affair, one must realise the atmosphere. A lot of men—quite insignificant from any national standpoint—were dressed up in authority at G.H.Q. and thought it a duty to humiliate any civilian of importance who happened to expose himself by some carelessness or error of judgment. They caught Birkenhead because he did not know the atmosphere at G.H.Q

The Generals also did not realise that the arrest of Birkenhead—a mere petty incident—would have far-reaching reactions. I do not think, in fact, that any of the parties concerned realised it at the time. They all sought to wash it out of their memories. It was a paltry thing—something to forget or be a bit ashamed of. Yet, none the less, in the background of consciousness the memory stuck like a burr.

Lloyd George and Bonar Law found at G.H.Q. in France not " men like gods," but military authorities who were quite prepared to put questions of passes and procedure on a par with their own urgent duties to the troops.

I will now tell the whole story. I went down from the line to Paris, to see Bonar Law. As he was Colonial Secretary, I had to transact much of my Canadian official business with him—so that I was frequently in touch with him. In Paris I found him with Lloyd George. Birkenhead was also there.

Lloyd George and Bonar Law had already arranged to go on a visit to G.H.Q. Birkenhead wanted to go up at the same time, and wished me to send him there by car. I said " No "—it would be better to go in the ordinary way of routine by train to Boulogne with the others. He understood and accepted my advice.

I also advised him to telegraph to Haig's private secretary for a permit to come into the military zone—which he did.

Subsequently the whole party, including myself, proceeded to Boulogne by train. Motor-cars were waiting for the Ministers. I got into my own car and drove straight to St. Omer by myself. I made it a strict rule never to take with me anyone who was not definitely vouched for and in effect

billeted on me by the Military—as certain jour-
nalists were. I understood the mentality of G.H.Q.

Lloyd George, then Minister of Munitions,
Bonar Law and Birkenhead then entered one
car. No passes were ready for any of them.
Lloyd George naturally was impatient, and simply
said, " Drive on." It thus escaped notice that no
pass had been issued for Birkenhead. On arrival
at St. Omer, there was accommodation prepared
at Haig's Headquarters for Lloyd George and
Bonar Law, but none for Birkenhead. He came
to me, therefore, at the Canadian Headquarters
and I offered to put him up for the night. He
then asked me for a car to drive him over to see
Churchill, who was at the time in command of a
battalion at the front. I told him I had no car available. He applied to the Army Service Corps pool
and obtained a car from them. He was wearing a
uniform as he was entitled to do because it was
convenient to travel through the lines as a soldier
and difficult to do so as a civilian.

The rest of the story is pretty generally known.
Birkenhead found Churchill and was just setting
out to go up to the trenches with him about 1 a.m.
in the morning when he was suddenly arrested
and brought back to G.H.Q. for not having a pass
to come into the military zone. He was confined
to rooms at the Hotel du Commerce, St. Omer,
for the remaining hours of the night.

In the morning he was asked to attend at the
Adjutant General's Headquarters. Macready, the
Adjutant of the Forces, then asked him the
following (no doubt carefully prepared) ques-

tions—If you are a civilian, why are you here in uniform ? If you are a soldier, why don't you obey the regulations ?*

After interviewing Macready he came to me at my quarters, and having been up all night, very sensibly went to bed. I went out at once to seek and inform Bonar Law. Churchill also had been active in getting in touch with the politicians at the Front, and sent the following letter :

Ploogsteert,
January, 1916.

My dear Bonar,

The arrest of F.E. in the present circumstances seems to me to be a very serious event. I received him here in virtue of a telegram from the A.D.C. to the C. in C. transmitted to me through the H.Q. of the IXth Division in wh. I am serving. Of this I enclose a copy. The act of placing the Cabinet Minister charged with the ultimate appeal in all Court Martial cases in arrest and removing him in conditions of indignity is one wh. cannot and will not end here in France. It will become public knowledge and will draw with it many other things. I am of course resolved to take any steps wh. the law allows. And I rely upon you to give the subject your most earnest and immediate attention as his colleague and friend. You shd. show this to Lloyd George.

Yours very sincerely,
Winston S. C.

* The late Lord Birkenhead gave me this account of the questions. General Sir Nevil Macready denies that they were put to Lord Birkenhead in this form.

Bonar Law was upset. The incident confirmed a view which had been growing in his mind that the mentality of generals was sometimes concerned with the day of small things. When Bonar Law was stirred, he could act forcibly. He interviewed Haig and told him quite frankly what he thought about the affair. He insisted that due apologies should be made to Birkenhead. I may add that the intention of the military up till this had been to send Birkenhead under escort to Boulogne, and deport him as one having no pass.

In the face of Bonar Law's remonstrances Haig agreed not only to stop this amazing plan, but he sent his private secretary to see Birkenhead, and to invite him to lunch at Headquarters. Explanations were made by Haig in the presence of Bonar Law and Lloyd George and accepted by Birkenhead.

Of course the story leaked out through officers returning on leave—and generally it assumed the most fantastic shapes, nearly always presented in a light unfavourable to the chief sufferer—Lord Birkenhead.

Birkenhead was a wronged man in this matter. At the worst he had been a victim of some act of technical carelessness—which the Adjutant-General should have ignored in the legal adviser of the Crown. The episode, as I have said, is trivial; the memory of it stuck.

CHAPTER XIX

DERBY

A FURTHER cause of weakening in the Asquith Coalition administration formed in 1915 was the perpetual battle in the Cabinet over Conscription. This raged intermittently throughout the year until by the time the autumn was reached it was admitted that a frank discussion and vote in the Cabinet would have broken the administration to pieces. Asquith, in consequence, followed his usual custom and prevented a discussion. The division of opinion here tended to follow party lines far more closely than on most of the War problems of the period—that is to say that the Conservatives were apt to be conscriptionists and the Liberals inclined to oppose compulsion, its strongest opponents, for instance, were Grey, Harcourt, McKenna and Runciman. This was the theoretical position. In practice it developed a good many modifications. For instance, the active fighting radical elements represented by Lloyd George and Churchill were conscriptionist from start to finish. On the other hand, Lord Lansdowne on the Conservative side early developed a passion for the voluntary system. We find here the germ of a

fundamental difference of view as to the aim of
the War and the methods by which it was to be
conducted which completely transcended party.
In the long run this divergence banded life-long
enemies together against life-long friends within
the Cabinet.

Asquith himself, however, took a purely party
view of conscription : that is to say, he was certain that the Liberal rank and file in the constituencies would not stomach it. He thought that
to carry a conscriptionist measure would disrupt
Liberalism—and so long as he could shelter his
opinion behind that of Lord Kitchener it was hard
for the conscriptionists in the Cabinet to effect
anything.

Sir John Simon also held to Asquith's view,
and envisaged a great host of Liberal adherents
flocking to his banner. When he resigned on this
issue on 11th January, 1916, on paper this host
ought to have appeared. Actually no one rallied
to the banner of freedom.

Asquith—and here he was followed by Simon
—could not understand that Liberals were also
human beings. Many Liberals had marched to
the front with the best. Their wives, their
fathers, their sons and their relations went
through the usual agony of anxiety. Like any
other people exposed to this stress they forgot
all about the opinions held by Liberal ministers
or Liberal Whips or Liberal Chairmen of Constituencies who were urging the Premier against
Compulsion. But they were human beings as
well as Liberal voters. And they said : " Well,

Jack has gone, why should not Cuthbert go too ? "

The truth is that Asquith had fallen into his besetting error of judgment—that of mistaking peace values for war values. The ideas of peace were a pleasant myth of the past, those of war were the only reality and quite different in character. Asquith clung to the myth throughout and ignored the reality.

One of Asquith's characteristic pieces of political tactics in this matter was used to counter Carson who was a strong Conscriptionist in the Cabinet. He would relate in private the story that he had seen Carson and Bonar Law just before the outbreak of war, and that Carson had said that the Regular Reservists, officers and men, in Ulster would refuse to obey the mobilisation orders and would remain behind to protect Ulster.

It is difficult to see exactly what this question had to do with the principal of compulsory service. Asquith, however, thought it had and he told the story many times.

However, in September of 1915, after the Battle of Loos, the tension in the Cabinet on Conscription became so great that even Asquith was compelled to adopt some kind of expedient to deal with the crisis. Nine Ministers met at Lord Curzon's house and resolved at all costs to bring the question to a head.

The Premier's answer to this revolt was simple and characteristic. It was not a policy—it was a man.

The Premier sent for Lord Derby, and sought

to cover the divisions in his own Cabinet by shovelling that issue out of sight behind Derby's broad back.

Probably no other man in public life could have served Asquith's turn in this scheme for postponement. For Derby's name was one to conjure with among the people—immensely popular, greatly respected, supported by his broad acres and the hereditary virtue of his House, he could claim support for a scheme simply by calling it by his name. This, indeed, was so obvious to his conscriptionist Conservative colleagues in the Government that they attempted to ostracise him for accepting Asquith's nomination as recruiting officer-in-chief. They said Derby was simply bolstering up a rotten voluntary system by his prestige, and that if he refused, Asquith could get no one else in England to do the job, and so must accept compulsion.

These colleagues actually induced Derby to attend at their meeting at Lord Curzon's house. There these opinions were put forcibly to him—but he remained firm in face of a minatory lecture. He took the view and argued that his scheme was the first and inevitable step to Conscription.

Derby's character and mentality are, I think, the most typical of all that I have come across in public life here. When I was fighting my first contest in the Manchester area, I tried very hard to get him to come to help me, but my effort was in vain. There was no personal reason for the refusal. His assistance would have been invaluable to me, because the cry against me was that I was a stomach taxer. So great was the Derby influence in Lancashire, that I would have derived great benefit by Lord Derby's appearance on the platform with me. But because he disapproved of my warm advocacy of duties on imported foodstuffs, or because I was an unknown man, he refused my appeal, even though I made it through Bonar Law.

When I was successful, the Chairman of my Committee asked me to fix a date for a celebration of the victory. I did so. I was told I must change it because it did not suit Lord Derby. I refused to do so. It seemed to me that if he would not help me to a victory, I would not help him to celebrate it. After that episode I rather took the line that there should be no Stanley influence in my constituency. I hoed my own patch of political land and was independent of that influence—and at the time we had never met.

Later, when I was fighting hard for the retention of the Food Taxes—the proposal to tax foreign imported wheat and meat while admitting the Empire product free—Derby was leading the movement for striking them out of the Conservative programme. It was really his power which forced the leaders to abandon the Food Taxes.

That power was the fruit of a tremendous personal popularity in the country. To appreciate its extent to the full, one had perhaps to know the north of England in the pre-war days. In the Palatinate, Derby in his public appearances received something just short of a royal welcome.

Party animosities were hushed and even the
opposing Press was often loud in his praise. And
this feeling was widespread in every constituency
throughout the county of Lancashire.

Yet, curiously enough, and here we have the
whole paradox of Derby's character and career
in a nutshell, he has never had a first-rate status
with his Ministerial colleagues.

Even when the Derby scheme failed—no one
knew better than Derby that it must fail and was
meant to fail, and that conscription could only
be built and was built on its failure—Derby was a
great national figure.

On the War Office becoming vacant by the death
of Lord Kitchener, some soldiers knowing Derby
from his recruiting work inside their office,
wanted him to succeed as War Secretary. He said
plainly he would prefer the post of Under-Secretary, though it was definitely inferior to his
general political status. He told Bonar Law that
he was prepared to serve under him at the War
Office—an offer which strengthened Bonar Law's
claim to the post.

When Lloyd George was appointed, he consented to serve under him in the same capacity,
and his adhesion brought an accession of strength
to Lloyd George in the critical months which
followed his acceptance of that office.

It was in these months that Derby was at his
strongest. Had he not attached himself to Lloyd
George's fortunes, many persons believed that the
Premiership was within his grasp. For when
Asquith fell, if neither Bonar Law nor Lloyd

George could have formed a new Ministry, Lord Derby would have been the choice of all the soldiers and some civilians with formidable Press support. He occupied, too, a relatively independent position in regard to the individuals whose disputes had brought down the Ministry.

What is the real Lord Derby like ? For on this point is a vital disagreement between popular opinion and Whitehall.

The popular approval given to Derby—greater than that enjoyed by most Prime Ministers and continued from year to year—is not based on any skill with the spoken or the written word. Derby is not a spell-binder—yet he speaks just well enough to get his personality over the footlights. It is that personality which begets his popularity— the high integrity, the sportsmanship, the amiability, the readiness to sacrifice everything to duty, joined to that tact and shrewdness which come from living much in the world.

Now we come to the Whitehal point of view. Whitehall does not deny all these qualities, but says that this imposing facade covers the weakness of a swithering viewpoint. Derby, it says, will agree in taking up a certain attitude but in the next ten minutes he will flop on to the other side if he meets an opposing influence.

Is this charge, which amounts to one of excessive amiability in counsel, correct ? Yes, it is true. But it is right to say that this form of indecisiveness does not go down to any root principle. Derby has never gone back on any

great cause. He has been meticulously consistent
in his service to the Conservative party. He has
never gone back on the leaders—though he might
well have done so, much to his profit, on more
than one occasion under the reigns of Balfour,
Bonar Law and Baldwin. He has often been an
alternative leader of the Conservatives, sometimes
a potential and once a probable Premier.

It would be interesting to speculate as to what
kind of leader and Premier he would have made.
I feel sure that he would have scored a success.
I do not make any reference here to the administrative side of such a Government. What I mean
is that this popularity would have been enlarged
even beyond its present sphere, and that the
critics of Whitehall would have ceased their
complaints. They would have said that his uncertainty was mere wise caution, and so the
experts would have joined with the populace in
adoring yet another " greatest " of living Prime
Ministers.

CHAPTER XX

BONAR LAW

BONAR LAW always had a strong streak of melancholy in his disposition. At the best of times he was never exuberantly gay—and in the summer of 1916 things were so bad with him that he became almost a tragic figure. He had always valued highly his old political associates in the Conservative party—not only the men who were leaders like Carson and Birkenhead, but many of the rank and file. And he had been for years on the best of terms with Chamberlain and Long.

Now his new conceptions of the necessities of the war began to press against his old personal and party loyalties.

As the year 1916 proceeded, he found himself doomed to an ever-increasing loneliness, until by the summer he stood absolutely alone. One working ally, it is true, he had in Lloyd George— but the alliance was not then based on friendship. As we have seen in the first volume of this narrative, he thought Lloyd George had treated him shabbily on more than one occasion, and attributed these incidents to the new War Secretary's insatiable greed for high office and personal ambition. He could not refuse to work with

Lloyd George because on all essential notions connected with the conduct of the war the two men coincided—but how much rather would he have been co-operating with the Tories !

The reasons for this growing isolation have already been traced up to a point.

We have seen how Asquith exalted Curzon at Bonar Law's expense, and how a good many of the Tory Ministers tended to listen to Asquith rather than to their own leader—and again, how the taking of the Colonial Office depressed his prestige and cut him from the centre of active management. Curzon, to put the matter bluntly, was getting ready to wrest the Conservative leadership from Bonar Law and he was being encouraged both by the Prime Minister and the trend of events.

Over the evacuation of Gallipoli, Bonar Law had been fighting hard against the majority of his Conservative colleagues—including Birkenhead. For the courageous attitude he had assumed in compelling the evacuation he had received no praise.   And Carson had resigned from the Ministry. This left him with Long alone as a really warm supporter, though his friendly relationship with Lord Lansdowne remained on the surface unimpaired. How long Lansdowne's friendship for Bonar Law had been undermined it is impossible to say.   And now Lansdowne and Long and many other lesser friends were about to join the band of the critics over the Irish issue. Yet Bonar Law's apparently growing weakness in friendship and party ties was in reality his growing strength in all that really mattered.

He had begun thinking for himself about the war instead of running in blinkers under the guidance of old prepossessions and ancient party friends. But I do not imagine that he ever really thought this out or it might have been a comfort to him.

In addition to his public worries, Bonar Law was also beset by private anxieties. His eldest son, James, had been to the front and returned. He had gone out a boy whom Bonar understood, he had returned a man whom Bonar found it hard to understand. The boy had seen both life and death to the full and had changed greatly and for the better. There was no question of a disagreement, but his father found a difficulty in adjusting himself to the new relationship. I suppose practically all fathers have been through the same experience.

Bonar Law's greatest love in these days was for this eldest boy. He had even tried for one afternoon at the outbreak of war to interfere with his taking his commission—and afterwards was ashamed of it.

Later on, when his second son, Charles, joined up, though the child was barely of military age, Bonar Law made no effort to hold him back. The lad lost his life in Palestine. For more than a month there was hope that he might be a prisoner in the hands of the Turks.

As to James Law, Bonar Law never tried to get him a staff appointment—which was a form of renunciation on his part, for more than one General actually made the offer.

When James returned to the front, his father suffered terribly from apprehension of the War

Office telegram—an apprehension which, alas, proved only too well founded—for James Law met his death in the air.

At no time had Bonar Law gone through such a continuous period of depression.

His eldest daughter, Isabel, now Lady Sykes, also meant much in his life. She was his comforter and shield all through the war. She subsequently became engaged to General Sykes when staying at my house near Leatherhead and I had the task of dissuading him from driving her back to town that afternoon. The secret, such as it was, was no secret to anyone except her father. The next morning she told him the news. He immediately called me on the telephone, beginning, " A terrible thing has happened "—yet ever afterwards he treated Sykes as his own son and had as much affection for him as if he had been born a member of the family.

Bonar Law's sister had all his confidence and advised him in everything. But her advice was not always valuable, for she cast about too much to find out in what sense he wished to be advised.

Much has been written of my relationship with Bonar Law. I think a plain statement of the truth about the terms on which we stood cannot do any harm.

It has been said that we were boys together in Canada. This is patently absurd. Bonar was twenty years older than I was and left New Brunswick at the age of thirteen. I came in touch with him because his firm—William Jacks & Co.— was agent for the Nova Scotia Steel and Coal

Company. Naturally I was interested in him, because while my father had been a Presbyterian Minister sent out from Scotland, with Church aid, to Newcastle, New Brunswick, his father had been a Presbyterian Minister—and one certainly assisted in the same way—at Richibucto, in the same province.

The first time I saw Bonar Law was in 1908 when I paid a visit to England. I went to see him at his flat at Whitehall Court, with no more romantic notion in my head than to establish a valuable business connection and sell him some bonds; for I was then placing Canadian Industrial Bonds on the British market on a very considerable scale.

My recollection is that I was disappointed with the shape of his head. I thought, " A man with a head like that cannot possibly go far." At that time I held by a theory that no one could achieve success unless he had a big head.

Bonar Law's account of the interview was that after a short time he got bored with me and became anxious to terminate it. As I would not go, he bought some bonds from me, and so got rid of me.

My real acquaintance with Bonar Law began some two years later, when I came over here in 1910.

This time I arrived in London as a rich man who had come through a fierce financial struggle with the spoils of victory, but was determined never to put those grave matters to the test again. It was true that I had had a success, but

I did not desire ever again to steep myself in the atmosphere of money-making.

I was looking for an interest in public life. I was concerned about the connection between Canada and Great Britain, which appeared to me to be in jeopardy. I found in the doctrines of Imperial Tariff Reform the best remedy for the danger. I was also convinced that the formation of an Imperial Zollverein involved a tax on British wheat and meat.

It was in this new mood that I met Bonar Law again. I went along to his house one morning.

My intention was to interest him. I succeeded so well that Bonar Law asked me to stay to lunch and I saw he really wanted me to stay.

The food was not very good, and I noticed with a little annoyance that I was given one glass of whisky and water, whereas my host helped himself twice to what appeared to be special whisky out of his own bottle. This keeping of a special tap in one's own house is a thing I have a prejudice against.

It was a week after that I found out that he was a teetotaller and his " special whisky " was a bottle of lime juice. I had remorse for my lack of charity. Henceforward I saw more of him, and it was plain that my conversation amused him.

Next, to my surprise, I found him dining with me. But perhaps his surprise was greater than mine, for he never dined with anyone if he could help it.

This was the more surprising because the food on Bonar Law's table was always quite execrable.

Its sameness was a penance and its quality a horror to me.

Bonar apparently neither knew nor cared about the cooking.

But this weakness in the cuisine was certainly not due to parsimony. On the contrary, money was poured out in profusion on the upkeep of the establishment. I should doubt whether any expenses of recent times in No. 11 Downing Street have been so great as Bonar Law's, when he eventually became Chancellor of the Exchequer in the second Coalition—although some account must be taken of the high cost of living of his day.

It was strange to see this methodical man—who had conducted a large business with close attention to the practice of administrative economies—so absolutely careless about his household accounts. It was, however, part of his attitude towards life. In some spheres it was essential to be meticulously careful—but the management of a household was one of those things which did not matter, and did not count.

It is obvious that this kind of carelessness is just as likely to lead to getting too much as getting too little. The phases alternate. At the very time when I was groaning under the miserable cuisine offered me by Bonar Law, I discovered that Lady FitzAlan had had a precisely converse experience. She had gone to tea with the Laws at a time when the rationing system was in full force. She was quite shocked at the array of cakes which confronted her at the tea-table of the Conservative Leader. She formed the opinion that Bonar

Law and his sister were inclined to do themselves
too well. How I wished at the time that Lady
FitzAlan had been right.

There was opposition to the rapidly growing
friendship between Bonar Law and me. The
hostility was not confined to Westminster. Some
of it found expression in Bonar Law's own domestic circle. His sister, Mary Law, was not at all sure
that I was good for Bonar. She objected to the
ribaldry of my remarks. She has since described to
me the scene at which this issue came to a crisis.

Bonar Law was lying on a sofa. Though he took
much exercise he had a desire for a recumbent
position whenever possible. It was as though
the somewhat tired aspect of his mentality demanded a physical expression. He was reading
with his glasses on (and talking at the same time,
as was his wont) in this favourite posture, when
his sister suddenly remarked, " I don't care about
the growing influence of Max Aitken here."

Bonar Law took off his glasses slowly and said
quietly, " Do let me like him." She then vowed
he should have his friend as far as she was concerned and never complained again of the part I
played in Bonar Law's life.

I can picture the scene so well because all
Bonar Law's little tricks of manner dwell in my
memory. For instance, when he was really per-
plexed by a problem he would first of all scratch
his head. Then he would take off his glasses.
Then his eyes, which were bright blue, always
assumed an absolutely innocent expression. I
used to be struck by this sudden appearance of

innocence on a face generally so wise and experienced.

When he retired temporarily from active politics in early 1921, I wrote a signed article on his character and career. In it occurred the statement that while the most unselfish of all men in the great affairs of the world, he was quite selfish in trivial matters. For instance, he always took the only comfortable arm chair in the room. On reading this, Miss Law instantly sallied out to Barkers and bought two new armchairs exactly resembling the old one. His room became disgracefully overfurnished as a consequence, but she had completely destroyed my ground of complaint.

What—to come to the crucial point—was the influence which I exercised over that life in its public aspect? In vital decisions none. Bonar Law himself invariably said that my attitude towards affairs, to the great problems of politics, always interested and concerned him, but that it never determined him. He weighed my opinion carefully but in his own mental scales. And that was the truth as I saw it too.

Of course I was always there ready to listen or to talk. I heard most of his speeches in advance, and faithfully fulfilled the role of the audience—but the speech and the opinions it voiced were his own.

One thing I did supply where there was a real need. I had an almost unlimited belief in Bonar Law's powers. His one weak point was that he had not this belief in himself. Is not his best remembered dictum " If I am a great man, then all great men are frauds " ? I did help to make up this deficiency in ambition, in the confidence of the self in the self—call it what you will—which marked Bonar Law to some degree or another to the very end of his career. I nurtured his ambition in the days before the war. I applied another kind of stimulus to his energies during the war. And these stimuli never failed me. He always reacted to them. I would appeal to his sense of the duty he owed to the public. Later on in the course of the struggle I would exact of him with a pertinacity bordering on cruelty an account of what his dead son would have required of him.

I never carried any gossip to Bonar Law—nor would he have been interested in it. He didn't care to know, as I admit I do, about the human frailties of associates.

He would not always accept my views of the motives underlying certain political actions or developments. I often had to resort to every art of exposition and to striking forms of expression to make him realise what was going on all about him.

But I never coloured the picture—that was part of my goodwill. I was punctilious in showing him nothing but the absolute reality. So I never suffered from any re-action from my description.

I think I went up in his estimation by refusing office in 1915. As a matter of plain truth I was never out for office and the fact that I was not a political "soldier of fortune" was a strong point in my armoury in those days. No office or promotion ever came to me through Bonar

Law.   He was anxious to hold me back rather than to urge me forward.

He believed that I was cleverer than anyone else and never would listen in silence to any attack on my character.

The same thing applied to the written word. I have seen since his death innumerable letters, of whose existence I had no idea, though I was managing his correspondence at the time, repelling assaults on me. With extraordinary delicacy he had hidden them away.

For my part I organised a very efficient system of effacing myself—particularly during his Premiership—and yet I was never out of his life.

No doubt my association did him an injury. Let us hope I did him some good as well. Birrell once said to him, after a speech of his in the House " You will go very far—if you will only get rid of Max Aitken." Perhaps he could have gone farther if he had taken the advice—but would he have had the will to go forward, even to the extent he did ? The two problems are distinct.

Anyhow, Bonar Law certainly ruined me. He became so much a part of my political life that Winston Churchill was justified in saying after 1923 that I had sat on a three-legged stool ; one leg was myself; the second was my newspapers ; the third was my relation to Bonar Law—now the third leg had gone and Churchill said I could no longer balance myself in politics.

It is true. When I lost that third leg I had no desire to sit again on the stool of party politics.

CHAPTER XXI

IRELAND AGAIN

BONAR LAW'S loneliness was increased by the Irish crisis which now rushed over the horizon. It was not of his own creating. It originated in the Dublin Rebellion of April, 1916, and in the visit Asquith paid to Ireland after this event. Asquith thought that this dreadful business had caused a shock of horror to the British and Irish peoples alike, and that the moment was ripe for some act of reconciliation.

Therefore Asquith with the very doubtful assent of the Tories in the Cabinet authorised Lloyd George in June to set up a negotiation with the rival Irish Leaders. Lloyd George succeeded in bringing Redmond and Carson together on the basis that the Home Rule Bill should be applied at once to Ireland instead of being left over to the end of the war, and that the six counties should be excluded from its operation.

The Irish leaders persuaded their followers to agree. But Redmond subsequently declared that the Government altered for the worse the terms offered him by Lloyd George and broke off the negotiation. The scheme of reconciliation therefore failed.

That is all I intend to say on a very complex matter. Since the negotiation bore no fruit it would be unprofitable to dissect its lifeless body. I propose to deal with this Irish issue simply as it affected the position of Bonar Law. The Tory Leader in the Commons was in favour of carrying out the plan and supported Lloyd George and Carson. With the exception of Balfour *all* the Tory Ministers and *practically all* the Tory magnates outside took the opposite view. Bonar Law's isolation was thus intensified.

He was stricken in the house of his friends because the operating force which destroyed the compromise between Unionist Ulster and Nationalist Ireland, was the hostility of the Unionists in the South and West, whom Lloyd George had omitted to bring into the deal. This body of opinion worked in Downing Street through Lord Lansdowne, a great Irish landlord, and Lord Long, sometime a Tory Irish Secretary. Bonar Law was instantly deprived of the countenance of those he thought his only two remaining friends in the Ministry, though Lansdowne's friendship was in reality by this time a non-existent asset.

Nor was this by any means the worst of the business. In forming his decision he had to struggle hard with an internal clash, which was painful to him, between his duty to his country and his allegiance to his old party cause. In reaching it he incurred the violent displeasure of at least two thirds of his quondam associates. He explained himself the motives which finally induced him to support the Lloyd George compromise on Ireland—when without any special suggestion on his part the Ulster Nationalist agreement had been attained—in a letter to his old and valued friend Lord St. Audries—

Downing Street,
27th June, 1916.

My dear St. Audries,

I have your letter of the 25th and I am very sorry to see that you take so strong a view on this subject. It would take too long to write you giving all the reasons which have made me take the other view, but it seems to me that now that the negotiations have reached this stage if our Party turns them down we shall simply have the whole of Nationalist Ireland in hostility to us instead of, as has been the case up to now, having for the first time in our history Nationalist Ireland divided and the official section of it on our side. We are getting the exact terms which would have been accepted at the time of the Buckingham Palace conference, and, in addition to this, there is the further consideration that if we turn down these proposals, obviously neither Asquith nor his Liberal colleagues can contemplate going on with the government of Ireland on what they will regard as a system of unnecessary coercion. I fancy, therefore, that Asquith would refuse to go on on the old terms for the sake of keeping us in the Government and would say to us " I am not going to coerce Ireland, you must do it." That would create a situation which seems to me impossible, for

whatever may be the feeling of members of
Parliament, I am convinced that in the country
we should have a very moderate amount of support for a policy of no Home Rule when Ulster
which represented the only backbone in the fight
in the past, is satisfied. In these circumstances
the only possible Government would be that of
the Liberals by themselves and now I do not
think such a Government could be carried on.

I am putting very roughly to you some of the
considerations which are influencing me and
which I shall put before the Party meeting to-
morrow. The upshot of my views is this : that to
go on, on the lines of Lloyd George's negotiations does mean a risk, but to reject them is
certain disaster.

Yours sincerely,
A. Bonar Law.

It will be observed at once what an immense
development in war mentality separates the writer
of this letter from the Bonar Law who had thun-
dered against Asquith for " putting the Bill on
the Statute book."

But not by patriotic and reasoned arguments of
this kind was the tempest to be assuaged. In
those days at Bonar Law's office there was a rain
of letters of denunciation and protest. They made
a huge pile which he divided into two separate
dockets—one labelled " Personally abusive," and
the other devoted to remonstrances from important people. The abusive letters again might be
divided into two categories. Class one begins

" Sir, you are a traitor who has sold his country for gold." Class two begins " Sir, I have been a loyal Unionist all my life but—"

To Conservative Peers, to Chairmen of Associations, and to Conservative M.P.s at the Front, Bonar Law replied firmly. But he felt none the less the alienation of his supporters on an issue which he had once made particularly his own. He would quote the old tag of Carlyle generally applied to Asquith : " I am their leader, therefore I must follow them," to point out that he was really paying the penalty for riding out in advance of his troop.

As to Tory sentiment towards him—he had plenty of opportunities of gauging this hostility. Lords Curzon and Robert Cecil went on a private mission to the Prime Minister to declare that the Conservative members of the Cabinet (except Bonar Law) had never, and would never, agree to the terms Lloyd George had offered Redmond. Lansdowne and Long had become his most bitter opponents—Long even hinting at resignation. Selborne did actually resign at the mere threat of putting Home Rule and Amending Bill into effect. Lord Hugh Cecil said that if a Bill to pass the Lloyd George proposal was produced, he would oppose it tooth and nail at every stage.

A typical letter of protest came from Lord Brentford, who was Sir William Joynson Hicks, written on paper with black edges—

22nd June, 1916.

My dear Law,

I have selected this funereal paper to describe

my feelings on the Home Rule compromise.

Seriously, I want you to know that there is a stalwart body of opinion in the Unionist party who will remain Unionist to the end.

At our meeting to-day Finlay told us that we could all exercise our right to communicate our views to our Leader.   Hence this letter.

Yours sincerely,

W. Joynson Hicks.

This epistle had a particular significance, because the writer was a prominent leader of what was called the " business men's committee "—a body particularly hostile to Coalition as such and, to Asquith and his Ministry—a " ginger group " which did not regard Bonar Law, quite apart from the Irish question, with any favour.

Finally a Conservative Party meeting was, after several postponements, summoned by Bonar Law. Immediately Lord Midleton protested against the exclusion of Conservative Peers—thus anticipating a similar protest over the famous Carlton Club meeting in 1922. Bonar Law answered, with deadly logic, that he was the Leader of the Conservative Party in the House of Commons, and was holding a private meeting of the supporters who had appointed him leader. None the less the party meeting was by no means propitious for him. He and Balfour harangued the audience in favour of the Irish settlement. Others spoke in a contrary sense. The meeting was adjourned without coming to any decision. It never met again.

This was one of the few occasions before the
Second Coalition of 1916 on which Balfour
and Bonar Law co-operated heartily. As late as
1915 Bonar Law always addressed his predecessor
as " Dear Mr. Balfour." Balfour never got further
than " My dear Bonar Law." Subsequently when
they were in various Ministries together—Balfour
used to write " My dear B.L."

Carson of course also had his difficulties—but
at least he had the advantage of not being in
office.

However, immediately after Lord Lansdowne's
intervention in the Lords and Redmond's protest,
Carson also showed signs of impeding the settlement. He explained that having successfully
accomplished the most distasteful task of per-
suading the Unionists of the Six Counties to
accept Home Rule plus exclusion, he thought the
Imperial Government ought to give some guarantees of protection to all the loyalists of Ireland.
He began to dwell on the naval necessity of controlling the south and west coast of Ireland—
which was the stock argument of the Tory opponents of the Irish compromise. He was
increasingly alarmed at the open demonstrations
of disloyalty throughout Ireland. He did not
say that he had changed his mind about the
advisability of sticking to the Lloyd George
agreement—but his written arguments could
hardly have been distinguished from those of
an opponent of that agreement. He complained
in the end that the " Daily Express " was rightly
or wrongly supposed to be the organ of Bonar

Law, and that its conduct had been such as to put the Carsonites in the gravest difficulties.

Now, all that the " Daily Express " had done was to support the plan when the Lloyd George scheme was launched, giving it a general blessing. Finally, when the dissensions in the Conservative ranks reached such a point that a party meeting had to be summoned, the " Daily Express " advised the Tories to listen to the advice of Bonar Law, Balfour and Carson, and not to that of the Tories in the Cabinet, who wished to wreck the settlement.

It will be seen that the defeated side in the Irish crisis were a little inclined to indulge in recrimination. Lloyd George, for instance, always maintained that had Asquith faced the Tory revolters firmly, he could have put the whole business through—having behind him all the Liberal Ministers, plus Bonar Law, Balfour and Carson.

So the July of 1916 closed sadly for Bonar Law. Yet there were several significant aspects of the Irish crisis, which were prophetic. For the first time Bonar Law, Lloyd George and Carson had worked together as a team.

In this Irish question Bonar Law had, as in the Gallipoli crisis, definitely disassociated himself from what might be justly described as the main current of Tory thought when it was manifestly wrong and out of date.

In the light of commonsense he refused to bow down before the idol of " Prestige " in the East and of the Dagon of " union at all costs " in the West.

It was this capacity for thinking clearly on the facts of the war as they emerged and of translating these thoughts into action by the exercise of cold moral courage which brought Bonar Law into the immensely powerful position he was to attain at the end of 1916. But his colleagues and friends in the summer of that year did not view the man or the matter in this light. They saw him apparently discredited and abandoned by supporter after supporter. They could not perceive that he had been forsaken by the people who were wrong because their minds did not move quickly enough for the urgency of the times, and that he must go to the top of any successful War Government which could be formed precisely because he had been right. Bonar Law's apparent failure in early 1916 was the measure of this coming success.

CHAPTER XXII

CHURCHILL DOWN

BONAR LAW, as he stood in the summer of 1916, has already been sketched at full length in a previous chapter. As the war proceeded and his mind attuned itself to new conditions it became more and more evident that his active assistance was essential to the winning of the war. He outstripped the other statesmen of the time in the two conjoint qualities required for the task—wisdom and character.

Lloyd George was viewed by men at this period in an ambiguous light. To the outside public he was becoming a hero. He was certainly becoming a nuisance to his colleagues. I give my own experience of him as a small contribution which may throw a little light on the subject. I had more than one interview with Lloyd George, especially in connection with railway transportation and engineering behind the front, with marked reference to concrete. He did not seem particularly interested in my views, or to seek my opinion. After the episode of his appointment to the War Office I got to know him better in a private way.

My modernised and romantic versions of Old

Testament events and characters certainly amused
him. A free rendering of the Bible story of the
life of David and other things with tales of the
judges, would hold his attention. But I never
felt anything like getting near to the real man
himself. To adopt the Bonar Law phraseology,
it did not seem certain whether he was a great
man or a great fraud.

This same dubiety of opinion was manifested
all round. The infallible instinct of the public
working through the Press was beginning, though
the needle quivered backwards and forwards, to
point to him as the saviour of the State. On the
other hand, we have seen him, and shall see him
again, regarded by many of his associates as a
purely ambitious intriguer caring for nothing
except his own aggrandisement. McKenna, the
most hostile witness, speaking of this period,
describes him as a kind of pest in council—never
helpful, always running down other people's
departments in order to seize a slice of authority
for his own. McKenna declares that he was not
the aggressor in his famous duel with Lloyd
George. The quarrel was forced on him because
he resisted Lloyd George's policy of " wrecking
before capture " other people's concerns.

But the balancing factor to Lloyd George in
the Cabinet in the early months of the war was out.
Churchill, the other brilliant mentality which
thought itself fit to ride the storm, had vanished
from the centre of power.

In 1916 Churchill was a character depressed
beyond the limits of description. When the

Government was deprived of his guidance, he could see no hope anywhere. He had remained with the Ministry in a subordinate capacity from May 1915 to the late autumn of that year, simply in order to press the Dardanelles scheme. With the evacuation of Gallipoli his last tie with Whitehall was severed. He turned readily enough to his long-nurtured ambitions for a command in the field. Churchill had been a " regular," and he possessed a mind singularly adapted to deal with a war of new methods and surprises. He might reasonably have expected a brigade—and I believe he would have secured one but for the intense prejudice manifested against him in certain quarters at home.

The night before his departure for the front I went to see him in his house in the Cromwell road. The whole household was upside down while the soldier-statesman was buckling on his sword. Downstairs, Mr. " Eddie " Marsh, his faithful secretary, was in tears. And it is a commonplace to Churchill that he should have evoked such a depth of sympathy in his private secretary. Upstairs, Lady Randolph was in a state of despair at the idea of her brilliant son being relegated to the trenches. Mrs. Churchill seemed to be the only person who remained calm, collected and efficient.

Churchill went to France and was offered by French, who was then nearly at his last gasp as Commander-in-Chief, an A.D.C.'s post at G.H.Q. or, in the alternative, a Brigade. Churchill chose the Brigade, but insisted first on obtaining some practical experience of trench warfare. For this purpose he served a month with the Grenadier Guards. After that Churchill was recalled to G.H.Q. and was actually given a brigade in Bridge's division. But the very day after this was apparently settled French happened to go home to London and told Asquith what he was doing. The Premier was apparently frightened and urged French, who was in no position to insist on having his way, to give Churchill no more than a battalion. This really was rough. A Premier may have to throw a colleague overboard sometimes to save the ship, but surely he should not jerk from under him the hen-coop on which the victim is trying to sustain himself in the stormy ocean.

The simile is not inapt. Asquith, as a politician, had a perfect right to remove Churchill, another politician, from high office. But surely he had no call to interfere, for political reasons, with the decision of the Commander-in-Chief in France, who judged Churchill's merits as a soldier and thought him worthy of a Brigade.

Thus pressed by Asquith, French simply hung the matter up. Before the question was really settled French was removed from the position of Commander-in-Chief in France, and Haig succeeded him. Churchill thereupon removed himself from General Headquarters and came to stay at Canadian Headquarters in France of which I had charge at that period. In the long run he only got a battalion at the hands of Haig.

My own opinion was that Churchill would have made an invaluable adviser to any Commander-in-Chief. He would have guarded his superior against all kinds of errors both military and diplomatic. His romantic initiative, which gave us the tank, would have been guided and checked in all directions by expert advisers. One Churchill on his staff might have saved French from dismissal.

Bonar Law was very strongly pressed to help Churchill to an appointment of this kind. He responded with an unswerving antagonism to Churchill. He thought that to give Churchill an influence on the conduct of affairs in France would be a disaster. Lloyd George would not give any countenance to projects for Churchill's preferment.

Churchill, as has been said, received the command of a battalion. I did not think it a crack battalion at that—though Churchill in the pride of possession and with due loyalty to his own command would hotly deny this.

I do not even know whether he was a good colonel. Such a judgment lies quite outside my province. So if I do not praise his conduct in the field it must not be supposed that silence implies a suppressed criticism.

He went into the trenches with the highest ideals—with the clear determination to do or die in the effort to succeed in a military career now that politics seemed closed to him. But it was an amazing waste of sheer brain and genius to make Winston Churchill a battalion commander.

Churchill very soon discovered the limits set

to his utility in this new field of endeavour. It is true that for a time he enjoyed the open air life of danger and seemed content to settle down satisfied with the command of a tiny province. But this mood did not last.

In the spring of 1916 he wrote me a letter foreshadowing his return to Westminster, and giving some excellent reasons for so doing.

> 6th Royal Scots Fusiliers.
> In the Field.
> 28. 3. 16.
>
> My dear Max,
>
> I am deeply impressed by General Lipsett, who seems to me to be a man of real merit and possibly even with genius as a commander. You know all about him and his work; but I daresay you will be interested to know my opinion. I am sure you cd. be doing no greater service to the Canadian army, than by aiding his promotion to the command of a division. Only merit and real qualities ought to count at a time like this. I believe both in big and in small affairs of war this officer is altogether exceptional in his judgment and *flaire*. Do think this over *pro bono publico*. Why don't you get hold of him now he is in England and talk to him?
>
> I did not feel able after all to take yr. advice; for though my instinct agreed with yours I had small but insistent obligations here wh. cd. not be hastily discarded for the sake of a personal opportunity. Now the situation is somewhat different, and I wonder vy. much what yr. views upon it are.

I was touched at the kindness wh. led you to take an interest in my affairs, and I shd. be vy. delighted to hear from you. I have really throughout this war tried only to do the right thing at whatever cost. But the problem wh. now faces me is vy. difficult. My work out here with all its risk and all its honour wh. I greatly value : on the other hand the increasingly grave situation of the war and the feeling of knowledge and of power to help in mending matters wh. is strong within me : add to this dilemma the awkwardness of changing and the cause of my, I hope, unusual hesitations is obvious. In principle I have no doubts : but as to time and occasion I find vy. much greater difficulties.

I did not feel in me the other night the virtue necessary for the tremendous task you indicated. My interests were too evident and one cannot tell how much they sway one's judgment.

Meanwhile the days pass easily and swiftly here : and at any time the necessity of solving these problems may flash away.

Yours vy. sincerely,
Winston S. Churchill.

Finally he received some political overture, which decided him to return. He was urged in the first instance by Carson, and independently by C. P. Scott of the " Manchester Guardian " and by Sir Arthur Markham, to come home and assist in a patriotic opposition. Churchill's function was to support the various ginger groups irre-

spective of party. At this moment, in the spring
of 1916, it was thought that Asquith might fall
on the question of a further tightening up of the
measure for enforcing conscription, and that a
first-class crisis and a reshuffle of the Ministry
might take place. Actually Asquith yielded to the
more vigorous members of his Cabinet and the
crisis and the Amending Bill passed in May 1916.
Churchill was therefore left out in the cold for
some time longer, and the feeling that the Empire
was being lost through his powerlessness gnawed
at his vitals.

When he returned to the House of Commons in
the autumn he immediately plunged into the
debates. He complained one day that the Government had failed to give the House a lead. The
next day he declared that Ministers showed a lack
of modesty in bringing forward a Bill to prolong
the life of the existing Parliament—worse still
they were going to put the Government whips on
to carry it.

Bonar Law made a witty and merciless reply.
" Mr Churchill," he said, " has given the House
two valuable lessons—which came with great
effect from him. One is that we should all conduct
ourselves with becoming modesty." (Laughter.)
" That is good advice from whatever quarter it
comes. The other is that the Government are
committing an unpardonable offence in putting
on Government Whips for a Government Bill.
That is from the same right hon. gentleman who
told us yesterday that the Government should
lead the House." (Laughter.)

The "Daily Express" gave considerable prominence to this episode. This drew from Churchill the following letter to me—

18. 8. 16.
41 Cromwell Road,
S.W.

My dear Max,

Freddie sends me the enclosed to forward to you. It explains itself.

It is a pity Bonar shd. be *personal* in rejoinders to me. I do not make personal attacks on him or try to decry his personal behaviour or qualities. Surely the wide field of political argument shd. afford sufficient scope at the present time, where everything is so uncertain.

Yours ever,
W.

It was strange to see this "Battling Butler" of politics so sensitive to a debating cross-counter.

At this time his thoughts seemed to be turning inwards as though he was anatomising his own soul. He always showed signs of despair in certain circumstances. On one occasion before this date I was disturbed because he was an obvious victim of depression and forebodings that distressed him. In consequence I asked him down to spend a day with me at Cherkley, Leatherhead, in the hope that I could distract his mind.

I borrowed a Canadian army car and called for him at his house. I drove him down to Cherkley

and we talked all the way about the war. I had
noticed that he had placed on the car an easel and
a box of colours. More mysterious still, a large
red despatch box was added. The house was
empty at the time. But Churchill's easel was
soon out and planted on the terrace, where we
look out on a view which has fascinated so many
politicians, including Asquith when he had his
interview with Bonar Law over Ireland.

Churchill had turned to his painting. It was
obvious that it absorbed his mind altogether. He
could not talk while he painted and did not want
to talk. I was glad to see him so engrossed in such
a calm amusement. Also I thought it would be
a good chance to get on with some arrears of work.
Like every other administrator in the War period,
I had to read innumerable and often badly written
documents, and always carried with me the residue
which had to be gone through. I had determined
on that day to make a clean slate.

Suddenly Churchill turned round and produced
the mysterious despatch box. " I cannot talk and
paint too," he said, " but I have not left you un-
provided for. That is why I have brought the
despatch case. In it you will find the whole of
my justification for the part I played in the Dardanelles Expedition. I will let you read my case."
And Churchill unloaded on the turf a vast mass of
printed, typewritten, and mimeographed matter—
enough for a man to ponder on for a week !

Churchill's charm lies so largely in his un-
expectedness and in his belief that everybody takes
everything as charmingly as he does. It is the

simplicity of a child which no contact with the world could ever spoil.

But Churchill then was Churchill "down." Practically he despaired of the Republic, and could see no rift in the clouds either for himself or the State. It is in these moments of depression that he is most fascinating.

Churchill " up " is quite a different proposition. I remember once a terrible scene with him when he was in a position of uncontrolled power and authority in dealing with public affairs which closely concerned me.

If any other man living had used such outrageous language to me as he did on that occasion I should never have forgiven him. Churchill on the top of the wave has in him the stuff of which tyrants are made.

. . . . . .

The balance of personalities on the Conservative side was rather curious. The majority of the Conservative members of the Ministry—Curzon, Chamberlain, Cecil and Long—undoubtedly leant to Asquith. Curzon was openly aspiring to the leadership of the party. In adopting this attitude in support of Asquith these Conservative leaders were, in an ever increasing degree, losing touch with their followers in the Commons.

No one could pierce through Balfour's reserve —but on the whole his temperament seemed to incline him towards Asquith. Certainly Lloyd George was his most severe critic in the Ministry.

Birkenhead was not very definitely attached to

any section of opinion. In policy he leaned towards the Conservative group hostile to Lloyd George, but he was at that time personally very much devoted to Bonar Law. As a matter of fact, the Curzon-Cecil-Chamberlain group whom he supported did not care for him. They said he was far too clever to be good. It was written :

" For, alas, it is seldom if ever
That people behave as they should ;
For the good are so harsh to the clever,
And the clever so rude to the good."

Carson, on the other hand, having left the Ministry as a critic of its lack of vigour, was rapidly becoming the leader of the discontented Conservatives or Diehards.

Carson's great ally was Gwynne, of the " Morning Post." Gwynne in turn was the Fugleman of the Diehards in the Press. In all that followed he should have been my natural ally. Gwynne had in the past influenced me greatly for many years. His conversations were illuminating and our friendship had been sincere.

This relationship came to a bad end by what was in effect an accident.

It was desirable that a piece of political information should be given out and I told the news early to Gwynne in confidence. Then Northcliffe came out with it in the " Times." I really had a perfectly good explanation of how this happened. But Gwynne seemed to me to be refusing to accept my simple disclaimer—while I did not then understand how much a journalist, with his passion for his newspaper, feels such an incident. I should have sympathised now and taken great pains to explain to Gwynne exactly what had happened. As it was I simply let the whole business slide.

This episode will provide an explanation of the fact that Gwynne, who desired to bring down the first Coalition Government just as ardently as I did, had no part or lot in what I did towards the work of destruction. No doubt there were others whose personal hostility kept them apart from me in the events of the autumn and winter of 1916.

The Gwynne episode perhaps explains one of the reasons why I had so many enemies. Once a man showed any hostility or distrust towards me, I would take no steps to conciliate him or to placate him. I could not be troubled. Even when my enemies told the most infamous falsehoods about me I could not be bothered to refute them— nor have I ever done so. Bonar Law often reasoned with me and even urged me to try and disarm the enemy, but I would not. It was the great weakness of my position and nature at that time. I had to go out on an enterprise which involved welding all kinds of different people and groups of politics together with this great weight of personal hostility hanging round my neck.

CHAPTER XXIII

THE NIGERIAN DEBATE

IT must not be supposed that the growing unpopularity of the first Coalition Government was so clear to every one at the time as it becomes on looking backward, or that most men would have predicted the fall of the Ministry. Indeed, it would have been pointed out that as long as Ministers held together, or even as long as the two party chiefs—Mr. Asquith, Prime Minister and Leader of the Liberal Party, and Mr. Bonar Law, Colonial Secretary and Leader of the Conservative Party—held together, there was no instrument for securing their overthrow.

Everywhere men still said that Asquith's leadership in the House of Commons was indispensable to the conduct of the war—that he possessed the unanimous and unswerving devotion of the Liberal Party; that he had more influence with the Tory leaders than Bonar Law himself—and further, that no other Premier could command any support from the Labour Party at all. Those who read this narrative must understand clearly how firmly this doctrine of the indispensability of Asquith was rooted in the minds of his colleagues and of Parliamentarians in general. They

287

thought it so sure a shield thrown over the existing Ministry that no political instrument could be forged which could break down that protection and menace what it protected.

But this view would have been wrong. There was such an instrument in existence, though, as usual in almost every crisis, politicians were not aware of it.

The weak point in the whole fabric was the position of Mr. Bonar Law and his relationship to his own party. Speaking to that party at the time the Coalition was formed, he had said :

"I say quite plainly that if I found that in this new position I had lost the confidence of our party I should feel I was of no further use to the Government. Certainly, so long as I myself believe that, whatever its defects, I can see no better way of carrying on this war, I should not oppose it, but if the party to which I belong had lost confidence in me I should not for a moment dream of continuing to be a member of the Government."

It followed, then, that if Bonar Law found himself with a majority of his followers against him he would be compelled to resign, and it could hardly be doubted that this would entail the most serious and possibly disastrous political consequences.

Now a section of the Conservative Party, called the Conservative Ginger group in contradistinction to its Liberal counterpart, formed with the latter a kind of guerilla opposition. It had gained greatly in prestige by the accession of Carson on his resignation in October. Its persistent attacks on Ministerial policy, though not personally directed against Bonar Law— indeed, many of his oldest friends and sympathisers were among the critics—nevertheless struck the Tory leader as well as the Liberal Prime Minister at whom they were really aimed. The Tory Diehards were thus blindly or subconsciously using against the Government a weapon of whose potency they themselves had no real conception.

Thus it happened that throughout the summer and autumn a division, marked by increasing bitterness, was springing up in the ranks of Toryism—one section accusing the other of disloyalty, and the other retorting that Bonar Law was helping to lose the war by holding up the trembling arms of Asquith. The two Tory protagonists, Bonar Law and Carson, were no longer on those terms of intimate cordiality which marked the history of the Home Rule crisis, and a trial of strength could not long be delayed.

It was the Nigerian debate which brought matters to the crisis.

For some time before that debate, I had been drifting somewhat out of touch with politics and politicians owing to the pressure of my Canadian military duties. My attention was recalled sharply by a warning which I received from Mr. R. D. Blumenfeld, the Editor of the " Daily Express," that things were far from well on the Conservative benches in the House of Commons, and that the

Nigerian debate might very likely prove a decisive trial of strength between the two divergent sections. The merits of the Nigerian question are not germane to my subject. It is sufficient to observe that the issue chosen was one calculated to collect the greatest number of Conservatives and Tariff Reformers in the " No " lobby, and to place Mr. Bonar Law in a position of some dialectic difficulty. But though the question of the sale of these enemy properties in West Africa might seem remote and trifling when measured against the vast issues of the war, to the seeing eye this was not so. The result of that division on the affairs of a distant dependency would stretch out far and wide, and its consequences would be felt on every stricken battlefield in Europe. The developments must follow one another in an inevitable sequence of cause and effect. The great bulk of the opposition would be Conservative, so that a defeat on the motion would mean that the Tory leader could only carry into the lobby a minority of his professed supporters. In that case, how could he be said to retain the confidence of his party ? No, he must resign office, and to pull out Bonar Law was to knock out the keystone of the Government arch. Some, if not all, of his colleagues would go with him, and the governing instrument must be proportionately weakened.

I was filled with concern for Bonar Law's position, not on any personal grounds, but because I perceived he was going to be placed in such a difficulty that a wrong choice of any sort might remove him, perhaps indefinitely, from the centre of war direction—and that such a removal would have the worst possible consequences on the conduct of the war.

I went to see him and found him in his room at the Colonial Office—a room which seemed singularly uncongenial to him. At one end of its vast expanse was his desk—thoroughly uncomfortable and most unsuited for business purposes. It was a place for a pompous man and Bonar Law was anything but pompous. I should say that one epithet always suited him : He was unassuming. His personality stamped itself in no way upon the casual acquaintance. It was indeed the precise converse of the type of personality which clamours for attention. For he was quite indifferent to the opinion which outsiders might form of him. In his immediate circle, on the other hand, he was most anxious to make himself agreeable and could wield great charm.

His personal habits reflected his individuality. At bridge, to which he was much addicted in his brief leisure at this time, he was a sound player—but he was also an easy one. He never would exact the penalties due to him, as the keen player generally does. He played regularly for half-penny points—to change this to penny points meant a " bust " to him. Contrary to the custom in his own circles, he settled his debts with cash on the spot instead of with a cheque next day. If he was winning he lost interest in the game. If he was losing he was anxious to play on—yet he certainly did not care for money. He invariably asked for and tried to arrange his bridge partnership with the most unsuccessful and least experienced player at the table. He never in my long experience criticised his partner or complained of bad luck.

He always went to bed at a fixed hour and in the very worst days of the war he was able to sleep well. But he read himself to sleep with the most ordinary kind of detective stories. Gone were the days when he had studied Carlyle and the classics to improve his mind.

Since all detective stories are really cut out of a few patterns, I once said to him, " Don't you get bored with the repetition and sameness of these tales ? " " Not more bored than usual," was his only answer.

One could bring him, like Asquith, by a little ingenuity to repeat the same story in response to the same lead. He had one about a man who suffered from gout all his life. He could find no remedy. He tried every sort of medicine, but with no effect. " At last," said Bonar Law, " he told me he had found a cure. He said that he was taking half a bottle of champagne for breakfast every day and the gout had disappeared completely. But," said Bonar Law in a tragic tone of voice, " in six months he was dead."

Occasionally, he would talk about himself. But no " leading " would make him do this. The inspiration for self-discussion had to be spontaneous.

Bonar Law had no decent regard for his food.

He liked little of it and plain—one course for preference—and simply swallowed it. The moment he had finished he started to smoke—generally a cigar, to be followed in turn by a pipe. Up till his final illness I only once knew him to touch alcohol. He took some brandy for an attack of indigestion. It did not cure him.

In the course of our interview at the Colonial Office I discovered that one thing concerned Bonar Law greatly. The bitterness of Carson's attitude towards him—a bitterness he did not return, but which he felt to be in such violent contrast with their former intimate friendship.

After this interview I sounded Carson to try to discover the origin of this particular bitterness. Carson was full of complaints about Bonar Law—particularly on the score of his " stubbornness " over the Nigerian business. Nothing, therefore, resulted from this attempt, and events followed their course, until the date for the discussion in the House of Commons which was fixed for November 8th.

The night before the Nigerian debate I again saw Bonar Law—he was agitated, but confident of success. This feeling was chiefly induced in him by the reiterated assurance of his friends that a division would not be challenged. My attitude was one of detachment. None the less I felt quite certain that a division would be forced—for this I had from the editor of the " Daily Express," who was far more likely than the Treasury Whips to know the plans of the Conservative Opposition. I also learnt from the same source that the division was

expected to be a very close one. Both these fore-
casts turned out to be correct.

On the night when the debate was still in progress, I dined with Birkenhead, who was gloomy
and despondent. He had been depressed by the
course which it had taken in the afternoon discussion, and feared defeat, and the consequent
resignation of Bonar Law. We went to the House
together. The atmosphere was somewhat electric,
civil strife inside a party always inducing greater
mutual exasperation than a contest with the
official enemy.

Bonar Law made a powerful statement of his
case—but he was subjected to much interruption.
He did not attempt to conceal his feelings against
Leslie Scott, but he showed no resentment towards
Carson, though the latter threw in some inter-
jections which were decidedly strong—at one time
accusing Bonar Law of " misrepresenting facts,"
and at another exclaiming, " That is not true."
The division was taken, and Bonar Law was
clearly sustained by a small majority of the Conservatives, but by a large majority of the House.
The feeling between the two Tory sections was
very strained. George Terrell, one of the Carsonite
Whips, met Birkenhead in the Lobby coming out,
and told us that Bonar Law's defeat had only
been averted by the votes of " the paid members."
" We will cross off the votes of the members who
are paid if you cross off those who want to be
paid," was the prompt and characteristic reply o
Birkenhead.

After the division I found Bonar Law in his

room surrounded by supporters who were con-
gratulating him as on a triumph and quite unaware
of the real significance of the division. They
had no idea of the critical nature of the situation,
nor any sense of the impending downfall of
the Ministry. They took the optimistic view
and made light of the division. Very different
were the feelings and forebodings of others. It
was clear that such attacks could not be continued
for long without a defeat in the Lobby ensuing,
and that apart from this, continuance must render
Bonar Law's claim to the confidence of the Conservative party nugatory, and his position in the
Government consequently impossible. It was
indeed this very fact which made the attacks so
dangerous. The opposition, or at least many of
them, were not out against Bonar Law—they were
out against the Government. But the fact
remained that it was only by damaging Bonar
Law's hold on his own followers that they could
menace the Ministry. And in effect this was
exactly what they were doing. They were pulling
out the linch-pin of the Government's coach.

The Ministry looked like having a short life, and
there were also certain cross-currents among the
Liberals in the Cabinet which were setting in
the same direction.

With these thoughts in my mind I urged Bonar
Law to resign.

My reasons were briefly as follows. He was the
only alternative Premier in the event—which now
seemed probable—of the existing Government
falling. Having resigned, he could at any rate

sustain the Administration for a time from outside, and, if Asquith fell, he would be there ready to take his place and reconstruct a fresh Ministry. On the other hand, if he stayed in he would be, in my opinion, infallibly destroyed—and as he was the guide in whom I placed my trust in the war, such a prospect could only be regarded with intense dismay. But destroyed he would be if he were forced out of office by the action of his own rebellious followers. Then he must infallibly lose the leadership—and face a catastrophe.

Bonar Law would not agree to this line of argument. He said that if he had been an individual Conservative Cabinet Minister it might have been sound enough policy to leave the Government without quarrelling with it, in order to help it externally and reserve his power in the interests of the country when the inevitable reconstruction of the Ministry came. That this course was the best one for his own safety and advantage, he did not deny.

But, anyhow, he was not, he declared, an individual. He was the leader of the Conservative party in the Commons, and even though his Tory colleagues in the Cabinet seemed inclined to repudiate his lead, yet he must continue to function as leader, even though his right to do so were denied in practice. Now, the withdrawal of the Tory Chief from the Cabinet meant, or might mean, the withdrawal of Conservative support from the Government—the return to party warfare —the fall of the Liberal Ministry—the attempt to substitute a purely Conservative one—in fact, the triumph of all the methods against which he had been battling since the outbreak of war. Therefore, as leader of the party he could not do something which in a private Minister might have been quite honourable—and would certainly have been to his personal advantage.

He was not to be turned from this resolution. Nor did there seem any escape from the dilemma.

It was obvious that all would be well if an agreement between Bonar Law and Carson could be reached, but it was equally impossible to discover in what the basis of such an agreement could reside. Bonar Law at the time desired in some form or another the continuance of the existing regime and no open breach : Carson desired the destruction of the Government; and, whereas Bonar Law could not enforce quietude by some strong action against Carson, Carson could prosecute his assault against Bonar Law.

The character and views of Carson became, therefore, a matter of vital importance to the solution of the problem. He had set the game on foot and seemed prepared to hunt it down. The popular view of him, though it struck home on the vital point of his courage, was in other respects almost absurdly inaccurate. He was pictured to great numbers of his countrymen as the typical representative of that honest, dour, and narrowly fanatical type which people the plains of Ulster. But since there was in addition something romantic in his appearance and fiery eloquence very foreign to the North of Ireland, he was conceived of as adding to the ferocity of Luther the fanaticism of Torquemada.

" A daring pilot in extremity,
Pleased with the danger when the waves went high,
He sought the storms, but for a calm unfit
Would steer too nigh the sands to boast his wit."

Something in the contour of a face which in deep and solid lines stands out like a Rembrandt portrait, and a gloom in repose which appeared to be almost entirely the product of his belief in consistent bad health, intensified this impression.

Carson certainly believed that he was subject to some disease which threatened his health or even his life. Before the war he thought a surgical operation would be necessary, and used to say so quite frequently. During the war he began to take the view that there was something wrong with his heart. Fortunately, these threats never really developed. None the less, his own feeling that he lived under a kind of menace gave the outside public a conception of his character which was quite contrary to fact.

In truth, Carson in opposition possessed beyond all the politicians of his time a peculiar charm and fascination of manner. In counsel he combined great breadth of view in taking up a position and unbending firmness in adhering to it once it was taken up. He thought the matter out carefully, and where his mind stayed, it fixed. That is not to say that I have not known him change suddenly from one opinion to another. A man cannot be judged on his vagaries, but on his continued record during the great crises of his life.

I observed him closely on two great occasions : in the Home Rule negotiations, when the late Lord Murray of Elibank and I endeavoured to negotiate terms at the time of the Buckingham Palace Conference; and in the crisis which led to the fall of Mr. Asquith's Government.

During the Home Rule crisis he showed great breadth and moderation of view, combined with unyielding tenacity. He was assailed on all sides by the cleverest men in England to compel him to change his ground; that ground was the threat of civil war, and a return to the time when heads were bartered for politics; it was shrewdly suspected, and not without legitimate reason, that his ground was bluff; he was pressed on all sides to admit it, and if he had done so it would have been fatal to his cause. Yet no one knows to this day whether it was bluff or not. I have seen many bluffs in great business deals, when the whole essence of the decision was to know when a threat was a reality; but I have never seen presented so impenetrable a front. Every word, every look, every letter was consistent, until what was either an heroic determination or a masterpiece of acting has left behind it an historic doubt.

Carson in office appeared in a different light to me. His resignation—from the first Coalition Government—impressed me at the time unfavourably. There seemed to be about it a certain element of petulance and of demanding miracles which made it possible to think that he was ageing and did not possess the immense self-restraint which kept Ulster in check during the critical months. It did not strike me at the time that the real explanation was that office in itself irked him and opposition fascinated him. At any rate he left the Government as an implacable enemy of the Asquith regime, and from that time forward, looking neither to right nor left, he strode straight on to its doom.

Certainly, during the negotiations relating to the fall of the first Coalition Government, he seemed to be the old Carson—vigorous in language, broad in view, inflexible in determination. He never aspired to office, but he never discouraged his partners by shrinking from the responsibility of taking it.

CHAPTER XXIV

TROUBLE IN THE CABINET

THE first striking intimation in outer political circles that all was not perfect peace in the Liberal wing of the Cabinet came in the form of a curious story widely circulated among politicians. It was to the effect that Mr. Geoffrey Howard, Liberal Whip, had telephoned to Lloyd George to remind him of the urgency of the Nigerian division. The answer came back from Mrs. Lloyd George that her husband was dining with Carson. In any case, Lloyd George put in no appearance at the House.

The story, as a matter of fact, was not accurate. Lloyd George was dining that night with Lord Lee of Fareham at his house in Abbey Garden, where several meetings had already taken place between Lloyd George, Carson, and Milner. All three had met that evening to discuss the general situation and the possibilities of co-operation, and it is claimed, the question of the Nigerian debate never came up at all. Lloyd George has always persistently denied that he refrained of set purpose from taking part in that division.

The implications drawn from the story however possessed great importance, for it implied that the Ministry was liable to assault from two sides, and that while Carson was attacking from the front, Lloyd George was executing a concerted movement on the flank.   The day after the division Bonar Law met Lloyd George at the War Committee, and the latter volunteered the statement the moment they met, that he had been paired.

Further confirmation of the view set going by the story that George had deliberately absented himself from the division, was soon to hand.   A day or so later I had occasion to go to the Treasury to see McKenna on other business. Without any opening on my part he asked whether I knew of Lloyd George's intrigue against Bonar Law, and spoke of the War Minister with the greatest bitterness.   I agreed that Lloyd George had tried to use the Opposition to defeat the Government.   Bonar Law had summed up his view of Lloyd George's attitude by remarking that Lloyd George was trying to take second place in the Government and lead the Opposition at the same time.   It was clear that if this was indeed true an entirely new factor had entered into the calculation, and the most powerful personality in British democratic politics was actively engaged on Carson's side.   All this gave food for reflection, but the events of the next few days were indecisive, and only went to prove the uneasiness prevailing in Ministerial circles.

On Saturday, 11th November, 1916, Churchill and Birkenhead came to my house at Leatherhead.   Bonar Law was to come the following day. In this plan no idea of politics whatever was involved.   The notion underlying the meeting was simply one of social and friendly relaxation from the strain and anxiety of the period. It was typical of the time, however, that this holiday rapidly turned into a series of warm political discussions. The truth of the matter was that it proved quite impossible for anyone to put the war and the responsibilities of the war out of his mind.

An atmosphere of tension began on the Saturday evening with an argument between Birkenhead and Churchill. They started to discuss the position and the future of the Government—Minister versus ex-Minister. Never at any time, I think, have I seen these two friends quite so far apart. My criticism of Birkenhead in the past had often been that though he was naturally sound in counsel he was too easily led astray from his own opinions by his loyalties and his friendships. On this occasion he showed an absolute rigidity in holding to his convictions, from which Churchill could in no way deflect him.

Birkenhead started with a tremendous attack on Lloyd George for fraternising with the opposition in the House of Commons and for deliberately abstaining from voting for the Government on the Nigerian debate. He quoted with approval Bonar Law's saying about Lloyd George's dual and ambiguous position—with a foot in both camps. He showed himself an out-and-out supporter of Asquith, believing that the existing administration both could and should be carried on in Lloyd George's despite.

Churchill's contribution to the discussion was made from a different angle.

He delivered a general attack on the Government with a defence of the position taken up by Carson which involved a certain amount of dialectic in praise of Lloyd George. So we had the curious spectacle of Churchill attacking the Government while lauding the second most important member of it. Equally strange was it to hear Birkenhead defending the Government while attacking Lloyd George bitterly.

One thing I noticed in the course of Birkenhead's conversation which reinforced my opinion that the Government was nothing like so solidly founded as he thought. There was a Franchise Bill before the Cabinet just then, and it was causing considerable dissension among Ministers. Birkenhead resolutely declared that if votes were not given to soldiers he would resign. Now, when all things are well with a Government, its Attorney-General does not fling threatened resignations about like this on minor issues.

The argument was strenuous and lasted late.

The next morning Churchill was due to go off early to see Lloyd George at Walton Heath—about three or four miles away. There Lloyd George had before 1914 a small house close to the golf course, and he retained it throughout the war. It was a most unattractive residence, much too small for his purposes, and it always looked as if the roof or the walls were leaking in wet weather.

I got up specially early to see Churchill before he started. My reason was that I thought Churchill might convey to Lloyd George, as the result of the previous night's talk, an erroneous impression of the Conservative attitude towards him. I told him that I was not in agreement with Birkenhead's position with regard to Lloyd George and that it must not be assumed that Bonar Law was either. I wanted to keep a possible avenue of agreement open by suggesting that I was certainly impartial in relation to Lloyd George and that Bonar Law was at least a potential friend. Churchill promised to tell Lloyd George what I said and he did so.

He came back in the course of the morning from Walton Heath. Later in the day Bonar Law arrived from London. He at once took me into another room in order to discuss the situation privately. He said that the crisis he had long foreseen, and which must in its nature force a readjustment of the conduct of national affairs was now clearly at hand. It was not a case for instant action, but for a preliminary discussion in order to be sure that when the moment came the decision he would have to take as Conservative leader would be a wise one. There were two dangers, he thought—the divisions in the Cabinet, especially on the Franchise Bill due for review next week—and, secondly, the growth of Parliamentary forces hostile to the Ministry. He discussed two alternative courses which seemed to be open quite calmly—one was to look on and acquiesce in the fall of the Administration, hoping that a better one might be formed out of the crash. The second was to appeal to the country and sweep

conversational tone. In vain—Churchill swept on
unheeding.

At last Bonar Law said, " Very well, if that's
what the critics of the Government think of
it—we will have a General Election." Churchill
was absolutely staggered by this remark.   I
don't suppose he foresaw in a flash the prospect
of his own defeat in his constituency. What
he did see was the elaborate sand-castles he had
been creating with the spade of his rhetoric
swept by one long low wave of the electoral
sea into nothingness.   In fact, he was obviously
frightened.· Churchill said afterwards that Bonar
Law's proposal to hold a General Election in
the middle of a war was the most terribly im-
moral thing he had ever heard of. It showed
that some men would do anything to retain
power.   Bonar Law said that Churchill's remarks
showed him just as ready as ever to use any
kind of instrument as long as it got him back
into office.

Birkenhead left in a temper. But he could not
be converted to the belief that the crisis was at
hand and that the fate of the Ministry was hanging
in the balance.

The more one reflected on the conversations
of this week-end, the more disquieting did the
situation appear.

The events leading up to and following on the
Nigerian debate itself had alarmed Bonar Law's
friends because they one and all implicitly believed
that Bonar Law's influence at the centre of affairs
was essential for the right conduct of the war.

They saw his whole position threatened by the crisis, or, at any rate, the influence they counted on diminished.

The week-end, however, had now brought with it a new menace.

Churchill had been greatly startled by Bonar Law's threat of a dissolution—but I doubt if he was as perturbed as I was by the suggestion.

For what did it mean ?

This clearly. If the Diehard Conservatives persisted in their course and forced Bonar Law to resign, Asquith, backed by Bonar Law and these Tory Ministers, who were notoriously under Asquith's influence, would appeal to the country against the followers of Carson.

This would mean in effect that all Liberal sitting members would be returned without a contest. On the other hand, the recalcitrant Tory members would have been opposed in their constituencies by Bonar Law Conservative candidates. These candidates would undoubtedly have swept the Diehards out of existence, for they would have had not only the support of the Conservative machine, which Bonar Law controlled, but the Liberal vote as well.

It must be pointed out at once that it was this special combination of the Tory and Liberal machine which made the power of dissolution such a deadly one in the joint hands of Asquith and Bonar Law. But a War dissolution which was simply a straight fight between the two historic parties or anything resembling it would have been a very doubtful experiment on the part of a Ministry.

CHAPTER XXV

LLOYD GEORGE AT THE
WAR OFFICE

ON the following Monday, 13th November, 1916, Lloyd George telephoned and asked me to go to the War Office. I hurried off immediately and on arrival was shown into his room. His surroundings there were different from those of Bonar Law at the Colonial Office. It is true that the room was big—very big—but it was better lighted and had not the unfurnished barn-like gloom of Bonar Law's. At the Colonial Office one felt the isolation of standing on a mountain peak in the dark. By comparison the War Office room was a valley—even if it was a large valley.

It was rather strange to see men like Lloyd George and Bonar Law, who had been brought up in their youth in small rooms, in these immense places. It did not affect them in the least, for they had long trained themselves to be quite indifferent to their surroundings. None the less, such rooms never seemed suitable for doing business in. Here Lloyd George carried on his activities. He was at that time a tremendous worker—a man of limitless energy. In addition he was sought out by all distinguished visitors from abroad. Already his reputation was so far established that the stranger would not be satisfied to go back to his own country unless he could say he had met Lloyd George.

Every day after lunch he used to sit down on one chair, put his legs on another and take a short sleep. If one found him in this position the floor round him would be littered with newspapers.

Sometimes he would lunch at the War Office, and would produce all sorts of supplies out of a cupboard at the end of the room.

His secretaries were always in and out. He rarely spoke on the telephone himself—though more frequently than Bonar Law. When, however, a message was brought in to him asking him to speak, the secretaries automatically left the room in a procession. This was not due to the personal or confidential nature of what he wanted to say. For on such occasions I would ask him whether he did not wish to speak privately—and he would reply, " Oh dear, no "—and go on with his talk. The retirement of his secretaries was, therefore, a matter of routine.

The object of this meeting of ours on the Monday was to discuss the general position. By this date it appeared clear that if events took their course Bonar Law would have to resign under the pressure of Carson, and would bring the Government down with him ; that Carson wished the fall of the Government ; that Lloyd George was profoundly dissatisfied with the Government ; that Asquith would try to persuade Bonar Law

a curious habit of putting his finger on the spot.

Lloyd George continued his harangue, declaring that the machinery for conducting the war was not functioning properly. This was partly due to having to put decisions before an immense Cabinet. The attempt to get round this difficulty by means of the War Committee* had been a failure, because Asquith, as chairman of that body was as dilatory and indecisive as in the Cabinet, and because, anyhow, the War Committee had not sufficient executive authority. His remedy was a real War Council of three with practically dictatorial powers.

After that he passed to his troubles at the War Office. He had much to do, but not enough to do, and not enough power to do it. He had his finger in many pies, but not in the War Office pie. In fact, he was impotent in his own office. This was because he was bound by the Kitchener-Robertson agreement, by which far too much

* I use the term " Committee " throughout to denote any body which was a mere Committee of the Cabinet with no executive power of its own and compelled to accept Cabinet authority. Such was the body known in succession as the War Council, the Dardanelles Committee and the War Committee. And the small War Committee of three which Asquith himself proposed to set up in 1916—an ideal which just petered out because Asquith never pressed it through— would have had much the same characteristics and weaknesses as the other bigger Committee.

I call a " War Council " a body capable of acting on its own initiative and responsibility without reference to the Cabinet—except perhaps on certain well-defined subjects or occasions. Such was the " War Council " Lloyd George now wanted to set up and did set up in the end.

The distinction between the two terms " Committee " and " Council " is vital for the understanding of the narrative.

power was given to the Chief of the Imperial General Staff.* This in itself might not have mattered so much had he not been at the outset an appointment unacceptable to the soldiers and had not Sir William Robertson shown a strong determination to have his own way in everything.

He said quite frankly that he had tried to mend matters by sending Robertson out to Russia on the original Kitchener mission, ended by Kitchener's death.

His object, he declared, was not especially to get rid of Robertson as C.I.G.S. as many of his colleagues declared, though he would be glad of a temporary relief from the existing tension. He was genuinely concerned to get at the truth about the Russian armies, so that we might give them practical assistance in the form of munitions.

He said he was so keen on this matter that he himself had actually arranged to go with Kitchener on the ill-fated ship and that Sir Maurice Hankey had been going with him. He had only been stopped at the last minute by the projected Irish settlement and the Premier's personal request to negotiate this never-ending crisis.

It would be an interesting speculation as to what would have happened if Lloyd George too had gone down in the ill-fated "Hampshire."

I have heard it said many a time by members of his entourage that he was preserved by the

* The Kitchener-Robertson agreement represented the terms of distribution of authority between the Secretary of State for War and the C.I.G.S., or Military Head of the War Office, and in effect deprived the Civilian Chief of much power.

I now return to the general discussion between
Lloyd George and me as to the obstacles put in
Lloyd George's way ever since he went to the
War Office. These he explained with great
vigour, fullness, and frankness. He was, he said
in effect, so circumscribed as to be absolutely
powerless. " I am the butcher's boy who leads
in the animals to be slaughtered—when I have
delivered the men my task in the war is over."
When he was at the Munitions he could take a line
at the War Committee and criticise or suggest
alternatives to the proposals of the General Staff.
Now his mouth was shut because he was simply
the mouthpiece of the General Staff at the War
Committee, and could not attack the views which
as Secretary of State he was officially supposed to
support, even when he disagreed with them. He
was, in fact, bound by the original agreement
between Kitchener and Robertson, by which the
former promised to leave strategy to the latter.
This arrangement did not suit Lloyd George at all
—and he gave me an instance of how it worked.

Early in September, 1916, he was anxious about
the position in the Balkans, and wished to reinforce the army at Salonika, but Robertson was
of the contrary opinion at an interview which
took place in the first week of September. Lloyd
George then wrote Robertson the following letter
on 4th September, 1916 :

" I have just seen the telegram announcing
the declaration of war by Bulgaria against
Roumania. This is an additional ground for the

anxiety I expressed to you on Saturday as to the possibilities in the immediate future in the Balkans. I expressed some apprehension that Hindenburg, who has strong eastern proclivities and has always been opposed to the concentration of Germanic forces in the west, would direct his attention to the crushing of Roumania, and that we ought to be thinking out every practicable plan for giving effective support to Roumania in the event of her being heavily attacked. We cannot afford another Serbian tragedy. We were warned early in 1915 that the Germans meant in confederation with Bulgaria to wipe Serbia out. In spite of that fact, when the attack came, we had not even purchased a single mule to aid the Serbians through Salonika. The result was that when our troops landed there, owing to lack of equipment and appropriate transport, they could not go inland, and Serbia was crushed. I hope we shall not allow the same catastrophe to befall Roumania through lack of timely forethought. There are three disquieting facts in the situation.

" 1. Hindenburg's well-known Eastern inclinations.

" 2. The declaration of war by Bulgaria against Roumania. I cannot believe that Ferdinand would have taken this risk, where it is quite unnecessary, unless he had received substantial guarantees of German assistance in the attack on Roumania.

" 3. The slackening of the German attack on Verdun. Hindenburg will certainly give up this foolish attack at the earliest possible moment. The abandonment of this operation will release hundreds of heavy guns and hundreds of thousands of good troops. If, in addition, he were prepared gradually to give ground on the Somme, making us pay for it as he retires, he could transfer several more divisions from the west to the east. He could give up four or five times as much ground as we have won during the past two months without surrendering any vital positions.

" 4. I can hardly think that the equipment of the Roumanian army would enable it long to resist an attack from an Austro-Germanic-Bulgarian force, armed with hundreds of heavy guns and supplied with enormous quantities of heavy shell. The Roumanians are very scantily supplied with heavy guns, and I doubt whether their supplies of ammunition are sufficient to enable them to get through a continuous fight over several weeks. I therefore once more urge that the General Staff should carefully consider what action we could, in conjunction with France and Italy take immediately to relieve the pressure on Roumania if a formidable attack developed against her. There may be nothing in my fears, but no harm could be done by being prepared for all contingencies.

D. Lloyd George."

This letter, Lloyd George said, produced no effect.

Lloyd George complained again of the fearful waste of time at the War Committee owing to the unwieldly size of it, and also of the bickering of its members. He personally had only to make a proposal for McKenna to oppose it, quite apart from the merits of the case. Finally, it was clear that he could not hit it off with Robertson at all in their present respective positions.

Lloyd George said that someone was giving away his private information to the newspapers and that he was always reading the arguments of his War Office opponents in the Press.

In effect he accused Robertson of being in communication with the newspapers, and conveyed to me the idea that he could prove his charges.

He then told me a striking story. One day, Northcliffe suddenly appeared in the room of his private secretary, J. T. Davies, at the War Office.

Davies naturally inferred that Northcliffe had come to see Lloyd George—and jumped up, as though to go in to his Chief and pave the way. Northcliffe waved him down. He had not come to see the War Secretary—but he had come to say something which could be transmitted to him. " You can tell him that I hear he has been interfering with strategy, and that if he goes on I will break him."

It is, indeed, most important in view of what is to follow, to keep clearly in mind the fact that Northcliffe was not a supporter of Lloyd George. Northcliffe, indeed, ardently desired the downfall of Asquith—but for another set of reasons he was just as hostile to Lloyd George. He was at this time the soldiers' man.

For instance, he attended a lunch at which he so conducted himself that everyone thought his speech a declaration in favour of the conduct of the War Government being handed over to the soldiers. I formed the same impression myself from a conversation I had with Northcliffe at this time. Certainly he appeared to be advocating a kind of Haig-Robertson dictatorship as a substitute for Parliamentary Government. All this, of course, was in direct antagonism to the way Lloyd George wanted to move. He thought the soldiers at home had too much power. Northcliffe thought they had too little.

Such, then, was the burden of Lloyd George's complaint.

I came away from the interview in a different frame of mind from that in which I entered on it. When I went my sole idea was that an alliance with Lloyd George might be useful in helping to solve the internal difficulties in the Conservative ranks and to place the whole political situation on a more satisfactory footing. My mood, therefore, was critical, cautious and even cynical.

I summarised in my own mind Lloyd George's position and contention as revealed in this long conversation. Briefly it was as follows :

(1) The machinery for conducting the War was fundamentally unsound.

(2) The troubles between Lloyd George and

Robertson at the War Office were disturbing and disorganising to the whole war-making system.

Under the first set of complaints came a double sub-heading : (*a*) We must have a small War Council—instead of a Committee, large or small ; (*b*) Lloyd George was sure that he could run the war and that Asquith could not.

Under the second set of complaints came : (*a*) The refusal of the military to take any interest in Lloyd George's strategic advice; (*b*) The Kitchener-Robertson agreement by which Robertson had real control of the War Office machine, to the exclusion of Lloyd George, the Minister.

I decided to abolish from my mind any issue concerning the refusal of the military to listen to Lloyd George's advice on strategic subjects. Further, I was not greatly moved by his complaint against General Robertson.

Lloyd George was on rather weak ground. He had vowed he would never go to the War Office while this agreement subsisted, but he had done this very thing. It was so easy for any one not sympathetic to him to reply to his grievance : " Well, you walked into your present position with open eyes." On the other hand, the fact that the War Secretary had made a mistake did not in any way alter the fact that the agreement was a bad one and ought to be done away with. Further, his statement threw a vivid light from quite a new angle on the situation in the Conservative camp and in politics as a whole.

The first alarm had been caused over the Nigerian debate by the risk that Bonar Law's essential influence on the conduct of the war might be impaired. Then fears of a fatal dissolution following Bonar Law's forced resignation and resulting in the permanent dictatorship of Asquith had become apparent. To these elements of natural danger was now added the conviction that it was imperative to create a small War Council free from the " dead hand " of Asquith's inertia.

All these considerations seemed to dovetail into one another—and to demand that somehow the forces and individuals working for the more efficient conduct of the war ought to unite in order to escape destruction and win success.

The next question which arose was this : What course of action was the best to pursue ?

The first practical step was to lay the question of an alliance before Bonar Law—but before doing this I determined to consult Sir Reginald Brade, Permanent Under Secretary of State for War, as to the view he took of the relations between the War Minister and the Chief of the Imperial General Staff.

I saw Brade that night. He is the essence of diplomacy, and possesses an extraordinary sound judgment of men and things; and these judgments are in no way subject to impulse. He played a far greater part in the conduct of the war than he will ever get credit for. But his post was officially subordinate and subject to the inevitable restrictions of permanent officialdom, and the very success with which he performed his duties nailed him more tightly to his chair in Whitehall; he could not be promoted because he could not be spared.

My special reasons for consulting him were that Bonar Law valued his opinion, and that he was removed from the political arena. He was impartial, and in addition could give counsel on matters relating to the War Office on account of a wide experience directed by a keen intellect. I knew well that if Sir Reginald Brade took the view that Lloyd George ought to be supported against Robertson it would have an effect on Bonar Law. At this interview Brade defined his position. He was not concerned with the personal aspect or individual equation involved in the dispute. But he thought that on principle the Secretary of State for War should be a superior authority to the Chief of the Imperial General Staff or to anyone else in the War Office. *

Further confirmed in my opinion that Lloyd George, Bonar Law, and Carson must at all hazards be brought together, I determined to set about the task without delay.

---

* The controversy regarding the powers and authority of the C.I.G.S., or Military Head of the War Office, although assuming considerable proportions at this time, is subsequently relegated to the background, and ultimately disappears from view.

CHAPTER XXVI

NEGOTIATIONS OPENED

IN this and succeeding chapters I am, for convenience, dealing with the narrative day by day.

Tuesday, November 14, 1916.

The next morning after I had seen Lloyd George I was ill in bed. Bonar Law, as was his custom on such occasions, came round to see me at the Hyde Park Hotel. I wanted, in a sense, to open the Lloyd George question to him then—but I was deterred by a variety of considerations. In the first place, I did not feel fit enough for what I knew was a vital conversation. Next, he had come round to visit an invalid friend, and it seemed rather a shame to take advantage of his kindness to bid him " stand and deliver " politically—for I knew he would dislike the topic.

Further, Bonar Law himself was full of the sale of enemy property in Nigeria, which was coming off that day. He was anxious that no foreigners should buy. One particular foreign firm was mentioned as a buyer. At his suggestion I communicated with Slaughter and May, solicitors to the foreign firm, and saw Burrows, of the Colonial

Office, who was in charge of the Nigerian Department. I then asked Bell, of the Colonial Bank, to go to the sale, with instructions to buy any properties that appeared to be going to foreigners, but not to compete with the British West Africa Trust.

That night Bonar Law came again and Lord Rothermere also. Again the occasion did not seem opportune, and though all three of us had a long talk on the war we did not touch on politics. Just as they got up to go I said to Bonar Law : " I saw Lloyd George yesterday." " Oh," he remarked in a curious way he had—expressing at once interest and disapproval in the intonation —but he stopped behind. I knew the moment had come and that much depended on the way I put Lloyd George's case. I was going to make myself the advocate for Lloyd George, and I knew I was not going to have an easy task, owing to the strong prejudice Bonar Law then entertained against the War Secretary.

The difference did not spring from any mutual incompatibility of temperament that makes it impossible for two men to work together even when their aims are the same. On the contrary, previous to the formation of the Coalition Government Bonar Law was probably in closer accord with Lloyd George than with any other member of the Liberal Ministry.

The root cause of the trouble was that Bonar Law had formed the opinion that in matters of office and power Lloyd George was a self-seeker

and a man who considered no interests except
his own.

He therefore regarded any proposal put forward by Lloyd George for a better ministerial
instrument for waging war as certain to contain
something to give its author a step upwards in
the first place—whether it had any other advantages or not.

He based this view on a whole series of incidents. First of all, when the Government was
formed Lloyd George had seized on munitions
for himself and joined in the intrigue which
relegated Bonar Law to the Colonial Office.
Then he had insisted on retaining the Deputy
Leadership of the House of Commons as
well.

Bonar Law was convinced of Lloyd George's
ability to manage the War Office, but he was still
of the opinion that Lloyd George was out for
his own honour and glory, and that he was not a
person to be trusted when national and personal
interests happened to clash. An unfortunate
incident in connection with the appointment of
a new Judge Advocate-General, which, since it
is of no public importance and its relation might
give pain to individuals, I will not quote, further
confirmed this adverse conviction.

A statement of mine that I believed Lloyd
George's plan included a small War Council
with real executive authority only stirred him to
attack Lloyd George afresh. He said he knew
all about these War Committees. Had not
Lloyd George treated him badly over the pro-

jected War Committee? In this he was really unjust to Lloyd George, as I proceeded to point out to him.

When the plan for a War Committee was brought forward by Asquith, the original idea was that the Prime Minister should be chairman and the only other two members should be Bonar Law and Lloyd George—and Lloyd George had said he would not serve unless Bonar Law did.

Now Asquith had a perfectly ridiculous idea of the importance of Lord Curzon in the eyes of the country and of the Conservative Party. When he was told that Curzon objected to Bonar Law going to the War Committee and might even resign if this happened, he was disturbed. One day Asquith, Lloyd George, and Bonar Law were all sitting together on the Treasury Bench, when Asquith, by some strange lapse of memory, spoke to Lloyd George as though forgetting Bonar Law's presence. He suddenly observed : " I've thought how to get out of that difficulty over Bonar Law and Curzon and the War Committee. Balfour shall be the third member. He's a Conservative and Curzon cannot possibly object to him. I cannot find room for Bonar Law as well, or else I should have to take Crewe in too." It did not seem to occur to Asquith that the selection of Balfour over Bonar Law's head would have been another heavy blow to Bonar Law's leadership of his party.

Lloyd George said nothing, but Bonar Law was very angry with him because he did not reply according to arrangement : " Then I won't

serve on the War Committee either." He seemed
to have no blame to spare for Asquith at all.
Yet such an attitude was transparently unfair.
Surely it was far worse for the Prime Minister
to think out a scheme to keep him off the War
Committee, and perhaps do him a mortal damage,
than for Lloyd George simply to acquiesce in
silence.

Bonar Law's attitude towards office in war-
time may be explained once and for all.   He
had no special belief in his own abilities as a
war administrator—rather the reverse.   He did
not think he could save his country and that
no other man could.   If this was a weakness in
his political character, then we must admit the
defect.   Nor did he care a scrap about personal
prestige and self-aggrandisement.   If the nation
or the party had said to him plainly : " We think
another man would do your work better than you
can," he would, I believe, have laid down office
with a huge sigh of relief.   But just as he never
sought responsibility, neither did he shirk it.   The
responsibility of leading the Tory Party had been
given to him and he had to take decisions as
to the way in which this tremendous influence
was to be used.   Now he could not manage and
control the party unless a certain amount of outward respect—in the shape of high office—was
shown him by the head of the Government.
He could not hold his post or control the machine
if his subordinates in the party hierarchy were
promoted over his head by Asquith.   That was all
he thought about, whether he was passed over

for the Chancellorship, or the Deputy Leadership, or the War Committee.

Bonar Law's position was indeed one of great weakness. He was little more than the titular leader of the Conservatives in the Cabinet. He had failed over and over again, as in the Dardanelles issue or on the Turkish crisis, to carry his Conservative colleagues with him. And this fact was weakening the cohesion of the Conservative Party in the Commons and the constituencies.

Curzon was opposing him on many issues and would say openly that no Conservative leadership now existed and that all the Tory Ministers were equal in the sight of Asquith. The leadership had been abolished by the mere fact of entry into the Coalition—and when this partnership was dissolved a choice of a new leader would be open to the party. He took this line quite frankly. He did not approve of Bonar Law as leader, and undoubtedly hoped to be chosen as leader of the party when Lansdowne disappeared.

This explains very adequately why Bonar Law preserved so jealously the rights and dignities of his post. He believed implicitly that weakness in his own titular position was in reality weakness in the party authority, discipline and cohesion.

We talked on and on that night at the Hyde Park Hotel, and I must say I found Bonar Law desperately " sticky." I retailed to him all Lloyd George's difficulties as I had been told them, and I also gave, for what it was worth, the personal impression I had formed of Lloyd George's sincerity in this dispute.

As the discussion proceeded Bonar Law made this position pretty clear. It could be summarised in the following way :

Lloyd George was dissatisfied with the way the war was being conducted. " Well, I'm dissatisfied too—so is the public—in fact, the Government is very unpopular. I know all that without being told." But, he continued, that was not the same thing as supplying a remedy—least of all did it appear that to satisfy Lloyd George's aspirations was to supply that remedy. You might abolish a personal grievance and the war might be conducted as badly as ever.

Furthermore, he desired to retain Asquith's personality as part of the machinery of Government. Bonar Law believed from the point of view of the conduct of the war that the control of the political machine was as essential as the preparation of big armies. He had said to Carson a day or two before our conversation that in the present House of Commons no one could control that machine as well as Asquith. Carson had acknowledged the strength of Asquith's position in the House.

Bonar Law thought there was no reason why, if Asquith would alter his conduct in certain particulars and eliminate some of the evils of the present regime, such as dilatoriness, he should not be able to carry on successfully.

Bonar Law then pointed out the gravity of the issue which was being put before him. In his case there was no opening for personal resignation, no via media in his attitude towards the Government. For, as the leader of the Conservatives, his line must be decisive to the fate of the Ministry. He must either sustain it or he must go right on and destroy it.

To sum up, Bonar Law distrusted Lloyd George and his ambitions. He suspected that Lloyd George's plan of a new executive War Council was not a considered scheme for reorganising the machinery of making war. He suggested it was a scheme for side-stepping Sir William Robertson's authority under the Kitchener-Robertson agreement. In other words, whenever the War Secretary and the C.I.G.S. had a difference about strategy, Lloyd George would carry the matter to his own court of appeal, the War Council, and overrule Robertson there.* Finally, the scheme was to exalt Lloyd George at Asquith's expense. This he was quite clearly not prepared to do—at least not without a great deal more thought and argument.

We were very late going to bed that night.

In the meantime Lloyd George had gone to France—but I had an arrangement with him by which I was to send him a telegram if I thought he ought to come back.

Wednesday, November 15, 1916.

On Wednesday I went to the War Office and settled with Davies (his secretary) to have a wire

* The division of authority at the War Office as a cause of crisis, ran for a time concurrently with the movement for a War Council, and was eventually submerged in the bigger issue.

sent, as we had previously agreed, calling Lloyd George home. A reply came saying he would be back on Friday.

Thursday, November 16, 1916.

A colleague of mine went to see Carson in order to discover how far Carson was acting with Lloyd George. He told me that he and Carson, who was hardening against Bonar Law, had discussed the certainty of an open and immediate rupture. Carson attacked the Prime Minister with great vigour, but he maintained that Bonar Law must take his share of the blame for the existing state of national affairs, because he held up Asquith's scheme, and without him the Prime Minister was helpless to resist the advocates of a vigorous war.

After this I went to Bonar Law in the afternoon. I told him Carson's sentiments, and informed him that Lloyd George was willing to dine with him on his return on Friday night. He replied that he had Sir Henry Wilson dining with him, and a suggestion that he should put off Wilson was negatived.

He wanted to hear Wilson talk about the war. "Lloyd George can come and listen to Wilson too, if he likes. I should say it would do him good."

I insisted that Lloyd George was practically coming back at Bonar Law's request. The greatest concession I could get was that Lloyd George could come if Wilson did not object; in fact,

CHURCHILL UP AND CHURCHILL DOWN

THE THREE C'S

Bonar Law actually telephoned to ask if Wilson had any objection, and the invitation was only sent after this doubt had been removed.

Now, I particularly did not want Wilson present at the first renewal of relations between Bonar Law and Lloyd George. If Wilson detested Asquith most of all the politicians, Lloyd George was easily next in the list of the men he hated. (Wilson and Lloyd George were reconciled in 1917, but the old difference broke out again later).

The contretemps was so unpleasant and the whole atmosphere so unfavourable for a discussion of this grave character that I sent a message through Davies to Lloyd George, asking him to telephone me when he arrived. I then advised Lloyd George to decline the invitation—which he did—returning straight home to Walton Heath, and joining me next morning at the Hyde Park Hotel.

Saturday, November 18, 1916.

Lloyd George arrived at my rooms in the Hyde Park Hotel to breakfast at nine a.m. He was in a state of profound pessimism; thought Bonar Law would prove immovable and was too much under Asquith's influence to be likely to consent to his own proposals. If Bonar Law would do nothing, he himself would resign and join Carson in opposition. The grounds of resignation would be the indecision of the Cabinet, his absolute impotence at the War Office and in the War Committee, and the refusal of his advice on Balkan affairs. We talked till noon. I pointed

out that if he resigned now, Asquith would try
to arrange with Bonar Law for an immediate
dissolution. He decided to withhold his resignation till Monday, while I made another attempt to
straighten things out. Lloyd George left at noon.
I went at once to Bonar Law, lunched with him,
and stayed till four p.m. We had the whole
matter out. I stated Lloyd George's objections
to the existing regime, and outlined Lloyd
George's proposals—in effect, that there should
be a War Council of three, Lloyd George (chairman), Bonar Law, and Carson. The Prime
Minister's relation to the Council was left as a
point to be settled in detail afterwards. My
two main contentions were that Lloyd George
was honest and sincere of purpose, and that the
state of inefficiency in the Government was
becoming intolerable and leading us towards the
precipice. Bonar Law more or less admitted the
truth of the last contention at once, but was
not certain that Lloyd George would do any
better; further, he doubted if Carson would
agree to join, and asked whether Carson (if
willing to join) could be got into the War
Council over the heads of the Unionist Cabinet
Ministers. On this point he foresaw the probability
of great trouble. He agreed, however, to meet
Lloyd George on Monday evening and discuss
the proposals with him, and indicated that he
would not mention the matter to the Prime
Minister, who might put some impediment in the
way of the conference.

Sunday, November 19, 1916.

I went over and saw Lloyd George at Walton Heath and informed him of the arrangements for the meeting. He went over much of the old ground again, but he remained pessimistic as to the prospects of coming to an agreement with Bonar Law.

None the less, the campaign had not opened so badly. Bonar Law was in possession of the outlines of Lloyd George's proposals, and was prepared to meet him in conference. I at once invited Carson to come to this conference, so that the first step to creating a triumvirate which would save the Tory Party from an open rupture and infuse a new vigour into the war policy of the Government had been taken. Future developments lay in the lap of the gods.

CHAPTER XXVII

THE MEETINGS OF THE TRIUMVIRATE

Monday, November 20.

I SAW Bonar Law early. To my surprise he told me that he had mentioned the Lloyd George proposals for a War Council to the Prime Minister—although he had said he would not do so. I complained that what Lloyd George had said to me had been told in confidence, but with the knowledge that I would disclose it to Bonar Law, and that he had done wrongly in divulging it to Asquith.

Bonar Law replied : " That is all very well, but I am not going to be drawn into anything like an intrigue against Asquith. I have had experience of what flows from this sort of conversation with Lloyd George. Lloyd George himself would do far better to go quite openly to the Prime Minister and tell him what he has told us." This sort of argument was not convincing, because if Lloyd George had gone alone to Asquith, his visit would have had no effect whatever. But if he could go with Bonar Law's support and authority, that would be a very different matter.

Bonar Law then gave an account of the conversation between Asquith and himself.

The Prime Minister had said that he thought that the whole proposal was simply a demand of Lloyd George's for more power, and that he had never really been loyal to the Cabinet. He felt doubtful whether even if Lloyd George got his War Council he would remain satisfied. These views were to some extent shared by Bonar Law. As to Carson's inclusion, the Prime Minister did not seem much exercised, but he remarked that he and some of his friends, including Conservative Ministers, had not formed a very high opinion of Carson's constructive abilities while he was in the Government. There was a good deal of rather vague dialectic about the discussion, and, as was frequent with Asquith, it led to no definite conclusion or result.

However, something did result, because Bonar Law had told the Prime Minister about Lloyd George's complaints of McKenna's persistent opposition, and at the War Committee that day McKenna was very pleasant to Lloyd George. Bonar Law also was willing to encourage Lloyd George, and promised to consider, *de novo*, his proposal to send Sir William Robertson to Petrograd.

He said to me : " You can go and tell Lloyd George that I am prepared to reconsider my position with regard to Robertson and the mission to Russia." (In other words, the removal of Robertson from the War Office.) In fact, he was ready to consider the whole position at the War Office

and to support a change there. He said he must
see Robertson personally first and explain his
new view to him. He would have no difficulty,
because it was now clear to him that Lloyd George
and Robertson could not work together under
the existing arrangement. He hoped that the
grant of supreme authority to Lloyd George
in his own office would be a sufficient solace,
but he said : " Of course, I see his scheme really
goes further than eliminating Robertson."

Monday, November 20.

This night the first meeting took place between
Lloyd George, Bonar Law, and Carson at my rooms
at the Hyde Park Hotel. The atmosphere seemed
unfavourable, not to say strained. Lloyd George
opened well enough with a repetition of his personal assurance to Bonar Law that he had taken no
part against him in the Nigerian debate, and Carson
confirmed this. But Bonar Law received his
assurances coldly. Lloyd George then stated his
main case with great skill and tact, nor did he go
too far in his demands. He only asked for his
War Council, and said the Prime Minister would
lead the Commons—a task he was pre-eminently
fitted for. Bonar Law had all along been of
opinion that Carson would never join an Asquith
Ministry again, but Carson seemed quite disposed
to come into the projected arrangement—so that
one difficulty vanished. Indeed, it may be said
that things would have been much worse but for
Carson's presence. The party broke up without a
decision having been reached. Carson and

Lloyd George went off together, and Bonar Law remained behind with me. He was still hostile to Lloyd George; he did not believe Lloyd George's Nigerian assurances, which he said Carson was bound to confirm, whether true or not, for he could not know what was in Lloyd George's mind. Bonar Law's main judgment was that Lloyd George's plans boiled down to one simple proposal—to put Asquith out and to put himself in. I made another strong effort to convince him; repeated everything Sir Reginald Brade had said about the principle which should govern the management of the War Office—namely, that the Secretary of State for War should be a superior authority to the Chief of the Imperial General Staff. This impressed him, and about this period he had an interview with Sir Reginald Brade, who said to him what he had told me.

Tuesday, November 21.

This day the negotiations went on with ups and downs. Carson had a long talk with Bonar Law in the latter's room at the House of Commons. This, although it improved their personal relations was not altogether to the good, because Bonar Law got the impression that Carson was not really working intimately with Lloyd George. But if Carson's support of Lloyd George should prove to be illusory, then the position of the War Minister would be greatly weakened. Yet the association was never really a matter for doubt. Following on this I arranged another meeting of

Lloyd George, Bonar Law, and Carson; again
there was a vigorous argument and some progress,
but no really satisfactory result, and—what was
more important—no really good atmosphere.
The trouble throughout was less a difference of
principle than the view which men took of each
other's mentality. The prospect was depressing
and the outlook was black.

There followed on this a meeting at my rooms
at the Hyde Park Hotel without Carson, and
this went the worse for his absence.

The whole question of the Prime Minister's
position under the new arrangement came up in
an acute form. Lloyd George said quite frankly
that Asquith must not be a member of the projected War Council. " For," he went on, " if
he is a member he must, in his official capacity,
dominate it—and if he dominates it, he will destroy
its whole utility—and the conduct of the war will
have gained nothing in efficiency." Bonar Law
was taken aback by this demand. He at once said
that my original version of Lloyd George's
proposals did not include this clause at all. This
was true, and the explanation was simple. I had
not thought it necessary to tell of this demand to
Bonar Law. I was not sure that Lloyd George
would insist upon this condition. I felt it
might make an insurmountable obstacle at the
outset of the negotiations. I wished to take the
easier obstacle in the first place. The bigger
jumps could be attempted later on.

I had also advised Lloyd George to try to settle
all the other points with Bonar Law first and come

to this one last, because it was the most difficult
of the lot. Lloyd George, however, at this point
threw my advice over and without any previous
notice to me boldly produced the whole of his
scheme—holding back nothing. And as it
turned out, he was wise to do so.

But Bonar Law did not hesitate, after Lloyd
George had departed, to criticise me severely.
The lot of the negotiator is never quite happy.

During the week further meetings took place,
and on Thursday there was a protracted and fruitful discussion.

On Friday, Sir Robert Donald, then editor of
the " Daily Chronicle," called to see Bonar Law.
Their relations were always friendly, and Donald's
conversation, unknown to himself, had considerable influence on the position. Donald made it
clear that Lloyd George was by no means alone
in the dissatisfaction which he expressed. The
movement in Liberal circles is well described by
Donald's own account of the growth of the discontent. He writes :

On November 24 I saw Mr. Bonar Law, and
told him that I contemplated having a critical
article on the direction of the war. I had heard
from many quarters that the War Committee
was most unbusinesslike, had become altogether
unwieldy, and was most dilatory in arriving at
decisions. Mr. Bonar Law suggested that I
ought to see Mr. Asquith before publishing an
article. I told him that I was not in the habit
of going to the Prime Minister, and pointed

out that it would be rather a disadvantage, particularly if I contemplated taking up a critical, although not unfriendly, attitude. Mr. Bonar Law still suggested that I might see the Prime Minister on Monday.

. . . . . .

I decided not to see the Prime Minister, as I felt I would not have a free hand. We published our article on the 29th—at, as it happened, a most critical time, when discussions were proceeding and negotiations beginning with Mr. Asquith. The article had precisely the opposite effect intended. It was intended to be helpful to the Government, but it was most useful to Mr. Lloyd George in pushing his scheme for the reform of the War Committee.

. . . . . .

I continue the narrative in diary form.

Saturday, November 25, 1916.

On this day, as agreed, Bonar Law, Lloyd George, Carson, and I met at one o'clock at Pembroke Lodge, Bonar Law's house. Carson spoke out very strongly on the impossibility of continuing the existing system—on the delays, the reversals of policy, and the bickering on the War Council, and of the presence of two kings of Brentford at the War Office—the Minister and the Chief of the Imperial General Staff locked in perpetual conflict.

As we were going upstairs immediately after lunch, Carson held me back, saying, " What do you think of all this ? " The question surprised me. I had taken it for granted, as indicated all along, that Carson was entirely in Lloyd George's confidence throughout. But the query suggested that he shared some of Bonar Law's doubts about Lloyd George. I replied that I was perfectly satisfied with the steps proposed and the situation arrived at, and then waited for him to explain himself. However, he made no further remark—possibly he was indicating an intention to resume his old relations with Bonar Law, and suggesting that he was not acting simply as Lloyd George's " man."

Before the meeting on Saturday morning I had drafted out a memorandum for the approval of the Triumvirate. Bonar Law made some corrections on my draft and after that it was adopted without alteration. It took the form of an announcement to be signed and published by Asquith.

It read as follows :

The War Council has, in my opinion, rendered devoted and invaluable service, but experience has convinced me that there are disadvantages in the present system which render a change necessary.

Some body doing the work of the War Council should meet every day. It is impossible that the War Council can do this while its members have at the same time to fulfil the exacting duties of their Departments. At the War Council, also, we have felt it necessary to have the advantage regularly of the presence of the

Chief of the Imperial General Staff and the
First Sea Lord. Their time is in this way taken
up sometimes unnecessarily when every moment
is required for other work. I have decided,
therefore, to create what I regard as a civilian
General Staff. This staff will consist of myself
as President and of three other members of
the Cabinet who have no portfolio and who
will devote their whole time to the consideration day by day of the problems which arise in
connection with the prosecution of the war.

The three members who have undertaken to
fulfil these duties are :

(Here was blank space for inserting names.)

and I have invited Mr. Lloyd George, and he
has consented to act as chairman and to preside
at any meeting which, owing to the pressure
of other duties, I find it impossible to attend.

I propose that the body should have executive
authority subject to this—that it shall rest with
me to refer any questions to the decision of the
Cabinet which I think should be brought before
them.

It will be seen that the names of the other members of the War Council except Lloyd George
were left blank, as in the text, but it was understood by all of us that Bonar Law's and Carson's
names were to be added if the Prime Minister
made no objection. Bonar Law and Carson
were indifferent, and willing to make way for other

men, but both agreed that Lloyd George was essential. The acceptance of this document marks a decisive stage in the negotiations, and also the primal definite, though not intentional, step forward to the fall of the first Coalition Government. The three men concerned had now reached an agreement which could be written down in ink. Bonar Law's view of the position of the Prime Minister in the face of this memorandum was so accurate as to be almost prophetic. If the Prime Minister, he said, accepted the scheme voluntarily, plus his own additions, all would be well with him, but if he allowed himself to be forced into acceptance he might well find his position as head of the Ministry untenable.

Lloyd George explained his attitude towards Asquith at some length and with considerable vehemence. He personally was perfectly prepared to work with Asquith; the trouble was that Asquith would not work with him. This, he said, was due mainly to the malign influence of McKenna, who, by suggesting to Asquith whenever a difference of opinion cropped up that Lloyd George was insincere or ambitious, poisoned their mutual relations. These innuendoes had had their effect on Asquith, and made business under existing conditions impossible. The conclave broke up, Bonar Law going to the Prime Minister to present the Memorandum, Lloyd George and Carson to the War Office to await his return, and myself home to Leatherhead.

At this point in the narrative it will be well to point out the salient features in the memorandum and also to explain the attitude of the various men towards it. The features of the memorandum were three :

1. The small War Council, with complete authority subject to the Prime Minister.
2. The personnel of that Council.
3. The relations of the War Council with the Prime Minister.

On the first two points there may be said to have been absolute unanimity—for there would have been no quarrel about personnel in any case. On the third point there were, in fact, degrees of divergence. Carson frankly wanted Asquith out of the Government, but he would take a lesser degree of elimination if nothing better could be managed. Lloyd George took a middle view— he did not want the Prime Minister to interfere with the war, but he was not bent on turning him out if it could be avoided. Bonar Law wanted to retain the Prime Minister if he would consent to a sufficient curtailment of his authority, but he wished to curtail it less than Lloyd George did, for, as I have already stated, Lloyd George wished to eliminate Asquith from the War Council altogether. All these facts will emerge quite clearly in the course of this history, but it will make the story clearer if they are stated here. The next move now lay with Asquith. What would he say or do ?

CHAPTER XXVIII

BONAR LAW AND ASQUITH

Saturday, November 25, 1916—(*continued*).

BETWEEN seven and eight that evening Bonar Law called me up on the telephone and gave me a guarded account of his conversation with the Prime Minister. The latter had listened to what he had to say and taken a copy of the Memorandum. In the main the Prime Minister went over the same arguments he had used before with Bonar Law. He would agree to the terms suggested if they represented Lloyd Geoge's final aims and were not merely an instalment of further demands for power. Personally, he did not believe that this was a final demand. He went on to raise the former objections to Carson's appointment to the War Council—the poor impression he had created in office and the difficulty of promoting him over the heads of other Conservatives in this summary fashion. Finally, he promised to give a definite answer on Monday. Bonar Law made it clear that, personally, he did not care a rap whether he was included in the new War Council or not, and went back to the War Office to meet Lloyd George and Carson.

It appeared that Bonar Law had been to some

extent influenced by Asquith's contentions, and as the latter's objections to both Lloyd George and Carson were largely personal, he found a difficulty in stating them in exact terms. Moved by these considerations, he did not press the matter then to any definite conclusion, but reiterated his own indifference to the new office and declared that nothing could be done until the Prime Minister's reply on Monday. This was agreed to.

Bonar Law's attitude, both in itself and its reaction upon that of others, was a very potent factor in these proceedings, and, indeed, in the whole conduct of the Coalition Government. Disinterested beyond his contemporaries and colleagues to an almost abnormal degree, he was capable of occasional flashes of personal ambition, which blazed out in the face of critical opposition from supporters or colleagues or of abuse in the public Press. This was curious in a man who was as a rule so impervious to abuse. None the less, although he cared nothing for what was said of him, such opposition roused him to a determination to assert his power and to great vigour of action for the moment. Then the fire died away, and he resumed an attitude of passive philosophy beyond and outside that of passion and strife. He was not really bored with life, but the original affectation that he was so had by long habit almost superseded the reality. He never told a lie in a great thing, and very seldom in a small one; in trifles he was selfish, though kind-hearted and capable of singular devotion to family

Memorandum written by Lord Beaverbrook on November 25, 1916, for the approval of the Triumvirate, showing alterations in Bonar Law's handwriting, as follows:

Page 1.—"their existing duties" into "the exacting duties." Deletion of "of the time."
Page 2.—"Chairman of these" into "Chairman of the body."

I The War Council has in my opinion rendered devoted & invaluable service but experience has convinced me that there are disadvantages in the present system which cannot always be remedy. The War Council ought to meet every day. It is impossible that the War Council can do this while its members have at the same time to perform their everyday duties of their department. At the War Council also we have felt it necessary to have the advantage especially of the first Sea Lord of the C.I.G.S. & in this way take their time in immaterial matters — yet sometimes unnecessary when every moment of their time is required for other work

2 I have decided therefore to create what I regard as a Civilian General Staff. This Staff will consist of myself as President & of three members of the Cabinet who will have no portfolios & who will devote their whole time to the consideration, day by day of the problems which arise in connection with the prosecution of the war. The three members who have undertaken to fulfil these duties are —

To these I have invited Mr Lloyd George & he has consented to act as Chairman of them.

and friends. In large matters he was of an extraordinary generosity, and would sacrifice the whole
comfort of his life for a friend or a cause.

But his distinguishing mark was undoubtedly
his freedom from self-interest. The idea of
whether he stood to gain or lose from a particular
decision in politics never entered his head. He
was therefore in this sense a great patriot, but he
fell short of greatness in that he did not possess
that supreme passion of patriotism which enables
a man to be ruthless for the public good.

His very capacity for loyalty and friendship
worked in this direction—for as a friend there was
no one like him. There are certain qualities in
friendship which every man knows, but no man
can define. In Bonar Law one realised them all to
a supreme degree.

This character the Prime Minister (Asquith)
understood thoroughly, and was by no means
inapt in playing on its various elements. Since
the formation of the Coalition Government, no
one had been a more loyal member of the Cabinet
in the face of much provocation, and the appeal
to loyalty was to the Prime Minister's hand. At
the same time, a kind of scepticism about strong
emotions and distrust of ardent passions or sharp
measures, mixed with a contempt for personal
ambition, made him by instinct, if not by reason,
regard the rise of Lloyd George to supreme power
as a dangerous portent in politics—and this side,
too, was open to the Prime Minister's attack.
The week-end passed, then, in a state of some
uncertainty.

Sunday, November 26, 1916.

I went over at night to see Lloyd George at Walton Heath. He was far from contented with the prospect of Monday's meeting. He felt sure that McKenna and his colleagues would be at the Prime Minister during the interval to refuse him all accommodation. He was strengthened in his pessimistic view of the situation by the fact that Asquith had belittled George's influence with the Liberal party and the Nation in talking to Bonar Law the day before. Lloyd George on the contrary in prophesying a rupture dwelt on his influence with the rank and file of the Liberals at Westminster and enlarged on the weight he would carry in the constituencies if Asquith persuaded Bonar Law to join in an appeal to the country.

Monday morning, November 27, 1916.

Early on Monday morning Bonar Law called me up from London on the telephone. " I am in a difficulty; come up at once," was the gist of his remarks. I noticed, however, a difference in the tone; for the first time he seemed to be taking a keen interest in the proposals for the reconstruction of the Government.

The Prime Minister's answer, which was in the form of a letter, was shown by him to Bonar Law in advance. Its most striking feature was some very disagreeable comments on Carson as a prospective member of the War Council. Carson, it was here written, had been vacillating in the Cabinet, and far from capable in general affairs.

He was perpetually striving after strength until this constituted a weakness.

Bonar Law pointed out that since this letter was an answer to the Memorandum he had submitted on behalf of Lloyd George and Carson as well as himself, it must be shown to them. Asquith, of course, could not object to this. Bonar Law then went on to say that it would be very unwise—in view of Carson's probable return to the Government—that he should read these reflections on his capacity. He made no objection to the references to Lloyd George. He thought, on the whole, it was better that Lloyd George should understand the light in which the Prime Minister viewed his activities. The Prime Minister then took out the peccant page and wrote in another of an innocuous character about Carson, and consented to the proposed disclosure to Lloyd George and Carson. Copies of the letter were delivered to both Lloyd George and Carson.

The letter from Mr. Asquith to Bonar Law is as follows :

The Wharf, Sutton Courtney,

Berks.

November 26, 1916.

My dear Bonar Law,

What follows is intended for your eyes alone.

I fully realise the frankness and loyalty with which you have put forward the proposal embodied in your paper note. But under present conditions, and in the form in which it is presented, I do not see my way to adopt it.

I take a less disparaging view than you do of the War Committee.* There is undoubtedly too much talk and consequent waste of time, but the Committee has done and is doing very valuable work; and is thrashing out difficult problems. I am quite open to suggestions for its improvement, whether in composition or in procedure. I may say, however, that I do not see how any body of the kind can be really workable unless the heads of the War Office and Admiralty are members of it. Our recent practice of sitting a good deal without the experts is a change for the better, and might perhaps be further developed.

But the essence of your scheme is that the War Committee should disappear, and its place be taken by a body of four—myself, yourself, Carson, and Lloyd George.

As regards Carson, for whom, as you know, I have the greatest personal regard, I do not see how it would be possible, in order to secure his services, to pass over Balfour, or Curzon, or McKenna, all of whom have the advantage of intimate knowledge of the secret history of the last twelve months. That he should be admitted over their heads at this stage to the inner circle of the Government is a step which, I believe,

---

* The War Committee was the large body of whose dilatoriness Lloyd George had complained in his talk with me at the War Office (Chapter VIII). The military and naval experts also attended it. It was simply a Committee of the Cabinet and had no power except to report to the Cabinet for or against a course. It must not be confused with the War Committee of Three (Chapter VIII) proposed by Asquith earlier in the year. This scheme of Asquith's never came to fruition at all.

would be deeply resented, not only by them and by my political friends, but by almost all your Unionist colleagues. It would be universally believed to be the price paid for shutting the mouth of our most formidable parliamentary critic—a manifest sign of weakness and cowardice

As to Lloyd George, you know as well as I do both his qualities and his defects. He has many qualities that would fit him for the first place, but he lacks the one thing needful—he does not inspire trust. . . . Here, again, there is one construction, and one only, that could be put on the new arrangement—that it has been engineered by him with the purpose, not perhaps at the moment, but as soon as a fitting pretext could be found, of his displacing me.

In short, the plan could not, in my opinion, be carried out without fatally impairing the confidence of loyal and valued colleagues, and undermining my own authority.

I have spoken to you with the same frankness that you use to me, and which I am glad to say had uniformly marked our relations ever since the Coalition was formed. Nor need I tell you that, if I thought it right, I have every temptation (especially now) to seek relief from the intolerable daily burden of labour and anxiety.

Yours very sincerely,
H. H. Asquith.

There was one curious feature about the Prime Minister's letter. The original letter had been written on " The Wharf " notepaper at Sutton

Courtney on the Sunday, but the substituted sheet was on blank paper. So the whole document looked rather odd.

This letter was, of course, tantamount to a flat refusal.

Monday afternoon, November 27, 1916.

On the afternoon of Monday the letter was considered by the three prime movers at a meeting at the Colonial Office. Bonar Law assumed the role of mediator between Asquith and Lloyd George. The present system of government, he agreed, could not, in the national interest, be allowed to go on, but it would be better if some *modus vivendi* between the two could be arranged. At the same time, he was most anxious to include Carson in the War Council. Unlike Asquith, he was a believer in Carson's capacities as a War administrator and had always been ready to bring him back into the Government on any favourable opportunity.

Finally, Bonar Law suggested that Lloyd George, who was not surprised at the Prime Minister's refusal, should go directly to Asquith to see whether or not they could come to an agreement.

Lloyd George then, as agreed, saw the Prime Minister, and conversations took place between the two men; they were of the usual somewhat indecisive character. In the meantime it became increasingly clear that the triumvirate were themselves far from united. Lloyd George and Carson, while not caring a button who had the titular

post of head of the Government, were determined
not to let the new War Council be run by Asquith,
and said so quite openly. If Asquith would accept
the titular role, well and good; if not, he must go.
But Bonar Law would not go as far as the other
two in this; he was restrained by a feeling
of loyalty to the head of the Government, and
was anxious to run Lloyd George and Asquith in
harness together. In consequence, he genuinely
assumed the task of mediator between the two men.

This holding-back attitude on his part undoubtedly annoyed Carson. Carson was seeing
a lot of Gwynne, the editor of the " Morning
Post," at this time.

Gwynne was a powerful personage, for he was
trusted by the Generals' party, was the confidant of
Carson, and definitely represented the views of
the group of Conservative members of Parliament most hostile to the Government. Of
course, he had in addition the " Morning Post "
as his sounding board, for though the newspaper
belonged to the Bathurst family, the policy was
controlled by Gwynne. But he had influence,
quite irrespective of his position in journalism,
owing to his personality and to the clear-cut consistency of his views on the conduct of the war.

It was, then, highly significant that on 23rd
November the " Morning Post," which, owing to
pre-war politics, had a natural tendency to be
hostile to Lloyd George, suddenly went right
about face and declared Lloyd George to be the
necessary man and the saviour of society. This
was clearly Carson's work.

I have dwelt on the attitude of the " Morning Post " because the Press became a very important factor in the solution of the crisis during this week. Lloyd George's strength in particular lay less in the Commons—and least of all in the Government—than in the country. And the Press was the only instrument for bringing this popular medium to bear. For this reason I was very anxious that Lloyd George should make it up with Northcliffe.

I had a strong belief both in Northcliffe's power and in his rigid patriotism. I did not share the dislike and disparagement of Northcliffe then rife in Governmental and political circles.

I felt sure that if it could be shown to him that Lloyd George was doing the right thing to win the war, he would support Lloyd George in spite of past disagreements. Still, the relationship between the two men was awkward, for, as has been previously recorded, Northcliffe had threatened Lloyd George recently over the " Roumanian Letter " —and the threat had been offensive in character.

Anyhow, Lloyd George would have nothing to do with the idea. But he is the most placable of men—one quite devoid of rancour in public affairs, and the day was not far distant when he was brought to make an advance. He said to me, in reply to my pressure : " I would as soon go for a sunny evening stroll round Walton Heath with a grasshopper as try and work with Northcliffe."

I replied that my experience of Northcliffe was

that he always carried out any bargain he entered into—but my plea was in vain.

I was now occupying a room at the War Office near the Secretary of State's quarters.

Sir Reginald Brade frequently called on me, though I was unwilling to call on him too often, because his office in the same corridor was like a public ante-room, with Generals and public men coming and going all day long.

One interview in the War Office room during this period stands out in my memory. Birkenhead attacked me, and with great and evident sincerity pointed out the enormous responsibility all of us who were planning to overturn the existing regime were assuming. He did not contest the fact that the intrigue (as he termed it from his point of view) would succeed, but he denied that an alternative Government could be formed. What, then, would happen to the country? I argued that his own position would be perfectly safe under a new Administration, but the suggestion annoyed him. He was genuinely alarmed at the situation and its development, and anxious to avoid a crash. He himself thanked his stars that responsibility in the matter would not rest with him.

Events were now fast approaching the actual crisis and came thick on each other. The Prime Minister could not be induced to come to a decision, but the men who were for a change in the conduct of the war were determined to compel him to do so. The manner and extent of their success will be exhibited in the ensuing pages.

CHAPTER XXIX

CONSERVATIVE OPPOSITION

BONAR LAW had now to make his vital
decision. The crisis had developed up to a
point which compelled him to inform his colleagues of the action he was taking and to disclose
all that had occurred. He must reveal himself as
definitely committed to a campaign for the creation of a War Council with dictatorial powers
over and above those residing in the Cabinet.
Finally, he must tell them that the fall of the
Government was almost certainly involved in the
acceptance or rejection of this scheme.

Thursday, November 30, 1916.

This was a day of great importance, because
it witnessed this first meeting of the Conservative Cabinet Ministers. At that meeting, at
which all were present except Balfour (who was
ill, and attended neither this nor any subsequent
conference), Bonar Law explained to his colleagues fully and frankly exactly what he had
done in connection with Lloyd George and the
Prime Minister. He read them the terms of the
joint resolution concurred in by Lloyd George,
Carson, and himself, and explained that he was
insisting on his plan of a small Council of three,

with supreme control, and real executive authority, and urging it on a somewhat reluctant Prime Minister. He made it clear that Lloyd George would be the chairman of this Council. Carson's name, as a Member of the Council, never came up, for agreement broke down on the principle of the new scheme before the question of personnel was reached.

Bonar Law, indeed, at the very outset found himself confronted with the uncompromising resistance of all of his old colleagues. Their objection to the new organ of war administration was, in fact, based not so much on an objection to its theory as on an objection to the proposed chairman. They saw in the whole plan simply a scheme for the further aggrandisement of Lloyd George, and they were absolutely determined not to proclaim a dictatorship with Lloyd George as dictator. Their attitude would have been very different, had Mr. Asquith been the probable candidate for the new post. It would not be fair to attach blame to the Conservative leaders for this mental attitude. For fifteen or twenty years in the past they had lived in an atmosphere of fierce political animosity in which Lloyd George was often the principal target. They had no reason to like him, and, as has been already pointed out, Lloyd George's conduct since the formation of the Ministry had been such as to destroy Bonar Law's original faith in his disinterested patriotism, and, further, had inflamed the inveterate distrust of his enemies. His colleagues had not undergone the process by which Bonar Law's doubts had been resolved. It is easy enough to blame them for rushing into violent opposition to the only scheme of reform which promised to save the country. But such a criticism would be unjust. The Conservative Cabinet Ministers were faced with a situation which had no parallel in their past experience; the precedents and modes of thought by which all public men had governed their political lives were useless and broken things; desperate situations require desperate remedies; but it required great imaginative insight to pierce through the superficial defects of the War Minister and see into the heart of the only man who had the courage, the genius, and the energy to rise to the height of the occasion. But if Conservative Ministers made a mistake in judgment (and this, of course, may still be open to question), it was certainly an honest mistake.

The popular judgment, never very far out in simple and vital matters, was sound.

The people were far enough away from Lloyd George to see him in better perspective. The majority of the newspapers, both London and provincial, were beginning to rally to him, and in countless trains and trams and omnibuses men were saying that "Lloyd George was the best man among the lot."

The Prime Minister at least was perfectly aware of this fact which made it impossible for him or anyone else to put forward an alternative candidate for the Chairmanship of the War Council.

We must continue the narrative of Thursday's

meeting of the Conservative members of the Cabinet. Bonar Law was completely taken by surprise at encountering such vehement unanimity in rejecting his scheme. But if he was taken aback, it is also clear that at this first meeting the Conservative members of the Ministry had equally no idea of the formidable nature of the movement they were opposing. Lloyd George, they thought, had been simmering with discontent, marked by occasional ebullitions of protest for months. This was just another of his " gags " to gain a little more power.

Bonar Law made it perfectly plain that he was not going on under the existing system of war control; that there must be great changes in the administration; that Lloyd George must be given the general direction of the war, and that Asquith must be kept apart from this executive side. Both Long and Lansdowne, in letters printed below, interpret, and rightly, his position to be equivalent to a threat of resignation if his general idea was not accepted. Yet his colleagues were not impressed. They could not believe that when Bonar Law found himself in a minority of one he could possibly proceed with his plan. If he did so, he would simply be ruined, and they could still carry on in the Government. They had forgotten the Bonar Law who had compelled the evacuation of the Dardanelles. They acted on " the meek and humble Bonar Law " hypothesis.

The majority, therefore, were quite certain of getting their way and were determined to reject the demands of Lloyd George and Carson. Much resentment was felt at being invited to work with these two. Lloyd George, it was said, was simply using Carson as a tool to stir up dissension and discontent among Tory back-benchers and so frighten the Conservative members of the Ministry into giving way to his inordinate ambitions. Well, Bonar Law might be frightened of Carson— but they were not. Carson could accomplish nothing against either the Conservative leaders or the Government as a whole. In fact, the feeling against Carson was so strong that Bonar Law thought it inadvisable even to mention his name in connection with the new War Council. Some feeling was manifested, too, against Bonar Law afterwards, Lord Robert Cecil complaining that Bonar Law was ruining the Conservative Party by dragging it at the coat tails of Lloyd George. But the general sense was that the whole business would blow over and was not serious.

The opponents of the War Council, however, did not wish to be left in the position of maintaining that all was going as well as possible with the best of all possible wars. For this was manifestly untrue, and the country was showing signs of resenting the attitude.

Several of the Conservatives put forward an alternative plan of rather a complicated character for a reconstruction of the functions of the Cabinet.

Since Lloyd George was unavoidable if his War Council plan were carried, the only way of disposing of the man was to destroy the plan. This the Conservative antagonists proposed to do by the somewhat ingenious method of setting up an alternative scheme of reform.

When Bonar Law, therefore, urged his original plan he was met by a counter-proposal. According to this, it should be agreed to set up a small War Council, to include the political heads of the fighting departments, and, on the other hand, to create what might be called a Home Council, consisting of the principal Ministers concerned with the Home Services.

The Home Council, however, would fall into the keeping of a nabob of the official hierarchy, and the dictatorship of Lloyd George would be avoided. One may readily perceive that there was something specious about this plan. It had, however, one glaring defect. The whole crisis had arisen out of the failure of the Administration to secure any unified control of the war. As a remedy for this evil it was now proposed to intensify it by setting up two bodies of practically equal authority, whose functions would be found so to overlap as to bring them into sharp and incessant conflict. The remedy was, in fact, worse than the disease. Bonar Law stood to his guns, and the conference broke up without a decision, all his colleagues declaring for the two-council arrangement, though, obviously, some with much hesitation.

The two letters received by Bonar Law from those who had been his closest friends in former days show very clearly the extent of the bitterness and hostility aroused by the proposals put forward at the meeting.

Local Government Board,
Whitehall, S.W.

My dear Bonar,

As I have told you before, I am profoundly anxious about the situation, and believe that it must have a very bad effect upon the prosecution of the war.

I believe you share this view, and that we only differ as to the remedy, and my object in writing to you now is to implore you to do all you can consistently, of course, with your own convictions, to carry your Unionist colleagues in the Cabinet with you.

I think you propose to approach the Prime Minister and demand the appointment of a committee of three without portfolios to " run the war " and do nothing else; and your intention is to resign if he is not prepared to give way.

I believe all your colleagues (Unionist) are doubtful whether this plan is the best, among them all of us who have had long and varied administrative experience. I share their view strongly. I observe that your plan has very powerful backing in the Press, but none the less I believe the course to be best which will make our views and objects plain and which places the facts as we see them frankly before the Prime Minister.

I believe the Government cannot " carry on " as it is.

I believe real reconstruction is absolutely necessary.

I believe that whatever changes are made it is vital that the men who are to wield these great powers should be vigorous both in mind and body, ready and able to push their policy regardless of any consequences other than those which will contribute to final and complete victory.

Is it not possible for us to agree on a line of action which will enable you to go to the P.M. and speak for yourself and all your colleagues ? Surely, when all are agreed that the present state of things exposes the Empire to grave peril, there must be immediate and drastic changes. It cannot be impossible to agree upon a policy which we can all support ?

Whether the precise plan be yours or the alternative favoured by your colleagues, or possibly even a third perhaps varying either of these, I personally do not so much mind. What I care for is that we should act together, act promptly, and use our combined strength to save the country from a grave danger.

Yours ever,

2.10.16.   Walter H. Long.

Bonar Law had no difficulty in pointing out the intrinsic absurdity of the whole "two-council" proposal. He asked who would be responsible for the transport of troops to France. The reply was that according to the Conservative plan this would fall to the Home Council, which would be responsible for shipping. " And suppose," he said, " the shipping authority orders troops to be taken across in cement barges towed by tugs because the transports are wanted for other purposes, do you suppose the War Council will agree not to have a word on that ? " This instance, and many others showing the impossibility of working the scheme, strongly confirmed Bonar Law in his original opinion. The obvious truth of the matter was that the plan had not been thought out so much on its merits as a means of winning the war as of meeting the cry for administrative reform without giving Lloyd George the conduct of the war.

None the less the letter from Long forms, in another aspect, an impressive document. Long stated, in a manner highly creditable to him, a position for which there was much to be said. It was reasonable to say that whatever reform of the existing war control was needed it was far better that all the Conservative Ministers should agree together on it and put it through.

At the same time, Bonar Law received another letter from Lord Lansdowne conceived in a very different vein. Lansdowne puts the very strongest pressure on him to modify his attitude of support towards Lloyd George, indicating clearly that he went on his course alone and at his peril. Lansdowne did not like the " alternative "—that is the two councils—and seems to have been in favour of the *status quo* as far as can be judged from his letter :

Lansdowne House,
Berkeley Square, W.
Dec. 1.16.

My dear Bonar,
The meeting in your room yesterday left " a nasty taste in my mouth." I did not like your plan, and I am by no means convinced that the alternative is all that can be desired.

You will, I have no doubt, have another talk with George, and we shall, I assume, hear the result.

I know you will not mind my making two observations.

1. I hope you will not commit yourself irrevocably to George until you have given us another opportunity of considering the situation. I underline the word " yourself " because it would be beyond measure painful to me to think that at such a moment you could entertain the idea of disassociating yourself from the other Unionist members of the Cabinet.

2. I think we all of us owe it to Asquith to avoid any action which might be regarded by him as a concerted attempt to oust him from his position as leader.

I am taking Grey to Bowood this evening, but shall be back on Monday evening at latest.

Yours ever,
L.

Bonar Law sent a non-committal reply :

Downing Street,
December 1, 1916.

My dear Lansdowne,

Thanks for your letter. It is not possible (I have not the time) to write giving you fully my view on the situation, but I am sorry that I did not say to you, as I happened to say to some of our other colleagues, that I would come under no obligation to George without telling them in advance.

Indeed, I have said the same thing to Asquith, who knew of my meetings with George, and I have said it to George himself.

I recommended both Asquith and George to have it out with each other, and I consider therefore that for the moment the matter is out of my hands.

I hope to see you on Monday, and though I do not say that I may not feel compelled to take action of which my colleagues do not approve, I am sure you will believe me when I say that rather than have to do this I would, if I could, give up political life altogether.

Yours sincerely,
A. Bonar Law.

The mildness of tone adopted in this letter really does Bonar Law something less than justice. Yet Lansdowne had been an old and valued friend, his co-partner and senior in the leadership of the party, and Bonar Law was at the time acutely aware of his own state of isolation. He was not influenced by the fact that the Prime Minister had been in possession for some weeks of a memorandum from Lord Lansdowne indicating the view that Britain ought to consider a policy of " Peace without Victory."

The truth of the matter was that Lansdowne having convinced himself that we could not possibly win the war and must fall back on a negotiated peace had completely changed his standpoint. He re-viewed all his colleagues, Liberal or Conservative, in the light of this new policy. Were they men in favour of Peace by Negotiation or "bitter-enders"? He had therefore, quite unknown to Bonar Law, changed his friendliness of many years for one of hostility to the Tory leader in the Commons. He sensed accurately enough that Bonar Law would fight Germany to the last gasp. He also saw with resentment Bonar Law drawing nearer to Lloyd George because they were like-minded men. Therefore Lansdowne would have gladly seen them both thrown out of the Government. For he obviously believed that he could bring Asquith round to his view of Peace by Negotiation, not as desirable, but as inevitable, if the opposing element in the Cabinet were removed. And the fear of this development was very generally shared in circles favourable to Lloyd George, though not, as has been said, by most of the protagonists in the Cabinet.

Lord Crewe has stated that in his opinion the Lansdowne memorandum was somehow connected with the crisis.

It was, but only in this indirect manner.

It accounted for the hostility of Lansdowne to the Lloyd George-Bonar Law plan for a change in the conduct of the war and for his violent opposition towards Bonar Law himself. One at least of his Conservative colleagues was informed by Lansdowne of his disappointment with his colleague and joint leader in the House of Commons, and others no doubt were favoured with the same opinion.

Lansdowne said that Bonar Law had no knowledge of European history or politics. He could hardly distinguish one Balkan state from another. It was absurd to suppose that he could read the mind of Europe as Lansdowne could in the middle of this terrific crisis. The inference was that Lansdowne was right in his policy of Peace by Negotiation and Bonar Law wrong in his determination to fight till Germany was beaten. Lansdowne developed and expressed quite a distrust of Bonar Law as a war-time Minister. Asquith, on the other hand, he felt certain, was open to conviction. If only Bonar Law and Lloyd George could be overcome, the way to peace was plain.

Lansdowne, therefore, in his conduct at this crisis was entirely obsessed by his zeal for Peace by Negotiation.

But neither Chamberlain, nor Cecil, nor Curzon, nor Walter Long was in his confidence or understood the motive underlying his action. So far indeed was Cecil from being in the Peace-by-Negotiation camp, that his conduct of the Blockade of Germany was one of the most resolute and efficient performances of the whole war. Further, Lord Robert Cecil wrote in the form of a Cabinet Minute an excellent reply to Lord Lansdowne's memorandum. No one put more clearly and firmly than he did the necessity for continuing war until a definite decision was reached. Yet he expressed his optimism and resolution in a balanced and tempered style.

The " Three C's "* then in conjunction with most of their colleagues seem to have regarded the Lansdowne memorandum as an academic essay on an unknown future. It was a brave and even lucid document. But it did not stir or interest them in the very least.

Bonar Law came back from Thursday's meeting badly shaken. In the light of the opposition he had encountered, it would be necessary to go over his whole position again. As was his wont on such occasions, he proceeded to analyse the situation in all its bearings and to consider his various possible lines of future action. For this purpose, as usual, he made use of me.

To begin with, he considered the charge made against him by his colleagues that he was supporting Lloyd George because he was frightened of Carson and that his desire to bring Carson back to the centre of control was dictated by expediency.

Was this charge true ? The answer was " No." " Do I believe that Carson is a good war administrator, a man of courage and character who ought to hold high position on his merits ? The answer is, " Yes." He reflected further :

* The " Three C's " were Curzon, Cecil and Chamberlain.

(1) Carson is ready to rejoin an Asquith Government if the War Council scheme is adopted. He does not insist as a condition that he should be a member. (2) Asquith is ready to take him into the Government though not in the War Council. (3) It follows that there is no menace from Carson whatever and no difference of interest or opinion between us. For if the War Council scheme is adopted we shall be friends together in the Government, and since we both believe in that scheme firmly we are likely, if it is rejected, to be friends together in opposition.

I have no doubt that Bonar Law misunderstood Carson's real attitude to Asquith. I was always convinced beyond question that Carson was determined throughout the autumn of 1916 to remove Asquith if he could from the direction of the war and to destroy him, if necessary, to gain his end.

In discussing this matter, Bonar Law always returned to the vital point : " What ought I to do about the War Council ? "

So far it had been rejected by Asquith and turned down in effect by all his Tory colleagues. If he persisted—and that to the point of resignation—he went on with Lloyd George alone. Or would Lloyd George resign even if he resigned ? Some experience of Lloyd George in the past made him uncertain on this point.

On personal grounds he would welcome the opportunity of getting rid of his responsibilities, but what would be the effect on the Government, on the country, and on the war of either a single-handed or a joint resignation ?

The Government was already too feeble. If he retired alone into private life, he merely weakened it further. The Government would go staggering along for some time in a condition of ever-growing incompetence. Was the war situation such that the fortunes of the Empire could stand such a development ? The answer was, " No." It is possible to judge now more correctly how far Bonar Law was right in his estimate of the danger. His retirement would have left Lord Lansdowne the sole leader and therefore the para-mount influence among Conservative Ministers while Lloyd George would have been so humiliated by his defeat that his influence in the Cabinet would have declined. In that case who can say that all we had fought for and all that we were to attain in the war would not have been sacrificed by a fatal " Peace without Victory."

It must be admitted that there was at the time a widespread suspicion abroad that several of the Liberal members of the Cabinet would welcome any opportunity of negotiating a peace before a military and naval decision had been arrived at. The finger had been pointed at several Ministers in this connection. The names bandied about in Tory circles were Runciman, Grey and McKenna. Mr. McKenna, the Chancellor of the Exchequer, was written down as a qualified supporter of any movement in this direction. I feel sure that he would deny this. But the mere fact that his name was widely mentioned in this connection shows how carefully the soil was being prepared to accept the seed of Lansdowne House.

Yet a whole series of minutes and recommendations and state papers issuing from Whitehall seemed to lead to the one definite conclusion that there was in the minds of men in authority a suspicion that a peace without victory was being contemplated.   It would be easy, though unnecessary, to call the witnesses.

The reason why McKenna was suspect in this direction is obvious. His duty was to collect money with which to finance the war. He found this a task of growing difficulty day by day. He was always warning his colleagues at one Cabinet meeting after another that the payment for great orders for stores and munitions abroad was not quite such an easy matter as they imagined. All kinds of steps had to be taken in advance. It was not like putting a penny in the slot and pulling a lever.

The opponents of McKenna put the case against him quite bluntly. They said he did not believe that Great Britain could finance a prolonged war : that in consequence he was for Peace by Negotiation.

But several of the Liberal Ministers were more or less suspect to the Tory newspapers and to the Tory rank and file on the issue of a vigorous prosecution of the war. Yet the leadership of the Peace-by-Negotiation party was in the keeping of a Conservative, and one of the leaders of the party at that. It was Lansdowne who belled the cat for those Liberal Ministers who despaired of a Military decision favourable to Britain.

In some cases popular instinct was correct. We were never nearer peace by negotiation than in the summer and early autumn of 1916.

On the other hand, if Lloyd George retired, he intended—and made no secret of it—to appeal to public opinion against the Asquith administration. The country would be asked to declare for Lloyd George and a vigorous war policy. " Believing what I do about the muddled conduct of the war," Bonar Law argued, " I should have to join in the campaign. My colleagues assume that they are representing the Tory orthodoxy in supporting Asquith. It is more probable that if I joined Lloyd George in such an assault the main stream of Tory opinion would go with me— and there would be a vast Press support. Asquith in the long run would fall."

But would not all this produce an equally impossible situation ? Would the Empire survive a weak Government on one side and a raging tearing campaign of criticism in the country on the other ? Again, the answer is " No."

Yet to do nothing, to submit, to carry on under a regime he did not believe in might be the very worst course of all for the nation. In these sombre and careful reflections Bonar Law passed the evening of Thursday.

Never had a man a more difficult decision to take. There were practically all the Liberals ranged behind Asquith, and reinforced by all the Tories in the Ministry, including even Birkenhead

—whose support of the Prime Minister impressed Bonar Law.

I went home that night to the Hyde Park Hotel and sat in my room on the fourth floor overlooking the Park. A cold north-east wind blew in from the night and the single lamp was so shaded as to give hardly a glimmer. And as I sat there alone I thought how vastly greater were the forces ranged against Bonar Law than those ranged on his side. The strength of the two contending parties seemed ludicrously disproportionate. If the opponents showed anything like good powers of management, might they not repel Bonar Law's attack? Ought men of good will to accept the inevitable? Should they bow before the strength of Asquith's position and his immense following in his own and the Conservative Party? Would it be better to compromise at once rather than to damage and weaken the Government? Or, on the other hand, ought they to go on to the bitter end, believing, as they did, in the need for a sweeping change in the management and direction of the war? Despite these doubts of the dark hour, reason showed plainly that we must go on.

Granted absolute conviction of right on each side—and I grant this freely and sincerely to our opponents on this issue of long ago—the matter was really one of psychological calculation. The external forces were arrayed in their entirety on Asquith's side. He had all the outer evidences— the oaths, the forms, and the ceremonies, the trappings of power and all the tempting baits existing office can hold out. Count heads on either front bench, and opposition to him would appear to be ridiculous.

His Liberal colleagues were, with the single exception of a hostile Lloyd George and a doubting Montagu, bound to him by indisseverable ties. Labour, it was said openly, trusted Asquith and had no love for the Lloyd George of the Ministry of Munitions. As to the Conservatives, Asquith had a far greater influence with the Conservative Ministers than their official leader. The front bench Tories were ready to throw Bonar Law over for him any day—as the event proved.

Above all loomed the immense conception—hardly doubted indeed even by most of his bitterest enemies—of the indispensability of Asquith as Prime Minister. Those who advanced to the attack of this political monument seemed in little better case than a pigmy slinging his stone at the Pyramids.

Yet Lloyd George with a flaming courage and Bonar Law with a cold determination, did advance against all these powers and principalities, apparently unsupported, and in the twinkling of an eye what seemed an easy victory was theirs.

No man to-day will recognise the desperate nature of their daring. It all seemed to happen so smoothly. At one moment Asquith was everything; in the next he was nothing. The great illusion of indispensability vanished in a night. Everyone, indeed, bowed down to the conquerors and accepted office and honours from them—but they did so not as to men who had performed a miracle of pluck, but as to men who had achieved some quite common political feat.

As a matter of fact, when Bonar Law and Lloyd George went into this issue they did so starkly as men doomed to inevitable defeat and political ruin in face of overwhelming forces, if Asquith had made full use of his powers and his majority in the House of Commons. They had nothing except patriotism and faith to sustain them against the all powerful myth that Asquith—bad or good as a war administrator—was indispensable, and that his opponents were like children playing by the seashore building up spade castles against the waves.

This was the great Asquith myth and it was false. Lloyd George and Bonar Law found afterwards that they could form a strong and reliable Government with the greatest ease. If every front bencher in the whole world of politics refused, his place in political life during the war would be instantly taken by a back-bencher, and in time of war hardly anyone in the country would notice the difference. The back-benchers were panting to take the place of the Right Honourables who had so far occupied the saddle—and I say this in no sense of irony. Everyone at that time thought that he could serve his country in office if he was too old to serve it in the trenches. Lloyd George or Bonar Law or anyone of standing who was commissioned by His Majesty to form a Government had only got to lift his little finger and his Ministry would be full—not of adventurers, but of men of solid reputation—Tory, Liberal or Labour—who were representatives of great constituencies and well seen by their neighbours. What did such men care for Asquith or Lloyd George as persons ? They cared for the war.

We shall see in the course of the narrative great Ministers changing their colours almost in a day. They strike the Asquith flag and hoist the Jolly Roger of Lloyd George. The man of mean mind will say they made the change purely for the advantages of office. I say nothing of the kind. They desired office so ardently in order that they might serve their country. When Sir Austen Chamberlain, a man whose name could not possibly be associated with any conception of sordid ambition, was asked on one occasion to accept a great post, he replied : " I must go ; I feel at last as if I was being ordered into the trenches."

That was what office meant to men in war times. No man, back bench or front bench, would refuse office in the war—as he might well have done in peace time. That was the central fact—but Asquith and his allied Conservative potentates did not perceive it until the smash came. Lloyd George had many of the Liberal back-benchers behind him when he became Prime Minister, just as Bonar Law had the Tory ones practically solid in his support. As soon as this fact was recognised, as it must be at the crisis, the front benches of Toryism would fall into line rather than resign their patriotic endeavours and their great positions to what they regarded as less able hands.

The Liberal front benchers proved of sterner stuff, but then they were more absolutely certain that Asquith would win out. As anticipated, there was no lack of Liberal back-benchers to fill their places.

What was at issue, therefore, in December, 1916, was a combat between a myth and a reality. The myth was that Asquith was the only conceivable Premier under whom men would serve. The reality was that men would serve under any efficient Premier.

But Westminster was blind in its belief in Asquith. It forgot completely all the outside forces —furious chairmen of Conservative organisations, men in munition factories, men in the trenches, Fleet Street—in fact, all the powers that cared nothing about the solemn observances of a consecrated Downing Street. All these forces, slow as they were to bring their weight to bear, began to turn in the direction of Lloyd George and away from Asquith.

CHAPTER XXX

LLOYD GEORGE FORCES THE CRISIS

Friday, December 1.

ON Friday morning I saw Lloyd George and discussed with him the proceedings at the Conservative meeting of the previous days. He had to face the fact that all the Conservative Ministers were hostile to Bonar Law's attitude—with the very doubtful exception of Walter Long, who leant towards some kind of compromise. I told him that Bonar Law had gone so far that on parting with his colleagues he had left them with the impression that he would either have the War Council or resign. I then asked Lloyd George in turn how he stood with his Liberal Cabinet colleagues, hoping to hear some better news. Lloyd George replied that he had absolutely no support at all in this quarter except from Montagu.

We were thus confronted with this extraordinary position : Dealing with the Cabinet alone, Lloyd George had only one Liberal adherent (who turned out to be a doubtful quantity), and Bonar Law not a single Conservative one.* As the third party in the controversy stood the Prime Minister, who so far had not shifted an inch in his refusal of the terms proposed by Lloyd George and Bonar Law.

The discussion then turned towards what outside support existed. Carson and his friends could be relied on. Derby was standing firmly behind Lloyd George. Montagu was encouraging Lloyd George, but his final attitude in the event of a clash was uncertain.

I then told Lloyd George the views that Bonar Law had expressed to me on Thursday night. From this account he was able to gather that Bonar Law thought that very careful consideration was necessary, and was indeed a public duty, before a definite rupture of the existing administration was forced on.

The news conveyed to Lloyd George was thus almost universally bad. None the less, he remained quite cool and undismayed. He was, he said, tired of all this indecision and playing about and abstruse calculation about the future. Whoever was for him or against him, he intended to go on, and would at once bring matters to an issue.

* The position taken by the Labour adherents of the Government was clearly stated by Mr. Henderson in a speech delivered at Northampton on the very evening of this day.

" Mr. Asquith," he said, " is the indispensable man to lead us to the end of this war and to lead us successfully. It is possible to put other men into the saddle and they might go faster. But there is not the same certainty as there is when you are following a leader tried and courageous as our present Prime Minister has proved himself to be. He is among the readiest I ever knew to take upon himself blame for the faults and failings of other men and especially of his own colleagues."

He thereupon sat down at the word and wrote a memorandum to the Prime Minister, outlining his proposals, and indicated in conversation with Asquith that resignation was not far behind if his terms were refused :

Memo. to Prime Minister.
December 1, 1916.

1. That the War Committee consist of three members—two of whom must be the First Lord of the Admiralty and the Secretary of State for War, who should have in their offices deputies capable of attending to and deciding all departmental business, and a third Minister without portfolio. One of the three to be chairman.

2. That the War Committee shall have full powers, subject to the supreme control of the Prime Minister, to direct all questions connected with the war.

3. The Prime Minister in his discretion to have the power to refer any question to the Cabinet.

4. Unless the Cabinet on reference by the Prime Minister reverses decision of the War Committee, that decision to be carried out by the department concerned.

5. The War Committee to have the power to invite any Minister, and to summon the expert advisers and officers of any department to its meetings.

The Prime Minister replied in the following terms :

10, Downing Street, S.W.
December 1, 1916.

My dear Lloyd George,

I have now had time to reflect on our conversation this morning and to study your memorandum.

Though I do not altogether share your dark estimate and forecast of the situation, actual and perspective, I am in complete agreement that we have reached a critical situation in the war, and that our own methods of procedure, with the experience which we have gained during the last few months, call for reconsideration and revision.

The two main defects of the War Committee, which has done excellent work, are (1) that its numbers are too large; (2) that there is delay, evasion, and often obstruction on the part of the departments in giving effect to its decisions. I might with good reason add (3) that it is often kept in ignorance by the departments of information, essential and even vital, of a technical kind upon the problems that come before it, and (4) that it is overcharged with duties, many of which might well be delegated to subordinate bodies.

The result is that I am clearly of opinion that the War Committee should be reconstituted, and its relations and authority over the departments, etc., more clearly defined and more effectively asserted.

I come now to your specific proposals. In my opinion, whatever changes are made in the composition or functions of the War Committee, the Prime Minister must be its chairman. He cannot be relegated to the position of an arbiter in the background or a referee to the Cabinet.

In regard to its composition, I agree that the War Secretary and the First Lord of the Admiralty are necessary members. I am inclined to add to the same category the Minister of Munitions. There should be another member, with or without portfolio, or charged only with comparatively light departmental duties. One of the members should be appointed vice-chairman.

I purposely do not in this letter discuss the delicate and difficult question of personnel.

The committee should, as far as possible, sit *de die in diem*, and have full power to see that its decisions (subject to appeal to the Cabinet) are carried out promptly and effectively by the departments.

The reconstruction of the War Committee should be accompanied by the setting up of a Committee of National Organisation to deal with the purely domestic side of war problems. It should have executive powers within its own domain.

The Cabinet would in all cases have ultimate authority.

Yours very sincerely,
H. H. Asquith.

This letter is, in effect, a recapitulation of the proposals put forward by Conservative Ministers at their Thursday meeting with Bonar Law. The penultimate paragraph shows the Prime Minister's approval of the scheme for two War Councils and not for one Supreme War Council.

Now that Lloyd George had gone forward, much turned on Bonar Law's final attitude. The narrative has indicated this already, but it can be made perhaps still plainer. He had overcome his distrust of Lloyd George and was genuinely on his side in the struggle, but he was oppressed with other considerations.

There were several differences between the situations of the two men. Lloyd George had quarrelled with his Liberal associates often enough since the war, and in any case he was not their official leader. Bonar Law had had differences of opinions with his colleagues too, but, after all, they were his followers. Lloyd George had to threaten his leader; Bonar Law, his subordinates.

And then again he had never been in complete agreement with Lloyd George as to the extent to which Asquith should be eliminated from the control of affairs. It is difficult to state exactly at all times the points of difference, but the two men's policies faced different ways. Lloyd George's policy favoured the greatest degree of elimination which was compatible with decency, and did not shrink from complete dismissal if the knot could be cut in no other way. In fact, by this time it would not be putting it too high to say that Lloyd George was moving in the direction of Asquith's destruction as Premier. Bonar Law did

not want this sudden extinction. He believed that
Asquith should keep the titular Premiership, while
handing over the driving power in the war to
Lloyd George—not in itself a bad or impracticable
idea.

He was also influenced in this last direction by
the proceedings at the meeting with his Conservative colleagues on Thursday and a very well
defined sense of honour and the determination to
commit no act approaching disloyalty towards
chief or colleague.

There is no doubt, however, that during this
time Bonar Law was acutely conscious of his
position of isolation. On the Friday night,
Bonar Law and I dined alone together at the
Hyde Park Hotel. We went over the old ground
again, I maintaining that nothing but bold
measures could save us from defeat in the war,
and that to preserve the Empire all private considerations must go to the wall. I said that the
difference between Lloyd George and Asquith
was that between two fire-engine drivers racing
for a fire. One man was so determined to get
to the fire with his engine intact and no spill on
the way that while the driver watched the ditches
and avoided the ruts the house would be burnt
down before he got there. The other was absolutely determined to get to the fire in time to
save the house and would cut corners and take
heavy risks of a smash to do it.

I quote this because the simile had an obvious
effect on Bonar Law.

I had, of course, reported to Bonar Law what

Lloyd George had told me and what action he had taken during the day. He realised how absolutely alone both Lloyd George and himself stood, and he kept on reverting to the position he had taken up the previous night, and restating the old difficulty of responsibility to the nation. On which side of the argument did duty lie ?

At last he said that he *must* see Lloyd George that night and at once. I had the means of finding Lloyd George at that time at any hour of the day or night, and I knew he was dining at the Berkeley Hotel. Bonar Law absolutely insisted on coming along with me too, so as to have an immediate interview, and come to some final decision. As we drove along in a taxi I realised that there was here a clash of temperament, or at least a divergence of mental process, between these two men. Both were sincerely united in a common aim, but in their intellectual method they were miles apart. In a big crisis Lloyd George was slapdash. As the odds rose against him, his courage rose to meet them. He was urged on to the fray less by a reasoned calculation of chances than by an impulsive instinct that what he was going to do was right and that his cause would prevail. To ultimate consequences, springing in the third or fourth degree in the casual sequence from his action, he would not look at all. This slap-dash attitude of his sometimes caused the observer as much anxiety for the issue as did the exact antithesis of that temperament which dominated Bonar Law. For the Tory leader always wanted to be sure that he had foreseen every possible consequence of his action—even the comparatively remote. He would work the possibilities out like a mathematical formula on his intellectual blackboard. Men have often accused him of indecision—even of moral cowardice—because he would not act until the solution had by this method become a perfect thing, an indisputable conclusion to his mind. Once the conclusion was reached, he was like granite—and because of this deep thought and care his judgment was practically never at fault. Such an attitude in a statesman is neither indecisive nor cowardly. It has its springs, on the contrary, in the highest sense of duty and wisdom.

Now, Bonar Law was going to put these ultimate questions to Lloyd George before he decided whether or not to go out with him into the nightstorm against the all-embattled forces of official politics. He was going to say to him :

" Suppose we follow your instinct that a crash must come and had better come, rather than endure the slow atrophy of the national power and will to war—what is going to happen in the next three months ? May we not so weaken this Government as to destroy the nation before we are ourselves strong enough to step into its place and conduct the war on an efficient basis ? Or, again, if we advance boldly, will all yet be well in the space of a few days ? Until these doubts are resolved I will not move. If they are resolved I will face anything."

But how would Lloyd George, the bold man of adventure, treat the doubts of his associate ? I felt the situation to be very critical as I entered the Berkeley Hotel, while Bonar Law waited in the taxi outside. Then the proceedings had about them a touch of farce.

Lloyd George was dining with the late Lord Cunliffe. There were also present at the dinner Lord Reading and Mr. and Mrs. Montagu. It was something of a feat to capture the War Secretary for such a social purpose. Lloyd George does not care for going into Society, and prefers to meet only his intimates. And he was already a European figure. Lord Cunliffe had, at any rate, the opportunity of discussing his own financial problems with an ex-Chancellor of the Exchequer, and it would not be surprising to learn that Mr. Lloyd George was listening—perhaps not altogether without relish—to criticisms of his successor at the Treasury, Mr. McKenna.

But the writing was on the wall—as at another feast but in a different sense. I did not approach the dinner table, but I beckoned to Lloyd George from some way off, and he came. He knew very well that only extreme urgency would have brought me to summon him at such an hour and at such a place. The guests looked rather staggered at seeing the War Secretary go out suddenly at a gesture from an ordinary back-bench Member of Parliament like myself.

As we left, I just had time to tell him in a few hurried words something of Bonar Law's frame of mind. I said he was in for a difficult interview, and I urged him to take calmly whatever was said by Bonar Law. We all three drove back to the Hyde Park Hotel.

Lloyd George behaved at the interview extraordinarily well. He also exercised consummate tact. Had he taken a strong combative or argumentative line, he might easily have compelled Bonar Law to take the opposite view, and so fortify his own fears of the results of going forward. What Lloyd George said was in effect : " You must decide as you think best. I will not bring any pressure to bear on you."

After this interview, which took place at the Hyde Park Hotel, I drove with Bonar Law to Pembroke Lodge. We went up to the sitting-room on the second floor. This room, as always, was insufferably hot. Bonar Law would have his fire perpetually made up and allow no ventilation. To add to the atmosphere, he always smoked strong cigars—with a pipe in between as a variant—and on occasions such as this he smoked rather more than usual.

I can still hear him speaking with that curious emphatic inflexion which always showed that he had come to the end of the period of interminable debate and made up his mind. So he had. He was going forward at any cost.

I came out happily into the cool air of the night and went home to the Hyde Park Hotel—to find I had to climb four flights of stairs because the lift was not working.

CHAPTER XXXI

THE PRESS AND THE CRISIS

IN the meantime the question of the attitude of the Press towards the contending parties became one of urgent importance. In such a crisis, with most of the old party loyalties dissolved or in process of dissolution, and with the spirit of war abroad in the country, the newspapers were in the main free to voice public opinion quite irrespective of ancient party bonds—and public opinion expressed through this medium might decide the result of the political struggle. So the views of men like Northcliffe, Robert Donald, Gwynne or Garvin carried as much practical weight as those of an equal number of men in the Cabinet.

My immediate medium was the " Daily Express." I did not at that time own the controlling shares of this newspaper, but I was on intimate terms with the editor. I had also taken pains to inform Sir Robert Donald, of the " Daily Chronicle," of what was going on.

Robert Donald was an important figure amongst the various editors or proprietors in a political crisis involving the Liberal party : because he was a man of strong character ; because he was a consistent Liberal; because he was trusted by Bonar Law; because he understood such important Press elements in the situation as the Robertson Nichol group; because he was not hostile to Lloyd George. Above all, he was a man devoid of prejudice or rancour, and a working journalist who could express himself logically and fluently, and meet and argue with the politicians on terms of equality. He was, in fact, in direct association with most of the leading public men involved.

Up till now the newspapers had been silent. There was, indeed, a certain premonition of coming trouble for the Government in Fleet Street, but nothing definite had been printed. The beams, which, like searchlights, were being projected hither and thither from the newspapers, did not show up to their readers clear and definite objects in a white light, but seemed simply to illumine a vague changing landscape with dark clouds hurrying across the sky.

The nation was now going to get the white light with a vengeance, and I must confess that the responsibility for the disclosure to the " Chronicle " and the " Express " was entirely mine. It is necessary to state this, because at the time Lloyd George was widely accused of inspiring the Press in his own interest during the crisis. The charge is untrue, so far as the " Chronicle " and the " Express " are concerned; whatever was done with these newspapers was done by me. It is true that there was an important publication of the news in " Reynolds " on the Sunday, with which I shall deal subsequently.

On Friday I gave Mr. R. D. Blumenfeld, the editor of the " Daily Express," an outline of the position and the line to take. Robert Donald had already informed the editor of the " Daily Express " on Friday evening of his intention to give publicity to the crisis on Saturday morning. Both papers came out against Asquith's direction of the war on Saturday morning.

The " Daily Express " on its front page wrote as follows :

A great political crisis has arisen in the past twenty-four hours. Nothing is certain except that the crisis which has been developing for some time is now upon us. The lack of unity which has characterised the deliberations of the Coalition Cabinet is no Cabinet secret. The war is the one thing that counts, and here it is generally felt that the Government has shown lack of initiative and courage. Here must be the change.

The suggestion of a new War Council was made, and the names mentioned in this connection were those of Lloyd George, Bonar Law and Carson.

The " Daily Chronicle " on its front page also voiced general dissatisfaction with the conduct of the war, and put forward the same list of names for the War Council.

Mr. Asquith, the statement continued, has been carrying on under a tremendous strain, and Mr. Lloyd George would be better released from the War Office in order to take up his new duties.

It will be seen that the only two newspapers publishing accounts of the progress of the new attempt to reconstruct a War Government on a better basis were the " Daily Express " and the " Daily Chronicle." To the man in the street, who was heartily tired of the incompetence exhibited in high places, their news contained the hope of salvation. The revolting section of the Press was viewed as a benefactor. To the narrower sect of the Liberals who were pertinaciously sworn to Asquith and the idea of an orthodox Liberal preponderance in the Ministry the whole business savoured of a conspiracy.

At this point the natural course would have been to explain the situation to Gwynne of the " Morning Post." The path was closed because of the personal quarrel I had indulged in with Gwynne, of which an account has already been given. Gwynne was the natural ally of Bonar Law in this struggle. He would have been a tower of strength to the Tory leader in combating the influence of those Conservative members of the Ministry who wanted to support the Asquith regime against Lloyd George and Bonar Law. Unfortunately, I was debarred from making any approach. Bonar Law never would make any arrangement for support with a newspaper. Carson never appears to have explained the real essence of Bonar Law's position in these critical days to Gwynne—a fact which, considering their political intimacy, has always appeared to me to be strange. Possibly the two men never happened to meet each other during the critical period.

The fact remains that Gwynne, in absolute and honest ignorance, was directing a cross-fire from the flank on Bonar Law, just as Bonar Law's Conservative Cabinet colleagues were attacking him on the front because he agreed with Gwynne's views on the Asquith Government. In a leader published in the "Morning Post," Gwynne accused Bonar Law at the worst of co-operating with those Conservative Ministers who were trying to support Asquith and the old war system of control—or, at the best, of being at least a half-hearted indecisive adherent of Lloyd George and of the doctrines of the "new regime." Actually at the moment this article appeared the Asquith Government was out, chiefly by Bonar Law's efforts, and the Tory leader was fighting side by side with Lloyd George in the endeavour to construct the new Ministry.

It is now necessary to discuss the more intricate and difficult problem of the part which Lord Northcliffe and his newspapers played in the crisis which displaced Asquith and substituted Lloyd George as Premier. There has always been a vague, if unsubstantiated, idea in existence that Lloyd George and Northcliffe co-operated in this matter and that Lloyd George's final victory was supported by Northcliffe. This idea is an illusion. When the battle between the old school and the new actually joined issue, Northcliffe supported Lloyd George against Asquith effectively and patriotically. But this was not done by pre-arrangement; nor did Northcliffe ever believe in Lloyd George any more than Lloyd

George ever trusted Northcliffe. Northcliffe supported Lloyd George in his storming of the Premiership because he thought him a lesser evil than Asquith. His heart was with the soldiers and sailors and never with the politicians.

I have already related that I attached so much importance to Northcliffe's influence that I urged Lloyd George very strongly to become reconciled to him. This move failed, and Lloyd George maintained an unswerving attitude on this point. He did not want Northcliffe's support in his campaign for the reform of the Government. He said he thought it would do him more harm than good. The mere fact of Northcliffe's adherence would damage him with the Liberal Press. Besides, he did not trust Lord Northcliffe to keep up a consistent attitude on any policy for more than a few hours.

Where I failed, Lord Lee of Fareham, who had great influence with Lloyd George, appeared to have achieved success. He had already, and with some difficulty owing to the antagonism between the two men, brought about a meeting at his house in Abbey Garden, and on Friday morning, December 1, 1916, he persuaded Northcliffe to come to the War Office to see Lloyd George again. I happened to meet them in the passage on the way to my own room and we exchanged a casual nod.

Whatever passed at that interview, Lloyd George did not give Northcliffe his confidence. At any rate, Saturday's newspapers showed the " Daily Express " and the " Daily Chronicle " well informed as to the situation. The North-cliffe newspapers, "The Times" and the "Daily Mail," on the other hand, published leaders favourable to the cause of the revolters in the Cabinet, but their news of the crisis was sketchy and inaccurate. Obviously Lloyd George had discussed general politics with Northcliffe and formulated his own complaints; equally obviously he had not revealed the innermost truth of the situation.

Next morning (Saturday, December 2) North-cliffe came down to the War Office once more. He interviewed Lloyd George again, and the War Secretary must at least have told him something pretty definite as to the state of his mind, for shortly afterwards the "Evening News" came out with posters "Lloyd George packing up." My own idea is that Lloyd George at the second interview underlined his points and certainly made it clear that he contemplated resigna-tion.

Afterwards, Northcliffe came to my room in the War Office. We talked at length. But I made no disclosures as I was uncertain as to the extent of Lloyd George's confidence in the great news-paper proprietor.

But Northcliffe was not fully informed on the political situation even after two interviews with Lloyd George, and the proof is contained in a letter Northcliffe wrote to me on the Saturday afternoon. The note is written in his own hand. After referring to a trifling matter of business, it proceeds :

Hope your man (Bonar Law) is not going to follow Simon into obscurity.   It looks very like it to-day.   We get some bushels of abusive letters about his negative attitude with great regularity.

The letter shows that Lloyd George had never told Northcliffe in the course of two interviews that Bonar Law was standing by his side.   The future Premier would not make a cónfidant of the greatest man in Fleet Street.   And so it remained to the end of the crisis.

In stating that Lord Northcliffe was not in active co-operation with Lloyd George I am simply telling the plain truth.   It must not be supposed that I am not fully aware of the great influence Lord Northcliffe's attitude had on the development of events.   Northcliffe had been foremost in denouncing the inefficiency of the Asquith Government and in interpreting and focusing the popular judgment in this matter.   And when the breach between the supporters of Asquith and the insurgent Ministers came to a head, he stood firmly behind the revolt.

CHAPTER XXXII

" THE LIFE OF THE COUNTRY "

Saturday, December 2.

WE may now resume the strict chronological sequence of the narrative, which was left at the point where Bonar Law made his final decision late on Friday night.

On the Saturday morning I called on Lloyd George at the War Office. I told him of Bonar Law's final decision in exact terms. The wording of my communication had been authorised by Bonar Law himself. A discussion took place as to what was likely to happen at a meeting of Conservative Ministers, fixed for the following day, at Bonar Law's house. Lloyd George had by him the Prime Minister's letter of Friday, December 1, which was by no means an acceptance of Lloyd George's demands. It was in effect a recapitulation of the proposals put forward by Conservative Ministers at their meeting with Bonar Law on Thursday. It was a scheme for two War Councils and not for one supreme War Council. It was an acceptance of the plans of Lord Curzon and his friends and a rejection of the plans of Lloyd George and Bonar Law and Carson. If Bonar

Law was overwhelmed by sheer weight of numbers at the Conservative Meeting on the Sunday, all was over and lost. If Lloyd George and Bonar Law were beaten—whether their defeat took the shape of humiliation or resignation did not matter much—the consequences would hardly bear thinking about. The whole drive and pith would have gone out of the Ministry. There would have been left as the Conservative leader an avowed advocate of Peace by Negotiation, and as the Liberal leader an inveterate procrastinator. Ultimately the two tendencies might have met and resolved themselves into a common purpose. For the Cabinet would have been dominated by two men, one of whom did not think victory possible, while the other's practice made it impossible. And if Britain wilted under these influences, the allied cause was ruined. On that Saturday the world was menaced with the prospect of peace which would have left a militant Prussia still unchained. But the triumph of Lloyd George and Bonar Law spelt Peace with Victory.

In the face of these gigantic issues which every man concerned felt hovering dimly at the back of his mind, Lloyd George acted with great simplicity. It was for Bonar Law, not for him, to bear the next onset. He therefore sent him the Prime Minister's letter of refusal—presumably to be shown to his Conservative colleagues. And to hearten him up he sent him also a single sentence which deserves to rank with Lincoln's speech at Gettysburg, because both are simple, heroic and inspiring, and both mark a turning point in the history of a great people.

> War Office,
> Whitehall.
> Dec. 2, 1916.

My dear Bonar,

I enclose copy of P.M.'s letter.

The life of the country depends on resolute action by you now.

> Yours ever,
> D. Lloyd George.

The blast of the trumpet !

Later that day I met Churchill and Birkenhead together. Churchill was almost wistfully eager for news. It struck me forcibly as being so much out of character for him not to be in the very centre of events.

Birkenhead evinced little curiosity, but considerable gloom. He warned me that if the Government broke and Lloyd George failed to form a Cabinet, the consequent effect on the war would prove a heavy burden.

But the main preoccupation was the thought of the next day's meeting.

Lord Derby was recalled by Lloyd George to the War Office that evening from a short visit to Lancashire.

The suggestion was at once put forward that as he was a supporter of the War Council plan and of Lloyd George, he should be asked to attend the Conservative Ministers' Conference on Saturday. This would at least give Bonar Law one ally in the Conference—and a powerful one at that. For Derby, although only an Under-Secretary, spoke for all the Chairmen of the Conservative constituencies and organisations throughout Lancashire. He was local opinion personified, and when he said he was on the side of Lloyd George it meant that many Tory big-wigs in Liverpool and Manchester would be for Lloyd George too. If they were not so already, they would be once they heard which side Lord Derby favoured. In this sense he was, and remains, unique. There are other Conservative peers in high political positions who are also territorial magnates. But anyone would at once realise the strength of Lord Derby's influence in the northern constituencies.

Derby, however, was not actually a member of the Cabinet. His right to attend the meeting would not of course be challenged, because of the position he held in the party and the country. On the other hand, there was the risk that his presence might cause resentment and do more harm than good. It might be said that Bonar Law was trying to pack the Tory Conference—and this argument finally carried the day. It was decided on Saturday that Derby was not to attend the following day.

This night of Saturday I spent with Bonar Law.

It could not be maintained that the position was free from doubt and anxiety. In attempting to strengthen the conduct of the war the revolters within the Government might end in weakening the Executive without displacing it or reconstruct-

ing it. The risk was not the damage to the rebels—
for which they cared nothing—but to the country
as a whole.

What was the balance sheet ? What was the
strength of the various parties, ideas, personalities,
and interests concerned ? On the debit side was
the unswerving hostility of the Conservative
Ministers.

On the credit side there was Carson. His
instinct had penetrated to the belief that we were
faced by a menace which might be described as
respectable defeatism. Carson's judgment was
determined and his position unassailable. He was
convinced beyond argument. He was a strong
reserve in a great emergency.

The immense asset was that Bonar Law had
made up his mind, just at the moment when the
Prime Minister seemed to be swaying between
defiance and surrender. Bonar Law had by this
time completed his usual mental process. He had
considered and calculated until the final solution
had become clear in his brain. Once his mind was
made up he never looked back, but marched
straight on in the field of action to the inevitable
conclusion.

Lloyd George was the final factor. Manifestly
emerging as a mighty leader, he was not so clear
in his mental process as either Carson or Bonar
Law.

It was not quite so certain whether he desired
to eliminate Asquith in a polite manner or to
smash him. But this at least was true that, in some
vague and inspired manner he represented all

those forces of national energy which were determined on a complete victory.

Carson, perhaps, saw his way clearly, for his mind had long ago been made up to the fall of the Government and all that it entailed. Bonar Law had hesitated between the conflicting duties which now occupied his mind. Lloyd George ran the greatest risk and incurred the heaviest responsibilities, for his decision would in the long run be paramount. Lloyd George, even if all forsook him and fled, could still form an Administration out of the Tory back-benchers which would be more alert and able than its predecessor, and could put forward a policy so vigorous and inevitable that it would receive the thunderous endorsement of the country. In these various moods men awaited the day of trial.

CHAPTER XXXIII

THE STORM

Sunday, December 3.

SATURDAY had been to me an exhausting day, and I awoke feeling weary. None the less, knowing that the critical day was now come, I went round that morning to Pembroke Lodge, where the Conservative Ministers were in session. I found Miss Law and Lord Stonehaven in another room, and I occupied a third one. Thence I sent a written note in to Bonar Law to let him know privately that I was there—if he wished to see me. It was not advisable that his colleagues should know, since they were ready enough as it was to charge me with possessing too much influence over him—a charge which was not true.

You must picture me waiting nervously and impatiently and wondering what was happening in the other room.

Things downstairs had taken an extreme turn—extreme indeed beyond all anticipation. All the Tory leaders had arrived with copies of " Reynold's " newspaper which contained a startling article. It was quite a different production from the statements in the " Daily Express " and the " Daily Chronicle." The " Reynold's " article said quite plainly that Lloyd George was prepared to resign if his terms were not granted and that he would then appeal to public opinion against the Government for mismanaging the war. Further it stated that Lloyd George was in active alliance with Carson : that Bonar Law would probably resign with him—and that Lord Derby was starting along the same road. Finally the article looked on the surface as if it had been directly inspired. It was like an interview with Lloyd George written in the third person.

No wonder the Tory Ministers were indignant at what they considered a monstrous breach of confidence taking the form of a public threat to them in the middle of a delicate negotiation. Indeed, it was hardly surprising that the tone of the meeting had changed since Thursday from one of passive hostility to Lloyd George's plan to an active determination to force an issue and compel Lloyd George to accept the domination of the Prime Minister or retire from the Government. It became rapidly apparent that Bonar Law stood absolutely alone. Opposed to him sat the whole array of the Tory leaders— Lord Curzon, Austen Chamberlain, Lord Robert Cecil, Walter Long, etc. The dominant note of the meeting was hostility to Lloyd George and to his plans for organising a War Council. It must be observed in passing that this attitude was assumed by the official representatives of a party which more than any other was responsible for the demand for a change in the Administration. The Tory Press had been indefatigable for months, both in London and in the provinces, in demanding a change from " Wait and see " in military and naval methods ; it both represented and created the opinion of the vast bulk of the Tory electorate who had rallied to the Lloyd Georgian view of affairs not from love of its protagonist, but out of sheer despair. Half the Tory party in the House of Commons (and this in the absence of the Service members) believed in Carson and more vigorous measures. Many others were only constrained from open concurrence by loyalty to Bonar Law and their party. In fact, every interest of national safety and of party expediency pointed in one direction yet the party leaders with one accord defied their chief, their followers, and their Press, and marched off in the other.

That these Party leaders were sincere and honest patriots, acting according to their lights, is not to be denied. Of course they were —and yet they were utterly mistaken.

The only explanation of this amazing fact must be sought in the hypnotic influence which Asquith —using his position as Prime Minister—had very subtly acquired over their minds. This influence alone makes the conduct of the Tory leaders explicable. They were, in fact, more Royalist than the King. They determined not only to support the Prime Minister against Lloyd George, but to compel the Prime Minister to advance far beyond his own intentions in a vigorous counter-offensive which was to turn Lloyd George out of the Cabinet. Never in political history was there a more confused situation. The Prime Minister only desired to be left in peace, and was not unprepared to make concessions in order to avoid a breach with Lloyd George, provided the price was not a break with other colleagues. His one fear, as he had explained, was that concessions might not avoid a final break. He was now to have his hand forced.

The following resolution was passed by the meeting :

We share the view expressed to you by Mr. Bonar Law some time ago that the Government cannot continue as it is.

It is evident that a change must be made, and, in our opinion, the publicity given to the intention of Mr. Lloyd George makes reconstruction from within no longer possible.

We therefore urge the Prime Minister to tender the resignation of the Government.

If he feels unable to take that step, we authorise Mr. Bonar Law to tender our resignations.

This resolution, like many such passed by committees, each member of which insists on inserting or altering phrases, is decidedly ambiguous. Its intention was to force a crisis by which the resignation of Asquith would compel Lloyd George to retire into private life or to attempt the formation of a Ministry. On his failure, which was thought certain, Asquith would return stronger than ever, and Lloyd George and his few friends would be thrown out of the Government on its re-formation. In any case, the decision, they thought, would prevent Lloyd George from dragging them at the tail of his coat. They did not believe in him, and they did not believe in the sincerity of his intentions. They looked on his activities as subversive of order and unison in the Government and the country. They charged him with inspiring the Press hostile to the Administration and held him responsible for attacks on several of their departments. They reverted to the accusation that he wished to be second man in the Government and also leader of the Opposition.

But all that the resolution says is that there must be reconstruction after resignation, and it might just as well mean that the Prime Minister should go as that Lloyd George must.

In fact, when the general terms of the Conservative resolution became known later on, after all the signatories had become members of the new Lloyd George Ministry, the outside public not unnaturally concluded that the resolution meant that Asquith should go—whereas it meant, to all its supporters except Bonar Law, that Lloyd George should go. I impute in this matter no discredit to the Conservative leaders. On the contrary, I think I can explain their motives. None the less, I must reveal the historic fact as to what their intentions were.

At last Bonar Law left the Conference and came in to me. He at once gave me an outline of the situation and of the attitude of his colleagues. He did not, however, show me then the actual text of the resolution, but he told me in general terms that it called on Asquith to resign.

Bonar Law's motive in coming out to see me was not to ask for my advice, but to clear his own mind. As I have already explained, he had long formed a habit of arguing out his pros and cons of any political problem which confronted him, with me as an attentive audience.

The problem he now faced was this. Should he adhere to the resolution ? He fully grasped that the object of that resolution was hostile to Lloyd George and intended to be helpful to Asquith—whereas his desire was to make Asquith part with a considerable portion of his powers (for war purposes) to Lloyd George. There was therefore a direct clash of intention between himself and his colleagues—yet these antagonisms might yet be covered by the terms of the resolution.

Seldom has there been, I should think, such a peculiar situation in the history of politics. The other Conservative members of the Government wanted to tell Asquith that he must resign office in order to crush Lloyd George finally and effectively. But Bonar Law had already told the Prime Minister that he would resign if Lloyd George's demands were not granted. So—as he argued it out to himself—all he was asked to do was to subscribe in written form to a simple threat of resignation which he had already made in words. The resolution on the face of it committed no one of the signatories either to Asquith or Lloyd George.

Then came to Bonar Law the broader thought :
" My colleagues and I are united at least on one
great and single thing. We all alike believe that
the present situation is intolerable—that the
Government must go and a new formation take
its place. They hope the new Ministry will be
formed on their pattern; I hope it will be formed
on mine. So let us agree to have a clean sweep of
the situation—and then let the best man win."

On this Bonar Law clinched his decision. He
marched out of the room and back to his waiting
colleagues. He gave his approval to the resolution, and promised to take it to the Prime Minister
that afternoon at three o'clock.

I must add a note of explanation.

The advice to Asquith of the Tory majority in
the Ministry was not to reconstruct but to resign.

For the benefit of those not versed in the
inside machinery of Downing Street it may be as
well to explain clearly the courses and alternatives
open to a Premier who finds himself faced with a
revolt or a weakness in his Cabinet.

(1) If he is certain that he has the confidence
of the country, he may do what Asquith did in
May, 1915. That is to say, he can remain in office
himself, but call for the resignations of all the
other Ministers. This Asquith did, without
objection, in 1915, in order to strengthen his
Ministry by the inclusion of a Tory element.

(2) If a Prime Minister faced with revolt is not
certain as to whether he possesses the confidence
of the country, or whether some other politician

Dec 2nd 1916

My dear Bonar

[illegible]

P.M's letter.

The life of the

[illegible] depends on

resolute actio[n] by

you now

Yours [illegible]

[signature]

Record of conversation between Bonar Law and Asquith, made by Lord Beaverbrook, on December 5, 1916.

might be preferred, he can put it to a simple test. He can resign—Ministry and all—and leave it to a possible rival to form an alternative Government. If the rival can do so, the test has decided against the existing Premier, and all is well from the constitutional standpoint. But if no rival can form a Ministry, then the resigning Premier returns to power with an immense accession of strength and prestige. He has proved himself the only possible Premier—so woe to the revolters in the Cabinet !

The Conservative Ministers wanted Asquith to take the second course—resignation—for one single reason. They thought it was the most complete and final way of crushing Lloyd George and dissensions in the Cabinet once and for all. They did not doubt that Asquith was the only possible Prime Minister—or they might have been more chary of giving the advice.

They were certain of it. What they wanted was to see it proved beyond all cavil by a failure of Lloyd George to form a Ministry. Then Asquith would come back to undisputed power and all his Ministers with him—save Lloyd George and possibly Bonar Law, or, if these Ministers chose to come in again under Asquith, they must do so as chastened and crippled colleagues.

Asquith, as we shall see, at first did not feel like this at all. He was frightened at the revolt and wanted to make some sort of terms with Lloyd George which would simply involve a reconstruction of the Ministry.

Even when a breach seemed unavoidable he would at the outset have preferred to follow the precedent of 1915, and at first proposed to do so because this course looked safer. But as the situation developed he found he could not do this because the conditions in 1916 were different from those of the preceding year. In 1915 he had the confidence of the country, and the Coalition was effected by mutual consent.

In 1916 he had not the universal confidence of the country or his own Cabinet. If he used the 1915 method to push his opponents out of the Cabinet, they would have fought him from outside and probably brought him down. The only method of crushing them finally was to show himself the only possible Prime Minister by resigning and proving that no one else could form a Ministry. This he thought wrongly that he could do.

When Asquith became converted by degrees to these ideas he changed his scheme from reconstruction to resignation.

To put the matter in a nutshell, reconstruction which left the Prime Minister still in office was only possible by means of an agreement with Lloyd George. The method was no good as a weapon against Lloyd George. If, on the contrary, there was to be an open breach, resignation became the only possible course.

.   .   .   .

I now return to my narrative. The Tory magnates departed at twelve noon and I remained

to lunch with Bonar Law's family. It was at
lunch that Bonar Law showed me the actual text
of the resolution he had agreed to with the others.
I was startled by the Clause denouncing Lloyd
George for communicating with the Press. Bonar
Law had not mentioned anything about this to
me. What did it mean ? I took the clause and read
it carefully. " In our opinion the publicity given
to the intentions of Mr. Lloyd George makes
reconstruction from within no longer possible."
If words meant anything these words meant this :

1. That the Tories would not countenance a
peaceable adjustment with Lloyd George.
2. That their reasons for taking this line was
that Lloyd George was abusing his position by
disclosures to " Reynolds."

The danger to Bonar Law lay in this publicity
clause. The rest of the document was one he
could safely sign in perfect good faith, though
he and his colleagues wanted different things.

But in the publicity clause was a definite accusation of a most serious character made against
Lloyd George. On the basis of this charge he
was to be destroyed and if he raised his voice
in the Country his opponents would retaliate on
him with this very accusation of his relationship
with the Press. And Bonar Law had counter-
signed the indictment ! It would be said that
Lloyd George's own ally believed this to be true
of him and set his belief down in writing.

I was aghast at the results that must follow.

For this would separate Bonar Law from Lloyd
George and bring him back to the camp of his
colleagues. In that case all the work of weeks
would be wasted, and the Government would
contrive to carry on the war as ineffectively as
ever. Or rather things would be worse; for Lloyd
George would have been thrown out of the
Ministry.

I thought that if Bonar Law took the document
to the Premier a split between Bonar Law and
Lloyd George might result. I therefore implored
Bonar Law in the most vigorous language to
insist on having the publicity charge deleted from
the resolutions—to throw it back in the teeth of
his colleagues and suffer anything rather than
accept responsibility for it.

Although I abhorred the publicity charge, I
did not blame the Tory Ministers for their anger
with Lloyd George.

I think the " Reynold's " article tried them very
highly. Here they had been from Thursday onwards in an extremely difficult negotiation which
involved the unity of their party, the future of the
Administration, and the fate of the country—and
were trying to bring it to some sort of successful end. Suddenly the whole business is
exposed in a truculent manner.

Bonar Law took the whole question of the
publicity clause much more calmly. He deplored
the publication in " Reynolds " because it had
savaged the Conservatives, but he was not involved in the charge. So long as he continued
to work in practice with Lloyd George what did

this newspaper article or the protest clause in the resolution really matter ? He was not going to be deflected in his course of policy by the incident at all.

I could not accept this view and I continued to press Bonar Law hard. But he did not take this persistency in good part.

At last I got quite heated and Bonar Law showed definite signs of impatience. He always swallowed his food in gulps and now he got up and left the table before the rest of us had finished. It was as though he resented my pressure and wished to be relieved from it. I finished my lunch quietly and then went up to his study, where he used to sit before the fire in a deep armchair, pipe going, and official documents heaped on the floor all round him.

I must say that I was a trifle doubtful of my reception. He might think me the pursuer come to renew the argument. But Bonar Law was never like that. He was the first to make advances after any kind of tiff or disagreement. He never sulked, and always made me feel that it was I that had a right to be angry.

He received my renewed arguments in a perfectly friendly way and he agreed to my suggestion that we should send for Birkenhead to discuss the question of the resolution on publicity.

Bonar Law agreed to this without making any real change in the view that the subject was trivial. The reason for selecting Birkenhead was that, though hostile to Lloyd George, he was loyal to Bonar Law, and with good reason. At the time of the formation of the First Coalition in 1915 he would never have obtained office but for the strenuous fight put up by Bonar Law on his behalf against all the rest of his Conservative colleagues, and also Lloyd George, who did not want him included in the Ministry. In fact he owed his political preferment to Bonar Law as much as one man can owe to another.

Birkenhead, however, when he arrived and heard the explanation, would give no assistance to the argument that the terms of the resolution ought to be altered. My contention was that the resolution assumed in advance that Lloyd George had inspired the " Reynold's " article. But he might have had nothing whatever to do with it and be able to clear himself. If the resolution had been hypothetical—if it had said " supposing Lloyd George has done this thing then other steps ought to be taken," it would not matter so much—surely the Conservative Ministers could be called together again and the resolution could be altered in this sense before it was shown to the Prime Minister.

Birkenhead replied that this could not be done. It would change the whole sense of the resolution against the intention of its authors. They believed Lloyd George was responsible for the article, and the resolution was definitely intended to be offensive to him on this ground. So nothing was changed. As the event proved, Bonar Law was right in thinking that this particular incident would not have any effect on the main course of events. None the less there was a big risk involved, and had the situation developed slightly differently

much more would have been heard of the cry of
" Trafficking with the Press."

Was Lloyd George the direct source of the
" Reynold's " article ? I have always believed that
he was not—though I have no proof ; still, it is a fact
that Lord Dalziel, the proprietor of " Reynold's,"
saw Lloyd George on the day before the issue.

But the publication can be accounted for by
other ways than by direct inspiration from the
War Minister. Lord Dalziel was an extremely
important person in the Liberal Party. Few
people realise how in his early days he had been
Lloyd George's closest rival in the race for the
support of the Radicals of the left. He had in
those times a better sense of the House of Commons than Lloyd George, and a finer understanding of the uses of debate. He was openly
pointed to as the future leader of the party.
Lloyd George has told me that he himself shared
this opinion of Dalziel's qualities in the early days.

Dalziel is a most lovable man, but he never
realised these high expectations others formed
for him. Perhaps he would not play the great
game because he was too much bound by com-
mercial affairs. Enough, however, has been
said to show that such a man was sure to be
intimately advised from many sources as to the
course the internal politics of the Cabinet were
taking. As a matter of fact I saw him with Neil
Primrose at his house during the crisis, but he
never asked me for any account of the position
—for he knew it too well. He only poked a
little fun at me—treating my efforts in a satirical

vein of humour. Dalziel was therefore perfectly able to write the article the Tory Ministers complained of by piecing together the various bits of information at his disposal without having recourse to one of the protagonists in the struggle. And this I believe is what really happened.

About three o'clock in the afternoon, Bonar Law started off to see Asquith, and I went with him as far as the Colonial Office. On that dreary winter Sunday afternoon Whitehall seemed more depressing than usual. We tried to get in by a side door. The attendant at the empty office seemed uncertain whether Bonar Law really was the Colonial Secretary or not. There was no fire in his room, and I lit it. Then I huddled myself up in this cold barn of an edifice over the flickering flames while Bonar Law went across to Downing Street. This wait was enough to depress anyone. It was the dark hour of this day of days—the most important and exciting I have ever passed in my life. In the gloom of the Colonial Office I had a sense of impending disaster. The mists seemed to creep up out of the afternoon and invade the room without a light. We were all mistaken after all ? Would nothing result from our efforts but two or three months of confusion—of weaker Government even than that which existed at that day ? All was chaos and night, and our plans might be swallowed up in the void.

For these few moments I doubted about my original preconception—that Asquith's position was the myth and our strength the reality. The dark hours must come some times in every crisis.

CHAPTER XXXIV

THE INTERVIEW

IN the meantime Lloyd George had rung me up from Walton Heath before we started out from Bonar Law's house for the Colonial Office. Naturally, he wanted to hear the result of the Conservative meeting. His voice came on the telephone, " WELL ? "—interrogation itself epitomised in a word. It was not possible to explain it all to him on the telephone, but he said he would go straight to the War Office, and there receive the news both of the Conservative meeting and the attitude taken up by the Prime Minister.

Bonar Law now came back and related his interview with the Prime Minister. He had explained to Asquith that while he was separated from his colleagues on the subject of Lloyd George and his war plans, all the Conservative Ministers insisted on the resignation of the Government, including the Prime Minister, as the only possible way out of the existing dilemma. His colleagues thought this method would put an end to Lloyd George's pretensions. Bonar Law himself thought it would have a very different result. Anyhow, there was the Conservative decision.

So much was said at the time about this interview, and so many echoes of the story still continue to reverberate, that it is absolutely necessary to try to form some clear idea of what actually took place.

For an actual charge of bad faith was levelled against Bonar Law in this connexion though it was abandoned when the real facts became known. The charge against Bonar Law was simply this— that he had failed either by accident or design to impress on the Prime Minister the extent of the hostility felt by his Conservative colleagues to Lloyd George and his claims. In other words he had'abused his position as an ambassador in order to misrepresent the views of his clients because he did not happen to agree with them personally. One could hardly imagine a more terrible accusation against any public man. In the case of a man of Bonar Law's character such a charge might be left to refute itself by its inherent absurdity. Still I think it ought to be met by a true and contemporary account of what happened.

Bonar Law was clear-headed, determined, fixed in his intention, and settled in his mind at this interview. He was the last person in the world to fail to give a lucid exposition of a political situation. And his word is the last in the world to be doubted when he states, as he did, that he explained the whole situation to Asquith with the most complete frankness.

Asquith, on the other hand, seized on nothing in the Tory resolution except the demand that he should resign. This single word RESIGNATION frightened him. He had not got by any means so far as the use of that last great weapon against Lloyd George. The point that caught his sole attention was not therefore the motives which induced the three C's* and Walter Long and others to urge him on to resignation—but the mere fact that they demanded that he should resign. The hostility of the Tories to Lloyd George, and the attack over trafficking with the Press, seemed to be quite occluded in his mind by the major issue of resignation. As to the attitude of the Tory Ministers mentioned, it is quite ridiculous to suggest that Bonar Law could have misled Asquith even if he had wished to. Asquith was in the closest communication with his Tory colleagues and was as well aware of what had been said at the Tory meeting on Thursday as if he had been present himself. But to know a fact is not necessarily to realise its significance. In spite of Bonar Law's patient and lucid explanation the Prime Minister obviously did not at that moment grasp the importance of that part of the resolution which accused Lloyd George of trafficking in Fleet Street. He did not realise that the feeling of antagonism between the two conflicting forces in his Cabinet had gone very deep down, and that no accommodation was really possible. The one word " resign " was before him and he feared it.

It may help to clarify the narrative if the reader will remember that Asquith always had three courses before him in dealing with the

* Curzon, Cecil and Austen Chamberlain.

Lloyd George revolt. Plan No. I was to grant Lloyd George's demands. Plan No. II was to continue his Government but to expel Lloyd George and his friends from it. Plan No. III was to resign and prove that the rebels could not form an alternative Ministry and that he was the indispensable Premier. We shall find in the course of the next forty-eight hours Asquith changing from one of these policies to another as the facts of the situation change or the strategy of the hour demands.

The effect of Bonar Law's communication and the word " Resign " was to impel Asquith violently in the direction of Plan No. I.

The gist of Bonar Law's statement when he rejoined me at the Colonial Office was that the Premier was getting ready to come to terms with Lloyd George. I did not regard this, as Bonar Law did, as an ideal solution of the crisis, for I thought that nothing would go well so long as Asquith was in power at all. Yet a sense of pleasurable relief accompanied the idea of a peace. The tension of the last two or three days had been too much—and if a compromise could be effected which would avoid the risk of merely creating a Government weaker than its forerunner, was there not something to be said for a truce ? This was a decision of the nerves rather than of the mind.

Bonar Law then proceeded to summon another meeting of the Conservative leaders (at Birkenhead's house, so as to be handy for Downing Street) while I went off, according to my promise, to meet Lloyd George at the War Office.

This was the most momentous interview of my life. The future of the country depended on the events of the next few hours. Lloyd George had been content to say that Asquith was a muddler and that an ordinary, efficient, and practical man of affairs should be placed in control of the war. None the less, this more modest plea barely concealed Lloyd George's real conviction that he was the only man for the crisis—the only adequate instrument for winning the war.

Lloyd George had already arrived at the War Office.

My first task was to tell him what had taken place at the Conservative Conference. Naturally, I was extremely anxious to see how he would take the news of the " Publicity Clause " in the resolution. Lloyd George showed no annoyance. He said " If this resolution is going to separate me from Bonar Law it matters. Is it going to separate us ? " I said it need make no difference so long as he did not wish it to. " Then," said Lloyd George " it is a matter of no importance whatever—and I don't care a bit about it." He regarded Asquith's change of front in dealing with Bonar Law's news from the Conservative camp as one more piece of evidence of the absolute instability of the Premier's mind and of the urgent necessity of taking the control of the war out of this man's hand.

But as a matter of fact Lloyd George did not need any encouragement at the critical hour which was to decide his fate and that of the nation.

He was firmly fixed in his purpose. The national interests must take precedence over any personal interest or concern. Private and party loyalties were things of no account. All that counted was to save the people from a ruin worse than anything that could be anticipated. He would be accused of treachery to his Chief, of the ruin of his party—these threats and accusations would in no way deter him from doing his duty.

At last came the expected message and summons from the Prime Minister. Lloyd George took it very coolly. He lit a cigar and considered impartially the interview which lay before him. I had never seen any man exhibit so much moral courage in the face of such great events. He considered that what he had to avoid was a settlement which was not really a decision. He would not be duped into accepting a position which gave the competent men no final and complete control of the conduct of the war. He must know how he stood in this matter once and for all before he left Downing Street. If this control was refused, events must take their course. He finished his cigar quietly ard left for Downing Street.

The result of this momentous interview was, after all these alarums and excursions, something of an anti-climax. Lloyd George and Asquith practically came to terms—that is to say, the functions and organisation of the War Council were to be as Lloyd George wanted, and Asquith would remain Premier. The only point that they did not settle was that of the personnel of the committee ; Asquith was anxious to include Henderson as a Labour representative, and wished to exclude Carson. It did not, however, appear likely that the negotiations would break down on the question of personnel.

At the end of this interview Bonar Law arrived at No. 10. Asquith informed him that he and Lloyd George had come to a complete understanding as to the status and functions of the War Committee—but that they were not entirely agreed as to personnel. He added that Lloyd George was in the house and suggested that he should come in.

Lloyd George appeared, and the Prime Minister again repeated the statement that there was complete agreement between them as to the nature of the Council, although they were not entirely agreed on personnel.

Could anything be clearer ?

This was the last private and personal interview which Lloyd George had with Asquith during the crisis. We shall see that on the morrow (Monday) Lloyd George tried in vain to arrange such a meeting.

About half-past six Bonar Law and Lloyd George returned to the War Office. Bonar Law then left for Birkenhead's house. The conference of Conservative Ministers there (Walter Long was not present) simply agreed to hold over the whole question of resignation.

Sunday evening then closed in peace, for the issue appeared to be settled and a substantial if not a complete victory gained by the reformers.

Such is often the way with the political crises,

for the political mind is a very curious thing. It can only be kept at a state of tension leading to big decisions so long as it can be concentrated on a single issue or problem. Relieve the strain for a moment; substitute some other question, if only for a few hours, and the politician will gladly grasp the chance to ride off on the side issue.

The night was, however, signalised by one curious incident. E. S. Montagu, Minister of Munitions, spent the evening with Asquith. He had been an encouraging supporter of Lloyd George, but doubts existed as to the point to which he was prepared to go. He desired the change in administration, but was unwilling to leave the ranks of official Liberalism, and the direful instance of Joseph Chamberlain was (rather absurdly, perhaps) held up before would-be seceders from the true fold. Chamberlain, it will be observed, lost the Premiership by changing his party, and this fact might be expected to act as a warning to Lloyd George and his backers. In any case, Montagu kept a leg in each camp. His position was obviously one of some difficulty. But his essential position was clear enough. The sum and aim of his policy all through the crisis was to keep Asquith and Lloyd George together. He considered that Asquith's strength lay in the confidence of House of Commons and of the Country, and Lloyd George's in the active conduct of the war. To combine these two forces was the path which led to victory; to allow them to separate, to antagonise, and so to nullify each other would be

"I have been through the hell of a time."—MR. ASQUITH
on December 6, 1916.

BONAR LAW

The Unknown Premier

a national disaster. It was an eminently reasonable view and—as this narrative shows—Montagu's opinion was widely shared by public men, including Bonar Law.

Lloyd George had been angling for Montagu's support by proposing Montagu's inclusion in the projected War Council as a kind of extra Liberal member to keep the balance even, and as a set-off to Carson. Montagu would only negotiate with Asquith's concurrence, and as Asquith had never agreed to Lloyd George's ideas of the personnel of the new War Council, the proposal never took formal shape. There is no doubt that Lloyd George played on Montagu's sympathies, which coincided with his interests, and a settlement by consent represented the apex of Montagu's ambitions. He might get on the War Council and yet keep Asquith and Lloyd George together. His influence was exerted for peace, and on Sunday night he persuaded the Prime Minister (against what had been settled earlier in the evening and without consultation with his colleagues) to issue a statement to the Press to the effect that there would be a reconstruction of the Ministry from within as follows :

The following official statement was issued at 11.45 p.m., 3rd December, 1916 : " The Prime Minister, with a view to the most active prosecution of the war, has decided to advise His Majesty the King to consent to a reconstruction of the Government."

This was the equivalent to the announcement

of a settlement between Lloyd George and Asquith.

E. S. Montagu's account throws light upon the position. Montagu says that agreement was reached on Sunday night while he was at Downing Street. He says that Lord Crewe came, but that the Prime Minister said little in front of Crewe, who was not cognisant of the negotiations.* The resolution of the Conservatives presented by Bonar Law opened up an entirely new and critical development. Lloyd George was sent for on Montagu's suggestion. When the Prime Minister was informed that Lloyd George was at Walton Heath he remarked, " That is the man for quick action." On Lloyd George's arrival, and after the conference with the Prime Minister, Lloyd George remarked to Montagu that an agreement was probable, but that he feared that Montagu was not likely to be a member of the new War Council, as Henderson had been considered.

Afterwards the Prime Minister told Montagu that all the Ministers would be asked to hand in their resignations, and he contemplated putting Runciman at the Admiralty. Thus, agreement with Lloyd George and Reconstruction, not Strife with Lloyd George and Resignation, was still the tendency that Sunday night.

Montagu begged the Prime Minister to put in writing his understanding with Lloyd George and send it to him that night. It was also decided to issue the notice to the Press.

---

* Lord Crewe has stated that he had been fully informed of all that was going on by the Premier by noon of that day. Presumably therefore the Premier did not trouble to repeat to him what he knew already.

Asquith's own account of the position on Sunday night was written from 10 Downing Street on that evening.

It is as follows :

I drove down to Walmer yesterday afternoon hoping to find sunshine & peace. It was bitterly drab & cold, and for my sins (or other people's) I had to drive back soon after 11 this morning.

I was forced back by Bongie* & Montagu & Rufus† to grapple with a " Crisis "—this time with a very big C. The result is that I have spent much of the afternoon in colloguing with Messrs. Ll. George & Bonar Law, & one or two minor worthies. The " Crisis " shows every sign of following its many predecessors to an early & unhonoured grave. But there were many wigs very nearly on the green.

The day which thus closed so calmly had been, indeed, sufficiently tempestuous to make peace grateful to the actors in this complicated and bewildering drama. The dénouement had been entirely unexpected. The day had begun by an attempt of the official Conservatives to come to the rescue of the Prime Minister and his Liberal friends against Lloyd George and to drive the latter out of the Cabinet. But, like the famous elephants of the Carthaginian army, their appearance as allies had struck more terror into the heart of friend than foe. The Prime Minister was frankly alarmed by the resolution which forced resigna-

* Sir M. Bonham Carter.   † Lord Reading.

tion on the Government, and hastened to make
terms with his formidable adversary while he was
still in the way with him, rather than face the perils
of resignation.

Lloyd George had obtained from Asquith the
official control of the war. But he had not got the
Premiership, and this last boon was presented to
him only by the efforts of his enemies. Unfortunately for Lloyd George's opponents, many of
them were busy picking up missing threads and
joining gaps in the lines of communication. As
Monday drew on they became cognisant of their
conjoint numerical strength, but not of their
concomitant moral weakness, nor of the powers
with which they had to contend.

The Conservative Ministers who had opposed
Bonar Law were especially indignant at the
developments of Sunday evening. They felt they
had been abandoned by Asquith, who had com-
promised with the arch enemy instead of destroying him. Many of their Liberal colleagues felt
precisely the same. Both sections thought the
Prime Minister had been bluffed by Lloyd George
and that the War Secretary held no real cards in
his hand. So when Asquith suddenly turned round
and decided to fight he had already inflicted a most
serious moral damage on his own cause by his
previous readiness to accept the Lloyd George
terms. After his attempted compromise on
Sunday Asquith lacked whole-hearted support in
either party. The tempest, then, which had subsided so suddenly on Sunday night began to rise
again the following day.

CHAPTER XXXV

THE HURRICANE

Monday, December 4.

ON Monday morning the illusory peace of Sunday evening vanished and the great storm winds began to blow once more. Part of the reason for the sudden shift must be sought in what had occurred at Montagu's house in Queen Anne's Gate late the night before. Lloyd George had not been satisfied that Asquith's verbal assurances at the afternoon interview, though more or less satisfactory in themselves, could be depended on. He wanted a ratification of his position as Mayor of the Palace for war purposes, in writing— for fear the weathercock might swing round. To obtain this vital document he employed Montagu, with whom Asquith was spending the evening, as his intermediary. Montagu undoubtedly desired keenly that Asquith should accept Lloyd George's terms. A rupture between the two men would force him to make a dangerous and doubtful choice—whereas, as has been already shown, there was always quite a good chance that he might be promoted to the new War Council as a counterpoise to Carson.

Finally, there is no doubt that, on the merits of the case, he thought Lloyd George right.

So on the Sunday night he tried very hard to get
the Prime Minister to sign some kind of docu-
mênt ratifying the treaty with Lloyd George
provisionally arranged a few hours earlier. Had
Montagu succeeded, all might have gone smoothly
for Asquith, for he would have been so deeply
committed to Lloyd George that it would have
been practically impossible for him to draw back
on the following day.   Again, had Montagu
failed to get anything in writing, Lloyd George
and Asquith might have come to a complete and
final settlement themselves—for nothing except
the personnel of the War Council remained to be
decided, and here there was plenty of room for
give and take—on the Monday morning without
any outside intervention having time to operate
in a hostile manner.

As it was, all that Montagu extracted from
Asquith was the disastrous statement to the Press
issued at 11.45 p.m. on the Sunday. This merely
announced the reconstruction of the Government.   But it came as an absolute bombshell
to the greater part of the political world. It
brought the politicians out the following Monday
morning buzzing like so many flies.   Downing Street was besieged. Imagine the surprise
of the Liberals—of Asquith's colleagues and
intimates ! Only Montagu, Crewe and Reading
knew anything at all about the Lloyd George
plan and the Bonar Law negotiations. The other
Liberal Cabinet Ministers had no idea that there
was any serious trouble until they suddenly
read in the newspapers that their Ministry was

to be reconstructed. They must have felt a justifiable sense of grievance in having been kept in the dark in so strange a fashion. Asquith in 1916, as in 1915, intended to act in these periods of internal crisis as though the Ministry was his private property instead of a joint stock company.

Early on Monday morning the uninformed Liberal Ministers—McKenna, Harcourt, Runciman and Grey—all called at Downing Street. Their note was one of surprise, dismay and protest. When they heard Lloyd George's terms they objected to them altogether. McKenna made himself the protagonist of this anti-Lloyd George attitude and voiced his own views and those of his colleagues in the most vehement fashion. To give way to the extent Asquith seemed prepared to do was, he said, to reduce the Premiership to a mere shadow, while all effective control of events would be transferred to the revolting Minister. It was a humiliation not to be endured by any statesman. Further, Lloyd George's assumption that he was the only man fit to run the war was in no way justified by the Cabinet experience of the last two years. But if he was to have control he ought also to have full official responsibility. It would be better for Asquith to go now, rather than linger on as a discredited ghost of a Premier until it suited Lloyd George to turn him out altogether. Better still would be to fight Lloyd George now, to refuse his terms and to crush the rebellion. The Liberal Ministers would swear a pact to stand by Asquith. McKenna thus at once put himself at the head of the non-compromising Liberals, and his bold and resolute action produced important results. Montagu, for instance, had considerable hopes of securing Grey's support for the policy of agreement and compromise, but found that McKenna had been before him and had secured Grey's adhesion to his own standpoint.

But of course the principal reaction of the line taken by McKenna and his colleagues was the effect on the mind of Asquith himself. He suddenly found rising up behind him a new army pledged vehemently to support him against Lloyd George's pretensions. He began to realise that he was not in such a weak and dangerous position as he had imagined the previous evening.

When, therefore, Montagu came to him later in the morning—once more at Lloyd George's urgent suggestion—to secure written ratification of the proposed settlement, he found Asquith in a far less pliable· and satisfactory frame of mind than he had been the night before.

For not only had the Liberal Ministers come to protest to the Prime Minister against his suggested course of action, but Tory Ministers had been too. The bulletin had said, "Reconstruction," but the Tories wanted resignation.

Lord Robert Cecil had been for some little time in close contact with the Prime Minister and had kept him in touch with sentiment in Tory Ministerial circles.

Apparently, as the result of his intervention,

a sudden doubt was spread whether the Prime Minister had been fully informed—or at least whether he really grasped the full vigour—of the intention of the Tory Ministers, excepting Bonar Law, to down Lloyd George at any cost and to insist on universal resignation rather than on partial reconstruction to achieve this primary end.

At any rate, the " three C's "—Curzon, Chamberlain, and Cecil—then waited on Asquith that Monday morning (saying also that they spoke for Walter Long) and put their point of view and their policy before him.* As has been explained already, Bonar Law, the previous day, had put Asquith quite clearly in full possession of the fact that all his colleagues were hostile to Lloyd George. But once more it may be said that knowing a fact is not the same thing as grasping its significance. Asquith was a worried man at the Sunday interview, and the word "Resignation" in the Tory resolution had alarmed him. Now, with the Tory leaders in front of him in the flesh he was reassured. He understood how deep was the severance between them and Bonar Law. It was explained to him that the plan of wholesale resignation rather than of reconstruction was only intended to make more certain the destruction of the common enemy. The three C's at the time never made any secret of their purpose. They were never in any doubt of the wisdom of their course. The object of their insistence on Asquith's resignation was this : Lloyd George and Bonar Law were to be given the opportunity of forming

* Sir Austen Chamberlain says he did not see Asquith until Tuesday morning.

a Government—which the Tory Ministers were certain they could not do. When this failure was admitted, Asquith would form a new Government—minus the revolters, who would have been completely discredited by their inability to obtain support for a Government of their own. The new Administration would go to work on harmonious lines and the elements that were responsible for discord and strife would disappear. The only weakness of this calculation was that it was based on a fundamental error. There was, in fact, no doubt from start to finish that Lloyd George and Bonar Law could form a stable administration. Yet it is fair to state that Lord Curzon had given Asquith a specific assurance that no Tory Minister except Bonar Law would serve under Lloyd George. Asquith accepted this assurance and repeated it to his Liberal colleagues.

If you put the two sets of interviews together you may realise something of their cumulative effect. Here were the Radical members of the Ministry urging a fight to the death against Lloyd George's pretensions and vowing unswerving loyalty to their old Chief. Then on the other flank all the oldest and the best of the Tories, the houses of Cecil, Chamberlain, Curzon and Long, appear to swear their fealty and to urge the most relentless method of suppression of Lloyd George. Asquith suddenly felt his strength that Monday morning, and thought he perceived the weakness of the enemy. He began to count noses in the Cabinet and the calculation seemed to prove his position impregnable. No wonder Edwin

Montagu, coming in later in the morning, got small comfort out of Asquith.

Lloyd George, however, did not content himself with sending Montagu as an Ambassador to clinch the deal of the previous night and so avoid a rupture with the Premier.

Finding that Montagu brought back nothing, he himself made repeated attempts on that Monday through his secretaries, Sir John Davies and Miss Stevenson, to get an immediate interview with Asquith. He was told on each occasion that it was impossible for the Prime Minister to see him at this moment. Seeing that the two men were only separated by a few hundred yards and considering the tremendous urgency of the issues at stake, such replies were tantamount to a refusal of the Prime Minister to see the War Secretary at all. And such a refusal could only herald a complete breach.

The true explanation of the sudden change of Asquith's attitude towards the Lloyd George proposals between Sunday evening, December 3, and Monday midday, December 4, is contained in his discovery of the number and strength of his own adherents and of their implacable hostility to Lloyd George. Now he wanted to fight.

But the negotiation was almost completed. How was he to break it off ? And what ground was the best on which to refuse accommodation with the War Secretary ? Asquith solved both problems at once by a single brilliant decision. It was on Lloyd George's activities in the Press that the Conservatives were anxious to arraign

and expel him. Well, that should be Asquith's
ground too, both for breaking off the negotiations
and in the subsequent contest.

But for this purpose the " Reynold's " article
would not serve. Asquith had condoned it by
treating with Lloyd George after its publication.
Some other Press article must be found, and here
to the Premier's hand lay ready a leading article
in " The Times " of that Monday morning,
December 4.

It was hostile to the Premier, who immediately
assumed that it was inspired by Lloyd George.
Basing himself on this supposition he wrote
Lloyd George the letter of complaint and hostility
published on page 252.

" The Times " leader was a very different production from the " Reynold's " article. It bore
no sign of having been inspired by Lloyd George.
It was news rather than comment, and it showed
exactly the amount of knowledge that an influential and well-informed journalist would
possess when he had read the other newspapers
and seen a few public men. It represented in fact
the kind of news that was fairly common property in political circles (outside the official
Liberals) on Sunday night. The article described
the Lloyd George proposals accurately—his protest against the cumbrous methods of directing the
war, and his demand for a small War Council. It
showed knowledge of the fact that Lord Carson
was working with Lloyd George—and that Bonar
Law was acting in support. The leading article
gave Bonar Law a rather patronising pat on the

back, and was markedly polite to Robertson and
the soldiers. But it was hostile to Asquith and
carried a sting in some of its implications.

" The testimony of his (Asquith's) closest supporters—even more perhaps than the pressure
of those who have no politics beyond the war—
must have convinced him by this time that matters
cannot possibly go on as at present. They must
have convinced him, too, that his own qualities
are fitted better, as they are fond of saying, ' to
preserve the unity of the nation ' (although we
have never doubted its unity) than to force the
pace of a War Council."

These words as quoted may have hurt Asquith's
pride—but did they not really translate accurately
enough the exact motives which had induced him
to agree to the essential element in Lloyd George's
demands ?

I have shown that Lloyd George had no deal-
ings with Lord Northcliffe in this matter. Mr.
Churchill states in the " World Crisis " that
Northcliffe had nothing to do with the article.
In this he is quite right. The leader was as a
matter of fact written by Mr. Geoffrey Dawson,
Editor of " The Times."

Dawson was perfectly familiar with the events
which led to the fall of the old Government and
to the formation of the new one. He possessed the
personal confidence of and had influence with
another group of opponents of the Asquith
regime which centred round Carson and Lord
Milner. For it must be remembered that while I
have described Carson chiefly in his relation to

Lloyd George and Bonar Law, he had also another
set of activities specially his own in connection
with his friends and supporters in Parliament and
the Press.

The first half of " The Times " leader was written
on Saturday, December 2, at Cliveden, where
Dawson happened to be staying with Lord Astor.
The concluding passages were added on the
Sunday after the writer had returned to London
and had talked with Carson.

It will be seen that Mr. Dawson was perfectly
well informed throughout on the political situation and in fact knew more than Northcliffe did.

Dawson did not attribute any tremendous significance to this leading article at the time of
writing. He was astonished later to learn that
Asquith had seized on it as the reason or excuse
for precipitating an open clash with Lloyd George.
Nor apparently did Northcliffe realise its significance immediately either. When, however, it
began to be hinted abroad that it was this article
which had provoked the crisis, Northcliffe, to use
an expression of the theatrical world, " took the
curtain."

But after all these years it may be permitted me
to record that what turned out to be a political
bombshell was not thrown into the arena by
those dreadful people, Lloyd George and Northcliffe, but by the highly respectable Dawson and
Carson.

Therefore Asquith, in assuming that Lloyd
George was the source of the article, made a
complete error and did Lloyd George a grave

injustice. If Lloyd George had been given a chance he could have cleared himself completely of the charge. Why did not Asquith ask for an explanation instead of writing Lloyd George a hostile letter assuming that he was somehow mixed up in the business or at least had the power to stop such articles appearing in " The Times " ?

The answer is that " The Times " leader was simply an excuse eagerly grasped to break off the negotiation and to join issue with Lloyd George just on the ground where he was most suspect—that of trafficking with the Press. It was not the cause of the breach—its only importance was that it was a handy weapon for doing something which Asquith had already made up his mind to do for quite different reasons.

Making all allowance for a vanity hurt by the sting contained in the tail of the article : admitting that Montagu erroneously confirmed the idea of the Lloyd George authorship* : granted that McKenna, as the opponent of compromise, described the terms as being insulting—because it showed clearly Lloyd George's intention of relegating the Premier to a position of absolute impotence in the conduct of the War—none the less it wrongs Asquith to suppose him capable of changing his whole policy at the crucial moment of his life because of a leading article in a newspaper. Such a theory denies him the qualities of clarity of intellect, of a sense of relative pro-

---

* Montagu had seen Northcliffe at the War Office when the visits were made to Lloyd George under the influence of Lord Lee of Fareham. Asquith was impressed by this news.

portion, even of the personal dignity which friend and foe alike have allowed him.

No. Plan I had failed because the hostility to Lloyd George in Asquith's own following, Liberal and Conservative, was too fierce to allow him to compromise with Lloyd George, and because the very strength of this feeling and following made Asquith think himself safe in tearing up the half accomplished settlement which he had never desired.

On the Monday then, Asquith turns to Plan II, the expulsion of Lloyd George from the Government practically for intrigue and disloyalty and trafficking with the Press. Hence his letter and the use made of " The Times " leader episode.

If, then, we envisage Asquith's mind on that Monday morning and afternoon, we shall see that he realises that his action on the day before had been precipitate. It had not squared with the real political facts. He had sought out Lloyd George because he wanted cohesion for his Government and not a great political upheaval in which Lloyd George and Bonar Law combined would make dangerous adversaries. But on the Monday he found this move had brought him not reconciliation but the indignant remonstrances of all his other colleagues and followers. In so far then as his predominant motive is a desire for tranquillity he sees he will not obtain it by completing his deal with Lloyd George—for then he will simply be courting a blow-up in the other anti-Lloyd George wing of the Cabinet. In so far as his motive in negotiating with Lloyd

George is fear of the consequences of refusing Lloyd George's terms, the immense accession of strength which now rolls up all round him makes that fear seem almost ridiculous. He is like a night-walker who has been frightened by the shape of a tree in the dark looming like some great monster—and then goes and looks at it by daylight.

He now decides upon Plan No. II, the expulsion of Lloyd George. The War Secretary has said he will appeal to the nation at large if he is compelled to resign. Well, Asquith still holds in reserve the dreaded weapon of a General Election with which he and Bonar Law had threatened the Carsonites and Churchill only a few brief weeks before. So long as he remains Premier and does not himself resign, however much he shifts his colleagues as in 1915, the initiative for a General Election now lies in his hands. But it is just at this point that the argument in favour of Plan No. II is about to be shattered to pieces. The projected Dissolution to wipe out the Die-hards and Grumblers was to have been a campaign jointly undertaken by Asquith and Bonar Law with both Party machines working in harmony to crush resistance.

But suppose Bonar Law will not play his part in the game ? Whatever the three C's might say or do, Bonar Law was the official leader and the Tory caucus would certainly in the main obey and follow him. In the clash between Tory and Liberal machines it was by no means certain that success at the polls would rest with the Government. In other words Lloyd George and

Bonar Law, simply thrust out of the Ministry
and left to agitate in the country, would be too
formidable a menace.

In the long run they might, probably would,
bring the Ministry down. If their Plan No. II
would not work what was the alternative but Plan
No. III ?

This issue was resolved for Asquith abruptly
early on Monday afternoon.

Shortly before question time Bonar Law followed Asquith into the Premier's room at the
House of Commons. He asked whether Asquith
was prepared to stand by the agreement reached
on Sunday and to continue the negotiation on the
matters left over. Asquith replied that he was not
so keen on the War Council plan as he had been.
When pressed he gave as reasons that all his colleagues, Liberal and Conservative, seemed to be
against it, and that Lloyd George was trafficking
with the Press. . . . Before the discussion could
proceed further, Asquith was suddenly called to
the Front Bench to answer questions. Such a
summons is imperative. No Minister can disregard it—any more than an actor can delay at
the call " The stage waits." After question time
Asquith attempted to avoid Bonar Law and so
dodge a continuation of the argument. He left
the House of Commons and went to Downing
Street. Bonar Law, however, was not to be put
off on such a vital occasion, and with his quiet
pertinacity pursued Asquith to Downing Street.
When he got there he found Grey, Harcourt, and
Runciman, waiting outside the Cabinet Room

with the Premier inside. He got hold of Bonham Carter and asked him to take in a message to the effect that he wished to see the Premier urgently and in advance of the waiting Liberal colleagues. He was duly admitted, but found McKenna closeted with Asquith. He then urged on the Prime Minister very strongly the necessity of standing by Sunday's agreement on the appointment of a War Council.

He drove home his arguments for the proposed change by repeating and reiterating them. Asquith at first made perfunctory replies—and when Bonar Law persisted he lapsed into a glum and obstinate silence. Failing to receive any satisfactory reply, Bonar Law made it clear beyond all possibility of doubt that if the War Council scheme was not adapted he would break with Asquith. He then left the Prime Minister, who still sat in sulky silence.

This interview is of primary importance in the sequence of the narrative, because it shows exactly how, why, and when Asquith abandoned Plan No. II for Plan No. III.

Plan No. II, it will be remembered, was reconstruction without resignation—plus a General Election to destroy the rebels. But the moment Bonar Law said finally that he would go out with Lloyd George, this plan became impracticable, because a General Election would find the Tory machine working against Asquith. Asquith's own mind had been already made up to refuse concession to Lloyd George under Plan No. I. Now Plan No. II vanished also. There remained only Plan No. III—Resignation and the definite proof that he was the only possible Premier.

It is rather curious to note how Asquith followed all along in his tactics plans which had been already laid down by the three C's. It had been so in demanding two War Councils instead of one Supreme War Council and in using " Trafficking with the Press " as a cry against Lloyd George—and again it was the Tories who all along had insisted on resignation and not reconstruction. Inspired or driven by Tories and Radicals alike he begins to believe that the stronger course recommended by his Tory friends may be the best one. He sees—what was obvious all along—that the Tory method was the right and constitutional method, and that you cannot vanquish such an enemy except by compelling him to make an open exhibition of weakness. Let Lloyd· George or Bonar Law try to form a Government, and Asquith will come back as the only possible Premier. It is a case for shock tactics and he will adopt them.

There does not seem to be anything in the least open to criticism in this attitude—change of attitude, if you like—in Asquith. When a great political crisis is in train, when both sides are battling quite honestly for what they believe to be the right, the facts of the situation change from hour to hour and men's minds must change with them.

The right tactics of yesterday may be the wrong tactics of to-day, and the tactics of to-day may need revision to-morrow. Asquith employed tactics exactly as the other side did, and shifted his method in the light of new information. Asquith knew that the group opposed to him desired, looking at their intention broadly, to put him out of power. He felt weak, and offered a compromise. His opponents accepted it, not because they thought it an ideal solution, but because they were prepared to give way to some extent rather than fight to the death. Then Asquith felt strong and threw down the gage of battle. His enemies picked it up because they had no choice. There is no censure to be applied to either side on the score of tactics. Asquith did what he thought best for his country. He believed his own Government to be not only an effective but also the sole possible instrument for carrying on the war. If he changed his plans it was only to meet some new development in the situation. And he showed not only keenness and coolness of vision but, at the end, undaunted courage.

Once he had made up his mind on Plan III he stuck to it unswervingly. In the face of one of the fiercest storms that has beaten on our political life he refused every kind of accommodation offered him by the other side. He was certain he was the only man who could form a Government and he would therefore agree to no other. If he was wrong in his ultimate judgment he sustained it with splendid tenacity.

His error lay not on the surface of tactics but deep in the heart of things. He forgot the imponderable forces which will immediately rally to a new Ministry when a new Premier holds up the banner of office. He did not understand much of human nature—and he was defeated by the human nature of war time.

Yet by the time that Monday—December 4, 1916—is reached, he has probably little choice except to declare for a fight to a finish. Passions have been heated in the controversy. He must prove himself indispensable if he is to stay, and to prove himself indispensable he must resign.

The whole issue is now to be put to the proof. The rebels must face the alternative of surrender or they must try to form a Ministry.

Ominous notes began to reach Lloyd George from Downing Street. The first began with a strong protest against the tone of " The Times " leader, couched in a manner which suggested that even if Lloyd George had not inspired the article he had the power to stop others of a similar character :

10, Downing Street, S.W.
December 4, 1916.

My dear Lloyd George,

Such productions as the first leading article in to-day's " Times," showing the infinite possibilities for misunderstanding and misrepresentation of such an arrangement as we considered yesterday, make me at least doubtful as to its feasibility. Unless the impression is at once corrected that I am being relegated to the position of an irresponsible spectator of the war, I cannot possibly go on.

The suggested arrangement was to the following effect : The Prime Minister to have supreme and effective control of war policy.

The agenda of the War Committee will be submitted to him; its chairman will report to him daily; he can direct it to consider particular topics or proposals; and all its conclusions will be subject to his approval or veto. He can, of course, at his own discretion attend meetings of the Committee.

Yours sincerely,
H. H. Asquith.

It is hardly necessary after what has just been written to comment at length on this letter. It clearly represents a complete change of front from the arrangements come to on the day before. On Sunday the Prime Minister thought the plan feasible, on Monday a leading article causes him doubt. No fair-minded man could say, after the reading of that letter, that it breathes out anything except a hard and almost threatening tone. The definition of the terms of settlement are couched somewhat in the form of an ultimatum addressed by one Power insisting on its rights to another—surely a remarkable change from the amicable agreement of Sunday. The War Minister replied at once in a far more friendly spirit :

War Office,
Whitehall, S.W.
December 4, 1916.

My dear Prime Minister,

I have not seen " The Times " article. But I hope you will not attach undue importance to

these effusions. I have had these misrepresen-
tations to put up with for months. Northcliffe
frankly wants a smash. Derby and I do not.
Northcliffe would like to make this and any
other rearrangement under your Premiership
impossible. Derby and I attach great importance
to your retaining your present position—effectively. I cannot restrain or, I fear, influence
Northcliffe. I fully accept in letter and in spirit
your summary of the suggested arrangement—
subject, of course, to personnel.

Ever sincerely,

D. Lloyd George.

Lloyd George's answer, though his repudiation
of any responsibility for " The Times " leader
was absolutely true, might be criticised in the
light of history on the ground that it was more
conciliatory than his actual attitude towards
Asquith. This criticism would hardly be fair. He
was ready to stand by the terms of the provisional
settlement he had made with the Premier on
Sunday afternoon—even though it fell short of
his full desires. A smooth answer might ensure
this settlement being ratified. If, on the other
hand, Asquith's note meant that he wished to
draw back from the arrangement and was, in
fact, courting a crash, then Lloyd George's
conciliatory reply definitely placed Asquith in
the position of the aggressor. This last fact would
prove important if the Liberals in the Commons
and the country were to be compelled to take
sides with one or other of the Liberal chiefs.

Derby's name was introduced into the letter with his consent and approval. Lloyd George's intention was no doubt to make a display of Conservative support which might be useful, particularly as practically all the other potentates of that party were ranged on the side of Asquith.

This Monday night was full of perturbation in the Liberal camp. The moderates still hoped for accommodation; McKenna and the extremists made ready for battle.

Montagu entertained at dinner the little troop of private secretaries known as the " Shadow Cabinet," consisting of Hankey, Bonham Carter, Masterton Smith and Eric Drummond. Montagu and his " Shadow Cabinet " decided to resort to the expedient of a Buckingham Palace conference in the hope of keeping the Government together in a reconstructed form. The plan failed.

On the same evening, according to Montagu, a meeting of Liberal members of the Cabinet, with the Prime Minister present, was held. The question of the Premier's resignation, and what would follow it, was discussed. No final decision was arrived at. At the meeting, Lord Buckmaster asked what their attitude would be if they were invited to join a Bonar Law and Lloyd George Government. McKenna said he would have no hesitation in deciding, as he was not likely to receive an invitation. According to other authorities, Buckmaster, McKenna and Runciman pledged themselves and their colleagues in most formal terms not to serve in any such

Government. Any Minister who dissented was in duty bound to make his position clear.

Mr. Arthur Henderson says he was late in getting to the meeting. When he entered, Mr. Asquith explained briefly what had happened, and said that the general opinion seemed to be that Mr. Lloyd George would not succeed in getting the Conservatives, except Bonar Law, to join a Government. Mr. Henderson did not agree. He considered that the Conservatives would join Mr. Lloyd George. He was then asked what about Labour ? Mr. Henderson said that Labour would join, too, as the terms offered would bring them in.

This evidence makes it perfectly clear that on Monday evening the Prime Minister was busily engaged in mustering his own array and counting up the forces on which he could depend. The basis of the calculation seems to have been this. Suppose the Prime Minister resigned and Lloyd George and Bonar Law were asked to form an administration, how many of the existing Cabinet Ministers could be counted on to refuse to join the new Government ? Asquith had heard what his Tory visitors had to say on this point in the morning. As a consequence, Asquith was able to inform some of his Liberal colleagues that Lord Curzon on his own behalf, and purporting to speak on behalf of the Conservative Ministers with whom he was acting, had given him an absolute pledge. Curzon's promise, couched in definite terms, was that in no circumstances would he, Curzon, or those acting with him take office under Lloyd George or Bonar Law.

Such had been the reinforcement proffered to the Premier in the morning, and now, at night, he was sitting there listening to pledges of refusal being considered or given by his Liberal colleagues. There is no doubt whatever that he had made up his mind that afternoon long before this meeting that the case for resignation was overwhelming and that reconstruction as in 1915 would not serve his turn at all. This time Asquith has got to prove, if it is safe, that he is indispensable—the one and only possible Premier. If the revolting leaders try to form a Government and fail, they are humiliated publicly and rendered impotent for mischief. Merely to accept the resignation of Bonar Law and Lloyd George would not serve this purpose.

And the same evening I had a talk with Neil Primrose, who did not conceal his certainty that the Prime Minister would offer no terms now, but would resign, and thus follow the Conservative plan for getting rid of Lloyd George and coming back without him. His predictions were verified in the letter which Asquith despatched to Lloyd George that night in reply to the note of conciliation Lloyd George had sent him.

Late at night I received an account of the proceedings at the meeting of the Liberal Ministers, which finally confirmed the news of Asquith's intentions.

The Conservative Ministers acting in support of Asquith were, however, not informed on Monday night of a decision which fitted in so well with their views.

CHAPTER XXXVI

THE PARTING

Tuesday, December 5.

ON this morning, Bonar Law, at Derby's request, breakfasted with him—the other guests being Lloyd George and Carson. Carson expressed himself in favour of what might be described as a " whole-hog " policy. He gave the opinion that a patched up arrangement between Asquith and Lloyd George was not possible. It would be unreal and therefore could not last—for any system founded on mistrust and jealousy is doomed to failure. The only solution, Carson thought, was for Asquith to resign and for Lloyd George to form a Government. If the present House of Commons would not sustain the new administration, then the new Prime Minister must appeal to the country. This, at least, in Carson's opinion, would present a clear issue as to whether the country wanted to go on with the war and fight it in an efficient manner or not. As it was, the Asquith administration was manufacturing Pacifists every day. In this statement Carson got nearer to the root of the matter than most of his contemporaries and colleagues were aware.

I went to see Lloyd George at the War Office

immediately on his return from Derby House. I saw the War Secretary, not in his own room, but in an ante-room usually reserved for his secretaries.

Lloyd George had just received the Prime Minister's official letter written the night before at 10, Downing Street. Its receipt clearly dictated the need for some instant course of action. For, while the Premier's missive was conciliatory in tone, its substance was an absolute repudiation of the agreement reached by Asquith and Lloyd George and ratified in Bonar Law's presence on the Sunday night preceding. Its effect was to make the rupture final and conclusive unless Lloyd George was to make an abject surrender to the Prime Minister.

10, Downing Street, S.W.
December 4, 1916.

My dear Lloyd George,

Thank you for your letter of this morning. The King gave me to-day authority to ask and accept the resignation of all my colleagues, and to form a new Government on such lines as I should submit to him. I start, therefore, with a clean slate.

The first question which I have to consider is the constitution of the new War Committee.

After full consideration of the matter in all its aspects, I have come decidedly to the conclusion that it is not possible that such a Committee could be made workable and effective without the Prime Minister as its chairman.

I quite agree that it will be necessary for him, in view of the other calls upon his time and energy, to delegate from time to time the chairmanship to another Minister as his representative and locum tenens, but (if he is to retain the authority which corresponds to his responsibility as Prime Minister) he must continue to be, as he always has been, its permanent president. I am satisfied, on reflection, that any other arrangement (such, for instance, as the one which I indicated to you in my letter of to-day) would be found in experience impracticable and incompatible with the retention of the Prime Minister's final and supreme control.

The other question, which you have raised, relates to the personnel of the Committee. Here again, after deliberate consideration, I find myself unable to agree with some of your suggestions. I think we both agree that the First Lord of the Admiralty must, of necessity, be a member of the Committee. I cannot (as I told you yesterday) be a party to any suggestion that Mr. Balfour should be displaced. The technical side of the Board of Admiralty has been reconstituted with Sir John Jellicoe as First Sea Lord. I believe Mr. Balfour to be, under existing conditions, the necessary head for the Board.

I must add that Sir Edward Carson (for whom, personally, and in every other way, I have the greatest regard) is not, from the only point of view which is significant to me (namely, the most effective prosecution of the war), the man best qualified among my colleagues, present or past, to be a member of the War Committee.

I have only to say, in conclusion, that I am strongly of opinion that the War Committee (without any disparagement of the existing Committee, which, in my judgment, is a most efficient body, and has done, and is doing valuable work) ought to be reduced in number so that it can sit more frequently and overtake more easily the daily problems with which it has to deal. But in any reconstruction of the committee, such as I have, and have for some time past had, in view, the governing consideration, to my mind, is the special capacity of the men who are to sit on it for the work which it has to do.

That is a question which I must reserve for myself to decide.

Yours very sincerely,

H. H. Asquith.

I was able to disclose to Lloyd George on the information I had received from various sources that this letter did not explain very precisely the Prime Minister's real intentions. He had two alternatives before him. (1) If Lloyd George sent a conciliatory reply, accepting the rebuff to his own proposals for an effective War Council, Asquith would simply reconstruct the Government. It would contain the humiliated Lloyd George and a chastened Bonar Law, if they so wished, as impotent members of the fresh administration. (2) If, on the contrary, Lloyd George and Bonar Law refused to accept the prospect of defeat and flung their resignations at the Premier's head, Asquith intended to deal with them in a more drastic fashion. He would resign and put his opponents to the humiliation of being unable to form a Government. Then he would come back as the only and inevitable Prime Minister. After that they could stay out or come in as they liked; they would be helpless in either case.

If Lloyd George would not submit, Asquith was going to smash him, not by reconstruction, but by revealing to the public Lloyd George's impotence to form a Government. It has been shown that this intention was really formed by Asquith on the Monday night before the letter was despatched to Lloyd George.

Lloyd George being fully informed of what was going to happen, then wrote his answer:

War Office,
Whitehall, S.W.
December 5, 1916.

My dear Prime Minister,

I have received your letter with some surprise. On Friday I made proposals which involved not merely your retention of the Premiership, but the supreme control of the war, while the executive functions, subject to that supreme control, were left to others. I thought you then received these suggestions favourably. In fact, you yourself proposed that I should be the chairman of this Executive Committee, although, as you know, I never put forward that demand.

On Saturday you wrote me a letter in which you completely went back on that proposition. You sent for me on Sunday and put before me other proposals; these proposals you embodied in a letter to me written on Monday :

The Prime Minister to have supreme and effective control of war policy.

The agenda of the War Committee will be submitted to him; its chairman will report to him daily; he can direct it to consider particular topics or proposals; and all its conclusions will be subject to his approval or veto. He can, of course, at his own discretion attend meetings of the Committee.

These proposals safeguarded your position and power as Prime Minister in every particular. I immediately wrote you accepting them " in letter and in spirit." It is true that on Sunday I expressed views as to the constitution of the Committee, but these were for discussion. To-day you have gone back on your own proposals.

I have striven my utmost to cure the obvious defects of the War Committee without overthrowing the Government. As you are aware, on several occasions during the last two years I have deemed it my duty to express profound dissatisfaction with the Government's method of conducting the war. Many a time, with the road to victory open in front of us, we have delayed and hesitated while the enemy were erecting barriers that finally checked the approach. There has been delay, hesitation, lack of forethought and vision. I have endeavoured repeatedly to warn the Government of the dangers, both verbally and in written memoranda and letters, which I crave your leave now to publish if my action is challenged; but I have either failed to secure decisions or I have secured them when I was too late to avert the evils. The latest illustration is our lamentable failure to give timely support to Roumania.

I have more than once asked to be released from my responsibility for a policy with which I was in thorough disagreement, but at your urgent personal request I remained in the Government. I realise that when the country is in the peril of a great war Ministers have not the same freedom to resign on disagreement. At the same time, I have always felt—and feel deeply—that I was in a false position, inasmuch as I could never defend in a whole-hearted manner the action of a Government of which I was a member. We have thrown away opportunity after opportunity, and I am convinced, after deep and anxious reflection, that it is my duty to leave the Government in order to inform the people of the real condition of affairs and to give them an opportunity, before it is too late, to save their native land from a disaster which is inevitable if the present methods are longer persisted in. As all delay is fatal in war, I place my office without further parley at your disposal.

It is with great personal regret that I have come to this conclusion. In spite of mean and unworthy insinuations to the contrary—insinuations which I fear are always inevitable in the case of men who hold prominent but not primary positions in any Administration—I have felt a strong personal attachment to you as my chief. As you yourself said on Sunday, we have acted together for ten years and never had a quarrel, although we have had many a grave difference on questions of policy. You have treated me with great courtesy and kindness; for all that I thank you. Nothing would have induced me to part now except an overwhelming sense that the course of action which has been pursued has put the country—and not merely the country, but throughout the world, the principles for which you and I have always stood throughout our political lives—in the greatest peril that has ever overtaken them.

As I am fully conscious of the importance of preserving national unity, I propose to give your Government complete support in the vigorous prosecution of the war; but unity without action is nothing but futile carnage, and I cannot be responsible for that. Vigour and vision are the supreme need at this hour.

Yours sincerely,
D. Lloyd George.

In fact the Asquith letter was nothing less than an open declaration of a breach. There was nothing for it but to go straight forward or else to admit defeat with humiliation added.

Lloyd George, as his letter shows, did not hesi-

tate. He gave in his resignation and he waved a
flag at the same time.   He was going to stand
before the public as the advocate of an efficient
war. Yet he had very few supporters. He could
count on the unswerving co-operation of Bonar
Law. Carson's offer of support remained a firm
one. Derby was with him, but outside the Cabinet.
Montagu was an uncertain factor—a few Liberal
under-secretaries might rally to his support. Other
backing there was none. The ranks of official
power seemed to be locked dead against him in
both the historic political parties. Could he win
through triumphantly and realise his ideal of
conducting Britain to victory over the Germans
—or would his political opponents prove too
much for him ?

It was true that Lloyd George possessed very
considerable resources (far larger than either his
Liberal or Conservative opponents in the Government realised) both in the House of Commons
and in the country. General public opinion is
reflected in the Press, and there Lloyd George was
strong.

The Tory editor of the " Morning Post " and
the " Globe " knew that he was the necessary
man ; the " Daily Chronicle " and the " Daily
Express " were also openly on his side—so, from
a rather different angle, were " The Times " and
the " Daily Mail." In the Commons the dissidents
of the Nigerian debate could in the main have
been marshalled by Carson against Asquith. Bonar
Law would have brought in the backbone of
the Tory Party, while Lloyd George showed

subsequently that he had well over a hundred Liberal supporters in Parliament.

The trouble was that all this support and countenance was in fact inoperative in the desperate struggle which was now going on inside the Cabinet. Westminster and Fleet Street might have been in Ecuador for all the good they were to the rebellion for efficiency.

To put it in a vivid way, Lloyd George and Bonar Law were like two men struggling with the bayonet in a trench against twenty opponents. The fact that they had in support a tremendously heavy long-range artillery which must soon blow the enemy's position completely to pieces did not help them in the least. The issue had to be decided hand to hand, and the long-range guns were under these conditions useless.

The same reason explains the practical disappearance of Lord Carson's name from the story during critical days and hours. So long as the fight was in the Cabinet he could do nothing. He was a general waiting to intervene—but with his army necessarily held in reserve. One has to think of the circle cast by a light in a reading-room when its rays are suddenly lessened by turning on all the high lights in the roof of the room. The narrow circle showed Asquith victorious; the high lights which might be turned on blotted out his glare and heralded the advent of the man destined to succeed to the seat of power.

When Lloyd George came to the ultimate wrench he stood up to it like a great man. He faced a group which seemed infinitely more powerful than himself and his friends. And yet he was absolutely clear that he could and must defeat them. "Here I stand—I can no other"— that was his attitude, and it was illuminating to see the spirit of the man—the courage rejecting all compromise. I saw it with my own eyes—and anyone who says that Lloyd George in this issue was animated by nothing more than personal ambition does not know his man. He was immediately put to the extreme test. Asquith's reply was prompt—and accepted his resignation.

> 10, Downing Street, S.W.
> December 5, 1916.

My dear Lloyd George,
 I need not tell you that I have read your letter of to-day with much regret.

 I do not comment upon it for the moment, except to say that I cannot wholly accept your account of what passed between us in regard to my connection with the War Committee.

 In particular, you have omitted to quote the first and most material part of my letter of yesterday.

> Yours very sincerely,
> H. H. Asquith.

 In the meantime, I feel sure that you will see the obvious necessity in the public interest of not publishing at this moment any part of our correspondence.

He was clearly rather frightened by the pro-

paganda part of Lloyd George's letter of
resignation with its appeal to the nation. He
pleaded for its suppression on the usual and useful
plea of the politician—the interests of the public.
Here is Lloyd George's reply :

War Office, S.W.

December 5, 1916.

My dear Prime Minister,
I cannot announce my resignation without
assigning the reason. Your request that I should
not publish the correspondence that led up to
and necessitated it places me therefore in an
embarrassing and unfair position. I must give
reasons for the grave step I have taken. If you
forbid publication of the correspondence, do
you object to my stating in another form my
version of the causes that led to my resignation ?

Yours sincerely,

D. Lloyd George.

As to the first part of your letter, the publication of the letters would cover the whole ground.

10, Downing Street, S.W.

December 5, 1916.

My dear Lloyd George,
It may make a difference to you (in reply to
your last letter) if I tell you at once that I have
tendered my resignation to the King.
In any case, I should deprecate in the public
interest the publication in its present form at
this moment of your letters to me of this
morning.

Of course, I have neither the power nor the wish to prevent your stating in some other form the causes which have led you to take the step which you have taken.

Yours very sincerely,

H. H. Asquith.

Lord Derby had made one last effort to avert the crash. He had visited the Prime Minister and implored him not to resign, but rather to come to an accommodation with Lloyd George.   Asquith declined to enter into any argument.   His mind, he said, was made up, and the motor which was to take him to Buckingham Palace with his resignation waited at the door.

So Lloyd George and Asquith terminated an association as Ministerial colleagues which had lasted for just eleven years and been of great reciprocal advantage.

It may be interesting to discover how Asquith viewed this separation immediately after the event.

Sir Robert Donald had a long talk with Asquith on December 7, when all was over, and asked him whether he thought Lloyd George, or some one acting in his interest, had courted the rupture. My narrative gives an exact answer to this question; but Asquith's own view must be one of historic interest. He said that Lloyd George had always been most friendly to him, and that no rift had occurred, in their personal relations. Lloyd George possessed unique gifts—a real *flair* for politics, foresight, and inspiration. He would not say that Lloyd George owed everything to him, but he owed a great deal. He had saved him over the Budget of 1909, when every one else in the Cabinet had turned against him, and also on another occasion when he might have been obliged to disappear from public life for a time.*

* Asquith was no doubt referring to the Marconi incident.

CHAPTER XXXVII

THE COURT-MARTIAL

Tuesday, December 5.

THE battle being now set between the two protagonists, it is time to describe how things were going on on this same day in the Conservative camp. Here there certainly reigned no more harmony than in the high places of Liberalism.

A most momentous meeting was held at eleven o'clock that morning at the India Office. It included the Conservative Ministers—Curzon, Chamberlain, Cecil, and Long—with the important exceptions of Balfour (who was ill) and Lord Lansdowne.

Balfour operated entirely independently throughout this crisis. On this Tuesday he wrote from his sick room two notes in succession to the Prime Minister.

The first letter was in the form of qualified approval of the proposed War Council with an acknowledgment of the need for appointing Lloyd George to the Chair. Further, Balfour assumed that his retention of the Admiralty would be undesirable in view of Lloyd George's recent attacks on his administration. Lastly he tendered his resignation. The letter is as follows :—

Private.   4, Carlton Gardens,
                        Pall Mall, S.W.
                              Dec. 5th, 1916.

My dear Asquith,

I have been mostly in bed since the political crisis became acute, and can collect no very complete idea of what has been going on. But one thing seems clear : that there is to be a new War Council of which Lloyd George is to be the working Chairman, and that, according to his ideas this Council would work more satisfactorily if the Admiralty were not represented by me. In these circumstances I cannot consent to retain my office and must ask you to accept my resignation.

I am well aware that you do not personally share Lloyd George's views in this connection. But I am quite clear that the new system should have a trial under the most favourable possible circumstances; and the mere fact that the new Chairman of the War Council *did* prefer, and, so far as I know, *still* prefers, a different arrangement is, to my mind, quite conclusive, and leaves me no doubt as to the manner in which I can best assist the Government which I desire to support. The fact that the first days of the reconstructed Administration find me more than half an invalid, is an additional reason (if additional reason were required) for adopting the course on which, after much consideration, I have determined.

                    Yours very sincerely,
                        Arthur James Balfour.

Asquith replied refusing to contemplate Balfour's retirement.

The second letter—marked " 4 p.m."—was a recapitulation of his reasons for believing that Lloyd George should be given the opportunity of presiding over a War Council, and re-affirming his resignation.

4, Carlton Gardens,
Pall Mall, S.W.

Dec. 5th, 1916. 4 p.m.

My dear Asquith,
I am very grateful for your note and its enclosure. I very highly value your appreciation.

I do not, however, feel much inclined to change my views. I still think (a) that the break-up of the Government by the retirement of Lloyd George would be a misfortune, (b) that the experiment of giving him a free hand with the day-to-day work of the War Committee is still worth trying, and (c) that there is no use trying it except on terms which enable him to work under the conditions which, in his own opinion, promise the best results. We cannot, I think, go on in the old way. An open breach with Lloyd George will not improve matters, and attempts to compel co-operation between him and fellow-workers with whom he is in but imperfect sympathy will only produce fresh trouble.

I am therefore still of opinion that my resignation should be accepted, and that a fair trial

should be given to the new War Council a
la George.

Yours very sincerely,

Arthur James Balfour.

Balfour in these letters shows clearly that,
well aware as he was of Lloyd George's hostility
to his administration at the Admiralty, he was
not going to let this fact stand in the way of the
success of a new regime. He preferred to eliminate
himself. The effect of his letters was therefore
helpful to Lloyd George, and made Lord
Balfour's final acceptance of a new office under
Lloyd George quite natural.

Bonar Law himself was not invited, and knew
nothing of the meeting at the India Office.
Birkenhead was not invited either. This gathering
was in fact a kind of court of enquiry to be held on
Bonar Law conduct and he regarded it as equivalent
to an attempt to oust him from the Leadership. At
this conference the Conservative Ministers took
the view that Bonar Law had separated himself
from them. They believed they were in the dark
as to Bonar Law's proceedings, and they were
uneasy as to what was happening.

They believed that Bonar Law had not in the
least made clear to Asquith the extent to which
the Conservative leaders were on his side in the
struggle with Lloyd George.

A full description has already been given of
what took place at this interview and shows that
Bonar Law did explain everything to Asquith, who
was too alarmed by the resolution to face the real

facts of the situation and square his momentary policy with them.

None the less, this tale about Bonar Law was gathering momentum because there was no one to contradict it. Bonar Law himself could not do so—for he was totally unaware of its existence. It gained currency and, naturally, it further estranged the other Tory Ministers from Bonar Law.

At this conference two decisions were arrived at : (1) To send the three " C's " back to the Prime Minister to assure him of the support of the meeting and to urge him to withstand Lloyd George to the uttermost. (2) To send Long to Bonar Law to summon him before a renewed session of the conference to be held at the same place at four o'clock. In fact, the General was summoned to face a court-martial—the tribunal being his own staff.

The conference between Asquith and the three " C's " was not really very important. The two sides simply went over the old ground with re-iterated emphasis—Bonar Law was responsible for a misunderstanding : Lloyd George must be curbed. Curiously enough, Asquith did not tell his visitors that he had definitely made up his mind to resign himself rather than attempt recon-struction. The news would have pleased his Tory interviewers, for it was in accordance with their advice—advice they urged consistently from start to finish. Still the Prime Minister did not tell them of his decision—though he seems to have hinted

The interview between Bonar Law and Walter Long was more dramatic in character.

Long appeared as the escort to conduct Bonar Law to the court-martial at four o'clock. When the Conservative leader realised the purport of Long's mission, he was furious. It took a good deal to rouse Bonar Law, but when he was really angered he could treat people very roughly. Immediately after the interview with Long he was in a state of real passion.

He had told the unfortunate emissary that he would not go to the meeting at the India Office at four o'clock, that he was the Leader of the party, and that it was his business to summon them to meetings and not theirs to summon him. If this was another of Lord Curzon's attempts to dispossess him of the leadership, he would appeal openly to the Tory party in the Commons and the country, and he thought the India Office Conference would find that the fact—whatever their ideas might be—would show that the great bulk of the party stood behind him and not behind them.

This, of course, was the truth. The back-bench Conservatives in the Commons and the Conservative organisations in the country hated the first Coalition. They recognised Asquith's lack of passion and zeal for the war instinctively, and thought Bonar Law had been " diddled " into accepting bad terms for the Tories in May, 1915. There are thousands of letters extant to show that this frame of mind existed in the Tories' local leaders. Some were written to newspapers, others to the Tory chiefs.

After this outburst of Bonar Law the ground was cleared for decisive action. The national situation was too serious for a complete breach of relations between the Tory chief and his colleagues to be contemplated without some further attempt at accommodation. Everyone concerned was too sensible to desire the prompt disruption of the Tory party. Bonar Law agreed to summon a conference of his own at the Colonial Office at five o'clock. It must have been a curious meeting. Was the chairman judging the board, or was the judge in the dock ? It is true that some kind of apology was tendered to Bonar Law for summoning the first meeting without his knowledge and consent, but the charges of bad faith were persisted in.

Like most meetings of this kind, it went in a very unexpected way. Long had explained to Bonar Law the story being told against him over the Asquith interview of Sunday. Now Bonar Law had his first chance of clearing himself of such an injurious suspicion. He told his audience quite simply that he had explained everything fully to Asquith on Sunday afternoon. They must take his word—or they must take Asquith's, that was all.

In an assembly of men who were bitterly opposed to Bonar Law's policy at this moment, such was the effect of his simple word of honour —his reputation for complete honesty and truth-telling through many years of stormy politics— that his associates without a single dissentient or a murmur of doubt or comment accepted his assurance. And if honour is due to Bonar Law, honour is due also to the men who believed him. This untrue charge, which was likely to pass into history, was killed here once for all. It has never been revived since—and I shall show that Asquith himself abandoned it when the crisis was over.

Tension at the Conservative meeting was thus immediately relieved. The whole conference was at once back to the frame of mind of the Sunday preceding. They would insist on the resignation of the whole Government, including the Premier. Bonar Law this time had no difficulty in agreeing to the proposal. In fact, the situation had developed in such a serious way that there was no real alternative to this method of procedure.

There was therefore no difficulty in drafting another resolution in the following terms and addressed to Asquith :

" C., C., and C. have reported to us the substance of what passed at your meeting with them this afternoon. After full consideration, we are unanimously of opinion that the course which we urged upon you on Sunday is a necessity, and it is imperative that that course should be taken to-day.

" We hope that you have arrived at the same conclusion, but, if this is not so, we are obliged to ask you to accept our resignations."

C., C., and C., means Curzon, Cecil and Chamberlain.

Inserted in the margin of this resolution is the following :

P

" We feel that we have no choice but to ask you to act upon our resignations, which we have already placed in your hands."

On the back of resolution is the following :

" That Mr. L. G. intends to publish the letters you read to us* to-morrow and we are anxious, therefore, to know this evening your reply, so that we may know whether we too shall publish our resignations."

Bonar Law approved of the resolution and of the elaborations, too.

Lord Curzon, who had practically made himself the leader of the dissidents, and was the most active supporter of Asquith in the Tory ranks, then made the following suggestion : Would it not be better to get the approval of the Prime Minister to the terms of the resolution, and then it could be published ? The meeting agreed to this plan—and Lord Curzon proceeded to Downing Street with the resolution. By the time he got there Asquith's resignation was already in the hands of the King.

Curzon returned with a statement to his colleagues that the resolution had been rendered useless by events. The Premier had resigned.

* These are the letters exchanged by Asquith and Lloyd George on Monday and Tuesday, December 4th and 5th, including Lloyd George's letter of resignation. It is evident that Asquith showed them to the three C's at their meeting on Tuesday.

CHAPTER XXXVIII

CHOOSING A PRIME MINISTER

THE meeting at the Colonial Office was hardly over when the definite news of Asquith's resignation was received. Bonar Law immediately took me over to the War Office to see Lloyd George. The problem of the new Premiership had to be faced.

The Government had now fallen, and the question was whether the old or a new Prime Minister would return. Asquith's whole procedure had been novel, but the constitutional doctrine is clear. If a Prime Minister has difficulties with his colleagues he can either call for their resignations and continue to act, as Asquith had done in 1915, or he can resign on the ground that his internal difficulties make it impossible for him to continue the conduct of His Majesty's Government. To resign and call on all Ministers to resign in order to force a minority out of the Cabinet is not a procedure which has any place in the practice of the Constitution, for it is obviously vexatious and unnecessary, since the minority can be made to resign by other means. The Crown, therefore, will assume that resignation is tantamount to impotence, and will not return to the resigning Prime Minister until all other

possible persons have been asked to form a
Ministry and have refused or failed. (It was on
this last eventuality that the Prime Minister and
his friends counted. with certainty.)

It was clear in the circumstances that either
Bonar Law or Lloyd George would be sent for
and asked to form a Ministry.

All the probabilities pointed to Asquith recom-
mending the King to send for Bonar Law as the
responsible Conservative leader and the head of
the largest individual party in the House of Commons. It was therefore absolutely necessary to
take a decision as to what Bonar Law should say
to the King. And the expectations were realised.
Bonar Law was summoned to attend at the Palace
at 9.30 o'clock that night. Was Bonar Law to
accept the offer of the Premiership or was he to
advise the King to send for Lloyd George ? It is
now necessary to give a complete account of the
conversation which ensued.

Bonar Law said to Lloyd George that he would
put forward his name to the King for the Premiership—as the man whose leadership was most
likely to win the war. By now Bonar Law believed
sincerely that while his judgment might be better
than Lloyd George's, Lloyd George had the more
drive—and that drive was wanted to win the war.
Thus with a characteristic and casual gesture
Bonar Law tossed away the prospect of the
glittering prize.

Why did he do it ? Why did he so often cast
away the prize he had won fairly and squarely
by his own efforts ?

It was due to his natural and inevitable disposition in regarding himself in relation to public affairs. He did not judge his own abilities himself. If public opinion or his colleagues designated him unmistakenly for an office, he would take it—because he would say that they were better judges of his capacity than he was himself. His own judgment was that Lloyd George was quite as good as himself for the supreme purpose of conducting the war, and that the ordinary public thought Lloyd George was better. He accepted this judgment—in fact, he preferred it. He was prepared to hold the stirrup of the great captain, provided he had a reasonable share in guiding the direction of the horse. How fruitful this combination was will be amply recorded in history. Lloyd George never went wrong until Bonar Law had to leave him.

Bonar Law's attitude of self-distrust is of course amazing to the ordinary politician. If this quality is a defect, Bonar Law will be judged very hardly. I cannot help this. The truth about Bonar Law must be told.

Those who worked on the " personal ambition " theory of Lloyd George's activities would have expected him to jump eagerly to seize on the offer. As a matter of fact, Lloyd George did exactly the opposite. "No,"he said in effect,"I don't want to be Premier. I have not been fighting for the Premiership, but simply to get rid of the Asquith incubus. Give me the Chairmanship of the War Council and (turning to Bonar Law) I am perfectly content and would prefer to serve under you."

It will be no use saying that this is a matter of hearsay or second-hand gossip. It was in my presence that Lloyd George told Bonar Law with the most transparent sincerity that he thought Bonar Law's premiership would be the wisest solution and that he wished to serve under him.

However astounding this record may be to Lloyd George's enemies, it is truth. Nor does the fact of this struggle of self-abnegation between Bonar Law and Lloyd George rest simply on my testimony. The whole written and accepted record of what happened in the course of the next hours and days bears it out.

The two statesmen finally came to this agreement : Lloyd George should have the Premiership if it was found possible to form an administration on these terms. Failing this (and there were serious obstacles in the way of a Lloyd George Premiership), Bonar Law was to take office, giving Lloyd George the Chairmanship of the new War Council.

The difficulties Bonar Law foresaw in forming a Lloyd George administration were twofold.

1. The difficulty of getting Asquith or any of his intimate supporters to serve in such a Ministry. Bonar Law they might swallow, but how could they accept Lloyd George ?

2. The difficulty of getting the Tories to serve under Lloyd George. If, on the other hand, their own leader in the House of Commons assumed the chief post, it would be past all bearing or belief that his principal Conservative colleagues should refuse to serve under him

It was agreed between the two men that while Lloyd George's Premiership should be aimed at as the ideal, Bonar Law's should be accepted as the practical solution if all else failed.

Bonar Law was received by His Majesty at Buckingham Palace at half-past nine o'clock that evening. He explained the position fully to the King and was asked to form a Ministry.

As had been arranged, he asked for time, and then went straight to Asquith. He had not yet abandoned hope that he would get Asquith to serve under him, though he would not under Lloyd George, and on that condition Bonar Law was prepared to take the Premiership. If, however, this could not be, it was better, in his view, that Lloyd George as the real protagonist should take the chief post.

Bonar Law then went on from the Palace to see Asquith to ask him whether he would serve in a Bonar Law Government. He began the conversation in this blunt way : "When a man has done another a serious injury no good can come from explanations." Asquith replied, "I have no feeling of hostility. You have treated me with complete straightforwardness all through." Bonar Law repeated these two sentences to me at the time and I wrote them down.

In effect they dispose, or should dispose, finally of the charge that Bonar Law misled Asquith at the Sunday afternoon meeting. Nor did Asquith or anyone else ever raise the accusation again. No doubt Asquith, on thinking things over calmly, realised that it was his own precipitancy which had led to the misunderstanding.

Bonar Law then asked Asquith if he would serve under him. Asquith replied in the negative.

Bonar Law then put forward the following offer to Asquith. If he advised the King to send for Balfour, would Asquith serve under him—thus tossing the offer of the Premiership away for the second time that day. Again Asquith said " No," showing clearly and with finality that he was in no mood for accommodation. By declining to serve under anyone he adhered resolutely to his plan of forcing Lloyd George or Bonar Law to try to form a Ministry.

On their failure his indispensability would have been proved.

Lloyd George and I then went to dine at Birkenhead's house. Birkenhead and Churchill were at the Turkish Bath of the Automobile Club that evening, and Birkenhead had rung up George to remind him of a dinner engagement. He mentioned that Churchill was with him and Lloyd George immediately requested that Churchill should be asked to come too. This suggestion, probably quite carelessly made, produced on Churchill's mind the natural impression that he was regarded as one of the new set of war administrators who were about to grasp the helm. Surely Lloyd George would not ask him to be included in a dinner party on this night of all others if he did not mean to offer him a real post—and a real post to Churchill meant nothing but war-service.

Apart from this deduction—a too hasty and

optimistic one as it proved—there were many cogent reasons why Churchill should expect an appointment under the new regime and why Lloyd George should give him one.

As has been said previously, Churchill had really been abandoned by Asquith because of his restless energy and his intrepid capacity for innovation. He had been ruined by his overpowering zeal for making war which had led him to disregard precedents and to forget the existence of old-established political animosities. Later Asquith had turned on Lloyd George for developing a precisely similar set of qualities. Who then could employ Churchill more suitably than Lloyd George—especially since now that he was to become Premier he could keep Churchill's activities under control ? Churchill in fact was a natural Lloyd Georgian and supported the new movement throughout in so far as he could do so after his retirement. He had come back from France at the express request of Lord Carson—so that he might reasonably regard himself as a member of the alliance which had overturned the Government.

He had, therefore, every reason for expecting office when we met at Birkenhead's table that evening. The company consisted of Birkenhead, Lloyd George, Winston, and myself. Bonar Law only was absent. The conversation turned entirely on the personnel of the new Ministry and everyone took a share in it on terms of equality.

It had been arranged that after Bonar Law had left the King and seen Asquith, Lloyd George was to meet him at Carson's house. Lloyd George invited me to drive along with him to the interview. But Birkenhead insisted that I should return at once to him to give Churchill and him news of what was happening. I was torn between the desire to hang on to Lloyd George and the insistence of Birkenhead, but eventually promised to return—much against my will.

On this drive Lloyd George told me particularly that he was worried about Churchill. The pressure brought to bear against his inclusion in the new Ministry was enormous. The whole situation was so shaky that if it was asked to bear an additional piece of weight it might collapse altogether. If he became Prime Minister, Lloyd George was not ready to run this risk. His difficulties, he said, were sufficient in any case. Here Lloyd George was as a matter of fact shying at a shadow. The event was to prove him quite strong enough to carry Churchill. Lloyd George, however, said that though he realised Churchill's abilities to the full, this was not an opportune moment for giving him the only kind of office which was worth his while. Churchill must wait a bit.

Lloyd George asked me to convey a hint of this kind on my return to the party which contained Churchill. He thought Churchill too confident of high office in the new regime. A refusal would be awkward. It would be better if Churchill was dashed a bit first. I went back to Birkenhead's dinner according to promise and met Churchill again.

This is the story of our meeting, at which

both of us can now in the after years afford to
smile. He has held great Government offices,
and I have found a different sphere of activity.
But this was not the light in which the event could
be looked at in that hour of Birkenhead's dinner.

I had by this time come to the conclusion that
I had been an important factor in forming the
new administration. Lloyd George, Carson and
Bonar Law had treated me as an equal. My sense
of values was destroyed for the moment.

I expected the Board of Trade, and had good
ground for my expectation. In fact I had been
promised the place. My mind was full of plans
for speeding up the management of the railways
in the military area in the North of France.

Here it will be convenient to state once and for
all, in a compact form, the opinions which guided
me in seeking, accepting, or declining office during
the war, and the feeling which underlay my
actions.

I had been offered minor office, as has been
related, in the formation of the first Coalition in
May, 1915, and had refused it. Again I could have
had office in July, 1915, when Lloyd George went
to the War Office and certain changes had to be
made in consequence. I did not want office then,
either.

And the reasons in both cases were the same.
In both cases the posts suggested had nothing to
do with the direct conduct of the war whatever.
I desired ardently to serve the country.

I did not want to be a sort of passenger on board
a War Administration just for the sake of being a

Minister. I wanted a war job for which I thought I had the talents and experience. Therefore I ardently desired the Board of Trade because it was an office of the highest importance in the conduct of the war and one in which all the experience of my past life would have been of the greatest service to me.

So when I came back to Birkenhead's party that night with Lloyd George's information stowed away in my pocket, I smiled on Churchill as a senior colleague might on an aspiring junior. I still, so to speak, walked warily—but I walked. Churchill also had every reason to suppose that he was sure of high office. We discussed as allies and equals the personnel of the new Government. Churchill suggested that I might be made Postmaster-General—a task suitable to my abilities.

Then I conveyed to him the hint Lloyd George had given me. I have a reason for saying that these are the exact words I used : " The new Government will be very well disposed towards you. All your friends will be there. You will have a great field of common action with them."

Something in the very restraint of my language carried conviction to Churchill's mind. He suddenly felt he had been duped by his invitation to the dinner, and he blazed into righteous anger. I have never known him address his great friend Birkenhead in any other way except as " Fred " or " F.E." On this occasion he said suddenly : " Smith, this man knows that I am not to be included in the new Government."

With that Churchill walked out into the street

carrying his coat and hat on his arm. Birkenhead pursued him, and endeavoured to persuade him to return, but in vain. So, really my patronising manner was lost on Churchill, as was his calm assumption of superiority over my assurance. We neither of us got office. Churchill was included later. Lloyd George gave Lord Ashfield, my old and valued friend, the Presidency of the Board of Trade I coveted. Birkenhead was the only one of the three present who had a real reason to be uncertain about his future, though he thought rightly enough that he was indispensable. Actually he was the only one of the three to be in the new Government.

CHAPTER XXXIX

FORMING THE ADMINISTRATION

Wednesday, December 6.

THE next morning, Wednesday, there was a meeting of the " Triumvirate " at Pembroke Lodge, at which I made a fourth. The question at issue was where to turn first in the direction of seeking support for the new administration. The most natural person to approach at once seemed to be Lord Balfour. He had been ill throughout the whole of the recent proceedings—and it seemed quite possible that he would take quite a different view of the situation from that of the three C's and Long. There was also the undeniable difficulty that Lloyd George had been openly hostile to Lord Balfour's administration of the Admiralty. Also he was undoubtedly the point of danger in the Conservative Party. Bonar Law and Lloyd George therefore went together to see him. They found him still unwell, but he received them.

In this conversation Lord Balfour did not commit himself definitely in any way to the new Ministry. He simply said that nothing could be decided until there had been an all-round talk at Buckingham Palace—an idea which Mr. Henderson had already put forward.

At this Conference, which took place immediately, there were present Asquith, Lloyd George, Bonar Law, Balfour, and Henderson. Balfour began the discussion. He expressed the view that in his opinion the right course was for Bonar Law to be Prime Minister, in order that both Asquith and Lloyd George might serve in the Government.

The main feature of the Buckingham Palace Conference was that everyone present—with a single exception—was anxious and especially anxious on one point—the retention of Asquith's services for the new administration in one capacity or another.

The exception was Asquith himself. He was neither worried, nor anxious to serve in any proposed new regime. His manner in fact was fairly like that of a schoolboy who has got an unexpected half-holiday. He was jocular with everybody. He showed this grave assembly an anonymous telegram he had received from Liverpool saying how delighted the sender was that he had been dismissed.

When the meeting came to business, which really was to discover what Premier, if any, Asquith would consent to serve under—Balfour, Bonar Law, or Lloyd George—Asquith simply said he had held the first place for eight years, and was now asked to take a subordinate position.

Still Asquith did not give an absolute refusal, but said he must first consult his friends. Bonar Law actually left the Conference under the impression that Asquith would yet come in to the new Government.

The truth was that Asquith's high spirits and disinclination to serve in a subordinate capacity were due to one single cause. He quite misinterpreted the situation and misunderstood the reasons for holding the Conference at all. He knew of course that Bonar Law had been asked by the King the previous evening to form a Government and he drew the inference that Bonar Law thought he could not form such a Government without Asquith's countenance and assistance. He looked, then, on the Conference not as an act of decent respect towards himself, based on a desire to preserve a complete appearance of national unity, but as an acknowledgment of weakness presaging ultimate failure. So they could not form a Ministry without him after all ! Well, he never thought they could. Anyhow, he had taken up his fighting position and decided to play the game to the end.

Asquith went away to consult his friends, with his mind already made up. It is doubtful if he needed any stiffening from the Liberal ex-Ministers who likewise did not believe that Lloyd George or Bonar Law could form a Ministry. They thought they had only to hold out resolutely and refuse all participation to secure Asquith's triumphant return and the rout of his opponents. They pointed out with some apparent reason that Curzon and his Conservative group in the Cabinet looked on Asquith, not Bonar Law, as their real leader. They would stand out, too. How was it possible, then, for the revolting Ministers to form a Government under these circumstances—with both front benches dead against them, and practically no House of Commons support except from the Carsonites and a few personal friends of Lloyd George ? They believed in the myth in preference to the reality.

As a result of their meeting this day Asquith sent a positive refusal within an hour and a half of the Buckingham Palace Cocnference.

10, Downing Street,
Whitehall, S.W.
December 6, 1916.

My dear Bonar Law,

Since we separated I have discussed the matter with ten of my late Liberal colleagues in the Cabinet.

They are unanimously of opinion that I ought not to join your Government. They think, and I agree with them, that I, and probably they can give more effective support from outside. They also think that we could not carry the support of the Liberal party for any such arrangement. I have no personal feeling of amour propre in the matter (as I believe you know), but I am more convinced, the more I think of it, that it would be an unworkable arrangement.

Yours very sincerely,
H. H. Asquith.

In the handwriting of Bonar Law, on the margin of this letter, is written : " I thank you for your letter and I greatly regret your decision."

McKenna and Buckmaster led the stalwarts at this meeting of Liberal Ministers, and succeeded in imposing upon their colleagues a self-denying ordinance pledging all Liberal Cabinet Ministers present not to take office. Henderson was there—but as a Labour man. Montagu says that Henderson and himself were in favour of them all joining Lloyd George—and that no definite decision was really taken. Henderson does not refer to this meeting in an account of this period available to me. Asquith's letter really makes it plain what the sense of the meeting was.

It was a cruel blow to Montagu. He was left in a very awkward situation. He said himself with a real flash of humour that he had to choose between deserting a sinking ship and boarding one that would not float. He had done his very best to secure an accommodation between Lloyd George and Asquith. But in doing so he had practically become one of Asquith's advisers, and so felt himself committed to follow Asquith's course.

It seems clear that he behaved with delicacy and propriety in refusing the offers which the new administration made to him.

Lloyd George was particularly anxious to retain his services,* and had him down on his new list of Ministers as retaining his old post at Munitions. Montagu says also that Lloyd George at one point offered him the Exchequer.

* So anxious was Lloyd George at this time to get substantial Liberal support that he approached Sir Herbert Samuel, but received a refusal.

A week later, when all the principal posts had been settled, Bonar Law made a renewed attempt to bring him in—this time offering the Financial Secretaryship to the Treasury.

Montagu replied as follows :

24, Queen Anne's Gate, S.W.

13. 12. 16.

Dear Bonar Law,

I have given very careful thought to your visit of this morning and your offer.

It is with great regret that I have come to the conclusion that the events of the last fortnight have placed me in such a position that I do not think I would be of much use if I accepted.

For this reason I must decline, but I need, I hope, not assure you that I wish you and the Govt. the greatest possible good fortune and that I hope soon to find means of proving my support and desire to assist.

Yours sincerely,

Edw. S. Montagu.

This letter would appear to be a complete justification of Montagu's conduct in this period. Later, when circumstances had changed, he joined a Government with which he had always been fundamentally in sympathy.

However, we have left suspended the absorbing topic of the day. Was Lloyd George or Bonar Law to be Premier ?

So far Bonar Law had been exploring the ground to see whether any manifest political advantage in the form of solidity for the new Government would be attained by his taking the Premiership himself.

The refusal of Asquith and the " Wee Frees " of Liberalism to accept his offer, cleared his hand. If they would neither serve under him nor under Lloyd George, then the Premiership should go to Lloyd George.

As far as the Conservatives were concerned, Bonar Law shifted his attitude slightly. He perceived, from the contents of shoals of letters from supporters in the House and from his knowledge of the party in the constituencies conveyed to him by the central office, that the Tory members of Parliament were in favour of the displacement of Asquith and the substitution of a Lloyd George-Bonar Law regime, and that Curzon would get the very feeblest kind of support if he quarrelled openly with Bonar Law, and endeavoured to take his place. Again this opinion proved to be perfectly well founded. The three C's and Walter Long never had the countenance of the Tory Party for their allegiance to Asquith.

At any rate, Bonar Law decided that, the Radical Asquithians being counted out, he could bring enough well-known Tory back-benchers into the Government of which Lloyd George was head, to make it secure. He therefore, according to the agreement between the two men, returned to the King and advised His Majesty to call on Lloyd George to form an Administration. The King thereupon commissioned Mr. Lloyd George with this task.

When night fell on this Wednesday, December 6, Asquith, sitting in the Cabinet Room at 10, Downing Street, gave expression to his pent-up feelings. He had been through a rough time and he felt it. No person among his circles of friends and supporters blamed him. There was no feeling of hostility towards him on Bonar Law's part. The other Conservative Ministers held him in the highest esteem. Men who believed him incompetent trusted his sterling honesty of purpose.

Asquith said :

"I have been through the hell of a time for the best part of a month, and almost for the first time I begin to feel older.

"In the end there was nothing else to be done, though it is hateful to give even a semblance of a score to our blackguardly Press.

"The colleagues to-day were unanimous in thinking—what seems obvious to me—that it is not my duty to join this new Government in a subordinate capacity. Apart from the personal aspect of the matter, it would never work in practice.

"So we are all likely to be out in the cold next week."

CHAPTER XL

THE FRUITS OF SUCCESS

IT has been said that Bonar Law was quite certain of sufficient Tory support to make the new Ministry a stable one.

Lloyd George, however, was especially anxious to include the ex-Conservative Ministers. The first thing he did on receiving the King's command was to ask Bonar Law to approach Lord Balfour on his behalf, and, in spite of past differences, to seek his aid. Bonar Law went to Balfour and found him sitting in a chair in his bedroom, wearing a dressing-gown. He offered him the Foreign Secretaryship. Lord Balfour jumped up instantly and replied : " Well, you hold a pistol to my head—I must accept."*

In this way he acted, much to his credit, as every single Tory Minister acted in those days. They thought of the cause of England, not of the particular Prime Minister, and it was this instinctive action on the part of the Tories which ruined the Asquith calculation.

Lord Balfour undoubtedly meant that the normal arrangements of politics, the etiquette

---

* Lord Balfour wrote me that he believed the first suggestion that he should take the Foreign Office was made as he and Bonar Law were walking away from the Buckingham Palace Conference. This was not Bonar Law's recollection

502

dictated by party conditions, were abrogated. He was simply being asked whether he would serve England, and he said " yes." This kind of consideration ought to be borne in mind if we are to judge the politicians of this period fairly.

Bonar Law, writing of this interview to me at the time, said of Balfour :

" Under all the circumstances I think that the part played by him was the biggest part played by anyone in the whole crisis. It was quite plain to me that he would have given anything, apart from the sense of duty, to be free from the responsibility of being a member of the Government. He knew that Lloyd George had been trying to have him removed from the Admiralty, and at that time it was at least doubtful whether Lloyd George could form a strong Government. Yet he took his decision without a moment's hesitation, and he did it, as he explained to me afterwards, for this reason—that unless the new Government succeeded then the only alternative was to return to the old situation with the conditions, if possible, even worse than before."

When Asquith heard of Lord Balfour's adhesion, shortly to be followed by that of the most important Conservative Ministers, he was completely thunderstruck. He had counted absolutely on Lord Curzon's definite assurances and on his general belief that no Conservative except Bonar Law would join Lloyd George. He believed he could depend upon eight Tory Ministers out of nine. This was the basis of his whole policy of declining to deal with Lloyd George.

In informing Lloyd George of Lord Balfour's adhesion, Bonar Law arranged with Lloyd George to sound the Liberals and see what independent support he could secure before they decided whether it was possible to form a Government or not.

This narrative will make it plain that all through Wednesday, December 6, Bonar Law and Lloyd George were in constant communication as to the filling up of prospective offices.

If such close contact seems strange and the Prime Minister's freedom of choice circumscribed by such co-operation, it must be remembered that in so far as Lloyd George failed to secure Liberal or outside support, the burden of filling the vacancies up with Tories would fall entirely on Bonar Law.

The Second Coalition was not a one-man show. It was a combination between two men of widely different type. That was the principal element in its success.

How these communications affected my hope— nay, my practical certainty—of getting the Board of Trade may be judged from the following note sent by Lloyd George to Bonar Law on the evening of Wednesday.

(Written in green pencil.)
My dear Bonar,
    Addison tells me 126 Liberal M.P.'s have already definitely promised support if I form

an administration and the numbers are still coming in.

Can I send for Milner and Stanley now ?

Please let me know per bearer.

Yours,

D. L. G.

The last short sentence but one spelt my undoing.

So my kingdom was taken away from me and given to Stanley (Lord Ashfield), who was offered and accepted the Presidency of the Board of Trade.

Of all these things I was ignorant for the greater part of Wednesday.

As it was, I met the Triumvirate at Pembroke Lodge in the morning by arrangement made the night before, and left the Conference feeling that I was quite in the van of the whole movement for forming the administration.

I was so sure of the Board of Trade that I told the Conservative Chairman at Ashton-under-Lyne my expectations, and warned him to be ready for a by-election on my accepting an office of profit under the Crown.*

I also asked my wife to go down to the constituency at once and begin the campaign for the inevitable fray, and she immediately started for Ashton.

This action was fraught with more important consequences than I could foresee.

And then on that Wednesday afternoon some-

* In 1916 any private member taking such office at any time had to re-submit himself to his constituents.

thing strange happened.   It was as though a
curtain had suddenly fallen between me and the
busy active world of politics in which I had been
living for days. At one moment everything has
been excitement—the abyss of despair or the ex-
hilaration of triumph. The day had been all too
short to fit the events into it. Only by staying up
late and rising early could one deal with the
constant stream of letters, telephone messages,
notes by hand, which poured in unceasingly in
the intervals of private and vital conferences.

The whole world seemed to turn round Whitehall or Kensington. The strained nerves felt that
this racket would be unending, and now came
tranquility in a most disturbing fashion.

A quietude like death settled on the Hyde Park
Hotel. There were no more calls from politicians
—no more agitated interviews. No special mes-
sengers arrived with notes. Even the telephone
bell ceased to ring. The reaction was tremendous.
It is said that people in a balloon do not feel any
sensation of motion, but simply think the earth
is drifting past them. There came to me this same
curious sense of detachment—passing by degrees
into boredom and then into anxiety, and finally
into a kind of desperation. I had been in the centre
of affairs and now I found myself translated to
the extreme circumference.

I had waited in all afternoon and evening,
expecting a message from the Prime Minister
which never came. The dark drew down and no
one came near me. There was no news of friend
or foe. At last I could bear it no longer and

walked out into the street. As by a magnetic impulse I was drawn towards the War Office, where all things must be settled. There the Prime Minister must be allotting the offices after his sensational and almost miraculous triumph. What I really wanted was a sight of Lloyd George. I reached the War Office, but a sense of propriety restrained me from going in. In that dark December night I walked round and round the square stone walls of the War Office like a lost soul.

As I was coming away I ran into Sir Reginald Brade, who told me in the most casual manner that Albert Stanley* would be the new President of the Board of Trade.

I returned to the quiet of my rooms—grateful now for the quietness which covered my disappointment.

Why was I so grievously disappointed at losing the Board of Trade ?

I had had the chance of taking minor office in May, 1915, but had declined because the duties involved were not concerned with the conduct of the war. I had been in a position to get a small place in July of 1916, but I had withdrawn because I was convinced that my existing activities were of more use than the Ministerial functions I might have fulfilled. I knew at this very moment that the new Prime Minister would offer me the Post Office. But what did the Post Office mean, since it had no relation to the conduct of the war ?

* Lord Ashfield.

But how I regretted the loss of the Board of Trade—for, as I believed, it would enable me to take over the management of the railways used for the Army in France.

So there entered into politics the figure of Lord Ashfield. The new President acquitted himself splendidly in his public office. He had always done everything supremely well in the course of his long and romantic career. Born in England and brought up in boyhood in the United States, he started life as an office boy of the Detroit Street Railway Co. at 75 cents per day. Thence he went up steadily stage by stage to the control of big business. Then he gave to his country the most brilliant of services in the war.

Ashfield has, however, to his credit something greater than all his business or political successes. It is not only that men believe in and trust his judgment—he secures the love and affection of all with whom he has to deal.

.   .   .   .

So ended my Black Wednesday. The next day, Thursday, December 7, was to be the decisive day for the various interviews which made the formation of the new Ministry a certainty.

At noon a deputation of Labour representatives waited on the new Prime Minister with a view to hearing what he had to say before they consented to support the Government. It was obvious from the proceedings that the deputation contained

members, particularly Mr. Sidney Webb, who did
not desire the Labour Party to join in and support
the Government. Subsequently, in fact, Labour
split into two groups, the smaller one Pacifist
and the larger Patriotic.

The new Prime Minister, however, rose to the
occasion. No man was more skilled in answering
what were meant to be embarrassing questions
in a way which turned to his own advantage in
debate.

Furthermore, he delivered to the deputation one
of those rare war speeches of his which alone will
make subsequent generations understand why
Lloyd George was the winning force in the war—
why men who distrusted him in all else trusted
him blindly in the supreme emergency of their
country.

It is a chopped sort of rhetoric, but, like the
Napoleonic bulletins—which in style it resembles
—it has the eloquence of energy, the soul of
conviction. He said :

" Don't let us make any mistake—the war for
the moment is going badly ; the country and
all the nations which hang upon the triumph
of Great Britain are in great peril. Bucharest
falling is not merely a question of one city
passing into the hands of the enemy ; it means a
good deal more than that ; it means, for the
moment, the blockade broken ; the work of the
fleet to that extent neutralised, and we are face
to face with the grimmest and most perilous
struggle that this country has ever been engaged

in. I felt that we were not waging this war in the way wars alone can be waged. I hate war; I abominate it. I sometimes think, Am I dreaming ? Is it a nightmare ? It cannot be a fact. That is a thing to consider before you go into it; once you are in it, you have got to go grimly through it, otherwise the causes which hang upon it will all perish. Delay in war is as fatal as in an illness. An operation which may succeed to-day is no good six weeks later on; may be, even three days later. So in war. Action which to-day may save the life of a country, taken a week later, is too late. I thought, rightly or wrongly, that there was delay, hesitation and vacillation and that we were not waging this war with the determination, promptitude and relentlessness—let us make no mistake about it— with which it must be waged. We cannot send men to carnage without seeing that, at any rate, everything is being done to give them a fair chance to win through to victory. They are prepared to make the sacrifice, and we, on the other hand, must support them with all the strength and all the will with which we are endowed. So it was I made certain proposals. I do not believe any Prime Minister, whoever he is, if he has the strength of a giant mentally and physically and morally, can possibly under- take the task of running Parliament and running the war. That is the conviction that I have received. I am still of the same opinion, and I shall certainly act upon it if I form an adminis- tration. Whoever undertakes to run the war must put his whole strength into it and he must make other arrangements with regard to Parliament.   The King, having failed to secure the adhesion of all parties—I wish myself there were no parties during the war—to the plan of forming a comprehensive national Government, invited me to form an administration.   Mr. Asquith and his colleagues decided that they would not serve under Mr. Bonar Law or under anyone else.   I regret that, but I do not wish to criticise it at the present moment.   The King's Government must be carried on.   You must have an administration to prosecute the war; and let me say this—it is what I have said to my colleagues and comrades in this office a few minutes ago—politicians make one fundamental mistake when they have been in office.   They think that the people who are in office, or who have been in office, are absolutely essential to the Government of the country, and that no one else is in the least able to carry on affairs.   Well, we are a people of 45,000,000 and, really, if we cannot produce at least two or three alternative Cabinets we must really be what Carlyle once called us —" a nation of fools."   Well, I don't believe it and I don't think that is the opinion of the country.   We are all very interested in ourselves and in each other, but with all respect to ourselves I think the country is looking out for something else ; it is looking out for a Government that will prosecute the war efficiently ; that is what it is looking out for, and therefore I am hoping to get the adhesion of that character and calibre to form an administration."*

This speech satisfied—as it well might—the greater number of the delegates that they were backing the right man. Lloyd George was given to understand that he could depend on the majority of Labour members to uphold the new Government.

Mr. J. H. Thomas, it is true, refused a Ministerial post, but on the ground that his assistance would be more valuable from outside.

Mr. Henderson, leaving the Asquithites definitely, became a member of the War Cabinet.

As to the Pacifist Socialists, their enmity was an asset in the Premier's favour.

At 1.30 the meeting broke up and Lloyd George left, assured that Labour would join the Ministry.

As has already been shown in the description of this meeting, there was a minority present which was more impressed with the diabolical skill with which Mr. Lloyd George evaded awkward points than with the general fervour and sound sense of his address. Among this minority was another future Premier. Sir Robert Donald has given me a record of the views Mr. Ramsay Mac-

---

* There is also a passage in this speech which bears out everything which has been said previously as to the lack of cordial relationship or alliance between Lloyd George and Northcliffe :

In reply to a question as to whether the policy of prosecuting small newspapers for expressing their opinions was to be continued, while larger papers were allowed to say what they liked.

Mr. Lloyd George said that he stated that he personally would treat Lord Northcliffe in exactly the same way as he would treat a labourer, and that if Lord Northcliffe was guilty of an attempt he would certainly take exactly the same action as he would in the case of a labourer. He did not think there ought to be any distinction, and that if a Government were not administered with complete impartiality it could not expect to be treated with respect in the country.

Donald expressed of this meeting a few days after the event.

"Mr. J. Ramsay MacDonald had breakfast with me and gave me an account of the interview between the Labour members and Mr. Lloyd George. Lord Derby was with Mr. Lloyd George when they were received at the War Office. Mr. Lloyd George spoke for about forty minutes, and described in very vague and general terms his programme with regard to Labour. He referred to the mobilisation of men for agriculture; the control of mines, and the taking over of shipping. He devoted a good deal of attention to the importance of keeping pigs. He said that the refuse of London could be used for feeding pigs. He told them about the condition of the country and the state of the war. MacDonald and Sidney Webb were present, as well as Philip Snowden, and some others who did not agree with Lloyd George, and they asked numerous questions, endeavouring to pin the new Prime Minister down to definite promises. He declined, however, to be caught. When he was asked, for instance, what he meant by the 'control of the coal mines' he did not say definitely; nor did he answer definitely questions about the treatment of labour. He was exceedingly amiable, but excessively indefinite. He was like a bit of mercury; when you thought you had caught him on one point he darted off to something else. When pressed with questions from MacDonald and Sidney Webb he avoided coming to close quar-

Q

ters by a diversion. Webb and MacDonald got rather upset. The majority of the Labour members were greatly impressed by the conversation. The first man to whom Mr. MacDonald spoke was J. H. Thomas. MacDonald told him he thought it was a poor performance. Thomas said he did not agree; he was very much impressed by what Mr. Lloyd George had said and thought they all ought to work for the nation. Mac-Donald wanted to know if he was looking forward to a position in the new Government. Thomas replied that he would not take it if he were offered one, but they had to work for the nation. MacDonald's impression was that Thomas would have taken office but that his Executive prevented him. He turned up at the Merthyr meeting late, and informed MacDonald that he had declined the most important office that Labour could occupy in the new Government. MacDonald congratulated him on refusing it, but he was still under the impression that Thomas would have accepted it if his Executive had agreed. Thomas he regarded as the strongest man among the Trade Union leaders in the Labour movement.

"Mr. Lloyd George was very amiable to Mr. MacDonald personally, and jocularly remarked that he might have to put him in prison, but he hoped he would come and breakfast with him the day he came out. Discussing Mr. Lloyd George's future, Mr. MacDonald said that he quite realised the possibility of his becoming the leader of the Labour Party."

CHAPTER XLI

THE TORIES COME IN

IT has been pointed out in the previous chapters that the new Prime Minister attached the greatest importance to securing the services of the Conservative members of the late Government. He could now be certain—with Bonar Law, Lord Balfour, Lord Milner, the Labour men and many Liberals behind him—of forming a sound Government. But he did not wish to exclude the Conservative leaders.

While Lloyd George had been negotiating with the Liberals and the Independents, Bonar Law had approached his own Conservative colleagues. He had made no headway with them.

On the Thursday afternoon, Lloyd George made a separate overture to Walter Long. He received a refusal. Long said he would support the Government from the back benches, but he could only act in concert with the other dissident Conservative ex-Ministers.

The general attitude of the other three Conservative ex-Ministers was summed up tersely at this time by an outside observer. "If," he said, "they think their refusal to serve will make it impossible to form a Ministry, they will refuse; if they see it can be formed without them, they will come in."

I do not subscribe to this judgment.

Lloyd George was very disappointed at failing to secure Long. He returned to Bonar Law and explained his anxiety to secure this group of Conservative leaders on the ground that the new Ministry should be formed on as broad a basis as possible. Would Bonar Law try again ? Bonar Law said he would not. It was then agreed to send another intermediary to Curzon separately. This envoy took with him a definite offer to Curzon of a place in the War Cabinet.* Curzon told Lord Crewe at the time that at this interview a strong appeal was made to his patriotism, and that it was this appeal which decided him to join the Ministry. I am perfectly prepared to accept this view that it was the motive of patriotism and not the lure of high office which induced Curzon to consent. It must be pointed out however that he did not follow Long's example in declining to take office apart from the group as a whole. On the contrary, he accepted for himself and without consultation with Cecil, Chamberlain, and Long. He ignored, too, the pledge he had given Asquith not to accept office under Lloyd George.

However, with his adhesion, it became practically certain that the others would not stand out. As we have seen, Long's attitude had not been unfavourable : Chamberlain could be relied upon as in May, 1915, to regard office as a public duty.

---

* As the new Executive body for the conduct of war which had been sketched out in advance under the title " War Council " henceforward becomes officially known as the " War Cabinet," the term War Cabinet, not War Council, will be used in the remainder of this volume.

Cecil seems to have been the most reluctant. Anyhow, an arrangement was made by which the Prime Minister should meet and confer with Curzon and Long, Chamberlain and Lord Robert Cecil, on the evening of Thursday, with a view to their joining the Government. This the Conservative Ministers eventually did on certain terms.

Their action in joining Lloyd George was utterly misunderstood by the public at the time. The rank and file of the Tory Party thought that the three C's had been fighting Asquith all through the crisis, and heartily approved of what seemed to be their conduct in adhering to Lloyd George as the successor to the Premiership. It has been shown that this popular view is baseless legend—the precise reverse of the truth. A Liberal colleague, on the other hand, has said : "Is not this the last limit in political cynicism—men who have tried to ruin Lloyd George and turn him out of the Government take office under him the moment it is shown that he has won out in the struggle ? The most violent supporters of Asquith against Lloyd George now transfer their allegiance to the victor ! "

I deny the truth of this charge altogether.

Is it really to be supposed that Sir Austen Chamberlain or the others would behave in this manner—that they would sacrifice every kind of personal loyalty or public principle in order to clamber back to office ?

The idea is essentially absurd, and depends on a

lack of understanding of the way the crisis developed, and of the unexpected positions in which contending personalities frequently found themselves.

The only real blame attaching to the three C's was misjudgment of the party and national temper—leading to a complete underestimate of the strength of Lloyd George and Bonar Law, and an equal overestimate of Asquith's position.

Suddenly it was clear that Lloyd George could not be driven out of a reconstructed Ministry —that Asquith was not indispensable as Premier —and that Bonar Law did stand for the Conservative Party in opposing a continuance of the Asquith regime.

The three C's must obviously reason as follows : " We have made a mistake. Lloyd George and Bonar Law are far stronger than we thought. But the only question is what course to pursue now in the public interest. It is just possible that if we refuse to have anything to do with Lloyd George's attempt to form a Government it may fail. Then we go back to Asquith again as Premier —but to what a new and altered form of Asquith administration ! The myth of the indispensable Premier will have vanished. Lloyd George and Bonar Law will be gone, carrying with them the sympathies of most of the Tories and of many of the Liberals. Other Ministers and Members will soon drift over to their side. All we shall have done by sticking to Asquith is to sustain the fugitive existence of a fatally weakened War Ministry. Is this the path along which plain

patriotic duty points us ? No. There is obviously
the other alternative of strengthening the new
War Government by joining it—provided that
we can be satisfied that the new Premier will make
no radical departures in policy with which we
disagree."

This would appear to be a perfectly logical,
and tenable position in war time. In peace time
politicians may be expected to pay to personal
loyalty the forfeit for a political misjudgment.

But the whole mentality of war politics was—
and quite rightly—different in character. Men
simply thought how they could best serve England. If they were men of long experience in
public office and carried weight in the country
they not unnaturally thought that experience
invaluable to the cause, and the confidence created
by their names a national asset in the conduct
of Government.

They could by their decision—as the position
appeared to them—either recreate an enfeebled
Asquith Government or create a strong Lloyd
George Government. From the national point of
view there could be no hesitation between these
two courses. The Conservative ex-Ministers chose
the right course.

Lloyd George himself, as we have seen, certainly
attached great weight both to their names and to
their capacity for public service.

In fact, the impartial observer might consider
that the new Premier, Mr. Lloyd George, made
immense concessions and too many pledges to
secure the adhesion of these statesmen. The

document I print below gives colour to this view.

But it is a sufficient justification of the alliance then concluded that Sir Austen Chamberlain, after being in office with Lloyd George for six years, resigned the Tory leadership and went into the wilderness with him in 1922 rather than abandon his cause.

To their credit these men came forward and said, " We will serve under Lloyd George if certain conditions are granted in advance—we will watch him and check him and work with him. We come in with him, not as captives, but on the basis of an honourable and joint agreement."

The interview, as has been stated, took place on December 7 between Lloyd George and the Unionist leaders, consisting of Lord Curzon, Lord Robert Cecil, Sir Austen Chamberlain, and Walter Long.

Here is the contemporary memorandum of what took place :

Memorandum of Conversation between Mr. Lloyd George and certain Unionist ex-Ministers, December 7, 1916.

On the evening of December 7, Lord Curzon, Lord Robert Cecil, Mr. Chamberlain and Mr. Walter Long, who had earlier in the afternoon been invited by Mr. Bonar Law, on behalf of Mr. Lloyd George, to join the Administration, had an interview with the latter at the War Office to discuss certain matters in connection with the proposed arrangements. Mr. Bonar Law was present during part of the interview.

The following were the main points which were touched upon in the conversation :

1. Convinced of the supreme necessity of setting up a stable Administration, the Unionist ex-Ministers inquired what support Mr. Lloyd George might expect to receive from the Liberal Party and his late Liberal colleagues, in the House of Commons. Mr. Lloyd George replied that, according to his present information, none of the Liberal members of Mr. Asquith's Cabinet was prepared to join him, having, it was believed come to an understanding with Mr. Asquith to the contrary; but that, in the event of his Administration becoming a settled fact, he was not without hopes of obtaining the services of one or more of their number.

As regards the Liberal M.P.s, he had received assurances of the support of 136, and believed that the numbers would grow. He anticipated a favourable reception of the new Government, when once formed, from the House of Commons.

2. In reply to a question whether, at a later date, if threatened with serious opposition, rendering the position of the Government difficult or untenable in the House, he would contemplate a dissolution of Parliament and a general election, he replied that in the last resort he would not shrink from such a step, and,

indeed, had mentioned it to the King, from whom no opposition was likely to be encountered.

3. As regards the attitude of the Labour party, Mr. Lloyd George stated that a meeting of the Labour M.P.s together with some representatives of the outside Labour organisation, had just been held, and had agreed to support his Government by as large a majority as accorded a similar support to Mr. Asquith earlier in the war, the minority consisting in the main of the professed Pacifists, and the majority containing the men—including Mr. J. H. Thomas, M.P. (who had not supported the Coalition Government at its formation)—on whom he would most wish to rely.

In reply to the question what assurances, if any, he had given to Labour members in return for their support, Mr. Lloyd George referred to several points which had been discussed between their leaders and himself.

(A) As regards personnel he had promised them—

1. A place in the War Committee* for Mr. Henderson.

2. The creation of a new Labour Ministry, to which the powers of the Board of Trade and the Ministry of Munitions, connected with labour, would be transferred, the office to be held by a Labour member.

* War Committee is here used as a term to indicate the new War Cabinet.

3. One other office of importance in the Government, either Local Government or Pensions or Insurance.

4. Two Under-Secretaryships.

5. One of the Whips.

(B) The Labour members had criticised the taking over by the Government of the South Wales coalfields alone, and had advocated a similar treatment of all the coalfields in the country. Mr. Lloyd George had informed them that the late Government had regarded the taking over of the South Wales coalfields as a first step, to be extended to the rest of the country. He regarded this, accordingly, as settled policy.

(C) A similar feeling had been expressed in favour of the State control of shipping on analogous lines. Here no pledge had been given; but Mr. Lloyd George was disposed to favour that policy, and to recommend the appointment of a single Controller of Shipping, with executive authority, to replace Lord Curzon as Chairman of the Shipping Control Committee, but to continue to be assisted by the latter.

(D) Mr. Lloyd George had acquainted the Labour members with his general intentions as regards industrial conscription, and had read out to them the resolution on the subject passed by the recent War Committee. They had not refused assent to such a programme, but had asked that just as the enforcement of military compulsion had been preceded by a period under the Derby scheme of voluntary enrolment, with a time limit, so a similar procedure might be adopted in the present case.

It was understood that these were the only assurances that had been given by Mr. Lloyd George to the Labour representatives.

4. A prolonged discussion took place on the proposed constitution of the War Committee; and the various alternatives of a Cabinet identical with the War Committee, a Cabinet somewhat larger than the War Committee, but mainly composed of its members, and a Cabinet separate from the War Committee were examined. The general conclusions arrived at were as follows :—

(A) The War Committee and Cabinet would be identical, that is, there would be no Cabinet apart or distinct from the War Committee.

(B) The latter would consist of four permanent members, the Prime Minister and three Ministers without portfolios, or at least without heavy departmental duties, namely, Sir Edward Carson, Mr. Henderson, and Lord Curzon, who would sit daily to deal with the war. Mr. Bonar Law, in consequence of his duties as Chancellor of the Exchequer and Leader of the House of Commons, could not be expected to attend regularly, but would have the right to be present whenever he desired, and would be kept informed of the proceedings.

(C) To their deliberations would be added,

as the occasion required, Mr. Balfour as
Foreign Secretary, Sir W. Robertson representing the War Office, and the First Lord of
the Admiralty (for which place the Unionist
members strongly pressed the claims of Lord
Milner).   Other Ministers and technical advisers would be summoned as required.

(D) The heads of the principal departments
of State would continue to administer their
departments, and would if the occasion arose
—e.g., in the case of departmental disagreement—be called into consultation by the
Prime Minister or the Leader of the House of
Commons, whose functions it would be to
decide.

(E) The new arrangement would relieve
the Ministers not included in the small War
Committee of Cabinet responsibility for the
acts of Government.   That responsibility
would belong exclusively to the War Committee, which, as stated above, would be the
Cabinet.

(F) Concerning other Ministerial appoint-
ments, Mr. Lloyd George explained that he
proposed that Lord Derby should become
Secretary of State for War, but without a
seat on the War Committee, at which the
War Office would be represented by Sir
William Robertson; Mr. Long, Secretary of
State for the Colonies; Mr. Chamberlain,
Lord Robert Cecil, Sir F. E. Smith and Mr.
Duke would retain their present positions.
Sir Robert Finlay would become Lord Chan-

cellor; Lord Curzon, President of the Council and Leader of the House of Lords; Sir A. Stanley, President of the Board of Trade; Sir George Cave (failing a Liberal member of the recent Administration), Home Secretary; Dr. Addison (failing Mr. Montagu), Minister of Munitions; Mr. H. A. L. Fisher, President of the Board of Education; Mr. Gordon Hewart, Solicitor-General; Mr. S. H. Lever, Financial Secretary to the Treasury.

(G) In reply to other questions, Mr. Lloyd George stated that he had no intention of asking Mr. W. Churchill or Lord Northcliffe to join the Administration. The suggestion that Lord Rosebery should be invited to accept the office of Lord Privy Seal was unfavourably received by the Unionist ex-Ministers.

5. The question was raised as to the desirability of taking further powers for the suppression of the kind of Press attacks which had done so much to discredit and finally to bring about the downfall of the late Administration— on the lines advocated in the earlier days of the Coalition Government. Mr. Lloyd George thought it undesirable to announce any restriction of the Press in the earlier days of the new regime, but suggested that an inquiry should be made as to what is done in France.

6. Questions were asked as to the relations of Mr. Lloyd George with the Nationalist members, and whether any assurance had been given with regard to military compulsion for

Ireland or a measure of Home Rule. Mr. Lloyd George believed that the Irish members were not unfriendly, but he had seen none of them, and had come under no obligation to them. No Minister joining the Government was being asked to join a Home Rule Administration. But it was obvious that no pledge could be given that Home Rule might not come on the tapis again at a later date.

7. As regards other controversial matters, such as the franchise, no Minister, whether on the War Committee or not, was committed in any way by joining the Government. The Prime Minister would explain that the Government had been constituted for war purposes only, and that would be, in all matters, the deciding consideration.

8. A question having been put as to the retention of Sir Douglas Haig as Commander-in-Chief in France, Mr. Lloyd George stated that he had no intention of proposing a change, if for no other reason, because there was no officer better qualified for the post.

9. After these explanations, the Unionist ex-members stated their willingness to accept office under Mr. Lloyd George, and the latter expressed his intention to inform the King without delay that he was now in a position definitely to accept the duty of forming an Administration.

A certain lurking distrust of the Prime Minister still seems to have animated the breasts of the

Ministers who accepted the terms thus offered. It was Curzon who wished them reduced to writing and sent to Lloyd George for countersignature. He asked Bonar Law to send such a document along to the Prime Minister. Bonar Law refused brusquely—" Send it yourself." By this remark he implied and meant that he was not a party to the arrangement come to between Lloyd George and his late enemies, and was not bound in any sense by the terms of the Memorandum propounded. It was strange that Curzon should ask him to act as his emissary to Lloyd George— particularly on an errand which implied distrust of the Prime Minister.

Lloyd George's position was now absolutely secure after Thursday's settlement with the Conservative ex-Ministers. He could count on the Tory Party almost to a man, since he had Bonar Law, Balfour, Carson, Long and the three C's in his Ministry. He had promises of support from at least 130 Liberal members, and the majority Labour Party solid behind him. The opposition of the Wee Free Liberals and of the Pacifist Socialists was obviously doomed to futility.

He possessed, therefore, in the House of Commons more than a comfortable working majority, and if trouble arose he still held in reserve, with the King's consent, the iron weapon of a dissolution. In the state of popular opinion and the obsolescence of the party machines it was not likely that his enemies would force him to the country.

The threat of dissolution was the rod which

every Coalition War Government held in reserve against its opponents. They had only got to say unanimously and with one accord : " We desire the confidence of the country in order to prosecute the war to a victorious conclusion " in order to carry the whole nation with them. The critics would have been simply swept away and drowned by the force of the electoral current, providing both parties were united in the appeal to the constituencies.

It was under these circumstances that the silence which had fallen on Downing Street and Whitehall was at last broken and Bonar Law came to see me. Obviously he had not called until the settlement with the Conservative ex-Ministers had been arrived at. Only then would it be clear as to what offices were vacant.

Bonar Law told me frankly two things :

(1) There had been no attempt by the Conservatives to impose any bar to my appointment, although Bonar Law expected something of this sort.

(2) But the Board of Trade was quite out of the question. He then offered me another office.

Possibly it was as much as I was entitled to or fit for. But at any rate it did not appeal to me, for it had no relation to the conduct of the war, and I refused it.

I do not pretend that the estimate Lloyd George had obviously formed of my political abilities was not wounding to my self-esteem. I believed that I could do first-class work of an active administrative kind in the war. Obviously the new Premier was no longer of this opinion. And Bonar Law clearly did not believe in my powers sufficiently to intervene on my behalf. It was the work I wanted, not the office.

On the Saturday silence was broken from the War Office. Lloyd George called at the Hyde Park Hotel. Lord Rothermere was already there, too. When Lloyd George appeared he brought with him Bonar Law as a body-guard—so there were four of us.

Lloyd George broached the question of the appointment to the Board of Trade. He said that, rightly or wrongly, he had given Stanley* the post, and there was an end of it. He then offered me another and smaller place. I declined in fitting terms and decided to continue my task and duties as Canadian Government representative.

Finally, Lloyd George left.

Immediately afterwards I received from him the following note offering to recommend me to the King for a Peerage.

(In L.G.'s own handwriting.)
War Office,
Whitehall, S.W.
Dec. 9th, 1916.

My dear Max,

There are two or three important business Departments which have no representatives in

* Lord Ashfield.

the House of Lords and therefore no spokes-men.

Would you allow me to recommend your name to the King for a Peerage. You could then answer for these Departments in the H.L.

Ever yours,

D. L. G.

I did not reply, but went down to the country instead. I was in an acute dilemma. I had in-formed my constituency that I had got a Govern-ment Office which I thought worth while. Now I had got nothing of the kind. If I went back there as an ordinary private member I should have placed myself in a position of extreme embarrassment. I had already telegraphed on Thursday to my wife to stop the campaign, and she came back on Friday. It seemed to me that a Peerage was the only way out of the diffi-culty, but I decided nothing for the moment.

On the Sunday evening Bonar Law suddenly swooped down on me at Leatherhead.

Derby had come to see him. He naturally, and rightly, imagined that Bonar Law knew all about the offer of the peerage and had come to remon-strate from his own special point of view. I was, he said, a Lancashire member and that there were several other Lancashire members who thought they had prior claims to a peerage. They would be furious if precedence were given to me.

Bonar Law was completely taken by surprise by this opposition. He had immediately motored down to tell me that he was convinced that I

should not go to the Upper House. He said he was
most unwilling to see a peerage conferred on me
as an intimate friend of his. It would be most embarrassing as a consequence of the crisis. I at
once said that I would withdraw any claim I could
possibly have. I withdrew as I had withdrawn
from previous possible offices at his request. And
I wrote Lloyd George that Sunday, December 10,
1916, a letter refusing the recommendation for a
Peerage. Bonar Law carried this letter away with
him to Lloyd George's house at Walton Heath.

So on Sunday night I felt myself in a sense dis-
Peered. The Peerage no doubt had been a
phantom one—and now even the phantom had
vanished.

Yet I was worried as to what sort of explanation
I was going to make to my constituency. My
ill-fated communication to Ashton-under-Lyne
about accepting an office of profit under the
Crown still weighed me down. However, I
went to London on the Monday prepared to
make the best of it.

On reaching the Hyde Park Hotel I found a
letter from Bonar Law, saying, to my astonish-
ment, that everything had been arranged and
I must apply for the Chiltern Hundreds.

I went to Bonar Law and said : " What is it
you want ? Last night you asked me not to
have my name submitted for a Peerage, and to-day
you withdraw your objection. "

Bonar Law replied in effect : " I have too often
stood in your way to suit my own convenience—
I will not do so any longer. Besides, we want

your seat at Ashton-under-Lyne for Stanley* and
the Board of Trade."

It will be seen that I was not altogether a willing
Peer. I would much rather have stayed in the
House of Commons with a suitable office. But
I had been jockeyed, or had jockeyed myself, into
a position in which I thought I had no choice.
The Peerage was a way of escape. I took it. It
would be absurd to deny that it was a very
foolish way of escape.

I had by this time also attained to a more sensible view of things and recaptured a juster sense
of political values. I saw now that the successful
issue of the crisis had been due to the working
of an immense number of forces. These forces
had indeed been co-ordinated to a certain extent,
but many of them had been working quite independently of any central direction. This un-
doubted fact reduced to real proportions my idea
of the part I had taken in the transaction.

Yet, curiously enough, at that very moment
the inner ring in politics started a myth about
my activities which persists to this day. The
chief authors of it were undoubtedly the defeated
Liberal Ministers, and from their lips it rapidly
spread outwards to the public at large.

It was said that I had managed Bonar Law, and
then pulled wires and got hold of Lloyd
George. In a word I was represented as the
inspirer and architect of Asquith's downfall.
This view was epitomised by the " Morning
Post " in the phrase " Bunty pulled the Strings."

* Lord Ashfield.

CHAPTER XLII

LOAVES AND FISHES OFFICES

IN the actual event the Conservatives accepted a War Cabinet with greater authority than the one which had been proposed to Asquith and to their own conferences. On the other hand, the personnel and constitution was not that originally suggested by the Triumvirate. Lloyd George became Premier and Chairman of the War Cabinet. Bonar Law became Leader of the House of Commons and part-time member of the War Cabinet—thus fulfilling in effect the role reserved for Asquith under the compromise.

How Lord Curzon came into the War Cabinet has already been related. The remaining two places fell to Henderson and Milner, while Carson went to the Admiralty.

The Prime Minister hesitated almost to the last minute as to whether Milner should come into the War Council and Carson go to the Admiralty, or Milner take the Admiralty and Carson to the War Cabinet. Indeed, Milner actually got a notice to attend the first meeting of the War Cabinet an hour before he had been notified that he was to be a member of it.

Milner's promotion was certainly the most

startling. In the declining days of the Asquith Government he had received the seventh refusal of the food controllership. Having consulted his friends, he finally asked Lloyd George's advice. Lloyd George strongly urged him to decline. I should imagine Lord Milner was as much surprised as anyone when his persistent neglect by consecutive Governments was crowned by the reward all politicians of the day coveted most.

Lord Curzon was in a position to congratulate himself. It is true that he had failed to overthrow Bonar Law and make himself the Tory leader. None the less, he had obtained a splendid office.

He was unselfish enough not to be content with his own promotion. He proposed to Bonar Law that the new Government should take in Lords Salisbury and Selborne—the most bitter antagonists of the new Prime Minister—and also Lord Midleton.

1, Carlton House Terrace,

S.W.

Dec. 8 (1916).

My dear Bonar,

I have been thinking over the contemplated arrangements in the House of Lords, where I understand I am to be Pres. of the Council and Leader of the House. Now if I am to be a member of the War Com. *sitting every day* I shall not have much time in the morning to get up all the subjects that are likely to be raised in the

afternoon and about which speeches or statements may have to be made. Crewe &
Lansdowne did it together, but both were
without serious official duties and neither was
on the War Comee. Thus they always had the
mornings to get ready. But even so their time
was fully occupied.

It is essential if we are to deal effectively with
H. of L. questions that I should have assistance.
It is true that there will be Derby, Finlay,
Crawford and, I hope, Milner. But all of these
will be absorbed in departmental work and *there
being no Cabinet* will know little of the collec-
tive intentions or the general work of the Govt.

I should like therefore to have one or two
lieutenants to help to do the work.

Selborne, Salisbury, Midleton are, I should
think, all available and all have experience,
insight and ability.

There still remain, I believe, undisposed of
the

> Lord Privy Seal
> Office of Works
> Chan. of Duchy (?)

Further, I think that when the Air Board has
got into the stride of its new work, I shall have
no time to continue that job which will require
another man. This may give another opening.
By the way, it may interest you to learn that
the solution to which the late War Com.—
quite erroneously, as I think, and contrary to
the views of all the experts—tried to force me,
viz., that Design & Supply should be handed

over to Munitions—has now been repudiated by the Air people at the Admiralty itself, who have unanimously petitioned Jellicoe to save them from Munitions and to give them entirely to the Air Board !

I have seen Lansdowne, who strongly recommends that I should obtain Salisbury as Lord Privy Seal if he will join. He says he will be far more effective than either Selborne or Midleton and does not think I can very well get on without him. Moreover, we shall disarm a rather formidable critic. Will you press this view on Lloyd George and let me hear. I do not think I can do the work otherwise.

Yours ever,
Curzon.

Bonar Law did not accept the suggestion, and these notables remained outside the Ministry.

Carson adopted the exact reverse of Lord Curzon's attitude. The moment that Asquith's fall was accomplished a kind of incuriousness seemed to descend upon him. He was like a man whose task is accomplished. He made no claim for himself. He gave up the War Council readily and took the Admiralty, which he really did not want. Nor did he make any claim for office on behalf of friends and allies in the House of Commons. A most grievous disappointment was thereby incurred by prominent members of the " Business Man's Committee," who had made certain at least of Under-Secretaryships when Asquith had been vanquished. And this feeling was not unreasonable. Once again it would appear that the Whigs were to have the best of it. All the smaller loaves and fishes were to go to Lloyd George Liberals, as in 1915, all the great posts in the Ministry had gone to Liberals without prefix.

I thought Carson carried this neutrality towards his old friends too far. Bonar Law did intervene on behalf of James Craig (Lord Craigavon), who seemed to me exactly the type of man who would be invaluable to his country in war time, and Craig did get office.

Carson's only recommendation was a City Banker, a man who had never been in Parliament and had no political experience whatever, whom he seemed to think would make a good Financial Secretary of the Treasury. Most astonishing of all, his nominee was a Liberal !

But Carson's mind was always filled with prejudice or free from it. This fact lends to his figure a real touch of historic interest. When he was in insurrection against a person or a Government the strength of his character was overpowering. He exhibited immense resource, he showed complete calmness in the face of risk and danger. His decisions seemed undeviating in their firmness. Here was a man, the onlooker was tempted to exclaim, fit to mount the throne of the Cæsars. Yet, the instant the opponent, Premier, or Ministerial system, was defeated and Carson reigned in their stead, with real powers of executive authority, an astonishing change came over his mentality. He became at once the orthodox

Minister, trusted by his permanent officials and ready to defend their errors loyally. In counsel he showed indecisiveness or even weakness. He seemed to throw away in power every single quality which had given him his authority in opposition and placed him in the Government.

When Asquith objected originally to Carson's inclusion in the War Council on the ground that he had shown no trace of executive ability in the Cabinet, Carson's friends thought Asquith was merely prejudiced. When Lloyd George left him out of the War Council it appeared to be an act of folly. It shook the faith of inside observers in the new Premier's capacity for judging men. It was said that he was promoting men of no real capacity at the expense of the proved and able.

Yet Asquith and Lloyd George were in essence right. Why? It would seem that Carson is by nature an insurrectionary. This part calls out all the great qualities of his mind. But reverse the roles and make him the Government instead of the rebel and something seems to dry up in his being. He changes back suddenly into a rather ordinary able lawyer-politician.

If the Conservatives had a voice on the appointments, they also had something to say about the exclusions. As will be seen from the Memorandum, they expressly insisted that the new Prime Minister should not give office either to Winston Churchill or Lord Northcliffe. Lord Northcliffe had taken the precaution of announcing publicly that in no circumstances would he serve.

Churchill was excluded. But Lloyd George at the time had no very high opinion of Churchill, believing that he had a leg in both camps and that Asquith was ready to give him the Admiralty back again should Lloyd George fail to form a Ministry. So, at least, he wrote in the following note, obviously tossed across the council table to Bonar Law :

Prime Minister.   10, Downing Street,
                              Whitehall, S.W.

My dear Bonar,
I think you ought to know that Asquith told Winston that if he came in he would put him in the Admiralty.

                                        D. L. G.

No spur could have been more effective than this in strengthening Bonar Law in his decision to keep Lloyd George in and Asquith out.

All these matters being amicably settled, the principal posts in the Government were allotted, while the official Liberals, deserted by their allies and instigators, sat down to nurse, under a thin veil of moderation, an implacable policy of revenge.

The Ministry, with the exception of the minor appointments, was now formed, and the inclusion of a number of men with greater business than political experience met a strong popular demand.

I propose to close my narrative at this point somewhat abruptly. The formation of the Ministry was assured. The appointments to subordinate offices are probably due to much the same causes in all Ministries, and are matters of private rather then of public concern. Generally speaking the Tories who had supported Carson and Lloyd George received inadequate recognition. This was a serious matter for the younger Tories, as they were mostly men of middle age whose party had been ten years out of office. On the other hand, the Liberals who were ready to serve received ready acceptance at the hands of the Prime Minister. This was natural, because it was the essence of the new policy to form a Ministry which would be national in appearance as well as in reality. But if these Liberal members had obtained an advantage, they were also exposing themselves to a greater danger. The refusal of the Liberal members of the ex-Cabinet to join the Government indicated in no uncertain manner that Liberals who accepted office must run great risks in a political future—after the war—into which no one could peer with certainty. Of the minor appointments, that of Neil Primrose as a Government Whip was the most significant, for it showed that some of the old Whigs were prepared to join with the Radicals, the Tories, and the Labour members against the new Whig leaders.

In this crisis the difference of opinion bore no relation to party politics. Every party was divided against itself. The Labour Party had to subdue its peace cranks. The forward and backward wings of the two great parties fought each other unceasingly. The divergence was in the main

not one of domestic principle, but of temperament, and methods and men chose their sides
accordingly. As to who was right and who was
wrong time alone can shew, history alone can judge.

For, indeed, a just survey of the matters at
issue would cover the whole field of Europe, and
would be concerned with military problems of
which the ordinary civilian is no more a competent judge than the average military man. We
should be concerned immediately with questions
about the attitude of our Allies, the disposition of
our forces, and many other problems so intricate
that they might be argued for years and never
he decided.

A friend of Mr. Asquith's has given a picture
of him on the critical day of his failure. " He was
sitting at the large table in the Cabinet room;
his back was to the fire. He looked a very lonely
figure and a tired man. He had a quiet and severe
expression. . . . My impression was that Mr.
Asquith was quite convinced that Mr. Lloyd
George could not form a stable Government.
Mr. Asquith was evidently not in touch with
public opinion, and had only prejudiced sources
of information in this case. He complained of the
Press attacks, but he never took any account of
the Press himself. He maintained a curious aloof-
ness, and regarded newspapers as not being of
much account. He took no pains either through
himself or his secretaries to keep in touch with
newspapers which were his supporters. He was at
some trouble to keep them at arm's length, and
they had to support him in the dark." The

observer was, in effect, witnessing the twilight of
the old regime while the new man strode on to the
stage to measure himself with Chatham.

But it would be a mistake to suppose that it
was a triumphant Lloyd George who entered the
portals of No. 10, Downing Street. I called on
him at the moment when he was taking over the
Prime Minister's premises. The battle had left
its scars. Lloyd George had shown immense
courage and supreme calmness at the critical
moments of danger, and he had to suffer the re-
action. Forming his Cabinet had really been a
terrible business. He had to go to Balfour, whom,
for months, he had been trying to drive out of the
Admiralty, and, really, it seemed that his political
existence had depended for a moment on Balfour's
nod. He had to make a private deal with Curzon,
who had been his arch-enemy in the whole affair.
He had to go to Tories like Walter Long to be
repulsed, and to his old Liberal friends like Samuel,
who turned him down. At the last moment
Montagu, his one ally, would not face the obloquy
of joining his Government. And then, after what
had happened, was any war administration to be
considered stable ?

Had not the very rapidity with which Asquith,
at one moment supremely confident and at the
next at the very depth of impotence, shown how
brittle a thing was a Premiership in time of war ?

There would not be, of course, much truth or
justice in these reflections. They are the thoughts
of a tired man whose stock of energy, vast as it is,
has become exhausted.

And then there is the Press. Cannot the Press pull down the Government without offering to rebuild ?

There was Northcliffe, for instance, in the background. The Northcliffe Press had supported him, it was true. But only because they meant the same thing for the present, not because they meant the same thing all the time. What power there was here of persistent detraction with no adequate opportunity of counter attack ! Perhaps his new Tory colleagues had been right after all in saying that the power of the Press ought to be curbed. Fleet Street would be attacking him next.

His prophetic vision might have foreseen a headline in the Northcliffe Press two days afterwards—" Bad Balfour Rumour "—which heralded a series of critical attacks on the new administration.

Perhaps he had been wrong to reject my advice about Northcliffe.

I give a telephone message :
" The Prime Minister would like to see Lord Northcliffe at No. 10, Downing Street."

I wait on the line. Northcliffe comes. He speaks.

" Lord Northcliffe sees no advantage in any interview between him and the Prime Minister at the present juncture."

In a moment Lloyd George is his own man again. If they can't be squared they shall be squashed ! His courage returns. His patriotism calls for the last ounce of his ability. His temperament responds as ever to the spur of danger. The nerve-weary despondent man vanishes.

In his place comes the man who is to advance by degree after degree from a position of preliminary weakness to one of supreme power. He is to be the idol of the nation, the Premier under whose ægis Germany was overthrown and the Empire saved. He is to attain an authority greater than that held by any British Prime Minister in history. For six years his smile means promotion and his frown banishment from office. He will dictate to Europe, fling out a great dynasty with a gesture, and parcel out the frontiers of races.

Everything is in his hands, and those hands will show that they have the power to use everything.

There, in this entry of his new day of glory, with the faded pictures of his predecessors on the walls around him, sits David Lloyd George, Premier of Great Britain.

And there for the present I leave him.

INDEX

Conscription (*see* Compulsion)
Views and attitude of Harcourt, Runciman, Churchill, Lloyd George, Simon, Grey, Carson, McKenna and Lord Derby, 246–251; Asquith's Coalition Government, 246 ; Proceedings in the Cabinet, 248

Conservative Party (in Opposition 1914–May 1915) and Home Rule, 13; and advisability of Coalition, *ib* ; open to support Government if war declared, 18 ; its dislike and mistrust of Winston Churchill, 25, 125 ; and despatch of B.E.F., 36 ; the Shadow Cabinet, 45, 125, 126 ; " Eager " to run the war, and selects Lord Long to lead revolt, 49, 52 ; its mild criticisms of Government, 87 ; and Lord Fisher's resignation, 104 ; welcomes Coalition, 128 ; and meekly accepts subsidiary offices therein, 135 ; and " Self-denying " Ordinance, 137 ; its great regard for Kitchener, 170, 177 ; *ib.*, undergoes complete change, 177, *et seq.*, " Ginger Group," 270, 288 ; favours Carson and Asquith in the critical 1916 period, 412

Conservatives, attitude in December, 1916, 412 ; they meet and pass a resolution, 413 ; Bonar Law's attitude, 415 ; advice to Asquith to resign, 417 ; the 1916 Conference, 429 ; favour a Lloyd George-Bonar Law regime in December, 1916, 500 ; Lloyd George War Cabinet in December, 1916, 517–520 ; War Committee, 522 *et seq.*

Constantine, King (*see* Tino, King)

Constantinople, and Russo-British Policy, 14, 53, 73

Cowans, General Sir John (Quartermaster General) and Kitchener, 179

Craig, James (Lord Craigavon), 538

Crewe, Lord, and Intervention, 20 ; his powerful address to Cabinet, 21 ; is nominated to proposed "Compulsion" Committee, 142 ; Asquith's high opinion of, 219

Cromwell, Oliver, allusion to, 74

Cunliffe, Lord (Governor of Bank of England) his relations with Lloyd George and with McKenna, 146 ; the latter brings about his retirement, 147, 148

Curzon, Lord, and the Coalition, 128, and Bonar Law, 142 ; nominated to proposed " Compulsion " Committee,

142; opposes evacuation of Dardanelles, 152, 164, 165 ; his ambition to lead Conservative Party, 165, 166; Estimate of, 167, 168 ; his *rapprochement* with Asquith, 169 ; his views regarding the settlement of the Irish Question in 1916, 271 ; leader of the Dissidents in December, 1916, 482 ; joins Lloyd George, 520 ; Achieves success, 535 (*see* Three C's)

D'ABERNON, LORD, 70

Daily Express, 42 ; on Nationalisation of Drink Traffic, 68 ; and Lord Beaverbrook, 69, 271, the Irish Question in 1916, 273 ; Reports the War Government Progress, 399

Daily Mail, on Shell Scandal, 113

Dalziel, Lord, 423

Dardanelles, initial British success at, 52, 72 ; and the Fisher-Churchill controversy, 99, *et seq.*, 120, 121 ; failure of Suvla Bay operations and repercussions in Cabinet, 151 ; evacuation or not? 152–168, 189; two Army Divisions removed to Salonica, 154 ; Lord Kitchener is despatched to report on, 157, 160, 190 ; successful evacuation of, 164

Davies, General, 157

Dawson, Editor of *The Times*, 445

Derby, Lord, appointed Secretary of State, 197 ; his compulsory service scheme, 201 ; Asquith sends for him in 1915—his scheme for Army Recruiting, 249, influence in Lancashire, 250 ; his recruiting scheme a preliminary to conscription, 251 ; appointed Under Secretary of War, 251 ; a possible Premier in 1915, 252 ; his general popularity, 252 ; how viewed by Whitehall, 252 ; consistently loyal to Conservative Party, 253

Dewey, Sir Thomas, 148

Disraeli, Benjamin, allusion to, 183

Donop, von, Sir Stanley, 60, 61

Drink Traffic, nationalisation of, Lloyd George and, 65, *et seq.*, 87

Dunkirk, Asquith and the " Dunkirk Circus," 228–230; Churchill's action in the matter, 228, 229 ; nature of Army landed there, and its intended effect on Belgians and Germans, 231 ; Asquith's views and attitude, 232, 233 ; French and Kitchener, 233 ; divergence of Asquith and Churchill, 234

INDEX

ship, 485 ; sees the King and then Asquith, 487; on Balfour's acceptance of Foreign Office in 1916, 503 ; collaborates with Lloyd George in forming the Ministry—Asquith is surprised, 504

Le Bas, Sir Hedley and Lord Riddell, 145

Lee (Lord) of Fareham, 401

Liberal Party (in power 1914 to May 1915) and Home Rule, 13, 125 ; and advisability of Coalition, 13, et seq. ; large majority of, for intervention in War, 36 ; dissension in, as to despatch of B.E.F., 41 ; resurrects Home Rule Bill, 41 ; again considers Coalition, 47–54; and Antwerp adventure, 49 ; and Shell Crisis, 56, 62 ; Fall of Government on resignation of Lord Fisher (19 May 1915), 56, 94–113 ; and Churchill, 126; annoyance in, at announcement of Coalition, 127 ; and " Places " in new Ministry, 132 ; first Coalition doomed to failure by intrigues of 133, et seq. ; opposes appointment of Bonar Law as Chancellor of Exchequer, 134 ; internecine strife in, 143 ; and Kitchener, 170, 186, et seq. ; disruption of, on appointment of Lloyd George as War Secretary, 210, et seq.

Liquor Control Board, 70

Lloyd George, D. (see George, Lloyd)

Long, Lord Walter, reference to, 31 ; estimate of, 51, 52 ; and Anti-Drink Campaign, 66 ; and Coalition, 128 ; his objections to Lloyd George and McKenna in new Ministry, 129 ; supports former's Balkan policy, 155; and Asquith, 169 ; his important interview with Bonar Law, 479 ; relations with Lloyd George in December, 1916, 517–520

Loos, Battle of, 178, 198

Lusitania, The, sinking of, 101

MACDONALD, J. RAMSAY, expresses his opinions in regard to Lloyd George's Premiership, 512

Macready, Sir Nevil (General), arrest of Birkenhead in France, 241, 243

McKenna, Rt. Hon. R., and intervention, 20, on despatch of B.E.F., 39 ; on Lord Fisher's resignation, 102, his friction with Lloyd George, 143, et seq. ; effects retirement of Governor of Bank of England re U.S.A. commitments, 146–149; character

of, 149, 150 ; and conscription, 246 ; relations with Lloyd George, 279 ; Peace negotiations, 378 ; Government crisis in 1916, 440 ; position in December, 1916, 498

Manchester Guardian, 134

Marlborough, Duke of, allusion to, 170

May, Sir George, 148

Middleton (Lord) and the Irish Crisis, 270

Military Service Act (see Compulsion)

Milner (Lord) joins Lloyd George Government of 1916, 434

Monk, General, allusion to, 170

Monro, General, urges evacuation of Dardanelles, 156, et seq.

Montagu, Edwin, S. (Financial Secretary to Treasury), is appointed on Shell Committee, 59, 60 ; his abilities and untimely death, 60 ; refuses to intervene between Lloyd George and McKenna, 144, 149 ; Asquith's high opinion of, 219 ; (Minister of Munitions) sees Asquith in December, 1916, 432 ; his account of the political position, 434 ; he, Asquith and Lloyd George, 437, his disappointment in December, 1916, 498

Morgan, The House of, 147–149

Morley, Lord, favours neutrality, 20 ; resigns, 21

Morning Post, 63

Munitions, Ministry of, supersedes Shell Committee, 64, 109–112

Murray, General Wolfe, 176

Murray, Sir, A. 237

NAVY, mobilisation of 21, 30

Negotiations in late part of 1916 ; Beaverbrook sees Lloyd George, 328 ; Bonar Law and Lloyd George, 329 ; Asquith and Lord Curzon, 331 ; Bonar Law's attitude, 332 ; Lloyd George goes to France, 335 ; Beaverbrook sees Law and others, 336 ; Wilson dislikes Asquith and Lloyd George, 337 ; Beaverbrook aids greatly in arranging a conference, 337–339

Neuve Chapelle, Battle of (10 March 1915) 56, 85, 198

Newspapers (see Press)

New Zealand contingent in Dunkirk, 232

Nigerian Debate, its introduction, 289 causes dissension in the Cabinet, 290 Birkenhead, Bonar Law, Leslie Scott etc., 293, 294 ; Carson's atti-

INDEX